THE PRACTICE OF JOURNALISM

a guide to reporting and writing the news

BRUCE PORTER

Brooklyn College of the City University of New York

TIMOTHY FERRIS

Graduate School of Journalism
University of California, Berkeley

D1603744

PRENTICE HALL, Englewood Cliffs, New Jersey 07632

Library of Congress Cataloging-in-Publication Data

Porter, Bruce
  The practice of journalism.

  Includes index.
  1. Reporters and reporting.   2. Journalism—
Authorship.   I. Ferris, Timothy.   II. Title.
PN4781.P59   1988   070.4'3   87-7375
ISBN 0-13-693706-3

For Al Johnson
City Editor of **The Providence Journal**
and
in memory of
Thomas A. Ferris
Newspaperman

Cover design: Ben Santora
Manufacturing buyer: Ed O'Dougherty

© 1988 by Prentice-Hall, Inc.
A Division of Simon & Schuster
Englewood Cliffs, New Jersey 07632

Printed in the United States of America

10 9 8 7 6 5 4 3 2 1

ISBN 0-13-693706-3 01

Prentice-Hall International (UK) Limited, *London*
Prentice-Hall of Australia Pty. Limited, *Sydney*
Prentice-Hall Canada Inc., *Toronto*
Prentice-Hall Hispanoamericana, S.A., *Mexico*
Prentice-Hall of India Private Limited, *New Delhi*
Prentice-Hall of Japan, Inc., *Tokyo*
Simon & Schuster Asia Pte. Ltd., *Singapore*
Editora Prentice-Hall do Brasil, Ltda., *Rio de Janeiro*

CONTENTS

PREFACE

The Practice of Journalism provides the beginning journalism student, whether graduate or undergraduate, with an introduction to the skills needed to perform successfully at entry-level print and broadcasting jobs involving reporting and writing the news. To this end, we have employed the techniques of journalism to investigate how journalism gets done, interviewing leading newswriters and reporters, spending time in newspaper city rooms and local and network television news operations, asking editors to send samples of the stories they consider exemplary of their trade, and combing through thousands of clippings for those that best illustrate the cardinal points of the field. Some of the resulting material is woven throughout the text and the examples; other information is found in the boxed interviews with accomplished journalists like Nora Ephron, Jack Newfield, and David Brinkley.

Part I contains a discussion of what makes for news and an anecdotal history of American journalism. Part II describes what it's like to work for a newspaper or a wire service. In Parts III—the writing section—the students are given pointers on producing accurate, lucid prose. Here, they are guided through the mechanics of composing straight news leads, structuring the straight news story, writing the standard pieces, from obituaries and fires to speeches, meetings and press conferences; and are introduced as well to the art of feature writing. Emphasis in this section is placed on common weaknesses and errors and how to overcome them. A chapter on self-editing encourages the would-be newswriter to improve his or her own copy, without relying upon others to do so. The section concludes with a detailed introduction to radio and television broadcast newswriting.

Part IV is concerned with reporting. It incorporates separate chapters on interviewing, public affairs reporting, and investigative reporting. In Part V, students are introduced to broader issues of press freedom, fairness and objectivity, ethics and taste, and the problem of separating facts from half-truths, assumptions and myths. A separate chapter on libel and privacy discusses these important areas of interaction between journalism and the law. The appendices include a style manual, bibliography and glossary.

Journalism is a richly varied field, with a colorful tradition to which we have tried to pay a full measure of devotion, but it is also a rapidly changing profession that demands an ever higher level of discernment and acuity from its practitioners. *The Practice of Journalism* therefore sounds the issues to a greater depth than is customary in introductory textbooks, and seeks to present its readers with examples and analysis that will reward the alert and discriminating mind. Though we concentrate on conveying the basic skills of the craft, we have endeavored always to explain why things are done this way, and to encourage the young journalist to explore new and more innovative pathways when they can.

Of course, no introductory test can provide exhaustive treatment of so variegated a profession, and every instructor will have his or her own preferences as to how to approach it. The chapters of this book consequently have been written as self-contained units, and need not be read or assigned in the order in which they appear here. We will have accomplished our purpose if we have helped make students feel excited by the challenge of reporting the news, and have aided them in acquiring the skills they need to make progress in the classroom and to put their lessons into practice in the wider world.

During the ten years that this book was being written, we incurred more debts of gratitude than we could ever fully acknowledge. We are especially grateful to the many colleagues who lent us the benefit of their expertise—especially to Joe Saltzman, Felix Gutierrez and Jon Kotler of the University of Southern California School of Journalism for their advice on broadcast newswriting, precision journalism, and press law, respectively; to Larry Pryor of the *Los Angeles Times* for his aid with the public affairs reporting chapter; and to Robert Potts, formerly of WCBS-TV, WNBC-TV and PBS, for his help relating to broadcasting. We are deeply grateful to publisher Forrest Palmer and his staff for permitting us to spend a week watching what went on in their news rooms at the *Danbury News-Times*. Thanks, too, for their special suggestions and general inspiration to Norman Corwin, Sue Horton, Jack Langguth, Luther Luedtke, Bryce Nelson and Clancy Sigal of USC, Anthony Mancini of Brooklyn College, Larry Pinkham of the University of Massachusetts, Penn Kimball, Luther Jackson, Barbara Belford, and Melvin Mencher of the Columbia University Graduate School of Journalism, H. L. Stevenson of United Press International, Walter Cronkite of CBS, David Brinkley of ABC, Robert Perry of the *Waterbury Republican*, and to the late Sheward Haggarty and Dwight Martin of *Newsweek*.

For research assistance we are indebted to Robert Ginsberg for his unrelenting pursuit of documents in the bowels of the New York Public Library, and to Pat Brierton, Eustice Clarke, Patricia Contini, Cynthia Hacinli, John Herzfeld, Judy Mitko, Carol Ramos and Marsha Ross. Thanks as well to Louise Fusco, Ann Orvieto, Blanche Bagley and Anita Stein of the Brooklyn College English Department, and to Myrtle Higdon and her co-workers at the USC School of Journalism, for responding beyond the call of duty to hundreds of cries for help over the years.

We gratefully acknowledge aid in gathering documents and material from Betty Cole Dukert of *Meet the Press*, Kendrick Frazier of *The Skeptical Enquirer*, Sidney Goldberg of the International News Alliance, Carolyn Horn of the *Los Angeles Times*, and Bruce Nathan and Ed Staats of the Associated Press.

We also wish to thank the following Prentice Hall reviewers who offered helpful insights: Mary Ann Yodelis Smith, University of Minnesota; Jon Christopher Hughes, University of Cincinnati; Rick Pullen, California State University; Patricia McNealy, University of South Carolina; Myron Schwartzman, Bernard M. Baruch College, C.U.N.Y.; Thomas Littlewood, University of Illinois, Urbana-Champaign; Charles Eisendrath, University of Michigan; Richard Hixon, Rutgers University; Michael Emery, California State University, Northridge; Richard Cole, University of North Carolina, Chapel Hill; Mary Pat Pfeil, Marquette University.

Most of all, our gratitude goes to our wives and children—to Lorna Scott Porter, Nell and Alexandra Porter, and to Carolyn Zecca Ferris, Alex and Francesca Zecca and Patrick Thomas Ferris—for their patience with the project over more than a decade of work, and for never giving up hope that someday it would come to a happy conclusion.

CREDITS

Our thanks go to the many individuals, magazines, newspapers, wire services and television networks who kindly consented to the reproduction of portions of their work in this book. Excerpts from these various sources are on the following pages:

Page 31: From *Public Opinion* by Walter Lippman. Copyright © 1922, renewed 1949 by Walter Lippman. Reprinted with permission of Macmillan Publishing Company.

Page 32: Reprinted with permission of the Estate of Edward R. Murrow.

Pages 54–55: Reprinted by permission of United Press International.

Pages 56–58, 92, 121, 123–24, 129–30, 151: Reprinted by permission of the Associated Press.

Page 71: Lyrics by Chuck Berry reprinted with permission; lyrics by Bruce Springsteen reprinted with permission; lyrics by Jacques Levy and Bob Dylan reprinted with permission of Ram's Horn Music and Jakelope Publishing.

Pages 84, 114–15, and 267: Reprinted with permission of *The Miami Herald*.

Pages 113–14, 153: Reprinted with permission of the *Chicago Tribune*.

From *The New York Times:* Pages 117–18, "Court Clears Prisoners' Move to L.I. Psychiatric Buildings," by James Barron, © 1972; page 121, "U.S. Is Set Back as O.A.S. Sides with Argentina," by Robert Reinhold © 1982; pages 140–41, "Reagan Presses for Tax Increase in Western Trip," by Steven R. Weisman © 1982; page 155, "Residents of Prospering Industrial Town in Iowa Show Few Signs of 'General Malaise'," by William Robbins ©

PART I Introduction

If it's extraordinary, and it affects us deeply, it's news.
                                        Walter Cronkite

News is what a chap who doesn't much care about anything wants to read.
                        Evelyn Waugh, in *Scoop*, a satirical novel about
                                        Fleet Street journalism.

1

WHAT IS NEWS?

Most definitions of news emphasize its freshness and popular appeal. The second edition of Webster's New International Dictionary defines news as "fresh tidings . . . gaining the interest of newspaper readers," while the Oxford English Dictionary calls it "new information; new occurrences as a subject of report or talk." We define news similarly, as *fresh information that interests or affects us*. That may seem plausible, but what, exactly, does it mean? Let's break it down.

First, news is *fresh* information. Old news is as worthless to a journalist as stale bread is to a baker. That's why reporters compete with one another to get the news first. When little fresh information is available, journalists try to emphasize a fresh angle; if the headline in the morning paper reads, BANDITS NET $100 THOUSAND IN AIR FREIGHT ROBBERY, the afternoon papers will headline the most recent aspects of the story: POLICE SEEK SIX IN $100 THOUSAND AIRPORT ROBBERY.

Second, news is fresh *information*. By information we mean the facts—what the reporter knows to be true—presented without bias or opinion. "The president broke his leg this morning." is information. It belongs in a news story. "Oh, the poor president!" is an expression of opinion, not of fact. It belongs in a news story only if enclosed in quotation marks and attributed to someone who said it.

Our third point is that news is what *interests* or *affects* us. The most important news has to do with changing patterns of *power*—that is, with changes that have some impact on us. If your next-door neighbor thinks the United States ought to launch a preemptive nuclear strike against the Soviet Union, that's

Editors deciding what makes news try to produce a mixture of what readers *need* to know with what they *want* to know. (Drawing by Ziegler; © 1978, *The New Yorker* Magazine, Inc.)

not news; your neighbor's opinion is unlikely to have much effect beyond the breakfast table, if there. But when President Reagan joked, while testing a microphone before a radio broadcast, that he was about to start bombing the Soviets, his remarks made news all over the world.

What affects us, of course, is not always the same as what interests us. The state of the economy affects us, but many of us find financial news dull and difficult to understand, and we follow it less closely than we should. At the other end of the spectrum, we may enjoy reading a profile of a movie star or a funny story about a cat up a tree, but we recognize that this sort of "news," like candy, is tasty but not very nourishing.

Even the most responsible newspapers carry a little froth—*The New York Times* runs stories about fashions and personalities, and the *Los Angeles Times* prints comic strips and horoscopes—but they also tell their readers what they need to know, not just what they might like to hear.

Finally, newsworthy information has to do with *people*. Newspaper editors and television producers try to keep the interests of their audience in mind. *The New York Times* reaches a better-educated audience than does the *New York Post*, and so the editors of the *Times* can afford to run longer and more sophisticated stories without worrying that they will lose the interest of their readers. But the "us" can also mean the editors and reporters themselves. Sometimes journalists will sense the importance of a story long before their readers do. Initially, for example, many readers reacted with indifference or indignation to the *Washington Post's* coverage of the Watergate scandal, but the *Post* persisted, and Watergate turned out to be one of the major stories of the decade.

WHERE DOES NEWS COME FROM?

News may be generated by *events* or by *issues*. By *events* we mean tangible happenings—like a burst dam or an outbreak of encephalitis—and also intangibles—like a change in the prime interest rate. "Things are in the saddle, and ride mankind," wrote Ralph Waldo Emerson, and much of the journalist's job consists of documenting that wild ride.

Issues are significant ideas about which people have differing views. Bombings of abortion clinics by "right to life" advocates are widely reported, not so much because of the damage caused by the events but because of what the bombings indicate about the deep emotions aroused by abortion as an issue. When demonstrators interfere with the launching of a nuclear submarine, the important news is not that the launch may have been inconvenienced but that the event dramatizes the issue of whether world security is improved by constantly building new weapons.

Some of the most interesting stories combine newsworthy events with pressing issues. When New York narcotics detectives kicked in the door of the wrong apartment and terrorized an innocent couple, the raid raised the issue of how much leeway the police should have to search private homes when they suspect that something criminal is happening inside. The crash of an L-1011 jet in a windstorm in 1985 raised the issue of whether federal aviation authorities should have funded deployment of a system that could have warned of the wind shear conditions responsible for the crash.

IMPACT AND INTEREST

One way to decide which news stories are the most important is to ask, "Which have the greatest *impact* and *interest*?" The impact of a news development may be *immediate* or *potential*. When President Reagan said in 1985 that he wanted to revamp the income tax system, the immediate impact was negligible, because Congress would have to debate the matter for months, but the story had considerable potential impact, because any such sweeping tax reform, if enacted, would affect nearly every American.

As improvements in travel and communications bind the world more tightly together, the impact of what were once considered local stories can often be felt far away. The cause of a trout dieout in the once-pure streams of the northern Adirondack Mountains in New York State, for example, proved to be sulfuric acid originating from factory smoke stacks in the Ohio River Valley, 400 miles away. The AIDS epidemic that struck America in the late 1980s began in Africa.

Some stories *interest* us, even though the events they report may have little impact upon our lives. People may not need to know about rock stars, spitball pitchers, or the Rhode Island judge who presided on hot summer days wearing nothing beneath his black robe but a pair of green running shorts, but many *want* to know these things, if only for their entertainment value. Such "human interest" stories remind us of the common bond of humanity that links all humankind; they lend empathy to the news. Roger Galluska, a 28-year-old reporter for United Press International, covered the 100th birthday of a Connecticut man named Henry Denninger. Instead of writing a story filled with cliches about the old man's long and happy life, Galluska reported that life no longer held any pleasure for Denninger. "It's my mind," Denninger complained. "I forget, lose track. I can't stand that. How do I feel? I wish I was finally six feet under the ground." The story, carried by hundreds of newspapers and radio and television stations across the country, drew thousands of letters urging Denninger to cheer up. "Please don't get tired of life, Henry," wrote a 12-year-old from Ohio. "We'd like to hear from you. God loves you." Galluska went back to get Denninger's reaction and found him sitting in bed amid a heap of letters. "There are some nice people around," the old man said. "It sounds very good to my ears."

The fact that human interest stories serve to entertain doesn't mean they can't have news value too. A cabinet member's personal religious views may be "human interest," but it was important news when James Watt, a secretary of the interior who advocated selling millions of acres of federally owned wilderness, said that conserving natural resources for future generations might be a waste of time, inasmuch as he believed that the Day of Judgment was close at hand.

WHAT MAKES NEWS?

Newspaper editors and the producers of broadcast news handle much more fresh, important information than they can report. Major news organizations like *The Chicago Tribune* or *CBS News* receive over a million words of copy daily just from the major wire services, and plenty more from their own reporters as well. They have space for only a fraction of all this information. How do they decide which stories to run, and how to "play"—that is, how much prominence to give—each story?

Personal judgment and taste play a role, of course. If the Earth were visited tomorrow by spaceships from the star Altair, every editor in the world would lead with that story. Below the blockbuster level, however, there's plenty of room for disagreement about which stories are the most important. In one study, sociologists examining the front pages of the nation's three leading newspapers—*The New York Times*, the *Los Angeles Times* and *The Washington Post*—found that the editors of all three newspapers led with the same story on only twenty-eight of 155 days. More than 80 percent of the time, the editors disagreed about what was the top news.

Another consideration is the audience. A typical issue of the *Midnight Globe*, a national weekly devoted to sex, scandal and gossip, featured Bing Crosby's "communication from the grave," a man who told of having been eaten by a great white shark, and an item headlined "Jesus Christ's Face Appeared on My Pancake." On the same day, *The Wall Street Journal* ran stories about American companies planning to build automobile engines in China, the decline of factory productivity nationwide and changes in the executive lineup at the R. J. Reynolds Tobacco Company. Evident here are the differences in education and sophistication of the two publications' audiences: *Journal* readers want hard facts, whereas *Globe* readers want to be entertained.

Newsweek magazine is read by 10 million people, many of them well-to-do college graduates who work in business and the professions. They look to the magazine for a wrap-up of important national and international news, and for news of trends and developments in art, music, books, movies, business, science, medicine, religion, sports, law and the media. The Belfast, Maine, *Republican-Journal*, a weekly newspaper with a circulation of 4000, is read by dairy farmers, wood pulpers and housewives who put up vegetables for the long harsh winter— rural people who work with their hands. They expect the *Republican-Journal* to inform them about news that hits close to home: that Willis Ladd broke five ribs when his tractor toppled over on him while he was cutting hay on a hillside last week; that the town council voted to spend $55,000 to blacktop the dirt road leading to Burkettville. A story in the *Republican-Journal* about a coup d'etat in Argentina would be as out of place as a story in *Newsweek* about the prize Ruby Adams took for her gladiolas at the Grange Hall in South Montville.

NEWS AND EDITORIALS DON'T MIX

Reputable newspapers express their editors' opinions through editorials, not on the news pages. Editorials can include opinion; news stories should not.

During the last days of *The Washington Star*, *The Miami Herald* ran a news story with this lead:

Chris-Craft Industries of New York may buy *The Washington Star* if Congress enacts tax benefits that would enable it to recover up to 96 percent of its business losses over the next three years, the corporation's chairman said Thursday night.

That's straight news: just the facts, no opinion. As it happened, the editors of the *Herald* felt rather strongly about Chris-Craft's plan to rescue the *Star*. But they reserved their opinion for the editorial pages the next day:

Only six days remain before Time, Inc., shuts down the presses of *The Washington Star*, leaving the nation's capital a one-newspaper town. Death for the distinguished old daily looms sadly close. If only some capitalist gambler would take a chance on rescuing the *Star*, that would be welcome news indeed.

But not the way Chris-Craft Industries tried to do it. Chris-Craft's motives were noble . . . but its method was totally unacceptable. . . .

Phrases like "distinguished old daily," "sadly," "welcome news indeed" and "totally unacceptable" are statements of opinion. Their place is where the *Herald* put them: on the editorial page, not on the news pages.

The most important considerations in deciding which stories make the top news are:

Consequence: How important is the story?
Proximity: How close to home is it?
Timeliness: How fresh, or "hot," is it?
Uniqueness: How rare or surprising is it?
Emotional appeal: How deeply does it touch our feelings?

The *consequence* of a news development can be gauged by asking *how many* readers it will interest or affect, and *how deeply*. A hurricane 1000 miles from land warrants scant coverage, because it threatens only a few passing ships; the same hurricane approaching the low-lying coastal city of Galveston, Texas, makes headlines, because the consequences of its striking the city could be widespread loss of life and property. A change in the leadership of France makes world headlines, for France is an influential nation; less attention is paid to events in tiny Albania, whose world influence is negligible. The obituaries of the famous and the powerful are viewed as consequential by more readers than are the obituaries of those who went through life leaving little trace of themselves.

Proximity means that readers are likely to care more deeply about developments close to home than those far away. Coverage of the murder of a 15-year-old boy during a fight outside a rock club in Van Nuys, California, filled three pages in the *Daily News*, a "valley" newspaper with a readership concentrated in the Van Nuys area. But the same story was allotted only twelve paragraphs in the *Los Angeles Times*, and the Chicago papers didn't cover it at all.

In a shrinking world, however, local stories can have "ripple" effects that spread for thousands of miles, and the rule of proximity consequently is becoming less persuasive. In 1975, a disastrous grain harvest obliged the Soviet Union to buy $200 million worth of wheat from the United States. At first the news might have seemed of interest chiefly to farmers in the Midwest, but it developed into a national story of considerable importance. By decreasing grain supplies, the sale had the effect of increasing the price of wheat, and of driving up bread prices in the United States by about 10 cents a loaf. And when terrorists in the Mideast held Americans hostage aboard a TWA airliner and, later, on an Italian cruise ship, the American press covered the stories with front-page headlines and special bulletins, as feverishly as if they were happening across the street.

The news is what's new: *Timeliness* counts. Journalists normally incorporate old information only insofar as is necessary to make the story intelligible or to put it in perspective. If Smith and Jones are battling each other in a well-publicized campaign for mayor, it serves little purpose to write a lead like this:

Gloria Smith, who is running for mayor against incumbent John Jones, continued to criticize her opponent today.

The public already knows that the two are engaged in a tough campaign; this lead contains nothing *new*. It is better to lead with fresh information:

> Mayoral candidate Gloria Smith today called incumbent John Jones "a chronic do-nothing whose reelection could wreck our city."

Ongoing stories that drag along for weeks or months can tax a journalist's ability to come up with fresh information daily. That's when the temptation looms to write a lead like:

> The dockworker's strike today entered its fifteenth day with no sign of an early settlement.

Such "calendar leads" tell us nothing new. They recall the "Saturday Night Live" newscaster who reported, week after week, "Generalissimo Francisco Franco of Spain is still dead today. . . ."

A story is considered timely—or "hot"—if it touches on a topic already on people's minds. When the Ford Pinto and other American cars were shown to be unsafe, newspapers began running stories each time an auto manufacturer recalled cars to correct mechanical defects, though editors previously had ignored such stories. In 1987, a story about a racial assault in a county north of Atlanta received heavy national play because the death of a black man being chased by a gang of whites in New York City had already heightened public concern about the problem of racial antagonisms.

The *unique*, the unusual, the surprising and the rare also make news. As John Bogart, city editor of the old *New York Sun*, counseled a young reporter, "When a dog bites a man, that's not news. But when a man bites a dog, that *is* news." A Rockefeller heiress attracted national coverage when she was found to be living frugally in a house trailer; were she living in luxury, her situation would not have made news.

The flavor of unusual stories is often ironic. The *Village Voice* reported that tough-guy movie actor Sylvester Stallone of "Rocky" and "Rambo" fame never served in the military and spent much of the Vietnam War giving acting lessons in a girls' private school. UPI reported that one of the items stolen during a burglary in Arlington, Virginia, was an anti-theft robot the size of a garbage can that had been programmed to shout, "Warning, intruder! I have summoned the police!"

We react to the news *emotionally* as well as intellectually. The recipient of the world's first artificial heart became something of a national hero; people appreciated his heroism in undergoing the rigors of a medical experiment that might benefit others. In politics and sports, an underdog or a comeback contender has great emotional appeal—as did the United States Hockey Team that beat the far-better-trained Soviet team in the 1980 Winter Olympics. A fatal fire in an old age home or a college dormitory may have stronger emotional effect than a fire in an apartment building, owing to the vulnerability of the aged and the tragedy of death at an early age.

Here, as always, the interests of the audience come into play. When seventeen sailors were lost in the Fastnet yacht race off the coast of England and Ireland in 1979, the story received prominent play on the American east and west coasts, where many ocean sailors live, but it was played less prominently in the Midwest, where boating is limited to going out on lakes.

SUMMARY

"News" may be defined as fresh information that interests or affects us. By *fresh* we mean that once everybody knows about it, it's no longer news. By *information* we mean facts—reporting what really happened, accurately and without bias. Journalists make news judgments not only in terms of their own views, but also in terms of their audience's as well. The average newspaper is a mix of what people *want* to read and what they *need* to read; the more serious and respected newspapers and broadcasters lean toward the latter side of the balance.

Journalists report on *events* and *issues*. In deciding what makes news, they consider each story's *consequence* (how important is it?); its *proximity* (how close to home is it?); its *timeliness* (how fresh, or "hot," is it?); its *uniqueness* (how rare or surprising is it?); and its *emotional appeal* (how deeply does it touch our feelings?). None of these criteria will make or break a news story in itself, but together they help determine which stories should be reported and how prominently each should be played.

2

REPORTING THE NEWS:
A BRIEF HISTORY

American journalists have been reporting the news since before the United States was founded. The concept of what news *is* and how news is gathered has changed over the years, shaped not only by reporters and editors but also by the laws and customs of society at large. This chapter offers a brief history of American journalism, a sketch of how it became what it is today.

THE EARLY DAYS

In early colonial times, newspapers were printed only by permission of the royal governors. News items or editorials critical of the authorities were regarded as criminally offensive. Troublesome editors might even be sent to jail for a few days to reconsider their views.

The first paper in America was a monthly newsletter published in 1690 in Massachusetts. Called *Publick Occurrences, Both Foreign and Domestick*, it consisted of four pages, with the back page left blank so readers could insert their own news and then pass the paper along to neighbors. In his first and only issue, the editor, Benjamin Harris, ran a story about New England farmers' grumbling over having to serve in a British expeditionary force being sent to fight Indians in Canada. This so annoyed the governor that he promptly ordered the paper suppressed on the grounds it contained "reflections of a very high nature."

Colonial papers circulated to only 500 to 1000 readers each. Geared strictly to the upper classes, they reported government proclamations, local real estate transactions and the comings and goings of merchant ships. They also reprinted foreign items from the London papers. Typically, the editor who wrote the week's news also went into the back shop to help set type and run the flatbed press. The press was a simple device operated by placing a sheet of paper on a bed of type and screwing down a heavy weight to make an impression. If the paper was banned or the editor run out of town by a mob, as sometimes happened, he could load his press and type fonts into a wagon and set up operation in another city.

One of the liveliest colonial papers, the *New England Courant*, was published in Boston in 1722 by three printers. Founded specifically to oppose the then controversial practice of smallpox inoculation being promoted by the Puritan Mather brothers, the *Courant* vented its opinion on other issues, too, aping the witty, urbane style of its popular contemporary, the London *Spectator*. In its first issue, the editor of the *Courant* asked readers to submit "short pieces, serious, sarcastic, ludicrous or other ways amusing." One of the first submissions was a dissertation on drunkenness. Slid under the paper's front door one night, it was signed "Silence Dogood." This turned out to be a pen name for the publisher's younger half-brother, Benjamin Franklin, then working as an apprentice in the back shop. The piece ended with a compilation of contemporary euphemisms for drunkenness:

> . . . They are seldom known to be drunk, 'tho they are often *boozey, cogey, tipfey, fox'd, merry, mellow, fuddl'd, groatable, Confoundedly cut, See two moons,* are *Among the Philiftines, In a very good Humour, See the Sun,* or *The Sun has fhone upon them*; they *Clip the King's English,* are *Almoft froze, Feavourifh, In their Altitudes, Pretty well enter'd,* &c. . . . If at any Time a Man of Sobriety and Temperance happens to *cut himfelfe confoundedly,* or is *almost froze* or *feavourifh,* &c, he may efcape the imputations of being *drunk,* when his Misfortune comes to be relayed.

Cotton and Increase Mather, continually attacked by the paper for their support of vaccination, liked neither the *Courant's* politics nor its irreverent style. To them, it was "full freighted with nonsense, unmannerliness, railery, profaneness, immorality, arrogancy, calumnies, lyes, contrarities and what not . . . all tending to corrupt the manners of New England." Governor Benjamin Shute of Massachusetts, however, had his own quarrel with the Mathers for their failure to support his Royalist party, and he allowed the paper to continue publishing.

Then, in one week's issue, the Franklins took after Shute himself, in an article intimating that the governor was being paid off by pirates not to interfere with their marauding of coastal shipping. Shute responded by clapping James Franklin in jail. Benjamin, seeing his chance to get free of his apprenticeship and be off on his own, promptly left for Philadelphia.

The first major step toward restraining the government from this sort of harassment and establishing a free press came with the trial of John Peter Zenger. Zenger, a German immigrant, was publisher of the *New York Weekly Journal*, a paper that campaigned against a repressive royal governor named William

Cosby. Incensed at the *Journal's* jibes at his administration (at one point the paper called Cosby's high sheriff "a monkey of a larger sort, about four foot high," who "has lately broke his chain and run into the country"), the governor ordered Zenger jailed on a charge of seditious libel.

Today the law holds that truth is a defense against a charge of libel, but in 1735 even a factual statement could be judged indefensibly libelous. As the judge in Zenger's trial put it, "It is nevertheless a libel that it is true."

Zenger's trial began on a broiling-hot August day in 1735. His lawyer was a well-known civil liberties advocate named Andrew Hamilton, then in his eighties. In a stirring speech, Hamilton urged the jury to ignore the technicalities of the law and to strike a blow for a free press. Said Hamilton, "The question before the court and you, gentlemen of the jury, is not of small nor private concern, it is not the cause of a poor printer, nor of New York alone, which you are now trying: No! It may in its consequences affect every free man that lives under a British government on the Main of America. It is the best cause. It is the cause of liberty. . . ." Hamilton called upon the jurors to create "a noble foundation for securing to ourselves, our posterity and our neighbors, that to which nature and the laws of our country have given us a right—the liberty—both of exposing and opposing arbitrary power . . . by speaking and writing Truth."

Despite instructions from the judge to the contrary, the jury returned a unanimous verdict of not guilty. The courtroom broke into cheers. Government control of the press would continue for many years, but an important precedent had been set: that the press could criticize government officials, as long as its reports were true.

Most papers of the period mixed opinion with the facts. In the years surrounding the American Revolution, publishers slanted the news according to whether they were pro- or anti-British. The *Boston Gazette*, an anti-British paper that a royalist editor called a "dung barge," ran an account of the Boston Tea Party written by Samuel Adams—the very man who had organized and led the mob that stormed the English merchant ship and dumped its tea into the Boston harbor.

The newswriting style of the period was ornate, and the essential news was often buried well down in the story. Still, some eighteenth-century newswriting makes good reading even today. This account of the first battles in the Revolutionary War at Lexington and Concord appeared in the *Essex Gazette* of Salem on April 25, 1775. It starts a bit slowly, but soon gets to the point (the spelling and punctuation have been modernized):

SALEM, April 25—Last Wednesday, the 19th of April, the troops of his Britannic Majesty commenced hostilities upon the people of this province, attended with circumstances of cruelty not less brutal than what our venerable ancestors received from the vilest savages of the wilderness. The particulars relative to this interesting event, by which we are involved in all the horrors of a civil war, we have endeavored to collect as well as the present, confused state of affairs will admit.

On Tuesday evening a detachment

from the Army, consisting, it is said, of 800 or 900 men, commanded by Lt. Col. Smith, embarked at the bottom of the common in Boston, on board a number of boats, and landed at Phip's Farm, a little way up Charles River, from whence they proceeded with a sense and expedition, on their way to Concord, about 18 miles from Boston. The people were soon alarmed, and began to assemble, in several towns, before daylight, in order to watch the motion of the troops. At Lexington, 6 miles below Concord, a company of militia, of about 100 men, mustered near the Meeting House; the troops came in sight of them just before sunrise; and running within a few rods of them, the commanding officer accosted the militia in words to this effect:

"Disperse you Rebels—Damn you, throw down your arms and disperse."

Upon which the troops huzzaed, and immediately one or two officers discharged their pistols, which were instantaneously followed by the firing of four or five of the soldiers, and then there seemed to be a general discharge from the whole body.

Eight of our men were killed, and nine wounded. . . .

Before the Revolution, dissident editors attacked the British; after the war they leveled their guns at their new government. The attacks drew counterattacks from other editors, and by the end of the eighteenth century the fuming and sputtering of the press had stirred up clouds of vituperation. Editorially, newspapers were divided by whether they supported the Republican party and Thomas Jefferson or the Federalist party, whose standard bearers included George Washington and Alexander Hamilton. Views differed violently, particularly over the French Revolution: The Jeffersonians supported the upheaval, and the Federalists lamented the fall of royalty and the established order.

One of the most skilled spleen-venters was a Federalist editor named William Cobbett, whose *Porcupine's Gazette* in Philadelphia sunk its quills into anyone who had an unkind word for the French king or George Washington. Cobbett's arch enemy was a fellow Philadelphian, Benjamin Franklin Bache, a grandson of Benjamin Franklin whom Cobbett nicknamed "Lightning Rod Junior." Bache, a Jeffersonian who published the *Aurora* across town, had already been beaten up for his strong anti-Washington editorials. When he tried to justify the anger of French revolutionists by accusing the French king, Louis XVI, of having had 8000 people put to death, Cobbett flew at him like a fighting cock:

Now who ever heard of this before? Who ever heard of a massacre at Paris, while poor Louis retained his power of King?. . . . This atrocious wretch Bache knows that all men of any understanding set him down as an abandoned liar, as a fool and a hireling. . . . He is an ill-looking devil. His eyes never get above your knees. He is a fellow of a sallow complexion, hollowed cheeked, dead-eyed . . . just like that of a fellow who has been about a week or ten days on a gibbet.

Journalists of the early nineteenth century still made little attempt to appear objective. Some became so emotionally involved in an event that they all but forgot to report the news. "TO ARMS! TO ARMS!" shouted *The Enquirer* of Richmond, Virginia, on August 27, 1814: "At length a blow is struck which must rouse the most listless and incredulous, a blow which would near 'create a soul under the ribs of death.' Prepare, prepare; the Philistines be upon you.

In what words shall we break the tidings to the ear? The blush of shame, and of rage tinges the cheek. . . ." And so on.

What had happened was that the British had attacked Washington, burned the Capitol and the White House and put the President and his government to flight. At the end of his two-column story the editor finally disengaged himself from his hysteria and, in a considerable feat of wishful thinking, concluded that the enemy occupation might not really be so bad:

> And after all, let us view this disaster coolly. What mighty feat has the enemy performed? He will attempt, no doubt, to magnify its importance; to give it a sort of eclat which must vanish at the touch of truth—they will sound it throughout Europe that they have seized the Metropolis of the U. States. . . . Let the truth be told, that Washington was but the other day a desert; that its population is only 8203, of all sorts and descriptions of people; that its defenders were few, inferior in number to the assailants. . . . Let these truths be told, and then let the British boast as they may. Our countrymen have beat them already; and with adequate opportunity they can do it again. As a *military feat*, we say, again and again, it is *nothing*, emphatically *nothing*. . . .

THE RISE OF THE POPULAR PRESS

Following in the spirit of Jacksonian democracy, newspapers in the 1830s and the 1840s came out of the clubrooms of the well-to-do and sought the patronage of the masses. Manufacturers had found a way to make paper more cheaply: The old hand-cranked flatbed press was replaced by steam-driven cylinder models that could turn out 4000 sheets an hour. And in 1844 the invention of the telegraph created a communications revolution. News of wars, disasters and elections no longer had to wait for trains and packet boats; it came over the wire in an instant, and readers could learn of it the very next day.

Along with the new technology appeared three remarkable newspaper publishers: Benjamin Day of *The New York Sun*; James Gordon Bennett of *The New York Herald*, and Horace Greeley of *The New York Tribune*. Day, who started the *Sun* in 1833 as an adjunct to his printing business, charged only a penny a copy instead of the traditional six cents. He employed a squad of newsboys—usually homeless waifs—to hawk the paper in the street, and published livelier news than the stuffy proclamations and speeches that filled the other papers. He hired an out-of-work printer named George Wisner and assigned him to report on each day's police blotter. Wisner became the first police reporter in the country. His stories, immensely popular, were mostly brief efforts to wring some amusement from the suffering of wretches:

> . . . William Luboy got drunk because yesterday was so devilish warm. Drank 9 glasses of brandy and water and said he would be cursed if he wouldn't drink 9 more as quick as he could raise the money to buy it with. He would like to know what right the magistrate had to interfere with his private affairs. Fined $1—forgot his pocketbook, and was sent over to Bridewell. . . .

> Bridget McMunn got drunk and threw a pitcher at Mrs. Ellis, of 53 Ludlow St. Bridget said she was the mother of 3 little orphans—God bless their dear souls—and if she went to prison they would choke to death for want of something to eat. Committed.

If Day was the great popularizer of the press, James Gordon Bennett might well be called the founder of sensationalism: the art of appealing to readers' emotions through the use of lurid detail. A Scottish immigrant, Bennett started the *Herald* in 1835 with $500 in capital. He did his first business over a board set up on two flour barrels at 20 Wall Street. His paper created an instant stir, and within fifteen months had overtaken the circulation of the *Sun*.

Part of Bennett's formula for success was aggressive news gathering. He outfitted special "news boats" in the harbor and sent them to intercept trans-Atlantic ships so the *Herald* could get the foreign newspapers first. He was the first to put reporters on special beats, covering business, society news and the courts. Before the telegraph arrived, he had *Herald* correspondents filing stories by carrier pigeon and the pony express.

As an editor, Bennett rid his paper of the flowery writing style then popular and began a trend toward plain English. Reporters were told to write "pantaloons" instead of "inexpressibles" and "legs" for "limbs." "Petticoats, petticoats, petticoats, petticoats," he shouted in an editorial responding to critics of his penchant for noneuphemistic prose. "There, you fastidious fools, vent your mawkishness on that."

Bennett excelled at reporting crime, sex and gossip. He ballyhooed the ax murder of a Broadway prostitute named Ellen Jewett until the whole country was following the case. Ellen was a peaceable harlot from a small town in Maine who worked in a "disreputable house" rather than on the streets, but Bennett painted her as a wanton siren who lured men to their destruction. The *Herald* created so much sympathy for her murderer that he eventually was acquitted.

The paper often ran salacious gossip about people identified only by their first initials, items that presaged the gossip columns popular a century later. And whereas the *Sun* made light of police news, the *Herald* concentrated on the gore:

> MYSTERIOUS CIRCUMSTANCES: On Monday morning, tracks of blood were seen in Anthony near Church St. and traced up to Broadway, and thence to a physician's door. Some persons of that neighborhood made a complaint yesterday morning that a serious occurrence had taken place in which one of the parties concerned had had his head dreadfully mangled with an ax. . . .

Bennett's excesses stirred a "moral war," launched against him by the city's established leaders, who tried to ostracize him from polite society. Editorials in other papers accused the *Herald* of "moral leprosy" and called Bennett a "polluted wretch." The more he was attacked, however, the more Bennett used the controversy to promote his paper. A rival publisher, Watson Webb of *The New York Courier and Enquirer*, became so furious at Bennett that, meeting him on the street, he hit Bennett with his cane, lacerating his scalp. The attack served merely to provide Bennett with a topic for the next day's editorial. "I have to apologize to my kind readers for the want of my usual life today," he said of the beating. "The fellow no doubt wanted to let out the never failing supply of good humor and wit which has created such a reputation for the *Herald* and appropriate the contents to supply the emptiness of his own thick skull."

For all his success as a newspaperman, Bennett had no interest in politics and did little to influence opinion. Quite the opposite was true of the third great publisher of the period, Horace Greeley. Short, pudgy, moon-faced, his suit rumpled, possessed of handwriting that few could decipher, Greeley arrived in New York in the early 1830s as an itinerant printer, his sole possessions wrapped in a red handkerchief. He founded the *Tribune* in 1841. From the start he sought to distinguish it from the competition by pledging to give no space to "immoral and degrading Police Reports, Advertisements and other matters which have been allowed to disgrace the columns of our leading Penny Papers."

Although Greeley soon found that he, too, needed crime news to attract readers, the *Tribune* achieved renown for its editorial page more than for its news columns. Nicknamed "The Great Moral Organ," the paper reflected Greeley's soaring idealism and his commitment to proposals for elevating the masses. "The Great, the all-embracing reform of our age," he wrote, "is the Social Reform—that which seeks to lift the Laboring Class, as such, not out of labor, by any means, but out of ignorance, inefficiency, dependence and want."

The budding labor movement, the antislavery movement, the western home-steading movement, temperance and extraterrestrial spiritualism all received the blessings of Greeley's lengthy and passionate editorials. His social conscience sprang from his horror over New York City's reeking slums, and his solution for most ills was a rural form of Marxism espoused by the French writer Charles Fourier. (Marx himself was the *Tribune's* London correspondent for ten years.)

When Greeley created the national *Weekly Tribune*, he gained a countrywide reputation. By the advent of the Civil War he was selling 200,000 papers, mostly to Americans in small towns of New England and the Midwest who shared his preference for rural virtues and who read his editorials as avidly as they read the Bible. Greeley, quipped Ralph Waldo Emerson, "did all their thinking and theory for two dollars a year."

More than a cornpone philosopher, Greeley was the first journalist to force the nation to confront the ideals written into its Constitution, particularly those pertaining to free speech. And as with H. L. Mencken after him, the fire from his editorials, particularly when directed against hypocrisy and small-mindedness, could be withering:

> Thousands will flock together to drink in the musical periods of some popular declaimer. . . . They go away delighted with the orator and themselves. The next day, they may be engaged in lynching some unlucky individual who has fallen under their sovereign displeasure, breaking up a meeting of an obnoxious cast or tarring and feathering some unfortunate lecturer or propagandist whose views do not square with their own, but who has precisely the same right to enjoy and propagate his opinions, however erroneous. . . . The shamelessness of the incongruity is sickening.

COVERING THE CIVIL WAR

With his cape overcoat, pocket compass, thick notebooks and long-tubed binoculars, the Civil War correspondent, or "special," was a familiar figure around most Army camps. Some 400 specials covered the war for the North alone, fifty of them from Bennett's *Herald*. It was not an easy assignment. They slogged along with the Army, sleeping in the mud and rain with the soldiers. The battles, involving as many as 150,000 or 200,000 men, were often hard to comprehend. Telegraph heads might lie miles from the action; reporters had to travel on horse or foot, sometimes through enemy territory, to file their dispatches. When they finally reached the telegraph key, they might find that it had been preempted by the military or by a rival reporter. Competition for the single strand of wire was keen, and the first reporter to get there would often hold open the line by handing the operator a Bible and telling him to send Genesis until the reporter got his copy ready. According to one account, possibly apocryphal, Joseph Howard of *The New York Times* spent so long putting his story into shape after the Battle of Ball's Bluff that the operator got to the Book of Leviticus before Howard was ready to file.

Because the wire might fail or be commandeered by a general at any time, reporters learned to structure their stories in short units, with the most newsworthy information first. That way, they would have conveyed the essential news if the transmission was interrupted. This style was to develop into the modern "inverted-pyramid" news format.

In the Civil War, as in nearly every war thereafter, the press encountered hostility from the military. Northern generals spent most of the first half of the war being defeated, and they were not happy to see their failures and ineptitudes spread over the front pages. General William Tecumseh Sherman, whose famous March to the Sea through Georgia eventually broke the South's back, banned reporters from his camp because he was convinced that their stories aided the enemy. "The only two really successful strokes out here," he wrote his brother, a senator, during the Vicksburg campaign, "have succeeded because of the absence of the newspapers or by throwing them off the trail."

Logistical problems promoted inadvertent errors by the journalists, and Civil War reporting was fraught with inaccuracies. Generals were reported killed who had never suffered a scratch. Battles were dated the wrong day. One account had Atlanta taken a full week before Sherman got around to his final assault on the city. Reporters who had neither the energy nor the luck to obtain accurate information relied upon rumor—the notorious "grapevine telegraph"—or simply made up their stories. In one typical instance, a story on the Northern victory at the Battle of Pea Ridge in 1862 was listed in the normally responsible *New York Tribune* as an "eyewitness account," when in fact the reporter had interviewed returning soldiers and "piped" the action and color from his imagination.

The sloppy coverage was due in part to the inexperience of correspondents who didn't know how to write about warfare. "Men turned up in the Army as correspondents more fit to drive cattle than to write for a newspaper," grumbled Henry Villard, a crack reporter who worked at various times for both the *Herald* and the *Tribune*. Editors abetted the process by demanding news, even if of questionable accuracy: War news sold papers. "Telegraph fully all news you can get," Wilbur Storey, publisher of the *Chicago Times* wired his specials. "And when there is no news, send rumors."

Government censorship occasionally intervened. At Bull Run, the first big battle of the war, Henry J. Raymond of *The New York Times* left the field at 2 P.M., convinced that the Confederates had been routed, and filed a vivid victory story from the telegraph head in Washington. That evening he returned to the battlefield, and was aghast to see Union soldiers fleeing in panic; their "victory" had become a humiliating defeat. The United States Secretary of War, Winfield Scott, prohibited Raymond and other reporters from sending word of the disaster. Readers in the North did not learn fully of the rout until a week later, when complete reports showed up in the *London Times*.

Confederate journalists maintained an attitude of optimism in the face of defeat, even while newspapers in Memphis and Chattanooga were moving their presses south to escape the advancing Union army. Casualty figures were minimized. The Confederate army never "retreated"; its backward movements were "improperly called a retreat by those who do not comprehend them," one Southern reporter wrote. In reality, he said, the movements were really "retrograde maneuvers."

Editors in the North, too, altered the news to make it more palatable. When reporter Henry Villard of the *Tribune* got a scoop on the Union defeat at Fredericksburg, he rode through trackless country and hitched a ride on a steamer to get to Washington. There he found the telegraph wire guarded by the military's censor for the War Department, so he sent the story along by train. His efforts went for naught when his editors in New York, horrified at the extent of the defeat, toned down the story to make the battle seem more like a draw.

As in all wars, reporters sometimes put themselves in considerable danger. One of the most intrepid newsmen was Villard's colleague on the *Tribune*, Albert D. Richardson. At the start of hostilities, Richardson risked being hanged as a spy by travelling through the South disguised as a banker and filing his stories in the form of coded letters to a New York bank, which then relayed them to his paper. During the western campaign, he and another reporter tried to run past the Confederate shore batteries at Vicksburg in a little steamer. The captain of their boat was killed and its boiler was blown up by grapeshot. The pair jumped into the river, only to be captured by the rebel forces. After months in prison camps, Richardson escaped. Aided by slaves, spies and a woman he later identified only as a "nameless heroine," he made his way across mountains and swollen rivers back to the Union lines at Knoxville, Tennessee. On his arrival, he rushed to the nearest telegraph office and cabled his editor, Horace Greeley, a dispatch that began: "Out of the jaws of death. Out of the mouth of hell." Then he went back to the front lines.

PICKETT'S CHARGE: AN EYEWITNESS ACCOUNT

Datelined "Field of Battle, near Gettysburg, July 2," here is the eye-witness account given *The Cincinnati Gazette* readers of the disastrous Confederate attack ordered by Robert E. Lee on the Union position along Cemetery Ridge that later became known as "Pickett's Charge." It was written under the pen name of "Agate" by reporter Whitlaw Reid who reported the story while standing at the center of the Union lines, the position most exposed to rebel fire. Notice how Reid gives the facts first, then ends the piece by telling readers what was significant about the battle—one of the early examples of interpretive reporting.

Ascending the high hill to the rear of Slocum's headquarters, I saw such a sight as few men may ever hope to see twice in a lifetime. Around our center and left, the rebel line must have been from four to five miles long, and over that whole length there rolled up the smoke from their two hundred and fifty guns. The roar, the bursting bombs, the impression of magnificent power, "all the glory visible, all the horror of the fearful field concealed," a nation's existence trembling as the clangor of those iron monsters swayed the balance—it was a sensation for a century!

About two the fire slackened a little, then broke out deadlier than ever, till, beaten out against our impenetrable sides, it ebbed away and closed in broken, spasmodic dashes.

The great, desperate, final charge came at four. The rebels seemed to have gathered up all their strength and desperation for one fierce, convulsive effort, that should sweep over and wash out our obstinate resistance. They swept up as before, the flower of their army to the front, victory staked upon the issue. In some places they literally lifted up and pushed back our lines, but that terrible "position" of ours!—wherever they entered it, enfilading fires from half a score of crests swept away their columns like merest chaff. Broken and hurled back, they easily fell into our hands, and on the center and left the last half-hour brought more prisoners than all the rest.

So it was along the whole line; but it was on the Second Corps that the flower of the rebel army was concentrated; it was there that the heaviest shock beat upon and shook and even sometimes crumbled our line.

We had some shallow rifle pits, with barricades of rails from the fences. The rebel line, stretching away miles to the left, in magnificent array, but strongest here—Pickett's splendid division of Longstreet's corps in front, the best of A. P. Hill's veterans in support—came steadily and, as it seemed, resistlessly sweeping up. Our skirmishers retired slowly from the Emmetsburg road, holding their ground tenaciously to the last. The rebels reserved their fire till they reached this same Emmetsburg road, then opened with a terrific crash. From a hundred iron throats, meantime, their artillery had been thundering on our barricades.

Hancock was wounded; Gibbon succeeded to the command—approved soldier, and ready for the crisis. As the tempest of fire approached its height, he walked along the line, and renewed his orders to the men to reserve their fire. The rebels—three lines deep—came steadily up. They were in point-blank range.

At last the order came! From thrice six thousand guns there came a sheet of smoky flame, a crash of leaden death. The line literally melted away; but there came the second, resistless still. It had been our supreme effort—on the instant we were not equal to another.

Up to the rifle pits, across them, over the barricades—the momentum of their charge, the mere machine strength of their combined action swept them on. Our thin line could fight, but it had not weight enough to oppose to this momentum. It was pushed behind the guns. Right on came the rebels. They were upon the guns, were bayoneting the gunners, were waving their flags above our pieces.

But they had penetrated to the fatal point. A storm of grape and canister tore its way from man to man and marked its track with corpses straight down their line! They had exposed themselves to the enfilading fire of the guns on the western slope of Cemetery Hill; that exposure sealed their fate.

The line reeled back—disjointed already—in an instant in fragments. Our men were just behind the guns. They leaped forward upon the disordered mass; but there was little need for fighting now. A regiment threw down its arms, and, with colors at its head, rushed over and surrendered. All along the field smaller detachments did the same. Webb's brigade brought in eight hundred taken in as little time as it requires to write the simple sentence that tells it. Gibbon's old division took fifteen stands of colors.

Over the fields the escaped fragments of the charging line fell back—the battle there was over. A single brigade, Harrow's (of which the Seventh Michigan is part), came out with fifty-four less officers, 793 less men than it took in! So the whole corps fought—so, too, they fought further down the line.

It was fruitless sacrifice. They gathered up their broken fragments, formed their lines, and slowly marched away. It was not a rout, it *was* a bitter, crushing defeat. For once the Army of the Potomac had won a clean, honest, acknowledged victory.

THE MODERN NEWSPAPER ARRIVES

After the Civil War, further advances in technology transformed both the appearance of newspapers and the way they reported the news. In 1866, a trans-Atlantic cable linked Europe and New York. Ten years later came the telephone. Now reporters could talk to news sources without having to go and see them, and stories could be called in from the scene and written instantly. This prompted the big urban papers to put out extra editions, or "extras," with newsboys screaming the latest headlines from every major street corner. The typewriter came along in the 1880s, but reporters resisted typewriters at first, preferring to write their copy by hand, just as 100 years later some journalists were reluctant to trade their typewriters for word processors. In the back shop, type was now being set up by simply punching out letters on a Linotype machine. Faster rotary presses could print, cut and fold 24,000 twenty-four-page papers in an hour.

The new technology allowed newspapers to enliven their layouts. Before the rotary presses, type had to be set in single-column files so it wouldn't fly off the presses as they revolved. Now, with modern lead-cast plates, stories could be set in columns of any width the editors wanted. Headlines didn't have to be stacked up like names on a tombstone, but could flow all the way across the page. In the New York *Morning Journal* the snowstorm of 1888 was heralded with a banner headline—B L I Z Z A R D—that dripped frosty icicles.

Editors started writing bold-looking headlines intended to grab the reader's attention. The reigning master of the new art was Horatio W. Seymour, wire editor of the *Chicago Times*, who specialized in puns and feats of alliteration. One head over a story about William Vanderbilt's last will and testament read:

HOUSE THAT VANDERBILT

Another one for a disastrous train wreck stated:

DEATH'S DEBAUCH

Seymour reached his zenith—or nadir—when he topped a story of a quadruple hanging in 1875 with the head:

JERKED TO JESUS

Journalists began looking for news that fell outside the traditional categories of crimes, wars, disasters and politics. Joseph Pulitzer told his staff on the *St. Louis Post-Dispatch* that news was anything "original, distinctive, dramatic, romantic, thrilling, unique, curious, quaint, humorous, odd or apt to be talked about."

Charles A. Dana, who had bought *The New York Sun* from Benjamin Day, emphasized what he called "human interest" stories: warm or humorous accounts of an Italian bootblack, a shop girl freshly arrived from the country or a "man bites dog" story pursued by his city editor, John Bogart.

Reporters began prying into facets of life not previously regarded as newsworthy. Jacob Riis, the police reporter for *The New York Tribune*, compiled a portrait of poverty on Manhattan's Lower East Side that became his landmark book *How the Other Half Lives*. Out West, Jerome Stillson of *The New York Herald* did a remarkable question-and-answer interview with Chief Sitting Bull in Bismarck, Dakota Territory, within months after the massacre of General Custer at the Little Big Horn River (see Box below). The story ran for fourteen columns and took seven hours and $2000—at that time a great deal of money—to send over the wire.

SITTING BULL TELLS THE *HERALD* OF CUSTER'S LAST STAND

Note reporter Jerome Stillson's attention to concrete detail in this interview with Chief Sitting Bull, on Nov. 16, 1877, after the Battle of the Little Big Horn.

I went on to interrogate Sitting Bull:—
"This big fight, then, extended through three hours?"
"Through most of the going forward of the sun."
"Where was the Long Hair most of the time?"
"I have talked with my people: I cannot find one who saw the Long Hair until just before he died. He did not wear his long hair as he used to wear it. His hair was like yours," said Sitting Bull, playfully touching my forehead with his taper fingers. "It was short, but it was of the color of the grass when the frost comes."
"Did you hear from your people how he died? Did he die on horseback?"
"No. None of them died on horseback."
"All were dismounted?"
"Yes."
"And Custer, the Long Hair?"
"Well, I have understood that there were a great many brave men in that fight, and that from time to time, while it was going on, they were shot down like pigs. They could not help themselves. One by one the officers fell. I believe the Long Hair rode across once from this place down here . . . to this place up here (indicating the spot on the map where Custer fell), but I am not sure about this. Any way it was said that up there where the last fight took place, where the last stand was made, the Long Hair stood like a sheaf of corn with all the ears fallen around him."
"Not wounded?"
"No."

"How many stood by him?"
"A few."
"When did he fall?"
"He killed a man when he fell. He laughed."
"You mean he cried out."
"No, he laughed; he had fired his last shot."
"From a carbine?"
"No, a pistol."
"Did he stand up after he first fell?"
"He rose up on his hands and tried another shot, but his pistol would not go off."
"Was any one else standing up when he fell down?"
"One man was kneeling; that was all. But he died before the Long Hair. All this was far up on the bluffs, far away from the Sioux encampments. I did not see it. It is told to me. But it is true."
"They kept in pretty good order. Some great chief must have commanded them all the while. They would fall back across a *coulie* and make a fresh stand beyond on higher ground. The map is pretty nearly right. It shows where the white men stopped and fought before they were all killed. I think that is right—down there to the left, just above the Little Big Horn. There was one party driven out there, away from the rest, and there a great many men were killed. The places marked on the map are pretty nearly the places where all were killed."
"Did the whole command keep on fighting until the last?"
"Every man, so far as my people could see. There were no cowards on either side. . . ."

In Washington, reporters began working in a pack called a "press corps." Their interest in the private lives of government officials was every bit as intrusive as it is today. When President Grover Cleveland was married at the White House, the press, barred from the ceremony, surrounded the building and then followed the President and his bride to a cottage in the Maryland countryside. The next morning, when the honeymooners awoke, their view of the forest was blocked by a gaggle of reporters trying to peek inside their retreat.

The exploits of foreign correspondents, typified by Richard Harding Davis of *Harper's Weekly* with his shining puttees and brace of revolvers, sometimes made better reading than the stories they covered. The most enterprising was probably Januarius Aloyisius MacGahan, from Ohio, who covered wars in Europe and Asia for *The New York Herald* during the 1870s. His ride across the Steppes of Russia to report the Battle for Turkestan, defying Cossacks and Turkomans alike, kept readers back in America on the edge of their chairs. He was hired away by *The London Daily News*, where his accounts of the Turkish massacre of Bulgarians prompted the Russians to declare a full-scale war on the Turks. MacGahan covered it despite a broken leg and other injuries, but then contracted typhoid fever and died just as the Russians marched triumphantly into Constantinople in 1877. An American warship brought his body back to the United States where it lay in state in New York's City Hall before being transported to his home town for burial. Bulgarians honored him for years afterward with an annual requiem mass at Tirnova.

Newspapers launched crusades on behalf of their cities and their readers. *The New York World*, taken over in 1883 by Joseph Pulitzer, helped raise money for a pedestal for the new Statue of Liberty just donated by France, and kept a staff of thirty-five doctors who gave out free medical care to subscribers. In Missouri, the *Star* led the way as Kansas City evolved from a muddy frontier village into a modern city. Published by William Nelson, a man of limitless energy who had made and lost a fortune in the construction business during the Civil War, the *Star* promoted street railways, parks and boulevards, offered rewards for the capture of desperadoes like Frank and Jesse James and campaigned against corrupt saloon owners and high gas rates.

Stunts carried out by reporters were plugged by papers to boost circulation. One of the most popular stunt reporters was a young Pennsylvania woman named Elizabeth Cochrane, who changed her name to "Nellie Bly" in honor of the Stephen Foster song of the same name. As a 22-year-old reporter for Pulitzer's *World*, Bly was sent on a trip around the world in 1889, to see if she could beat the time set by Phileas Fogg, hero of Jules Verne's *Around the World in 80 Days*. The paper ran a contest for guesses of how long she would take; it drew more than a million entries. Bly ended up doing the trip in seventy-two days, six hours, eleven minutes and fourteen seconds. To celebrate her victory, Pulitzer hired a special train to bring her across the country from San Francisco to New York. Bly sent dispatches from every stop.

The most spectacular stunt in journalistic history occurred in 1871 when *The New York Herald* sent its reporter, Henry Morton Stanley, out to find a Scottish missionary named David Livingstone, lost in Africa while trying to find the source of the Congo River. Stanley, a Britisher who had covered the Indian wars in the West, was given $5000 and a blank check for any additional cash he might need. He set out from Zanzibar with two other whites, sixty natives and a pack train of 150 animals. Nine months later, having lost most of the natives and one white companion to fever and tribal wars along the way, he stumbled into a village on Lake Tanganyika where tribespeople had told him a strange white man lived in a thatched hut. There he encountered a gaunt, frail creature. Stanley's account made journalism history:

> Doffing my helmet, I bowed and said in an inquiring tone, "Dr. Livingstone, I presume?" Smiling cordially, he lifted his cap and answered briefly, "Yes."

Stanley had been sent on his mission by the new publisher of the *Herald*, James Gordon Bennett Jr. The son of the paper's eccentric founder, he was soon to strike people as even more bizarre than his father. Several years after Stanley's expedition, Bennett was ostracized from polite New York society when, during a dinner party in a sumptuously furnished brownstone, he urinated in his host's fireplace. Rather than live with the censure that followed, Bennett boarded his yacht, the *Lysistrata*, and set sail for Europe, never to return. In France, he founded the *Paris Herald* and ran both of his papers from aboard ship. He entertained frequently and lavishly, but despite constant practice never developed the ability to hold his liquor. Rabidly anti-Catholic, he was in the habit, when inebriated, of ordering his secretary to compose diatribes against the Catholic church and wire them to New York for publication in the *Herald*. The secretary invariably filed the editorials in a wastebasket, much to his boss's gratitude the following morning.

The junior Bennett shared his father's genius for calling attention to the *Herald*. A story headlined A CARNIVAL OF DEATH alleged that animals had escaped from the Central Park Zoo and were mauling pedestrians all over the city. The last paragraph of the story admitted that the whole tale was a hoax, but for days many New Yorkers who hadn't read that far shivered behind their locked doors for fear of being eaten by a lion.

Pulling the levers of power from the fastness of his yacht, Bennett, a tyrannical employer, brooked no criticism. Once he summoned a *Herald* staff member to Paris for a conference. The man's editor objected to the trip, wiring Bennett that he was "indispensable." Bennett wired back demanding a list of other employees who the editor considered similarly "indispensable." When the editor complied, Bennett fired every person on the list. Said Bennett, "I will have no indispensable man in my employ."

YELLOW JOURNALISM: THE WAR
BETWEEN PULITZER AND HEARST

The tradition of sensationalism begun by Bennett Sr., and amplified upon by his son, reached its crescendo in the "yellow journalism" that reigned near the turn of the century. The term had been used earlier to depict a tawdry press, but its popularity grew out of a skirmish between Joseph Pulitzer's *New York*

World and William Randolph Hearst's *New York Journal*. In 1896, the *World* had begun running a cartoon called Hogan's Alley, a single-panel montage populated by a gaggle of slum children making sarcastic comments on people and events in the news. The "kid" given the best lines was a widely grinning character dressed in a bright yellow robe. Envious of the instant popularity of the feature, Hearst pirated its cartoonist, R. F. Outcault, over to the *Journal* by doubling the man's salary. Pulitzer retaliated by hiring another cartoonist and ordering him to reproduce the "yellow kid" for the *World*. Soon, each paper was plastering its own Yellow Kid on walls and billboards all over the city. To the public, the character symbolized not only the growing war between the publishers but also the tawdry tactics each paper employed.

When newspapers battle for circulation, they almost always try to satisfy the worst in readers' taste rather than the best, appealing to the lowest common denominator. In this game, Pulitzer was clearly no match for Hearst. The child of a well-to-do family, an immigrant from the Austro-Hungarian Empire, Pulitzer had bought the *St. Louis Post-Dispatch* and later the *World* intending to establish them as papers offering the highest ideals. "Every issue of the paper," he told his staff, "presents an opportunity and a duty to say something courageous; to rise above the mediocre and conventional; to say something that will command the respect of the intelligent, the educated, the independent part of the community."

Hearst, the boisterous son of a millionaire California silver miner, honored different newspaper ideals. Kicked out of Harvard for paying too much attention to band music, fireworks and practical jokes, "Little Willie," as he was then called, was presented with the *San Francisco Examiner* by his father as a gift. He infused its staff with a principle that was to govern every Hearst paper since: Front page stories and headlines should be so bold and startling as to make readers rise slowly out of their chairs, murmuring, "My God!" In 1895, Hearst bought the ailing *New York Journal*. Within a year, he had not only overtaken the popular *World* but had dragged Pulitzer into a dogfight that almost killed Pulitzer's once fine paper.

Yellow journalism took several forms, not all of them unworthy. Hearst launched a series of crusades against big business interests who were trying to take over city franchises for running the subways and furnishing electricity and gas without paying market value for them. The *Journal* was the first newspaper actually to go into court to try to block a piece of public larceny—all the while, of course, braying about its own uprightness. WHILE THE *WORLD* TALKS, ran a typical head, THE *JOURNAL* ACTS. Hearst sent Mark Twain to cover Queen Victoria's Golden Jubilee for the *Journal*, and Stephen Crane, the immensely popular author of *The Red Badge of Courage*, to cover the Greco-Turkish War of 1897.

The Sunday sections of the *World* and *Journal* battled each other with "sob sister" columns aimed at titillating working-class women and with phony science stories designed to astonish their readers. Headlines like REAL AMERICAN MONSTERS AND DRAGONS and half-page drawings of ghastly looking and totally fictitious beasts would accompany legitimate stories about fossils. There was also a lot of tittering over sex. When the *Journal's* star reporter, Alan Dale, interviewed a French actress named Anna Held for the *Sunday Journal*, the headline read:

MLLE. ANNA HELD RECEIVES ALLAN DALE ATTIRED IN A NIGHTIE

The story scandalized the city, and the clergy called on libraries to ban the *Journal* from their racks.

Hearst thrived on what his biographer, W. A. Swanberg, called the "crime and underwear genre." The most famous of these stories was the murder of Willie Guldensuppe, a masseur at the Murray Hill Turkish Baths whose hacked-up body was found in the East River and at other locations in the city. To find out who the man was and who killed him, Hearst organized a special "murder squad" of thirty reporters; Hearst himself careened around town in horse cabs urging them on. To give proper credit, Hearst's staff did a much better job of solving the case than did the police. One reporter, himself an habituee of the Murray Hill baths, recognized Guldensuppe from the special calluses masseurs develop on their hands. Other squad members traced the oil cloth used to wrap up Guldensuppe's parts to a woman named Augusta Nack, the masseur's mistress. Nack subsequently admitted killing him with the help of another boy-friend, Martin Thorn, a barber.

The *Journal* concealed its discoveries from the police, preferring to announce them in print under a banner headline: MURDER MYSTERY SOLVED BY JOURNAL. To keep rival reporters out of the *Journal* operation, Hearst rented the entire East Side apartment house where the police were grilling Nack, cut the telephone wires to the building and posted his men outside as guards. All the while, his paper was running lurid full-page accounts illustrated with draw-ings of Nack, the oil cloth, Thorn, the murder weapon and various pieces of the unfortunate Guldensuppe's body.

The Spanish-American War, some historians maintain, might never have happened had it not been for the war hysteria whipped up by sensational and, in many cases, totally erroneous stories in the press. Not surprisingly, the two worst offenders were the feuding pair of publishers in New York City.

Before hostilities broke out in the spring of 1898, the anger of the press was directed at the Spanish military governor of Cuba, General Valariano Wey-ler, soon to be nicknamed "Butcher" Weyler for his heavy-handed effort to put down a rebellion by Cuban insurgents. Some of the press tales of torture and inhumane conditions at prison camps were undoubtedly true, but some were the exaggerations of rebel forces, and others were made up by American reporters who got no closer to Cuba than Key West, Florida. Atrocity stories boosted circulation. Predictably, the most avid atrocity hunter was Hearst, who had long been fulminating on his editorial page for the United States to declare war. In 1897, he sent his best circulation boosters, Richard Harding Davis and the artist Frederick Remington, to Cuba on the yacht *Vamoose* to dig up grisly tales. Remington, then famous for his paintings of western cowboys, never had his heart in the assignment. After arriving in Cuba, he is said to have wired back to New York:

> HEARST, JOURNAL, NEW YORK
> EVERYTHING IS QUIET. THERE IS NO TROUBLE HERE. THERE WILL BE NO WAR. WISH TO RETURN.
> REMINGTON.

Hearst shot back:

> REMINGTON, HAVANA
> PLEASE REMAIN. YOU FURNISH THE PICTURES, AND I'LL FURNISH THE WAR.
> HEARST.

Remington stayed on, reluctantly.

Davis, by then a wealthy man who had been paid $500 by the *Journal* just to cover the Yale-Harvard football game the previous fall, pressed the hunt with zeal. His most famous prewar piece was a long account of an execution of a captured Cuban rebel by a firing squad in Santa Clara. Davis ended his dispatch as follows:

> As . . . I looked back, the figure of the young Cuban, who was no longer a part of the world of Santa Clara, was asleep in the wet grass, with his motionless arms still tightly bound behind him, with the scapular twisted across his face, and the blood from his breast sinking into the soil he had tried to free.

The piece, entitled "The Death of Rodriguez," created a national sensation and was read on the floor of Congress. But it was soon eclipsed by the next big story, the sinking of the battleship *U.S.S. Maine* in Havana Harbor and the loss of 260 American seamen. To this day, no one knows how it happened. The best guess is that the ship accidently struck a mine that had been stationed to protect the harbor. The American press, sure that the Spanish treachery was to blame, went into paroxysms of fury. The *Journal* offered $50,000 for clues and ran a large page one drawing—completely fictitious—purporting to show the ship lying at anchor over a mine with wires going to a detonator on shore marked with an *X*. The *World* sent down a diving expedition, but even though the Spanish authorities let it get nowhere near the wreck, the paper claimed to have made "discoveries" that implicated Spain. Day by day, the *Journal* headlines increased in frenzy:

THE WARSHIP MAINE WAS SPLIT IN TWO
BY AN ENEMY'S SECRET INFERNAL MACHINE
THE WHOLE COUNTRY THRILLS WITH WAR FEVER

To their discredit, a majority of the country's newspapers, though lacking the *Journal's* flare, were equally bellicose. The government in Washington found it increasingly difficult to avoid declaring war. One of the few journalists who resisted joining the bandwagon was Edwin Lawrence Godkin, editor of the highly respected *New York Post*, who editorialized:

> Nothing so disgraceful as the behavior of two of these newspapers this week has been known in the history of American journalism. Gross misrepresentation of the facts, deliberate invention of tales calculated to excite the public and wanton reckless-ness in the construction of headlines which even outdo these inventions have combined to make the issues of the most widely circulated papers firebrands scattered broadside throughout the country.

President McKinley finally gave in and asked for a declaration of war in April, and some 500 reporters went off to watch the fun. Most acted less like journalists than tinplate soldiers in a comic opera. The Associated Press hired a flotilla of press boats and cruised in and out of naval actions, oblivious to the shelling. Reporters participated in infantry charges, and even led a few them-selves. Richard Harding Davis, now working for *The New York Herald*, led soldiers at the Battle of Las Guasimas. Stephen Crane captured a town on behalf of the *World*. James Creelman, a *Journal* reporter, was shot in the left arm in heavy fighting around a blockhouse at El Caney. Creelman wrote that while he was lying on the ground:

> Someone knelt in the grass beside me and put his hand on my fevered head. Opening my eyes I saw Mr. Hearst . . . a revolver in his belt and a pencil notebook in his hand. . . . Slowly he took down my story of the fight . . .
> "I'm sorry you're hurt, but"—and his face was radiant with enthusiasm—"wasn't it a splendid fight! We must beat every paper in the world."

Hearst was in a sweat to get into the action himself. He had outfitted a ship with a printing press and a staff of twenty writers and artists, and he steered the vessel so close to a naval engagement in Havana Harbor that Commodore Schley of the United States Navy ordered a shot fired across his bow to keep him back. At one point in the battle Hearst spied a dozen or so hapless Spanish sailors stranded on the beach, their ship having been sunk. Waving his pistol, Hearst jumped overboard, waded to the beach and "captured" the sorry little band. Then, he steamed back into the heart of the American squadron, this time signalling, WE HAVE PRISONERS FOR THE FLEET. He proudly turned his charges over to the United States commander.

THE PRESS COMES OF AGE

By the early 1900s, the excesses of the yellow journalists had dismayed much of the public. Pulitzer's *World* lost both circulation and reputation in its war with Hearst; it did not regain both until the 1920s, and then only by returning to its former high ideals. Journalists abandoned much of their clowning and sensationalism, and set out more seriously to inform readers about news that mattered.

Newspaper English shed its ornate veneer in favor of the spare, matter-of-fact prose of today. The modern five W lead, with its familiar who, what, when, where and why or how, was becoming firmly established as the most efficient way to present breaking news. An impetus grew from within the craft to set standards that celebrated responsibility and professionalism. Journalism schools sprang up, first one at the University of Missouri and then one, started by Pulitzer, at Columbia University, where students were trained in the ethics of the craft as well as in the use of its tools. *The New York Times*, bought in 1896 by Adolph Ochs, earned a reputation for accuracy, hard digging and thoroughness that inspired journalists all over the country. Publishers began to appreciate that fair, objective reporting was good for circulation in the long run.

The maturation of the press meant less emphasis on personalities, including those of cavorting reporters, and more emphasis on the facts. In the coverage of World War I, the relatively anonymous wire service reporters—especially those for E. W. Scripp's United Press—scored well. The press corps still included several flamboyant journalists left over from the old days. Richard Harding Davis, working for a syndicate of papers, went to war accompanied by his wife and ensconced in a $1000-a-day suite aboard the *Lusitania*. Floyd Gibbons of the *Chicago Tribune*, a highly energetic correspondent who criticized his colleagues as "lazy louts who won't get out after their own news," chose to sail aboard the British liner *Laconia*, hoping it would attract attention from the German U-boats.

It did. On February 25, 1917, the ship was torpedoed off the southern coast of Ireland, and sank within twenty minutes. Gibbons helped get passengers into lifeboats, then spent most of the icy night interviewing people about their experiences. Two hours after landing in Ireland, where he was treated for exposure, Gibbons filed one of the most vivid accounts of the war. It included the following paragraphs, based on an interview with the chief steward in lifeboat number 3:

> . . . As the the boat's crew steadied its head to the wind, a black hulk, glistening wet and standing about eight feet above the surface of the water, approached slowly and came to a stop opposite the boat and not six feet from the side of it. "What ship vas dat?" The correct words in throaty English with a German accent came from the dark hull, according to Chief Steward Ballyn's statement to me later.
> "The *Laconia*, Cunard Line," responded the steward.
> "Vot did she weight?" was the next question from the submarine.
> "Eighteen thousand tons."
> "Any passengers?"
> "Seventy-three," replied Ballyn, "men, women and children, some of them in this boat. She had over two hundred in the crew."
> "Did she carry cargo?"
> "Yes."
> "Vell, you'll be all right. The patrol vill pick you up soon," and without further sound, save for the almost silent fixing of the conning tower lid, the submarine moved off.

World War I lent itself to few such dramatic accounts. Unlike the action during the Civil War, which could sometimes be watched in safety from atop a hill, the battlefields of World War I in France consisted mostly of flat open ground that offered no promontory from which reporters could view the conflict. Venturing anywhere near the action meant a serious risk of getting shot, blown up or gassed. Gibbons, who accompanied the United States Marines at the battle of Belleau Wood in 1918, poked his head above a trench to watch an attack and got a machine gun bullet in the left eye. He survived, but wore a black patch for the rest of his life.

Another problem was the strict censorship imposed on news by the United States Army. In a system that was to become familiar in World War II and again in Vietnam, battle news came out of central press briefings at headquarters. Military blunders were covered up or played down, and officers treated reporters with suspicion. Probably the shortest interview in history was given by the United States commanding general, John J. "Black Jack" Pershing, to a 23-year-old United Press reporter named Westbrook Pegler. Pegler, who later became an acid-tongued columnist for the Hearst papers, was the youngest journalist overseas. One day he strode into the press tent and announced breezily that he was going over to have a talk with Pershing, who prided himself on giving no personal interviews. A half hour later, Pegler returned, put paper in his typewriter and began banging out a story. Dumbfounded, reporters crowded around to see what he could possibly have gotten out of the old man. "This correspondent had an interview with General Pershing today," the copy read. "The General said: 'Pegler, get the hell out of my office.'" End of story.

Because most war news emanated from one official source, it took considerable pluck for one reporter to get an exclusive story. The fiercest competition raged between the two wire services, the AP and UP; the story that came in first over the wire at newspapers back home was usually the one that ran in the paper. One of the biggest scoops came to Fred Ferguson of the UP at the Battle of St. Mihiel, the first all-American action in the war. In a briefing just before the attack was launched, all reporters were told, step by step, how it was to proceed. The idea was that they would go out to the battlefield and see how the plan worked in practice, then come back and send out their stories.

In a stroke of genius, Ferguson decided to write his story *before* the attack began. He outlined the American battle plan just as it was supposed to happen, then instructed the Army press officer to wait until the action started and wire off each section of his story as reports came in from officers in the field verifying the plan's success. That arranged—secretly, of course—Ferguson offered to take his car and drive his Associated Press colleagues on a tour of the battle. It was late at night when they all got back. The AP reporters were nervous because they'd been out of touch with their office all day, but their consolation was that Ferguson hadn't had a chance to call in either.

Back at the press tent, they discovered how badly they'd been gulled. Not only had Ferguson's copy gone out long ago, and, indeed, was that minute actually running in most of the country's newspapers, but there awaited him an exultant telegram from his boss for the whole press corps to read. It read:

CONGRATULATIONS ON YOUR GREATEST SCOOP

In the 1920s, editors began exploiting the full power of photographs to help tell the news. With the pictures came jazzy new tabloid-style newspapers in Boston, New York, Chicago and Philadelphia. Printed half the size of a normal paper, the tabloids usually featured a large page one photograph taken with the new Graphlex or, later, Speed Graphic, camera. Stories and headlines were written in a fast and snappy style; the content of news columns—a steady run of crime, sex and scandal—was a throwback to the days of the Bennetts and Hearst.

In New York, a feverish press war fought out in coverage of messy divorce cases and lurid murder trials raged between three new tabloids, the *Daily News*, the *Daily Mirror* and the *Evening Graphic*, whose excesses soon earned it the nickname, "Porno-Graphic." A *Daily News* photographer with a miniature camera strapped to his ankle snapped a picture of a murderess, Ruth Snyder, as she was electrocuted at Sing Sing prison. The picture, run under the single-word headline, DEAD!, sold a million extra copies of the paper.

The twenties have never been surpassed for famous trials and the attention paid them by the press. The anarchists Sacco and Vanzetti, charged with the murder of a payroll guard in Brockton, Massachusetts, occupied the front page from the time of their arrest in 1921 until their execution in 1927, when they were given the entire front page of *The Boston Globe*. From Chicago came the "thrill killing" of 14-year-old Bobbie Franks by two well-to-do Chicago teenagers named Isaac Loeb and Frederick Leopold. Reporters kept the country's eyes riveted on their trial while the famous criminal lawyer Clarence Darrow saved them from the electric chair with his closing arguments against capital punishment.

For sheer drama, few journalistic events of the era equalled the eight-day trial in 1925 of a Tennessee biology teacher named John T. Scopes for violating a state law against teaching about Charles Darwin's theory of evolution in the public high school. Nearly 200 reporters, among them H. L. Mencken of the *Baltimore Sun*, journeyed to the Bible belt town of Dayton to watch the show. The story was not so much whether Scopes was guilty; he freely admitted violating the statute. Rather, this was the contest of ideas, as reported in the battle between two legal titans: Darrow, whose fee was being paid by the *Baltimore Sun*, and William Jennings Bryan for the prosecution. A former secretary of state and thrice a presidential candidate, the 65-year-old Bryan had now taken up the cause of religious fundamentalism. As its chief defender against the inroads made by scientific discovery, he maintained that the Bible should be read as a literal history of humanity on Earth. Bryan encountered his most stringent test on the seventh day of trial, now so crowded and raucous that the judge moved it outdoors. As recounted in *The New York Times*, Darrow began by asking Bryan if he seriously believed the miracles reported in the Bible were meant to be taken for absolute fact:

> . . . Joshua and the sun was another miracle that Mr. Darrow wanted to know about. How did it happen (according to the Bible) that the sun stood still, when the earth moves around the sun?
> It was the language of the day, Mr. Bryan said, and if anything stopped, it must have been the earth.
> "Now, Mr. Bryan, have you ever pondered what would have happened to the earth if it had stood still?
> "No," replied Mr. Bryan. "The God I believe in would have taken care of that, Mr. Darrow."
> "Don't you know it would have been converted into a molten mass of matter?"
> "You testify to that when you get on the stand," retorted Mr. Bryan. . . .

The journalism of the 1920s was marked by increasing coverage of common people: bootblacks and cab drivers, gamblers and street musicians. Sportswriters like Ring Lardner and Damon Runyon drew vivid portraits of athletes and street riff-raff. Their stories were sometimes sentimental, but they opened the eyes of many readers to the human richness and diversity of their cities, and mined a vein of realism and descriptive writing that has enriched journalism ever since. A nineteenth-century daily might well have turned up its nose at the funeral of Florence Mills, a much-loved black dancer. But when she died in 1927, at age 32, W. A. MacDonald of the *Boston Evening Transcript* covered her funeral in Harlem, and paid her mourners the simple tribute of assuming that they were worth writing about with respect. His closing paragraphs:

> The bearers lifted the great copper coffin. High above the heads of the people the bank of roses moved slowly down the aisle. The people pushed out into the greater crowd outside. Block after block it jostled for position. Along 137th Street to the Corner of Seventh Avenue moved the procession and past the corner where all the traffic was stalled on the avenue. As it passed through that crowded sea the hats of Harlem came off. You could see it as a great movement along the avenue. An airplane roared overhead. The police whistles shrilled, sharp, imperative; automobiles moved slowly at the sound.
> Florence Mills, to whom a little chorus girl, leaning over the casket, had said, "Bye-bye, honey," rode up Seventh Avenue.

During the Depression of the 1930s, with hardship afflicting almost every neighborhood and European countries falling to Fascist dictators, readers hungered for explanations of the decade's great social upheavals. In response, journalists began paying more attention to economics, sociology and the realities, as opposed to the dramatics, of international affairs. They wrote more stories that involved issues and ideas: How to ease unemployment, then running at 25 percent; what to do for Oklahoma farmers whose land had blown away in the wind; whether America should become entangled in the political struggles of Europe. "Interpretive reporting," as it was called, emphasized the last of the five Ws—it sought to reveal *why* things happened and *how* they affected people's lives.

Walter Lippmann, a columnist for the *World* and later for *The New York Herald-Tribune*, hailed interpretive reporting as the "new journalism," and predicted that it would eventually drive the sensationalistic press out of business. His prediction has in great part come true. Wrote Lippmann:

> [Sensationalism] is not, I believe, enduring. . . . It selects from the events of the day those aspects that most immediately engage attention, and in place of the effort to see life steadily and whole it sees life dramatically, episodically, from what is called, in the jargon of the craft, the angle of human interest. This is highly effective—for a while. But the method soon exhausts itself. When everything is dramatic, nothing after a while is dramatic; when everything is highly spiced, nothing after a while has much flavor; when everything is new and startling, the human mind just ceases to be startled. But that is not all! As the readers of this press live longer in the world, and as their personal responsibilities increase, they begin to feel the need of being genuinely informed rather than of being merely amused and excited. Gradually, they discover that things do not happen as they are made out to appear in the human interest stories. The realization begins to dawn upon them that they have been getting not the news but a species of romantic fiction which they can get much better out of the movies and the magazines. . . .

MODERN TRENDS

The technology of putting out newspapers is changing more rapidly today than ever before. The smell of glue pots, the rustle of copy paper and the rat-a-tat sound of typewriters are all but gone from the city room. Reporters sit at their desks and punch their stories silently into computers. The copy desk edits them electronically and presses a key; the stories then become available to the back shop. There, the clanking Linotypes with their pools of molten lead have been replaced by electronic equipment that produces plates for the press as quietly as a cat walks. The only noise left on newspapers is the press itself, still a glorious, roaring monster that, on large urban dailies, is two stories high and two blocks long. It can turn out 70,000 copies an hour.

Dramatic changes in news gathering were generated by the arrival of radio and television, with their power to bring major news to vast audiences almost instantly. The explosion of the Space Shuttle Challenger in 1986, for example, was seen instantly by millions of television viewers. And so quickly did broadcasters bring news of the attempted assassinations of President Reagan and Pope John Paul II in 1981 that many viewers knew more about the story than did the reporters at the scene. The time lag in conveying the news dropped from weeks in the eighteenth century, to hours in the nineteenth century, to seconds today.

The first "newscast" was broadcast on August 31, 1920, over a radio station in Detroit called "8MK," later to become WWJ, but it was not until the late 1930s and World War II that radio was used to inform mass audiences of the news. And none used radio more effectively than the chief of CBS European correspondents, Edward R. Murrow.

Murrow, who had been with the network since 1935, spent most of the war in London, with occasional forays on bombing missions over Berlin or with British tank units in Africa. His power as a broadcaster lay in the precision of his delivery—he sounded as if he were cutting out the words with a knife—and in his gift for describing a scene of action. Murrow's most famous series of broadcasts were delivered during the Battle of Britain in the fall of 1940, when the Germans sent 300 bombers and 600 fighter escorts against London to try to knock England out of the war. On many nights, listeners could hear the wail of fire engines and bombs crashing in the distance. But one night when Murrow spoke it was quiet:

> I'm standing again tonight on a rooftop looking out over London, feeling rather large and lonesome. In the course of the last fifteen or twenty minutes there's been considerable action up there, but at the moment there's an ominous silence hanging over London. But at the same time a silence that has a great deal of dignity. Just straightaway in front of me the search lights are working. I can see one or two bursts of anti-aircraft fire far in the distance. Just on the roof across the way I can see a man wearing a tin hat, a pair of powerful night glasses to his eyes, scanning the sky. Again, looking in the opposite direction, there is a building with two windows gone. Out of one window there waves something that looks like a white bed sheet, a window curtain swinging free in this night breeze. It looks as though it were being shaken by a ghost. There are a great many ghosts around these buildings in London. The searchlights straightaway, miles in front of me, are still scratching that sky. There's a three-quarter moon riding high. There was one burst of shellfire almost straight in the Little Dipper.
>
> Down below in the streets I can see just that red and green wink of the traffic lights; one lone taxicab moving slowly down the street. Not a sound to be heard. As I look out across the miles and miles of rooftops and chimney pots, some of those dirty-gray fronts of the buildings look almost snow-white in this moonlight here to-night. And the rooftop spotter across the way swings around, looks over in the direction of the searchlights, drops his glasses and just stands there. There are hundreds and hundreds of men like that standing on rooftops in London tonight watching for fire bombs, waiting to see what comes out of this steel-blue sky. The searchlights now reach up very, very faintly on three sides of me. There is a flash of a gun in the distance but too far away to be heard.

Murrow also helped bring television news to maturity when, in 1954, he broadcast a documentary on Senator Joseph McCarthy that awakened the public to the Senator's browbeating and bullying as the newspapers never had. Television, in fact, became the medium through which most Americans absorbed the biggest stories of the sixties, seventies and eighties: the deaths of John F. Kennedy, Martin Luther King and Robert F. Kennedy; Chicago's Mayor Richard Daley, his face twisted in anger as he shouted insults at Senator Abraham Ribicoff during the 1968 Democratic National Convention; and the clockwork cool of John Dean as he unraveled the Watergate conspiracy before the United States Senate.

Television also brought home the battle of the Vietnam War. The crackle of machine-gun fire intruded into American living rooms as families sat down for dinner. People saw soldiers die on camera. Although the TV producers avoided televising the goriest shots, the very matter-of-factness that suffused the business of death and destruction helped awaken the public to the senselessness of the war. One of the lasting images from those years came during a story by correspondent John Laurence of CBS, who showed an American GI casually setting fire to a peasant's thatched hut with his Zippo cigarette lighter. Set against images like that, the patriotic injunctions of the politicians began to ring hollow.

But even though television has become proficient at telling people *what* is going on, it has never been very good at telling them *why*. Evening newscasts dart like waterbugs across the surfaces of the stories; the script for a thirty-minute network newscast would fill only a few columns on a single page of a newspaper. And television needs pictures. Given the choice, most producers will air a less newsworthy story with visual appeal over a weighty story that can be presented on camera only by what is disdainfully called a "talking head."

Print journalists, unable to compete with radio and television in terms of immediacy, have evolved toward greater depth in their reporting. Depth calls for expertise, and reporters for the major newspapers are better trained today than ever before. Many have advanced degrees in journalism and have studied law, science, political science or history as well.

The "new journalists" of the 1960s and 1970s stretched the boundaries of nonfiction writing. Tom Wolfe and Gay Talese wrote profiles that purported to delve into the thoughts and feelings of their subjects—a claim that might have seemed insupportable, had it not so often been based upon thorough reporting. Hunter S. Thompson, writing for *Rolling Stone*, made his witty doom-struck consciousness the centerpiece of his coverage of presidential politics. But his reporting was exemplary, a fact that was sometimes overlooked in the glare of his lively style. In his book *In Cold Blood*, which described the circumstances surrounding a quadruple murder in Manhattan, Kansas, Truman Capote revealed the killers' lives and those of their victims with a kind of detail and nuance that previously had been almost exclusively the province of novelists.

By the 1980s television may have become the medium through which most people learn of most news, but it remained to newspaper reporters to unearth practically all the big investigative stories of the last three decades, from the Pentagon Papers and the massacre at My Lai to the Watergate conspiracy and the illegal diversion of profits gained from selling arms to Iran to guerrilla forces trying to overthrow the government of Nicaragua.

Print and broadcast journalism complement each other more often than they compete head to head. People may hear a story first from the nightly newscast, but they still pick up a paper the next day to read about it in greater detail. With both print and electronic reporters at work, journalism in the future is likely to experience changes as dramatic as those that have occurred since Benjamin Franklin was setting up type by hand and helping his brother publish "short pieces, serious, sarcastic, ludicrous or other ways amusing" on a flatbed press.

SUMMARY

American newspapers are older than the United States itself. Colonial papers circulated mostly among the upper classes and were printed by permission of the royal government. Editors freely mixed opinion and fact, but those who criticized public officials risked jail. Andrew Hamilton's defense of publisher John Peter Zenger set in motion the process that ultimately led to a constitutionally guaranteed free press.

The popular, or "penny," press came along in the 1830s and 1840s, when publishers such as Benjamin Day and James Gordon Bennett lowered the price of their papers and appealed to a mass readership by emphasizing police news and gossip. Their generally tawdry influence was offset in part by Horace Greeley, publisher of the *New York Tribune*, which became known as the "Great Moral Organ." Greeley's editorials, read throughout the country, sought to remind readers of the lofty ideals upon which the country had been founded.

Civil War correspondents, or "specials," risked their lives to report the war, but editors sometimes delayed or rewrote reports of defeats suffered by the armies of their side. Toward the end of the nineteenth century the laying of the trans-Atlantic cable and the invention of the telephone speeded coverage of distant events, and reporters came into their own as personalities: The exploits of Nelly Bly, Henry Morton Stanley, Richard Harding Davis and others drew as much attention as the news they covered. Rotary presses made possible large, lively headlines and innovative newspaper makeup.

The trend toward sensationalism begun in the 1830s reached its crescendo in the 1890s during a circulation war between Joseph Pulitzer's *New York World* and William Randolph Hearst's *New York Journal*.

In the early twentieth century, the founding of professional journalism schools and the growing success of *The New York Times*, a respectable newspaper, led journalists to abandon much of their clowning and turn to serious news gathering and objective reporting. With the rise of radio and television, the imperatives for print journalism shifted from immediacy to depth, context and analysis. The result, despite a shrinking number of newspapers, was a richer variety of news.

PART II The Working Press

The press and the judiciary "both sustain democracy not because they are responsible to any branch of government but precisely because . . . they are not accountable at all."

Irving Kaufman, U.S. Court of Appeals

"The press is a disorderly and unpredictable lot, but that is the point. The press is meant to be outside the established order."

Anthony Lewis, Columnist, *New York Times*

3

WORKING FOR A NEWSPAPER

Most young journalists find their first jobs on small-town rather than big-city newspapers. The smaller papers generally require less experience of the reporters they hire, and they provide broader training. Beginners get to cover a wide variety of stories from the day they start work, rather than being shunted into anonymous desks in the corner of a large city room. Small-town editors are usually more willing to go over a novice's copy and offer advice on how it might be improved.

Covering a town or small city affords an insight into how communities function. Small towns have nearly the same number of government departments as large ones, but planning boards, zoning commissions and welfare agencies that employ only a dozen or so people are easier to comprehend than are those that employ hundreds or thousands.

Small-town reporters can get closer to the news they cover, can see more clearly how their stories affect people's lives—and can pay more directly for their mistakes. The newspaper office may be a storefront on Main Street, where irate readers can come in to complain about factual errors, and the mayor who was so approachable yesterday can loom menacingly today when he complains that he was misquoted.

HOW A NEWSPAPER IS ORGANIZED

Newspapers large and small are headed by *publishers*, and they are divided into five major departments. The *advertising* department sells the ads that earn most of the paper's income. In the nineteenth century, when paper was inexpensive and wages low, newspapers ran few advertisements and survived on the two or three pennies per copy they charged readers. Today the newsstand or subscription price barely pays for the paper on which the newspaper is printed; advertising revenue is what keeps the publisher in the black. The *business* department handles the finances. The *production* department, or "back shop," is the mechanical end of the paper, where stories are transformed into type, and the newspaper is run off the press. The *circulation* department gets the paper out to newsstands or to readers' homes.

Reporters work in the fifth division, the *editorial* department, which gathers, writes and edits the news. Headed usually by an *executive editor*, the editorial department is split into two parts. The "news side" handles breaking stories, or hard news, as well as background stories tied to daily headlines. On the other side are various departments, or "desks," that produce the rest of the reading matter in the newspaper, sometimes referred to as "soft" news. How many desks there are, and how many people work them, depend on the size and sophistication of the paper.

Most dailies have a *sports* desk that covers local sports and edits wire service stories about sports elsewhere. Larger papers have *business* desks specializing in financial news; *entertainment* departments to review plays and movies and cultural news, and *Sunday* departments whose job is to fill the expanded Sunday editions of the papers.

What once was the "woman's page" most papers now call the *family/style* or *modern living* section. Along with presenting news of weddings, fashion and food, modern living reporters cover problems of everyday life—from dealing with divorce to coping with teenage drug habits.

Papers print their opinions on public issues on the *editorial pages*. On most small papers the editorial page is a one-person operation. Along with writing several editorials a day—with or without consultation with the paper's publisher—the editorial page editor edits the letters to the editors section and lays out the syndicated columns that appear on the page opposite the editorial page, known as the "op-ed" page.

The news side, where young reporters start out, is usually organized according to where the news comes from. International news is handled by the *foreign* desk, domestic news by the *national* desk. Because small papers get these two kinds of news from the wire services rather than from their own out-of-town correspondents, the foreign and national desks may be consolidated into a *wire desk*, headed by a *wire editor*.

The *city desk*—often called the metropolitan desk—is presided over by the *city editor* and covers local news. The *state desk* watches over the suburbs and outlying towns. Photographers work for the *picture desk*, whose editor handles photo requests from all the departments.

After finishing a story, a reporter submits it to the editor of his or her desk. The editor makes sure that the story reads clearly and contains all the necessary information, and then passes it along to the *copy desk*. There, copy editors check the stories for spelling, grammar and sense, and make sure they conform to the paper's style. The copy editors also write the headlines.

PROFILE OF A NEWSPAPER: *THE NEWS-TIMES*

Rather than generalize about a reporter's job, in this chapter we describe what it is like working for one newspaper, *The News-Times* in Danbury, Connecticut. Danbury is a New England mill town of 60,000 people built along the Still River in the southwestern part of Connecticut. Once a prosperous center for the manufacture of hats, the city fell on hard times after World War II when derbies, homburgs and other formal headgear began to go out of style, largely because of the advent of low-slung automobiles. Then came a torrential flood, in 1955, that laid waste to much of the downtown business district. A subsequent urban renewal project destroyed many of the city's graceful nineteenth-century Victorian buildings and replaced them with acres of parking lots. Today, Danbury is in the midst of an economic boom created by people and corporations moving into the area from New York City, fifty miles away. The largest of these, the Union Carbide Company, employs almost as many people as made their living from hats in the city's heyday.

Located in a red brick building on Main Street that formerly housed a First National supermarket, *The News-Times* is an amalgam of two other newspapers, the *Danbury News* and the *Danbury Times*, which merged in 1937. The paper has a circulation of 64,000, which means it goes to 64,000 households. Because each household may contain more than one reader, the paper's actual readership is estimated to be about two and a half times more than its circulation. Whereas

Increasing numbers of American cities are served by only one newspaper, its hyphenated name testimony to the many papers that once thrived there. (Drawing by H. Martin; © 1981 *The New Yorker* Magazine, Inc.)

once, the paper found most readers inside Danbury itself, now about 60 percent live outside the city, in eighteen surrounding towns in Connecticut and three across the line in New York State. Those towns are increasing in population while Danbury is shrinking, and the paper looks to them for growth in circulation. It likes to be perceived not as a Danbury paper but as a regional one, serving the whole southwestern section of the state. For this reason it removed the word "Danbury" from its name in 1974.

Like most dailies in the country, *The News-Times* is no longer owned by local people. In 1961 it was brought by Ottaway Newspapers, Inc., an out-of-state corporation that owns thirteen other papers in the Northeast. Ottaway, in turn, was purchased in 1975 by a larger corporation, Dow Jones & Company, of New York City, publisher of *The Wall Street Journal.*

Opinions differ, sometimes heatedly, over whether corporate ownership of local papers is good or bad for the freedom of the press. On the positive side, large companies can raise the money it takes to modernize a newspaper and make it more efficient. This, in turn, can lead to hiring additional reporters, which can mean better news coverage. On the negative side, once ownership passes out of local hands, so does ultimate control over how the paper looks, what news it covers and what opinions it expresses on its editorial page. The publisher is no longer his or her own boss, but must report regularly to company headquarters in another city. The result can be a blander newspaper with little independent spirit.

The argument remains largely academic, however, because the trend in newspaper ownership seems to be moving inescapably in the direction of bigness. At the end of World War II, a majority of the country's approximately 1750 daily newspapers were independently owned. By the 1980s, local families controlled fewer than 400 of the papers, or less than 25 percent.

THE REPORTERS

Reporters on *The News-Times* are organized to cover news on two levels. One level of coverage is handled by the state staff, which consists of eleven reporters assigned to cover the rural and suburban towns outside Danbury. Each reporter is given one or two towns and is responsible for reporting everything that happens there, from burglaries and auto accidents to government meetings and concerts at the high school auditorium. Most government business in the towns transpires at night, so the suburban reporters work evening hours, usually from 3 or 4 o'clock in the afternoon to midnight or 1 o'clock in the morning. Their boss—who on most papers would be the state editor—is called the "night editor."

The other level of news is reported by the "dayside" staff of nine reporters who work out of the newsroom in Danbury. A few work on general assignment and cover breaking news in the city, but most specialize in a particular "beat," such as education, the environment or business and finance. Whereas reporters in the outlying towns cover day-to-day events, the beat reporters in Danbury are more interested in issues that affect the region as a whole. If a reporter responsible for the town of New Milford wrote a story about a parents group trying to rid the schools of books it regarded as offensive, the education beat reporter in Danbury might do a story about censorship in the schools throughout the region. Because the Danbury staff work in the daytime, their editor is called the "day editor."

"Before we divided up the staff this way, the readers couldn't see the forest for the trees," says Edward Frede, executive editor of *The News-Times*. "We would do a story one week about how elderly people in one town were having a hard time finding places to live. Then the next week we'd do another story about elderly people in another town having the same kind of difficulties. But no reporter was tying it all together, doing a story about the old people throughout the whole area having the same kind of problem."

A DAY IN THE LIFE OF *THE NEWS-TIMES*

When it comes to the rhythm of a day's work, each newspaper has its own pace and style. Some editors work at putting out a paper as if it were a race with disaster, spreading panic throughout the newsroom as deadlines loom. Others betray little emotion, even when stories break just before the final press run. Reporters on morning papers, or "AMs," usually have ample time to write their own stories, but big-city afternoon papers, or "PMs," are geared for speed. Deadlines race by all day long, and copy has to be updated as the stories develop. On breaking stories, time is so short that a reporter's job may have to be handled by two people: a "leg" man or woman who calls in raw facts from the scene and a "rewrite" person in the city room who writes the copy.

The News-Times is an evening paper but, unlike its big-city counterparts, it works toward one major deadline, 11 A.M. Its day starts when Robert Bollman, the stubby, grey-haired chief of the copy desk, arrives with his English muffin and container of coffee at 5 o'clock in the morning and sits down to work.

Bollman fills what would be three different jobs on a larger paper. As copy chief, he oversees the work of five copy editors. He also acts as wire editor, because the copy desk edits national and foreign news as well as local copy. In addition, he is the paper's *news editor*. As the main link between the newsroom, where the paper is written, and the back shop, where it gets printed, the news editor holds a critical job in the editorial department. Bollman "makes up," or "lays out," the major news pages, designing them so the most important stories attract the most attention. He also keeps track of the "news hole," or open space reserved for news. As the paper moves toward deadline, Bollman watches the news hole fill with stories. On late-breaking news, he has to know exactly how much space is left so he can advise the day editor, who then tells reporters how much they can write. When a major story breaks shortly before deadline, Bollman and the managing editor must decide which stories to discard to make room for it.

By the time Bollman comes to work some of the news hole has usually been filled. Copy from the suburban towns has been written the night before, edited by the night editor, laid out in the suburban pages and set into type. Such special sections as modern living and the editorial page have been written, edited and "closed" the previous day.

Bollman's concern centers on the day's breaking news—police stories, fires and automobile accidents that occurred during the night, news from the state capitol in Hartford that affects the area and a welter of national and international news arriving at the paper over the AP wire. To see what his choices are for the day, Bollman first consults his "budgets," or lists, of upcoming or completed stories. One budget comes from the night editor; it suggests suburban stories that might be important enough for page one. Another budget comes from the day editor; it lists Danbury stories and those of the paper's beat reporters that are all written and ready to run.

It's a blustery day in mid-December that threatens to produce a blizzard. The day budget tells Bollman that the paper's political reporter, Thomas Ahearn, is in Hartford, the state capitol, for a press conference called by the National Association for the Advancement of Colored People. Its announcement concerns the Adult Correction Institution, a federal penitentiary located in Danbury. In a phone call to the NAACP, Ahearn found out that the group is planning to charge negligence on the part of prison officials in connection with a fire at the prison that resulted in six deaths six months before. As one of the largest employers in the area, the prison interests many readers; this morning's charges will make a good story for page one. Bollman sees that the press conference is set for 9:30 A.M. and that Ahearn thinks he can phone in a story by 10, in plenty of time for the 11 A.M. deadline.

Among other stories listed by the day desk is one expected from Kristin Nord, the paper's education reporter. It's an "advance" about a ruling expected later that week from the Federal District Court on an appeal by a student at Danbury High School who was suspended during a race riot at the school a few months before. Bollman decides the story can go inside the paper, on the page reserved for Danbury news. When the judge actually issues his ruling, that can go up front.

Bollman also reviews the news budgets issued by the Associated Press. One AP budget lists stories from around the state and New England, another the news from its national and foreign bureaus. Like many small PM papers, *The News-Times* ignores all but the most crucial national and international stories. It assumes that readers will follow these stories via the TV networks and *The New York Times*, which circulates in the Danbury area. "We see our main job as providing news and background about events that concern readers where they live and work," says Frede, the executive editor. "If we also tried to supply the news from the world outside, we wouldn't have room for anything else." At any rate, today is a slow news day on the world front. An Israeli delegation is arriving in Cairo for negotiations; the Mideast oil states are meeting to consider increasing oil prices. In Washington, farmers from the Midwest are asking to meet with the President to argue for increased price supports.

Looking over the AP budget for the region, Bollman spots an obvious page one story: A disastrous fire early that morning at Providence College in Rhode Island has killed seven woman and badly burned fifteen others. No one from Danbury was injured, but quite a few students from the area attend the college.

By now it is 8 A.M., and others are arriving for work: Frede; the managing editor, James Smith, who oversees the daily news operation; and Doug Hulette, the day editor. Beat reporters have also checked in. Some will be working on stories for that day's edition. Jason Isaacson, the city hall reporter, is writing a piece about threatening telephone calls received by a woman active in the local Democratic Party. She is scheduled to testify at a party hearing against another Democratic official charged with helping a Republican candidate in the previous election.

Others are piecing together stories that may not run for a day or two. Health and welfare reporter Mary Connolly is wading through a four-volume study that predicts what the region's health needs will be for the next five years. Business reporter Bob Chuvala is making phone calls for a story he's writing for tomorrow's paper about unemployment in the region.

At 9 A.M., Bollman meets with his managing and executive editors to show them what he's planned for page one. A good picture has come over the UPI telephoto wire on the Providence fire. It shows a frightened girl in a dormitory window protecting her face with a curtain as flames dance nearby. *The News-Times* likes to use pictures and to print them large, for dramatic effect. Sometimes, however, the editors' quest for a dramatic shot leads them astray. A week after Thanksgiving, just as the Christmas season was getting under way, Bollman put a large picture on page one of a deer that had been killed by the local dog warden after the animal crashed through the picture window of a real estate office. The picture showed a grinning warden holding up the deer's head as if it were a hunting trophy. Blood was spattered on the animal and smeared all over the office floor. Readers were horrified at the spectacle; they feared their children would inevitably associate the bloody deer with Santa Claus's reindeer, and they flooded the paper with angry letters.

At 9:20 A.M. Ahearn, the political reporter, calls from Hartford. The NAACP is running late. The press conference won't be held until 10, but he still thinks he can get a story in by deadline. Bollman starts looking for other stories he would promote to page one should Ahearn's fall through.

Locally, the only other breaking news that morning are two items from police and fire reporter Ruth Lockwood, both strictly routine. A fire alarm had been sounded at a local nursery school, but the "fire" turned out to be only a smoky oil burner. In addition, a 13-year-old boy was arrested for assaulting the owner of a grocery.

At 10:40, however, Ahearn calls in to dictate a story on the press conference. It's a good one. The NAACP is charging that after the prison fire started the firehoses were not hooked up in time to be of use. The group also said that afterwards the prison hospital had refused to admit a badly burned prisoner merely because he lacked the proper papers. The man later died.

By 10:50 the news hole is filled. If anything major happens in the ten minutes remaining before deadline, an existing story will have to be dropped from the paper to make room. The Providence fire leads the paper in the upper right-hand quarter of page one. The "off-lead" story, on the left side, is the NAACP. Underneath is another AP story from Hartford: The police have finally identified a 17-year-old girl who was killed by a car last year as she was hitchhiking. The girl was buried anonymously, and the search for her identity had aroused national interest. She turned out to be a runaway from Alabama.

To balance these somber stories, Bollman fills out page one with two light pieces—one detailing the discovery of thirty cases of 100-year-old French wine in the basement of a mansion in Albany, New York, and the other telling how the U.S. Labor Department in Washington D.C. has rewritten its dictionary of job descriptions to make them more sexually neutral. "Bat boys," for instance, would now be known as "bat handlers."

One hour later, the "six-star" edition—each edition is marked by a different number of stars at the top of page one—rolls off the press and is rushed to newsstands in Danbury to catch the lunch crowd. The suburban editions—that is, the five-star, four-star, three-star and two-star editions—start coming out twenty minutes later. Filled with news from a different set of suburban towns, these editions are trucked out to points north, south, east and west of the city. The last edition, the one-star, hits the street at 2:45. It goes to the fifty-five news boys and girls in Danbury who deliver it to readers' doors by the time the people get home from work.

A little after noon, Bollman puts on his coat and goes home. Work has already begun on the next day's paper. Hulette, the day editor, gets Chuvala's unemployment story, checks it over and adds it to tomorrow's budget, along with Mary Connolly's 1000-word piece on the health survey. Ahearn plans to do a follow-up on the NAACP press conference by getting reaction from prison officials. The city hall reporter is doing a story on the mayor's appointment of a woman to the police department, only the second in its history.

At 3 P.M. Hulette turns the desk over to the night editor, Mac Overmyer. The eleven suburban reporters in Overmyer's charge begin trickling in to tell him what they'll be doing that night. In the town of Woodbury, correspondent Jack LeMenager will be checking rumors that a large corporation is trying to buy 200 acres of farmland for construction of its new headquarters. In New Fairfield, the board of selectmen will be discussing a controversial new conflict-of-interest ordinance for town employees. In Ridgefield, angry residents are expected to turn out that night for a zoning board hearing on the proposed extension of a large shopping center.

By 5 P.M. the newsroom is nearly empty. Steve Collins, the editorial writer, has gone home after finishing his last editorial for tomorrow's paper, a blast at South Korea for not cooperating in the investigation of a U.S. Congressional bribery scandal. The executive editor, Frede, is putting on his coat. He has just finished a thorough reading of the day's paper and has sent out several complimentary notes, or "warm fuzzies," as he calls them, to reporters whose pieces he liked.

It is sleeting outside. Overmyer starts getting calls from reporters about meetings that will be cancelled that night. LeMenager phones to say he's called five sources but can turn up nothing on the land purchase in Woodbury. A call comes from the Ridgefield reporter, who says that, despite the bad weather, the shopping center hearing is jammed to overflowing, and that, judging by the list of people scheduled to testify, it won't be over until near midnight.

At 8 P.M. Ron Galluska enters, dressed in a Santa Claus suit. He is a feature writer who works on stories for the Sunday department. Tonight he's doing a first-person account about playing Santa Claus to neighborhood children. For authenticity, he glued on his false eyebrows with rubber cement. Now the glue is beginning to burn his skin. "I don't know why I do stuff like this," he says. A photographer picks him up, and they go off into the ice storm.

At about 10, the newsroom begins filling again as suburban reporters return to make phone calls and write their stories. Overmyer's two assistant editors have arrived, and the three confer about which stories will go where. Overmyer goes home at midnight. It has been a slow night for news. By 4:50 A.M. all the suburban pages have been laid out and sent to the back shop. Outside the sleet has changed to freezing rain, and the trees look like crystal.

In a few minutes, Bollman arrives with his English muffin and coffee. He says the roads are a sheet of ice, and he had a hell of a time getting in. Now that he's here, though, the new day is ready to begin.

REPORTING A BEAT

As explained earlier in this chapter, beat reporters specialize in particular areas of news, so that they can cover them in depth. On larger papers, they frequently have had special training in their fields, particularly in areas involving the sciences, the law and business and economics. On smaller papers, beat reporters, who often have taught themselves a beat, may cover more than one area of news.

"The news today is much more complicated and it requires more expertise on the part of reporters," says Frede of *The News-Times*. "I think it's more important to give the trends, and the background of major stories than it is simply to tell about specific events. Stories explaining energy consumption, transportation needs and the economic effects of some government program are bigger news in my book than who held up the local bank or broke into the department store. It may not seem as dramatic, but it affects a lot more people."

In Danbury, reporters generally develop a beat after they've spent a year or two reporting on the suburban towns. Beat reporters need not turn in a story each day; often they go two or three days before coming up with something substantial. Sometimes they think up their own story ideas and get them approved before starting out. Frede and other editors supply their own ideas, and some of the best stories originate with readers who view the newspaper as a court of last resort.

Mary Connolly, the paper's health services reporter, is 29 years old and a graduate of the University of Missouri School of Journalism. One day she learned from a friend that a Danbury woman had been complaining to neighbors of receiving inordinately high hospital bills. Connolly went to see the woman, a 57-year-old liquor store operator whose husband had been taken to Danbury General Hospital two months previously with a blood clot in his stomach. Doctors conducted tests and a surgeon performed a five-hour operation, but thirty-one hours after entering the hospital, her husband died.

In a week or two the bills started coming: from the surgeon, the anesthesiologist, three internists, two cardiologists—and the hospital itself. These bills added up to $8126 for her husband's day and a half in the hospital. The woman had no medical insurance and would have to sell the liquor store to pay off the bills.

Connolly's front page story about the bill caused a furor. Readers wrote angry letters. They called the paper; they called the hospital. In the end, the hospital refused to lower the bill, although one group of doctors cut their fees in half. But its annual fund drive, then under way, was crippled by the bad publicity. Several people returned the hospital's requests for a donation with a copy of Connolly's story—and no money.

The hospital was so mad at Connolly that it called the paper's publisher to try to have her taken off her beat. The paper, however, stood firm. And after a period during which hospital officials refused to talk to her, eventually they began giving her stories again. "They saw I wasn't going to go away," says Connolly, "so they decided they had to deal with me." Her story won two state press awards.

The police reporter for *The News-Times* is Ruth Lockwood, a 36-year-old mother of two boys. With her large frame and her brown hair swept haphazardly into a bun, Lockwood looks more like a fifth-grade music teacher than someone whose job is to chase fire engines and ambulances. "I'm not the kind of police reporter who hangs out at the police station or has a flashing red light on my car," says Lockwood, the only reporter on the paper who never attended college. "But I get along just as well without all that, just by being me." She has, in fact, cultivated reliable sources, in both state and local police departments, who slip her details on stories that higher officials are reluctant to give out. Her informants on the Danbury force are so loyal that once, when the police chief tried to cut her off from crime news because of a derogatory story she had written about him, she received a fat envelope in the mail containing the unlisted home numbers of every police officer on the force, including the chief's.

Lockwood keeps an elaborate statistical file on all the major crimes as well as what happened to the culprits who were caught. She compiles a log of pending cases to follow in the courts, broken down by categories such as rape, arson, fraud and police brutality. This gives her ready background when final verdicts come down or when she has to do a piece on crime trends.

Lockwood's day begins at 6:30 A.M. when she drops by the regional State Police barracks in nearby Southbury. At midmorning she visits the Danbury police and fire departments to check for news that occurred over the night or early that day. She keeps alert to picture possibilities, especially those of dramatic accidents. "The rule on *The News-Times* is that accident pictures must be *unusual*, as well as dramatic," she says. At one Danbury intersection that runs under a low-slung viaduct, the tops of so many too-tall trailer trucks have been sheered off by the overpass that the paper no longer runs pictures of the wrecks.

Local police and fire news occasionally involves sizable disasters. In Lockwood's ten years on the paper, the biggest stories were the bombing of the police station by the Pardue brothers as a diversionary action for a bank robbery, the fire at the federal penitentiary and the midair collision of two airliners over nearby North Salem, New York, which killed fifty-four persons. Lockwood caught the plane crash by chance: "It was a Saturday and I was all dressed up in high heels going to a wedding," she said. "I was driving along when two fire trucks passed me. I figured it was more than a brush fire so I decided to follow. The first thing I saw when I got there was a man. He was all gray and burned. It was a horrible sight, and I remember standing there and asking myself, 'Gee, I wonder if I should take a picture.'" She took the picture, then rushed to a phone to call the desk, which ordered all available reporters out to help her cover the story.

By now Lockwood's family has gotten used to the occasional late-night calls from the police that send her out on stories. Especially understanding is her 13-year-old son: "He once got to go with me on a drug raid," she said. "He thinks my job is really neat."

STARTING OUT

Young reporters start on *The News-Times* by covering the suburban towns. As town reporters, the paper's frontline news gatherers, they are responsible for daily accounts of routine news; they are also expected to come up with feature stories for the suburban and Sunday editions. Between covering meetings, chatting with town officials and residents to cultivate news sources and coming in voluntarily to help cover major stories, they sometimes work ten to fourteen hours a shift.

Overmyer, the state editor, gets as excited over important news as do his young reporters, and he takes pains to walk them through problems and to console them if they've done something wrong. In the process, he has won a good deal of affection and engendered a lot of enthusiasm in his staff. "At present they're dedicating about 70 percent of their lives to the paper," he says. "I find myself spending more time urging them not to drive their health into the dirt than spurring them on. They do their own spurring."

A 34-year-old journalism graduate of Ohio State University, Overmeyer has vivid memories of his own early days on the paper. He was assigned to cover the town of Bethel, a community east of Danbury with about 3000 people. It was just before Christmas, and Bethel had scheduled the annual Christmas tree-lighting ceremony on the village green. But instead of the excited children and carol singing that usually accompany such events, the ceremony served as an excuse for the town's business and political leaders to hold a loud cocktail party. At one point during the boozing, someone staggered out to flick on the Christmas tree lights, after which the party continued into the night. Overmyer's story the next day began:

> The town lit its Christmas tree last night. No one sang carols. No one wished anyone Merry Christmas. The only cheer was in the bottles of whiskey over at the Chamber of Commerce where the celebration took place.

The uproar was immediate. Furious town officials and businesspeople called the paper's editor and demanded that Overmyer be fired for "insulting the town." Wondering by now whether his story was such a good idea after all, Overmyer, then 26, was understandably unnerved by the response. But his editor, an unexcitable old newspaperman named Forrest Palmer, not only refused to take his reporter out of Bethel but told Overmyer: "From now on, if you get any complaints, you tell them to talk to me."

The furor subsided, and, to Overmyer's amusement, the tree-lighting ceremony the next year followed a different course: "Everyone was out there on the green singing carols," he said. "There were men, women, a lot of children. They were handing out candy canes. It was like it should be. And I couldn't help thinking that my story had been responsible."

Town reporters learn to juggle several stories at a time, hunting for fresh news while keeping up contacts that may pay off in the future, and following up on stories covered in the past. Following is a look at one day in the life of Cathy Shufro, a typical, 25-year-old reporter for *The News-Times*. A liberal arts graduate of Brown University, Cathy was hired two years earlier, and since then has worked out of the paper's bureau in New Milford, a factory and farming town of 17,000 people located fifteen miles north of Danbury. The bureau, which consists of two reporters and a receptionist, occupies a storefront office on Main Street, next to a laundromat and across the village green from the red brick Town Hall. Cathy shares an old farm house in the country with several other young people and a Newfoundland dog named Erica. Her diary covers one mid-December day:

8 A.M.—I wake up. No, I tell myself, you can't wake up yet. You didn't get to sleep until 3. Come on, don't start thinking about the story. Don't think. I go back to sleep.

10:30—I cautiously look at the clock. Late enough to get up, I guess. Sleeping is a problem since my natural inclination is to wake at 8 no matter when I went to bed.

11:45—Leave for office. I have a 12:30 appointment to eat lunch with the YMCA director and talk over some problems he has, but I have calls to make first. I drive past Whiting's dairy farm and notice he's bringing in the cows, past a house being proposed as a new restaurant, see a young colt at the horse farm nearby and pass some town crewmen I know sweeping the ice pond. I live in the town I report on, and that's important. I know how these people feel about things. And the townspeople seem to appreciate that I'm a New Milfordite, too. I very much like this town, despite its problems.

12 noon—Call Walter Burke, head of the press club at the Canterbury School, a local boarding school. I ask him if he would include *The News-Times* on his mailing list. He says just last month they had a student sent to a national track meet. Now he tells me! He says he considers the weekly *New Milford Times* to be the hometown paper so he doesn't bother with us. I tell him we sell almost as many copies every day as they do each Thursday, and we joke about the merits of each paper. He is willing to keep in contact and takes my name and number; he says he will have another teacher call me about a new computer program the school has.

12:15—Leave fifth message at the Century Brass Co. to inquire about water problems at the factory. The Housatonic River has washed away a river bank near the plant, and they're trying to get the federal government to pay for fixing it. They say the manager is in Waterbury. I ask for his number there and they say he is en route. Getting through to Century is even harder than getting through to JP Stevens (the local branch of a textile company that had made national headlines because of its labor problems). At Stevens they now recognize my voice, which can be a liability. They don't like the press, so I used to state my name in an authoritative tone without saying I was a reporter and found it got me through more effectively to the boss. I called Stevens last Thursday and kept calling, and by Monday I got them to call back. So I await Century. Will it be the millennium before they call?

12:20—Call union organizer at textile union in New York. Main object is to find out progress of probable injunction request against JP Stevens. The company has refused to bargain with them. The injunction should come this week or next, but the National Labor Relations Board isn't at liberty to tell me in advance. Usually I can get it from the union, since press coverage is in their interest. The organizer knows as much about the injunction as he's read in my article in our paper. He refers me to legal department. I ask about his plans so I'll know where to reach him—he travels a lot. We talk briefly about the AFL-CIO convention going on in Los Angeles and he tells me what's going on there. I find it fascinating. Call legal department. Both people I want are out.

12:30—YMCA director calls, cancels appointment. Discuss situation at Y for half an hour. Board of directors may resign because of big controversy with regional headquarters in Danbury. The argument's over who gets to spend money on what project. All off the record at this point. I need background just in case, I tell him. Maybe at 4:30 we can meet, he says.

1 P.M.—Woman calls and cancels a Wednesday interview about an orphanage she wants money for in the Philippines. Doesn't know when she can reschedule,

GETTING A JOB

Finding one's first reporting job on a newspaper is not easy, but anyone with talent who goes about it with care and diligence can usually get work. A few words of advice:

First, put together a resume that summarizes your background. Keep it to a page or two at most. Long resumes get ponderous, and suggest to editors that you don't understand the importance of being concise.

Choose a region of the country where you intend to apply for the job. Then draw a circle about 100 miles in diameter around its largest city, make a list of every newspaper inside the circle from the *Editor & Publisher International Yearbook* in your college library and write the managing editor of each.

Accompany the resume with a brief cover letter describing when you will be ready to work, the job you want and your chief qualifications—such as editorship on a campus paper or literary magazine, a summer job on a local weekly or unusually high grades. Opinions differ on what tone a cover letter should take. Some argue for the hard sell, a letter that shouts how wonderful you are and what the newspaper will miss by not having you on its staff. Generally, though, editors rely more on an interview to form an opinion of an applicant's worth. A brassy letter may well turn them off.

Along with the resume and cover letter, send along one or two stories you've written for your campus paper, or some other sample of your writing. Avoid mailing a whole sheaf of material. Editors have to read copy all day, and will not welcome dozens of news stories sent in by a novice. If you're a promising journalist they will see that from a few clips as readily as from a bundle.

The object of all this is to secure a personal interview. When job openings occur editors are more likely to remember applicants they've met in person. Then, too, jobs often open up unexpectedly, sometimes between the time you write a letter and the time you show up for the interview. Editors with a job opening to fill sometimes hire the first qualified applicant who walks through the door. So end the cover letter by requesting an interview, even if no jobs are available. Say when you plan to be in the area and that you will call for an appointment.

At the interview, be yourself. Anyone who regularly interviews prospective employees can easily tell when someone is putting up a false front. Give some thought to questions you might be asked. Editors like young people who have done some pondering about their future and know something about the field. Why *do* you want to become a journalist? What kind of reporting would you eventually like to do? What can you contribute to the paper?

Study the newspaper in advance of the interview. Does a local columnist strike you as interesting? Does the makeup seem innovative? Is the paper running an investigative series? Editors take pride in their product and like it when a prospective employee shows interest.

and so I tell her I don't know then if I can do the story at all. She is much taken aback and quickly agrees to a new appointment.

1:05—Call the new director of the local youth commission to set up interview and get to know him a little. His group counsels kids and runs recreational programs. He is out of town until Thursday. I ask one of his social workers what's on agenda for tonight's meeting of the commission, which I must miss in favor of school board. I've seen the agenda, but it's too vague for me to gauge the importance of anything in it. What can you make out of "director's report," "counseling report"? Ask for secretary, who usually knows what's happening, but she's out. Leave message.

Editors want to hire reporters who are inquisitive and curious, so don't be afraid to ask questions. How many reporters does the paper have, and how is their coverage organized? Where do young people start out? What are the prospects for advancement, if you did well, on a beat that appeals to you?

Editors also like to hire personable, lively, cheerful people, who will represent the paper to its advantage. The way you act in the interview tells them a lot about how you would cover a story. Enthusiasm and a desire to make yourself useful count for a lot.

Along with an interview, many papers require job applicants to take written tests. These may include a current affairs quiz, to see if you know what's going on in the world; a test of vocabulary, spelling and grammar; and an exercise that tests your ability to write a hard news story under deadline pressure. The latter usually involves a scrambled fact sheet on a police story, such as a fire or an accident. The paper may also ask for a brief autobiography or an essay on why you want to become a reporter.

Note that The News-Times gets several hundred applications for the eight or ten jobs that open up each year, and so can be choosey about whom it hires. Before being granted an interview, applicants are tested on their spelling, vocabulary and general knowledge of the news of the day. Then they are asked to write an accident story from a set of notes and a weather story based on facts they can make up themselves. One tests newswriting skills; the other, an applicant's resourcefulness.

"I'm impressed," says Executive Editor Frede, "when a young person comes here from out of town and, when writing the weather story, she bothers to look up the names of real shopping centers in the directory and puts in real street names, or asks someone what the mayor's name is. It's that extra little effort that shows us why we should hire her over someone else."

When it comes to a person's background, editors tend to hire reporters who reflect their own outlooks on life. A liberal arts graduate from the University of Connecticut, Frede prefers people who have studied something else besides journalism. Of the reporters on his staff, twice as many majored in other fields—history, English, psychology—as majored in journalism. He does, however, expect applicants to have taken some journalism courses. "Applicants have got to demonstrate to me that they've made some effort to learn the craft," he says. "Journalism is a skill like everything else. While it doesn't take as much training as, say, medicine, I get irritated when someone asks me for a job without having bothered to learn the fundamentals."

In the end, however, enthusiasm as much as skill wins the job. "When I talk to young people I've got to be able to see an excitement for journalism as a way of life," Frede says. "They've got to convince me that journalism is what they really want to do, that they're not just after a job."

1:15—Woman comes in door. Kay, our receptionist, is out, so I listen to the lady elaborate on a press release of monumental unimportance—new officers for some club or other. I'm polite, chat about weather, etc. I figure 10 percent of my time is spent on similar stuff, commiserating with those whose newspapers are delivered late, saying we're sorry but, no, the groom can't be in the wedding pictures along with the bride. Sometimes it's a nuisance, sometimes a pleasant diversion.

1:30 P.M.—Catch a quick lunch.

2:15—Call Pettibone School for a feature story about program they have for children with learning difficulties. Phone is busy as usual. This is my tenth call to school in two days, always to find phone busy. Call office of superintendent of schools. I'm pretty sure he just takes it off the hook. Call school board chairman in town of Shepaug, which I also cover. Need to pick up what happened at a meeting I had to miss in favor of another one last night. She's out of town for rest of week. Try the superintendent of schools. Not there. The school business manager. Not there, leave message.

Do some briefs on upcoming meetings, etc. Some details left out, so I make calls to fill in. What time is the meeting? Where?

Run across the street to mail letter. Call the union lawyers again. They're not in. Finally reach principal at Pettibone School. We talk for quite a while. Tells me she is starting a newsletter for parents of children with math problems. I ask to be put on list. She worries about having photos of kids with learning problems in the paper because the class is a remedial one, and their parents might object. Says she'll check. We set up time for interview. First time I've spoken with her so I take time to find out about her, her background, etc.

3:30—Call Century Brass vice president in Waterbury about its river problems. He says money for the job is in a U.S. Senate Bill, but someone has put a rider on the bill for funding the B-1 Bomber program, which means it probably won't pass. His version of what's going on is a little different from mine. He says he'll check with his lobbyist in Washington, can I call him in the morning? Story can wait because I have a more pressing story in tonight's meeting of the New Milford School Board.

Call Doug Hulette, the day editor, to ask about legalities of taking photos in connection with the Pettibone School story. Do we ever need release? Doug is not my editor, but Mac Overmyer doesn't start work today until 4:30 and I always get busy well before then.

It is sleeting out, on top of ice and snow.

4:45—Call union lawyers again for info on injunction. No word yet, he says, and promises to call. I plan to bug him and the union organizer and the public relations man at the Labor Relations Board tomorrow. One of them should let me know. Labor Board man is very helpful—he's taken a special interest in me, tells me about his old days with United Press in Kansas in the 1930s. It's nice to call him. Also I've learned a tremendous amount of labor law from him.

Youth commission calls and cancels meeting because of weather.

Call local superintendent's office to find out if tonight's meeting will be cancelled because of the weather. They're rude, as usual. The secretary tells me *of course* the school board will meet.

Drive home at 5:30 to get dinner before my meetings tonight. My window keeps icing up; cars are going very slowly. I slip and slide. Hope they'll cancel school board!

6 P.M.—Call school board chairman. He says he will cancel meeting since seven members say they refuse to drive in sleet. I call Overmyer and tell him both meetings are cancelled. He tells me to take the evening off. As my days go, this was a short one. But I am tired. Not sure why.

SUMMARY

Most journalists find their first jobs on small-town rather than big-city newspapers. Small papers proceed at a slower pace, permitting editors to give reporters closer supervision, and small communities, where government is on a more human scale, provide an excellent journalistic training ground.

This chapter examined a days' operation of *The News-Times* of Danbury, Connecticut, whose population is 60,000. Young reporters there start out by covering one or more of the twenty-one rural and suburban towns surrounding Danbury. As the paper's frontline news gathers, the suburban reporters are responsible for a daily account of routine news as well as writing feature stories for suburban and Sunday sections. After a year or two in the towns reporters move into Danbury, where they develop a speciality, or beat. Whereas suburban reporters limit their coverage to what happens in their own towns, beat reporters—whether concentrating on politics, business or the environment—look at trends throughout the whole western part of the state.

4

WORKING FOR
A WIRE SERVICE

No one newspaper or broadcast organization can cover all the world's news by itself. There's just too much going on. A few American newspapers make a serious effort in this direction: *The New York Times* has a staff of nearly 500 reporters and photographers in thirty foreign and eighteen domestic bureaus, while the *Los Angeles Times* has twenty bureaus scattered from Washington, D.C., to Peking and New Delhi. But even giants like these need help. That's why they subscribe to the wire services. The wire services gather the news and transmit it to the hundreds of newspapers and broadcasters that pay for the service. If an oil tanker sinks off Capetown or a prime minister falls ill in London, the editors of the *Sacramento Bee* or the *Detroit Free Press* don't normally send one of their own reporters to cover it. They rely on a wire service reporter to do the job.

There are two major wire services in the United States—the Associated Press (AP) and United Press International (UPI). Other nations have wire services too; among the most prominent are the French Press Agency (AFP) and Reuters in Great Britain. UPI, a private concern, sells its service to clients, and the AP is set up as a cooperative among its clients, but in practice both work in much the same way.

To fulfill their mission as the world's most wide-reaching news-gathering organizations, the AP and UPI have mustered imposing arrays of human and technological resources. Each employs more than 1000 reporters, editors and photographers. The AP has 120 bureaus across the United States and sixty-three in other nations; UPI, seventy domestic and 102 foreign bureaus. Every day, these bureaus dispatch news stories and photographs by satellite channels and telephone lines to wire service headquarters in New York: to AP headquarters in Rockefeller Center or to UPI on East 42nd Street. There, editors fashion this flood of information into a steady stream of copy and photographs and send it out over the wires. Clients pay for the service according to their actual or potential circulation; a major daily like *The Chicago Tribune* may pay ten or fifteen times as much for the same AP or UPI line as does the *News-Times* in Danbury, Connecticut.

Each wire service moves the news in two cycles per day. One cycle, from noon until about midnight, is intended primarily for the nation's morning newspapers; the other cycle, from midnight till noon, is intended for afternoon and evening papers. The most important news of the day moves on the *A* wire. Stories considered somewhat less newsworthy move on the *B* wire. An account of a major California earthquake would make the *A* wire, but a minor tremor, one that did no more than rattle windows, would be consigned to the *B* wire. A plan to reduce nuclear weapons stockpiles would make the *A* wire if advocated by the president, but the same plan, if advocated by a small group of professors, might go on the *B* wire—because the professors, unlike the president, have little power to turn their political preferences into reality.

Both AP and UPI offer specialized services: sports wires, financial wires that carry spot business news and updates on the stock markets and feature services that carry book and movie reviews, consumer service features and profiles of television stars. Broadcast wires offer copy edited and rewritten for reading on the air. Here the stories are cut shorter than they would be if intended for newspapers, and they are edited for the ear. (See also Chapter 11, *Writing for Broadcast*.)

Technologically the wire services stand with one foot in the past and one in the future. To some of their smaller clients they still send copy clanking through a mechanical printer at sixty-six words per minute. Clients who have invested in electronic data-processing equipment can receive wire service copy at 1200 words per minute, pumped directly into the memories of their computers. UPI "slow-scan" service feeds the news to many of the nation's cable TV subscribers. Those who have home computers can access the UPI report by subject, reading what interests them without waiting while other stories troop by on the TV screen. As the technology develops further, both the AP and UPI are phasing out transmission by land lines. Instead, they beam the news via satellite directly to rooftop antennas at each client newspaper or broadcasting station.

In recent years, the AP and UPI have been experimenting with computerized combinations of their general and special-purpose wires. Pouring out copy at high speed, as suggested by the AP's name for its computerized "Datastream" service, these new wires are intended primarily for smaller newspapers that need a variety of news but cannot afford to subscribe to all the special-purpose wires.

In addition to their national wires, the AP and UPI also have regional wires in some areas. State wires are especially useful to clients in big states like New

"GET IT RIGHT, GET IT RIGHT NOW": WIRE SERVICE CREDO PUT TO THE TEST IN COVERING THE ASSASSINATION OF A PRESIDENT

Veteran UPI staffer Merriman Smith had been covering the White House for twenty-two years when he witnessed the assassination of John F. Kennedy. Riding as a pool reporter in the President's motorcade in Dallas, Texas, November 22, 1963, Smith heard shots and saw the cars ahead speed up. He grabbed a radiotelephone mounted under the dash of the car, called the Dallas UPI bureau and dictated a bulletin reporting that shots had been fired at the President's motorcade. He and the other pool reporters followed Kennedy's car to Parkland Hospital. In an article for *UPI File* recounting how he covered the story, Smith relates what happened next:

I ran to the side of the bubble-top.

The President was face-down on the back seat. Mrs. Kennedy made a cradle of her arms around the President's head and bent over him as if she were whispering to him.

Governor Connelly was on his back on the floor of the car, his head and shoulders resting in the arms of his wife, Nellie, who kept shaking her head and shaking with dry sobs. Blood oozed from the front of the Governor's suit. I could not see the President's wound. But I could see blood spattered around the interior of the rear seat and a dark stain spreading down the right side of the President's dark gray suit.

(Despite the shock of the grisly scene, Smith is careful to observe it in detail.)

From the car telephone I had radioed the Dallas bureau of UPI that three shots had been fired at the Kennedy motorcade. Seeing the bloody scene in the rear of the car at the hospital entrance, I knew I had to get to a telephone immediately.

(Smith's first reaction is to recognize that he must get the news out at once.)

Clint Hill, the Secret Service agent in charge of the detail assigned to Mrs. Kennedy, was leaning over into the rear of the car.

"How badly is he hit, Clint?" I asked.

"He's dead," Hill replied curtly. . . .

I spotted a telephone. . . . It took two tries before I successfully dialed the Dallas UPI number. Quickly I dictated a bulletin saying the President had been seriously, perhaps fatally, injured by an assassin's bullets while driving through the streets of Dallas . . ."

(Smith carefully reports only what he knows to be true. Despite what the secret service man told him, Smith cannot assume the President is dead until a doctor has pronounced him dead.)

Wayne Hawks of the White House staff ran by me shouting that Kilduff would make a statement

---

York and California, so large that covering them would exhaust the resources of all but the largest newspapers and broadcasters. Metropolitan, or "local," wires serve major American cities. Because their clients are relatively few, principally just a particular city's newspapers and broadcasters, local wires tend to flourish in boom times, when clients can afford them, and to die when financial times are hard, and clients cancel their subscriptions to save money.

Like the content of newspapers, the choice of stories emphasized by the AP and UPI reflects the needs and interests of the audience. An account of the slaying of a petty counterfeiter in his home in Westchester County, New York, would be of little interest to the editor on the AP national desk, because only the readers in the New York area are likely to take an interest in such an item. If the murder victim were more prominent, the story might make the state wire. A sensational crime—like the murder of physician and bestselling "Scarsdale Diet" author Herman Tarnower, shot by his former lover, the headmistress of a prestigious girls' school—will attract sufficient national interest to be covered on the *A* wire.

shortly in the so-called nurses' room above and at the far end of the hospital.

I threw down the phone and sped after them. We reached the door of the conference room and there were loud cries of "Quiet!" Fighting to keep his emotions under control, Kilduff said, "President John Fitzgerald Kennedy died at approximately 1 o'clock."

I raced into a nearby office. The telephone switchboard at the hospital was hopelessly jammed. I spotted Virginia Payette, wife of UPI's Southwestern division manager and a veteran reporter in her own right. I told her to try getting through on pay telephones on the floor above.

Frustrated by the inability to get through the hospital switchboard, I appealed to a nurse. She led me through a maze of corridors and back stairways to another floor and a lone pay booth. I got the Dallas office. Virginia had gotten through before me. . . .

(*Learning that Kennedy's body is to be flown to Washington at once, Smith hurries to keep up with the story.*)

Charles Roberts of *Newsweek* magazine, Sid Davis of Westinghouse Broadcasting and I implored a police officer to take us to the airplane in his squad car. . . . As we piled out of the car on the edge of the runway about 200 yards from the presidential aircraft, Kilduff spotted us and motioned for us to hurry. We trotted to him and he said the pool men could take two pool men to Washington; that [Vice President Lyndon B.] Johnson was about to take the oath of office aboard the plane and would take off immediately thereafter.

I saw a bank of telephones beside the runway and asked if I had time to advise my news service. He said, "But for God's sake, hurry."

. . . I called the New York bureau of UPI and told them about the impending installation of a new president aboard the airplane.

(*Smith risks missing the plane in order to report the important news that Johnson is about to take the oath of office.*)

Aboard Air Force One, on which I had made so many trips as a press association reporter covering President Kennedy, all the shades of the larger main cabin were drawn and the interior was hot and dimly lighted. . . . I wedged inside the door and began counting. There were twenty-seven people in this compartment. Johnson stood in the center with his wife, Lady Bird. U.S. District Judge Sarah T. Hughes, 67, a kindly faced woman, stood with a small black Bible in her hands, waiting to give the oath. . . .

(*Jammed in a sweltering aircraft carrying the body of the president, Smith, despite his distress, has the presence of mind to note salient details and describe the scene.*)

At 3:45 EST, the wheels of Air Force One cleared the runway. . . .

Mrs. Kennedy went to the rear lounge and took a chair beside the coffin. There she remained throughout the flight. Her vigil was shared at times by four staff members close to the slain chief executive—David Powers, his buddy and personal assistant; Kenneth P. O'Donnell, appointments secretary and key political adviser; Lawrence O'Brien, chief Kennedy liaison man with Congress, and Brigadier General Godfrey McHugh, Kennedy's Air Force aide. . . .

(*Throughout the flight Smith continues to note the concrete, specific details.*)

READING AND WRITING WIRE COPY

News items are dispatched (or "moved") over the wires as they become available, in approximately the order of their timeliness and importance. Wire service editors move the most newsworthy stories first, and let the less newsworthy ones wait their turn.

If a newsworthy story is lengthy, however, running it in full might make clients wait too long for the rest of the news. So editors often move stories in segments of 200 to 400 words in length, interspersing other news. In the old days, when wire copy moved slowly, this was practically a necessity. Today, high-speed transmission makes it less so, but editors still often transmit stories in segments, if only to assist clients who are in a hurry to rip the first few paragraphs off the machine and get it on the air or into the editing process. The result can be a mosaic of *leads, adds, new leads, inserts* and *subs*.

The *lead* is, of course, the top of the story. It may run from as little as a sentence up to several paragraphs. Then the dispatch is signed off. An *add* soon follows, continuing the story down through several more paragraphs. If the story requires rewriting or updating, a *new lead* is moved. If only the lead paragraph or paragraphs are new, they can *pick up* the earlier copy at a designated point somewhere in the body copy. If the entire story is rewritten, it is called a *write-through* (sometimes spelled *write-thru*). *Inserts* can be designated for placement within a previously moved story. *Subs* are paragraphs substituted for paragraphs in a previous story.

Wire service editors indicate the news priority of important stories by designating them *urgent, bulletin* or *flash*. A flash is news of the very highest priority. Flashes are employed very seldom, and are kept short:

> a1041
> fa
> AM-Landing,
> FLASH
>
> SPACE CENTER, HOUSTON (AP)—Man on the moon.

A flash is always followed by a complete lead, which moves as a *bulletin*:

> a1042
> ba
> AM-Landing, 20
>
> SPACE CENTER, HOUSTON (AP)—Astronaut Neil A. Armstrong set foot on the Moon today at 2:56 A.M. Greenwich Time and said, "That's one small step for a man, one giant leap for mankind."

The *bulletin* should promptly be followed by an *add*, marked *urgent*.

Entire dispatches also may be designated urgent, to help distinguish them from less exceptional dispatches. A flash should be written in but a few words, a bulletin in no more than about fifty words, an urgent in no more than about 150 words.

A major developing story can generate many new leads, adds, inserts and subs. To keep order, each segment of wire service copy is labelled with a set of code numbers and letters. To see how these work, let's look at several stages in the AP's coverage of a Space Shuttle landing:

> a143
> ba
> PM-Space Shuttle, 3rd Ld, 50
> BULLETIN
>
> CAPE CANAVERAL, FLA. (AP)—Astronauts John Young and Robert Crippen survived the scorching heat of their white-knuckled descent through the Earth's upper atmosphere today and directed rocketship Columbia toward an airliner-like landing on California's Mojave Desert.

The "a143" at the top of the code in the bulletin designates that this was the 143rd segment dispatched on the *A* wire in this cycle. The lowercase letters "ba" immediately below are a *priority* code; "b" indicates a bulletin, and "a" means the *A* wire. "PM" means that the dispatch is being transmitted during the twelve-hour PM cycle. "Space Shuttle" is the slug; computer people sometimes call the slug the *keyword*. This was the third lead to the Space Shuttle story so far that cycle, so it is designated "3rd Ld," followed by the approximate number of words in the segment, 50.

In writing wire copy, remember that all adds, inserts and subs must be keyed to the transmission number of the most recent lead. In the case of the Space Shuttle bulletin, the first add looked like this:

a145
ua
PM-Space Shuttle, 3rd Ld, 1st Add a143, 100
URGENT

CAPE CANAVERAL, FLA. (AP)—Mojave Desert.
   The Columbia's heat-shielding tiles, problematic throughout the shuttle's development, passed their test. . . .

The add then went on for several paragraphs. Here, the priority code was "ua," designating an urgent, and the add was preceded by a line designating the number of the latest lead to the story. Also included are the final words of the previous segment, so that there can be no doubt about where the add belongs.

The safe landing of the shuttle was a more important event than its beginning or its descent from orbit, so when the shuttle landed, a new lead was called for:

a146
ba
PM-Space Shuttle, 4th Ld, 30
BULLETIN

   EDWARDS AIR FORCE BASE, CALIF. (AP)—America's rocketship Columbia and her two pilots swooped safely back to Earth today, surviving a blazing plunge from orbit and a heart-stopping landing on a hard-sand runway in the Mojave Desert.
   MORE

Two adds followed, with an instruction of where to pick up the older copy dispatched prior to the landing. Then came reaction from the president, calling for an insert. (Here the priority code "r" indicates regular priority):

a154
ra

PM-Space Shuttle, Insert a146, 60
EDWARDS AIR FORCE BASE: insert after 18th graf: From Shuttle

From President Reagan in Washington came this message: "Congratulations on a job well done. I'm very proud."
A crowd of about 150,000 persons—waving flags like crazy as Columbia headed in—let out a collective cheer when the landing wheels appeared and a louder one when first the back wheels, then the front hit paydirt.
Columbia came, 19th graf.

The codes employed by the wire services have changed over the years and doubtless will continue to change, but the underlying principle remains the same: Every piece of copy moved over the wire should be numbered, and, if the copy is tied to previous copy on the cycle (as are all new leads, adds and inserts), then the number of the earlier story and the place of the new copy in it must be clearly marked. In addition, every segment is signed off by the wire operator with the bureau number and the time of day. In this way, clients can quickly piece together copy to create fresh, complete stories, and they can tell at a glance where each segment came from and when it was transmitted.

THE INFLUENCE OF THE WIRE SERVICES

The major wire services are probably our most influential news organizations. They have *direct* influence: Wire service copy is printed in newspapers and broadcast verbatim every day. They have *indirect* influence: Journalists often employ information gleaned from wire service dispatches, and don't always credit the information to its source. And they have *editorial* influence: Many editors follow their lead when deciding which are the most important national and international stories of the day.

The public tends to notice only the most *direct* influence, when wire service stories are printed in newspapers with an identifying "bug"—(AP) or (UPI)—following the dateline, or when a radio newscaster says, "Here's the news, from the WKRP newsroom and the wires of the Associated Press."

Indirect influences operate when local editors and radio and television broadcasters incorporate material obtained from the wires into their stories. Sometimes newspapers rewrite two or more wire dispatches into a single story. Reporters sometimes consult wire service copy to verify or supplement information in a story they have covered—to learn the police estimate of the size of the crowd at a political rally, for instance, or to background a story on a local propane tank leak with news of a similar accident in another state. Television reporters rushing to an assignment often take with them a swatch of wire copy to read in the car on the way to the scene. The clients aren't obligated to credit the wire services: A newspaper story written from wire copy may or may not carry a byline reading, "From combined wire services." TV correspondents often attribute information to the wire service only when they aren't sure it's accurate, and local radio announcers may read an entire newscast word for word as it came in on the wires ("rip and read," in broadcast parlance) without saying where they got it.

The wire services wield *editorial* influence over the nation's newspapers and broadcasters by choosing which stories to cover and which to give the most space on the wire. Twice daily, at the start of each *A* wire cycle, the editors of

---

WIRE SERVICE EXPERIENCE "BEST IN THE WORLD," SAYS AP VETERAN

William F. "Nick" Carter worked for the Associated Press for forty-five years, first as a telegrapher and then as a reporter and rewrite man in New Jersey and New York City.

What makes a good reporter?

First, you have to be interested in the news. Not everyone is, you know. You can tell by looking around the office which of the young reporters are going to work out. They're the ones who, when the copy boy comes in and slams down a fresh edition of a newspaper on their desk, reach out and pick up that newspaper. Right away. They want to know what's in it. They're *interested* in the news.

You have to have an inquiring mind. It's essential that you be curious about everything. That's the only road to success in this business.

And you have to develop a talent for expressing things quickly and accurately, with as few wasted words and as few fumbles as possible. An emergency may come only once a month or once a year, but when it does you have to think fast. You've got to be able to form that lead in your mind, to wrap up that story in one sentence that has those five elements in it—who, what, where, when and why—that we've all heard so much about, and we all find so difficult to handle in practice.

When things were slow, I used to sit and practice trying to develop the knack of writing a lead. I'd make up stories—train wrecks and things like that—and try to write the lead. It's like riding a bicycle; you've got to know you can do it. Once you've got it, the rest is easy. I've never seen it fail: A reporter may fiddle around and fiddle around trying to get the lead, make a dozen false starts, but once he's got the lead, he just goes sailing through the rest.

What advice would you give a student who is thinking of becoming a reporter?

Keep your nose in a book all the time. Study geography. It's a subject every reporter needs but too many of us neglect. History. You should have a solid grounding in history. And vocabulary. Never pass up a word you don't understand. Look it up, mark it down, try it out in a sentence, make it your own. Even if it's a word that oughtn't to be flung into a news story, you still may need it.

Did you find it difficult to maintain accuracy under the constant deadline pressure of wire service reporting?

You're always on deadline, or feel as if you are, because you've always got to worry about the competition. The AP breaks its skull every day of the week trying to be accurate. If it didn't it would soon be in hot water, because hundreds of eyes are watching it—the eyes of all the desk editors on all the client newspapers. You can't permit much inaccuracy when you've got all those eyes on you.

What are the best and worst aspects of a career in the wire services?

The heartbreaking thing is that you don't often get to see your stuff in print under your byline. Although the AP and UPI may be generous with bylines, the editors of the newspapers using the story tend to strike the bylines off. I would too. As a newspaper editor, why should I run a lot of bylines of wire service reporters? So even if your byline goes out over the wires, it usually won't get into many papers.

Another drawback is that the wire services are eternally shorthanded. Our bureau chief in Washington, at the end of his career there, said "When I came here we had sixty-seven reporters working in this bureau, and when I left we had 127, and all the time I was here we were one reporter short." The wire services are so busy just getting the report out each day that they haven't much time to worry about the deeper meaning of things, the spiritual side of things.

On the good side, you get to work your tail off, cover all sorts of stories, get terrific experience. There's enough interesting work to go around, and not enough drudgery to break anyone's spirit. The best place in the world for a young reporter to get experience in journalism is at AP or UPI.

the AP and UPI list what they consider to be the top stories of the day. These lists, called "news digests," "schedules" or "news budgets," are consulted by editors across the country. If UPI says that a NATO meeting in Brussels is more important than a typhoon in Tahiti, newspaper editors will tend to play the NATO story more prominently than the typhoon—except, say, for editors in Hawaii, where people have reason to be concerned about Pacific storms. If the AP regards a flareup in the Mideast as the most important story of the day, network news directors will either schedule the Mideast for the evening news or muster a good reason why not.

This means that the editors of the two major American wire services rank among the most influential of all journalists. In making up the news digest, they are guided chiefly by common sense and time-honored news values like timeliness and impact. "An enormous number of considerations are at work when the news schedule is shaped every day," says UPI Editor-in-Chief H. L. Stevenson. "The most important consideration is what's happening *now*. If the hostages have just been released at 2 A.M., that's clearly the most important story. But if it's the seventh day of somebody's saying the hostages *might* be released today, the story drops in importance." Professional editors tend to agree about what makes news, and so in practice the AP and UPI news schedules on a given day contain many similarities. "Most days, the schedule pretty well sorts itself out," says Stevenson. "Events almost dictate it. We're looking at the whole world, and there's always something big going on out there."

WIRE SERVICE REPORTING

The wires make a good training ground. Walter Cronkite, David Brinkley and Howard K. Smith are only a few of the many journalists who started as wire service reporters. Some work for local newspapers before landing wire service jobs; others are hired by the AP or UPI right out of school. Some stay a few years, then move on to less hectic and perhaps better-paying posts; others make the wires their careers.

Wire service reporting is characterized by variety and efficiency. "We look for people who are alert, curious, and who are generalists rather than specialists," says Stevenson of UPI. "You may be covering a disaster one day, then a sports event, put in a day of routine desk work, then the next day do a political story. The work is varied. You're not catalogued or put into a pigeonhole."

Speed is essential. Newspaper reporters need to file by the deadline for the next edition, television reporters must complete their reports in time to air on the next newscast, but the wires run constantly, day and night, and their deadline usually is *now*.

UPI and the AP compete vigorously, circulating daily "logs" in-house to assess how they did the previous day against the competition—meaning how many client newspapers used their version of the story rather than the opposition's.

The key to winning in the logs is often speed, because editors and broadcasters tend to use the stories that reach them first. Wire service reporters are expected not only to get it *right* but to get it *right now*. It's not hard to spot them at news events: They're the ones rushing to the telephone, notes in hand, to dictate a lead nearly as fast as they can talk.

Looking back on his forty years with UPI, reporter Jack V. Fox saw four elements in the competition with the AP: "Who got it first? Who got it best? Who *wrote* it best? And what might be called the 'flim-flam.' Who got the exclusive angle, the scoop?"

The wire services' emphasis on speed can make for a hair-raising risk of inaccuracy. An AP reporter in Memphis in 1966, overhearing that civil rights activist James Meredith had been "shot in the head," thought he'd heard, "shot dead," and wrote a bulletin saying so. Meredith, though wounded, survived. On November 8, 1918, United Press (which merged with the International News Service to form UPI in 1958) declared that the World War was over—three days too soon. A senior editor, travelling in Europe, had been told by what seemed a reliable source that the armistice was being signed, and had cabled the erroneous report over the telegraph lines so clogged that he could not be reached for confirmation.

Reporter Fox of UPI was caught on the horns of the speed-accuracy dilemma on July 21, 1961, when he stood on the deck of the aircraft carrier Randolph watching astronaut Gus Grissom splash down in a Mercury capsule following a suborbital flight into space. A young Navy lieutenant viewing the distance recovery through binoculars suddenly said, "Uh, oh!" Lowering the binoculars, he told Fox that the capsule had sunk, taking Grissom with it. Fox was tempted to send a bulletin reporting this tragedy, but, as he later recalled, "a bell rang in my head and a small voice said to me: 'Don't do it, don't do it.'" Fox ran forward, burst onto the ship's bridge, questioned a startled admiral and learned that although the capsule had indeed sunk, Grissom had escaped safely.

THE LIMITATIONS OF THE WIRES

For all their technical resources and diligence, the general wire services are spread thin trying to cover all the news all the time. Often they are obliged to emphasize speed over depth of reporting, immediate developments over background and context, high-visibility news over the less accessible information sought by investigative reporters. A noisy protest demonstration over chemical pollution at Love Canal will get wire service coverage, for example, but the far more subtle, complicated and ultimately more important story of chemical pollution throughout the national ecosystem requires more time and money than the general wire services normally have available.

The demands of editors for deeper, more reflective, better-written copy to supplement the AP and UPI has led to the emergence of "supplemental" wire services like the *Los Angeles Times–Washington Post* service, *The New York Times* news service, and the United Feature Syndicate's Independent News Alliance (INA). These services are relatively small—the *Los Angeles Times–Washington Post* service moves about 50,000 words a day, compared to over 1 million words per day for the AP or UPI—but they are also popular; hundreds of newspapers subscribe to them and run their stories. As Sidney Goldberg of the INA puts it, "We don't try to cover all bases. We don't tell papers they can depend on us for spot news of the day—we leave that to AP and UPI. We try to expand on spot news and give a new dimension to the coverage, through background, analysis, personal journalism." To accomplish this, the INA relies on freelance contributors, whereas the wire services run by the major newspapers use copy written by the papers' staff reporters.

If the virtues of the wire services include speed, efficiency and broad coverage, their liabilities include hastiness, shallowness and blandness. Wire service editors are usually too busy and shorthanded to assign a reporter to take days tracking down a hard-to-get story or putting together a subtle feature; assignments like these, though not unknown in the wires, are rare. Still rarer is the sight of a wire service crusading for a cause, the way a newspaper might crusade against higher taxes or fight to preserve a wilderness region. "We can't crusade because we [serve] papers of every complexion under the sun," general manager Wes Gallagher told *The Wall Street Journal*. "A crusade that pleases one is anathema to another."

The wire services listen attentively to their clients. They get used to newspaper editors, publishers, producers and newscasters calling with questions or complaints. Sometimes the calls are friendly: "You say $40,000 is missing in that armored car hijacking and the AP says it's $14,000. Who's right?" Sometimes they are less friendly: "Where the hell is the tornado story? We go to press in thirty minutes!" Occasionally, clients express disagreement with the editorial judgments of the wires: An editor may protest that a wire service photo taken at the scene of an air crash was too gruesome, a local television producer may ask for more coverage of ski conditions, a publisher may complain that an expose of corruption among highway contractors was unfair to local business-people.

Listening to the clients makes sense—after all, the clients are paying the bills—but it can also make wire service editors overcautious. Newspaper publishers tend to be older, wealthier and more conservative than the general public, and the wire services can go overboard in trying to avoid offending their sensibilities. Consider the case of the elephant who ate the windbreaker. UPI editors in New York anguished at length over the story, about a boy whose nylon windbreaker had been gobbled up by an elephant at the St. Louis Zoo. A zoo-keeper telephoned the boy three days later to say that the jacket had passed through the elephant's digestive tract and was available if the boy wanted to reclaim it. The boy told the zookeeper no thanks. The UPI editors, amused by this odd little story, debated how to word it so as not to offend their clients with the image of the defecated windbreaker. Finally they decided that the item could run if the jacket were said to have simply "reappeared." Even this version seemed in dubious taste to some editors. One newspaper ran the item only after deleting everything that happened after the elephant ate the windbreaker—which must have left readers wondering what the story was doing in the paper in the first place.

Faults and all, the wire services are part of the sinew of modern journalism. Relied upon to some degree by nearly every journalist in America, they put their reputations on the line every day, minute by minute. If they did not exist, we should quickly have to reinvent them.

SUMMARY

There are two major wire services in the United States: the Associated Press (AP) and the United Press International (UPI). Their aim is to gather all the news of importance to Americans from around the world every day, a task so demanding that it is beyond the capacities of almost every newspaper. For this reason, thousands of newspapers and broadcasting stations subscribe to one or both wire services. Most depend on the wires for most of their news from most of the world.

Each staffed by more than 1000 editors, reporters and photographers, the wire services run their top stories on what they call the *A* wire in two cycles per day. They also have a variety of lesser wires, among them the *B* wire for less pressing news, financial and sports wires, municipal and state wires and broadcast wires with copy rewritten for easy reading on the air.

Wire service editors move stories in order of their newsworthiness, often dividing them into segments of 200 to 400 words in length. They move *new leads*, *adds*, *inserts* and *subs* to update and improve developing stories. Priority codes attached to important stories designate them *urgent*, *bulletin* or, most newsworthy and least often employed, *flash*. Each segment is numbered, and each new lead, add, insert or sub must be clearly keyed by number to its story, along with a clear indication of where it belongs in the copy that has already moved.

The major wire services are highly influential in at least three ways. First, their stories are picked up and printed in many newspapers each day, especially in smaller papers that cannot afford to maintain reporters of their own far from home. Second, information provided by the wires often is incorporated into news stories, with or without crediting its source. Third, each wire service twice daily transmits a list of the stories it considers the most important of the day, and these lists are consulted by thousands of editors deciding which stories to run in their newspapers or newscasts.

Reporting for a wire service means covering a wide variety of stories and covering them quickly, because the wires are always running, and the deadlines are usually immediate. The rigor and diversity of such experience makes the wires a prime training ground for young reporters, and a career for those who thrive on the pace.

Various supplementary wires are offered by such competitors as *The New York Times* News Service. These do not cover much breaking news but instead concentrate on features, analysis and "in-depth" stories.

PART III   Writing

An honest tale speeds best being plainly told.
Shakespeare

In all narration, there is only one way to be clever, and that is to be exact.
R. L. Stevenson

5

WRITING PLAIN ENGLISH

FOUR VIRTUES

Good writing is characterized by *accuracy*, *clarity*, *economy* and *vitality*.

Accuracy

Joseph Pulitzer offered his reporters three words of advice: "accuracy, accuracy, accuracy." No reputation is more valuable to a journalist than a reputation for accuracy, and nothing does more damage to a news story—and to its author's reputation—than inaccuracy. An editor can correct occasional lapses in style or reorganize a story if its news priorities are scrambled, but rarely can an editor correct a reporter who mistakenly writes that a fugitive has a tatoo on his left arm when he means the *right* arm, that Bob Wilber was indicted when he means Bob *Wilbur*, or that illegal poker games were held at 312 Wood Avenue when the correct address was *213*.

In addition to its intrinsic merits, accuracy promotes a readable style: As philosopher Arthur Schopenhauer wrote, "The first rule of good style is to have something to say." When persistent problems in style arise—for example, when a writer can't seem to find a way to phrase a given paragraph clearly— the problem often is not with style but with content.

Consider this example, taken from a newspaper excerpt of a book about millionaires: "It is put forward in this section that there exist definite money types."

What does this tangled thicket of a sentence mean? If we rewrite it for clarity, we arrive at something like this: "Definite money types exist." What are "money types?" Reading further, we find that the author means to say that all millionaires are not alike. This is hardly news. The problem in style resulted from the author's trying to make a statement that was devoid of meaningful content.

When wrestling with a tough problem of style, try asking yourself, "What am I trying to say here?" Once *the idea* is clearly in mind, the style will usually fall into place.

The following describes five ways you can help yourself achieve accuracy in newswriting:

Conduct Ample Research. Understanding the background of a story can help you identify what's new about it today. Whether the story calls for as little as reading newspaper clippings and making a few telephone calls, or whether it involves weeks of toil in the stacks of a library, research lends authority to a writer's work, and authority in turns generates a comprehensible and engaging style.

Be Thorough in Your Legwork. The reporter's goal should be to learn as much as possible about the subject at hand—not just enough to get by. By the time you sit down to write a story, your notebook should contain several times as much material as the finished story will require. That way you're free to use only the choice material: the liveliest and most informative quotations, the most pertinent background material, the most telling details and evocative descriptions. Your readers may feel that the resulting story exemplifies a more pleasing "style," but the real difference is in the thoroughness of the reporting.

Take Accurate Notes. The worst time to make mistakes is when taking notes, because errors made at the source are the most difficult to correct. Quotations must be written down precisely as the words were spoken; paraphrases are insufficient. Check the spelling of names. Note all pertinent information; don't neglect relevant material merely because you doubt that you will use it in the story. And *do* take notes whenever possible; never trust to memory unnecessarily.

Edit Your Copy. Only under extreme deadline pressure should a journalist hand in a story to an editor without first having edited and checked it. Whenever time permits, edit your copy for greater economy of phrase, precision of language and efficiency of structure. Proofread as well, correcting spelling, punctuation and typographical errors.

Editing involves a psychological shift of gears, from the heat of authorship to the cool skepticism of analysis. Acting as self-editor, the journalist should ask: Is the vital news in the lead? Is the body of the story structured coherently? Have I included everything important that the reader will want to know? And, most important, is the story accurate in every detail? Only when a writer is prepared to stand behind every word should the copy go to the editor. (We discuss editing in more detail in Chapter 10.)

Use the Dictionary. To stand behind every word of a story means, literally, every word. When in doubt about the spelling or meaning of a word, look it up. Frequent use of the dictionary is a sign of strength, not weakness.

Clarity

Sound writing is as clear as a mountain stream and as simple as stone. As Walt Whitman wrote, "The art of art, the glory of expression and the sunshine of the light of letters is simplicity; nothing is better than simplicity. . . ."

The writer's goal is to communicate, not to show off in print. "Read over your compositions," Samuel Johnson advised, "and wherever you meet with a passage which you think is particularly fine, strike it out." The following are suggestions on how to achieve a more lucid style:

Be Specific. One of the great advantages of specific writing is that it creates a picture in the reader's mind. A *tattered green coat* is more interesting to read about than a *garment*; a *kiss* evokes a deeper response in readers than does a *demonstration of affection*; a *shattered mirror* is more readily imagined than *damage to the furniture*; a *welder* is better envisioned than a *worker*.

Choose the most specific language that accords with the facts. Good newswriting—and good writing generally—is built not upon sweeping generalizations and grand abstractions, but upon the specific things that fill the real world: flowers and mud, trees and clouds, perfume and bus exhausts, real people and the words they really speak.

General	*Specific*
abode	bungalow
auto	red convertible
illness	leukemia
appliance	stove
crime	murder
wooden furniture	oak chair
fruit	banana
poetry	sonnet
laborer	lathe operator
insect	wasp
The following year she ascended the corporate ladder.	In March 1987, Allied Industries promoted her to district manager.
He left the metropolis in a penurious condition.	He hitchhiked out of Chicago with 80 cents in his pocket.

Another advantage of specific language is that it conveys more information than the general. A reporter who writes *nuclear physicist* tells us more than one who writes *scientist* or *professor*. *Convicted rapist* is preferable to *felon*, *senator* to *politician*, *Parisian* to *European*, *gold* to *precious metal*.

Generalities have their place. If thieves make off with sixty ounces of gold bullion, 5000 silver coins, and thirty platinum necklaces, for example, the reporter may find it necessary to lead with *precious metals*. But abstractions and generalizations, when unavoidable, should still be as specific as possible. At least *precious metals* is more specific than *booty* or *loot*.

Use Concrete Language. This rule is closely related to the preceding one. It expresses the same conviction—that a writer ought to be no more abstract than necessary.

Abstract	Concrete
He showed signs of fatigue.	His eyes were red and his voice hoarse with fatigue.
Obviously perturbed, the judge cautioned spectators on the need for silence.	The judge slammed down her gavel and demanded that the laughter stop.
Inclement weather discouraged bathers.	Rain soaked the empty beaches.
Fire did extensive damage to the building, much to the disadvantage of its inhabitants.	Fire gutted the tenement, leaving twenty-eight persons homeless.

Excessive preference of the abstract over the concrete can lead to a disease that Fowler's *Modern English Usage*, a leading reference work, describes as "abstractitis." Fowler writes:

> The effect of this disease . . . is to make the patient write such sentences as *Participation by the men in the control of the industry is non-existent*—instead of *The men have no part in the control of the industry*; . . . *The availability of this material is diminishing* instead of *This material is getting scarcer*; *A cessation of dredging has taken place* instead of *Dredging has stopped*. . . . It may no doubt be said that in these examples the meaning is clear enough, but the danger is that, once the disease gets a hold, it sets up a chain reaction. A writer uses abstract words because his thoughts are cloudy; the habit of using them clouds his thoughts still further; he may end by concealing his meaning not only from his readers but also from himself.

Use Natural Language. A journalist's prose is printed in newspapers and magazines, not engraved in marble; its language should be that of intelligent but unpresupposing conversation. Write *died*, for example, not *deceased*; *ended* not *terminated*; *said* not *stated*; *jailed* not *incarcerated*. When in doubt, consider how you would tell the story to an interested stranger, and try to achieve the same natural, unassuming tone in your writing. A student describing a fight in a bar wrote, "The altercation ceased abruptly upon the arrival of the authorities." It seems unlikely that he would have used this same language in conversation. More likely, he would have said, "The fight stopped when the police arrived." And that's the way to write the story.

Avoid slang except in direct quotations, and be wary of it even then. Most slang goes out of vogue quickly, and what seems like a clever expression today may turn sour tomorrow. Moreover, slang typically is understood by but a minority of the general public.

SLANG, ABSTRACTION BOTH HINDER COMMUNICATION, SAYS MARK TWAIN, NOTED EXPERT

Slang may seem distant from flowery or excessively abstract language, but they have in common that both tend to confuse readers. In a passage of his book *Roughing It*—cited by Robert Morsberger in his *Common Sense Grammar and Style*—Mark Twain illustrates the limitations of both slang and flowery language by bringing together Scotty Briggs, a miner accustomed to frontier slang, and a young minister addicted to a mock-intellectual style full of circumlocution and grandeloquence. Asks Scotty:

"Are you the duck that runs the gospel mill next door?"

"Am I the—pardon me, I believe I do not understand?"

With another sigh and a half sob, Scotty rejoined: "Why you see we are in a bit of trouble and the boys thought maybe you would give us a lift, if we tackled you—that is, if I've got the rights of it and you are the head clerk of the doxology works next door."

"I am the shepherd in charge of the flock whose fold is next door."

"The which?"

"The spiritual advisor of the little company of believers whose sanctuary adjoins these premises."

Scotty scratched his head, reflected for a moment, and then said: "You ruther hold over me, pard. I reckon I can't call that hand. Ante and pass the buck."

"How? I beg pardon. What did I understand you to say?"

"Well, you've ruther got the bulge on me. Or maybe we've both got the bulge, somehow. You don't smoke me and I don't smoke you. You see, one of the boys has passed in his checks and we want to give him a good send-off, and so the thing I'm on now is to roust out somebody to jerk a little chin music for us and waltz him through handsome."

"My friend, I seem to grow more and more bewildered. Your observations are wholly incomprehensible to me. Cannot you simplify them in some way? At first I thought perhaps I understand you, but I grope now. Would it not expedite matters if you restricted yourself to categorical statements of fact, unencumbered with obstructing accumulations of metaphor and allegory?"

Another pause, and more reflection. Then, said Scotty:

"I'll have to pass, I judge."

"How?"

"You've raised me out, pard."

"I still fail to catch your meaning."

"Why, that last lead of yourn is too many for me—that's the idea. I can't neither trump nor follow suit."

The clergyman sank back in his chair perplexed. Scotty leaned his head on his hand and gave himself up to thought. Presently his face came up, sorrowful but competent.

"I've got it now, so's you can savvy," he said. "What we want is a gospel sharp. See?"

"A what?"

"Gospel sharp. Parson."

"Oh! Why did you not say so before? I am a clergyman—a parson."

"Now you talk! You see blind and straddle it like a man. Put it there!"—extending a brawny paw, which closed over the minister's small hand and gave it a shake indicative of fraternal sympathy and fervent gratification.

"Now we're all right, pard. Let's start fresh. Don't you mind my snuffling a little—becuz we're in a power of trouble. You see, one of boys has gone up the flume."

"Gone where?"

"Up the flume—throwd up the sponge, you understand."

"Thrown up the sponge?"

"Yes—kicked the bucket."

"Ah—has departed to that mysterious country from whose bourne no traveler returns."

"Return! I reckon not. Why pard, he's *dead*!"

Shun Pretension. Insecure writers sometimes try to compensate for their anxieties by assuming what Wolcott Gibbs of *The New Yorker* called an "amused and godlike tone"—that is, by affecting an air of superior knowledge and wisdom. Sometimes the tone is literally godlike. In one story, apparently apocryphal, a reporter covering a mine disaster in Harwick, Kentucky, led his dispatch with the words, "God is close to the people of Harwick today." His editor wired back, "Forget mine disaster. Interview God."

"Lapel grabbing," a milder form of pretension, turns up when a writer tries to force the reader to a conclusion. Such posturing usually creates more problems than it solves. If a tragedy has occurred and is related clearly and accurately in a news story, nothing is gained by telling readers that it was "tragic." If someone is lucky enough to escape harm in a dangerous situation, readers will understand, without being told, that the survivor was "fortunate." Nine times out of ten, news stories are improved by eliminating such lapel-grabbing terms as "amazing," "miraculous," "sad," and "ironic."

Lapel grabbing at the conclusion of a story creates a "capper," or what Gibbs called "the tricky or vaguely cosmic last line." "And so another violent crime has victimized an innocent citizen of our troubled city, where fear stalks the streets . . ."—that sort of thing. Don't do it. If you have accurately reported and competently written a sad or comic story, your readers will understand that it is sad or comic. If not, the readers are unlikely to weep or laugh on cue. The most effective tone is neutral, informative, unpretentious.

Be Direct. Aesop's credo—"Grasp the nettle firmly"—is good advice to newswriters. Indirection, the habit of smuggling fresh information into a story as if the readers were already in on it, suggests timidity. Be direct. When the mayor says she plans to run for reelection, write, "Mayor Wilma Peters announced today that she intends to seek reelection . . ." not, "Mayor Wilma Peters today announced her intention to run for reelection." The latter, an indirect form, implies that the reader already has heard of Mayor Peters's intentions. If so, the announcement is hardly news, and you'll need a more newsworthy lead. Make it direct: write, for example, "His left arm was broken, and he was taken to the hospital," not, "His broken left arm prompted his being sent to the hospital." Write, "They called him a fascist," not, "They made reference to his alleged fascist leanings."

Economy

Words can be set down on paper at little expense, but this does not make them free: Reading takes time, and time is valuable. Effective writing, consequently, is economical. Every word should pull its weight. Never use two words when one will do.

Cut excess words—what editors call *deadwood*. As Wolcott Gibbs advised, "The more 'as a matter of facts,' 'howevers,' 'for instances,' etc. you can cut out, the nearer you are to the kingdom of heaven." Write, "A bay is a horse," not, "A

BREVITY IN NEWSWRITING CAN BE SIMPLE AS A SONG

Rock songwriters, like journalists, have to say a lot in a very few words. For sheer economy of phrase it's difficult to top, say, the first two lines of this Bobby Fuller classic:

Breakin' rocks in the hot sun,
I fought the law and the law won.

Like a good straight news lead, Fuller's single sentence states the essence of the news and draws us into the story.

In songwriting, as in newswriting, the key to descriptive imagery is efficiency, simplicity and the use of concrete, specific language. In these lines from his "Johnny B. Goode," Chuck Berry not only creates a clear picture, but manages to alter our perspective on it three times within four sentences; we see Johnny first from nearby, then from the perspective of the engineer in a passing train, then as he's seen by passers-by:

He used to carry his guitar in a gunny sack,
Go sit beneath the trees by the railroad track.
The engineer could see him sitting in the shade,
Strumming to the rhythm that the drivers made.
People passing by, they would stop and say,
"Oh my, but that little country boy could play!"

Copyright © by Chuck Berry

Some of Bruce Springsteen's and Bob Dylan's narrative songs resemble newspaper feature stories in their vivid, economical description of action. This is how Dylan and co-author Jacques Levy described the death of mobster Joey Gallo:

One day they blew him down in a clam bar in New York.
He could see it coming through the door as he lifted up his fork.
He pushed the table over, to protect his family,
Then he staggered out into the streets of Little Italy.

Copyright © 1975, 1976 by Ram's Horn Music and Jackelope Publishing.

And here is Springsteen's account of a crime story:

Down in the part of town
where when you hit a red light you don't stop
Johnny's waving his gun around and threatening
   to blow his top
When an off-duty cop
snuck up on him from behind
Out in front of the Club Tip Top
they slapped the cuffs on Johnny 99.

Copyright © 1982 by Bruce Springsteen

bay is a *type of* horse," and, "Pinochle is a card game," not, "Pinochle is a *kind of* a card game." Don't waste words stating the obvious, as did the writer who reported that a man threatened his ex-wife's life "prior to her murder," and that the unfortunate woman's body was "afterward" taken to a funeral home, as if anyone would assume otherwise.

Needless words frequently crop up in the form of excess *modifiers*. Modifiers are words that qualify other words; they include adjectives and adverbs—for example, "she has *"red* shoes." or "she left *promptly*." Modifiers are part of the language, but when used too frequently they can turn into parasites that bleed prose of its vigor. As Gertrude Stein wrote, "Adjectives are not really and truly interesting." When writing, you can simply delete redundant modifiers.

Qualified experts	They could hardly be experts if they weren't qualified.
Loud shriek	It couldn't be a shriek if it were quiet.
Complete destruction	If incomplete, it's damage, not destruction.
Totally surrounded	It must be total or it does not surround.
Thoroughly hopeless	Either there's room for hope or there's not.

Some other common redundancies include:

Circled around
Fell down
Divided up
Invited guest
Old adage
Past history
At the present time
Got into his car and drove away

Often, a word and its modifier can be replaced by a single word that says the same thing as do the modifier and its subject. *Extremely happy*, for instance, means *delighted*. *Rather pretty* becomes *attractive*. *Most unsightly*? *Ugly*. *Not very enthusiastic*? *Dubious, cool*, or *skeptical*.

A prime offender is the modifier *very*, which is frequently employed by lazy writers to pump up tired words when fresh words could do the job of both.

Very stupid	Idiotic
Very far	Distant
Very near	Nearby
Very large	Enormous
Very intelligent	Brilliant

Multiple modifiers can be cut back or eliminated altogether. An *old, sunken ruin of a ship* is a *hulk*. A *heavy canvas covering* is a *tarpaulin*. A *large angry aggregation of unruly persons* is a *mob*. Retain modifiers only when you are sure that you can't say the same thing in fewer words.

Beware, too, of the tendency to tack back and forth unnecessarily between two sides of a question—the "on-the-one-hand-this, on-the-other-hand-that" syndrome. Its symptoms include sentences beginning with *but* or the woefully belabored *however*. Tacking denotes nervousness or lack of organization. A strong writer leaves a straight wake.

Eliminate needless words. Make long phrases into short phrases, long sentences into short sentences. The nineteenth-century author Sydney Smith wrote, "In composing, as a general rule, run your pen through every other word you have written; you have no idea what vigor it will give your style." We may not want to take Smith's advice literally, but most of us would benefit from honoring its spirit. This is how Mark Twain described a successful young journalist at work: "Whenever he saw anything that could be useful . . . he wrote it out, then went over it and abolished adjectives, went over it again and extinguished other surplusages, and finally when he got it boiled down to the plain facts with the ruffles and other embroideries all gone, he laid it on the city editor's desk."

Vitality

Good writing is energetic. It employs meaningful words and wastes none of them. Here are a few techniques that can help you achieve a lively style:

Use Strong Verbs.   Verbs are the motors that move sentences. Avoid tired, overworked, commonplace verbs.

Weak Verb	*Strong Verb*
An explosion *occurred* that blew up the shed.	The shed *exploded*.
His arrest by police *took place* at dawn.	Police *arrested* him at dawn.
She *was employed* as a dish washer at Monte's Cafe.	She *washed* dishes at Monte's Cafe.
The sight *caused* him to gasp.	He *gasped* at the sight.

Try not to overuse the verb *to be*—the verb form that incorporates is, are, was and were. *To be* expresses an identification or association between two things or categories, as in the sentence, "A Chevrolet *is* a car," or, "They *are* outfielders." As such, it performs a valuable function in the language, but twentieth-century English has worked it almost to death. The vitality of writing can be greatly increased by simply replacing *to be* with more interesting and informative verbs.

Weak Verb ("to be")	*Strong Verb*
The position that the Senator took *was* that the bill should pass.	The Senator *urged* that the bill be passed.

Weak Verb ("to be")	Strong Verb
The man who kicked the extra point *was* Sullivan.	Sullivan *kicked* the extra point.
The subject of her talk *was* house painting.	She *talked* about house painting.
They *were* enlistees who *were* in the army for two years.	They *enlisted* and *served* in the army for two years.
Pneumonia *was* what Gordon suffered from.	Gordon *suffered* from pneumonia.

Beware of sentences beginning with *there is, there are, there was, there were.* Such sentences can almost always be arranged in a livelier way.

Weak Verb	Strong Verb
There were green pennants tacked up on the wall.	Green pennants were *tacked* up on the wall.
There was a vase of flowers that decorated the table.	A vase of flowers *decorated* the table.
There were fourteen references to unemployment in the speech.	The speech *contained* fourteen references to unemployment.
There are two buildings on the site.	Two buildings *stand* on the site.
There was no reason given by her for her change of plans.	She *gave* no reason for changing her plans.

In using verbs, as in other aspects of your writing, strive to employ the fewest and the most appropriate words that will do the job. Instead of using the long word *procrastinate*, for instance, use the more brief *delay*. Render such fancy verbs as *finalize* or *implement* more readable by translating them into *finish* and *do*. You can also often condense long verb phrases into a word or two; *elected to the presidency* can become *elected president*; *fell rapidly* can become *plummeted*; and *proceeded very quickly on foot* is fleeter as *ran*.

Prefer the Active Voice. A sentence written in the active voice first introduces the actor, then tells us of the action (this is the role of the verb) and finally mentions the object of the action, if any. Most neutral, spontaneous English is arranged in the active voice.

Bob Williams threw the ball.
The mayor flew to Cleveland.

Sentences written in the passive voice reverse this order. The object of the action appears first, and then is acted upon. The two preceding sentences read like this when recast into the passive voice:

The ball was thrown by Bob Williams.
Cleveland was the destination of the mayor's flight.

In general, prefer the active voice. Sentences written in the active voice tend to be clearer, more economical, more vigorous and easier to understand than those in the passive voice.

Passive Voice	*Active Voice*
The feature story was written by her.	She wrote the feature story.
Blindness was suffered by Bach.	Bach went blind.
Traffic jams were created by the heavy rains.	Heavy rains created traffic jams.

The active voice also promotes strong verbs.

Passive Voice *(Weak Verb)*	*Active Voice* *(Strong Verb)*
The charge *made* today against Smith by the District Attorney *was* arson.	The District Attorney today *charged* Smith with arson.
The shattering of store windows *was caused* by the explosion.	The explosion *shattered* store windows.

In addition, using the active voice helps to clear away deadwood.

Passive Voice	*Active Voice*
The porch was destroyed by a car *which* rounded the corner and skidded across the lawn.	A car *rounded* the corner, *skidded* across the lawn and *destroyed* the porch.
The murder weapon *was* sold by a Tucson gunsmith.	A Tucson gunsmith *sold* the murder weapon.
A guilty verdict *was reached* by the jury in the Wilcox case.	The jury *found* Wilcox guilty.

Sentences that describe action normally should run forward in time. An exception to this rule is the lead paragraph of a straight news story; the lead may run backward in order to move the heart of the story up front. ("Four jugglers were injured today when two cars of a circus train jumped the tracks . . .") This exception aside, a sentence usually reads more clearly if it recounts events in the order in which they occurred. Habitually writing backward in time makes the reader work like a salmon swimming upstream. Here is an extreme example:

> Wilcox broke his wrist when he struck the sidewalk after plunging from the second story window from which he had jumped.

The needless words ". . . when . . . after . . . from which . . ." can be eliminated by reorganizing the sentence chronologically, as shown:

> Wilcox jumped from the window, plunged two stories, struck the sidewalk, and broke his wrist.

Notice that among its other virtues, the time-sequence sentence is cast in the active voice.

Prefer the Positive to the Negative. Positive language conveys more information than does negative language. An apple, for instance, is *not* many things: It is not an orange, a loaf of bread, a lake, a mule or a starry sky. Nor is it musical, articulate, or the king of Spain. We can make a long list of things that an apple is *not*, but we will have used a lot of words to accentuate the negative. A positive sentence like, "An apple is green." tells us more than the negative sentence, "An apple is *not* orange." Positive sentences also tend to sound more satisfying than negative sentences.

Negative	Positive
Not fat	Thin
Not happy	Unhappy
Not interested	Uninterested
Not legal	Illegal
She did not feel well.	She felt sick.
The boat didn't sink.	The boat stayed afloat.
They could not find any signs of life.	They found no signs of life.
There were not many members there.	Few members attended.
He was not detained.	He was released.

Use Simple Declarative Sentences. Most writing can be improved by more frequent use of simple declarative sentences. "The best sentence? The shortest," wrote novelist Gustave Flaubert. You may employ complex sentences occasionally, for the sake of variety, but whenever possible, keep your sentences short and simple.

Complex Sentence	*Simple Sentence*
After graduating from Ohio State University and obtaining her Ph.D. in Chemistry at the University of Chicago, she joined the Department of Agriculture, where she now directs a task force studying the causes of wheat blight.	She graduated from Ohio State University and received a Ph.D. in Chemistry from the University of Chicago. She now directs a Department of Agriculture task force studying the causes of wheat blight.
Pointing out, "I'm the shortest one here," he volunteered to attempt the rescue.	He volunteered to attempt the rescue. "I'm the shortest one here," he pointed out.
Rather than return to New Jersey where he faced a twenty-year prison sentence, he opted to remain in Costa Rica, and expressed his desire in words to that effect.	He said he would remain in Costa Rica. If he returned to New Jersey, he would face a twenty-year prison sentence.

Complex sentences can get quite tangled, with unintentionally hilarious results. This misplaced phrase turned up in an AP dispatch:

> The President's helicopter settled on the grass landing strip that serves Plains as an airport and spent the next few minutes hugging and kissing relatives and friends.

This sentence appeared in the St. Paul *Sunday Pioneer Press*:

> While enjoying an outdoor cocktail party, two rare trumpeter swans flew unconcernedly over our group.

This one was taken from a student newswriting paper:

> Mrs. Beerbaum, bleeding from a superficial head wound, worked six weeks as a receptionist.

This one, from an unpublished novel:

> Helplessly, Roger watched from his study while his stomach tied itself into knots.

And this one, from a radio advertisement:

> All good things must come to an end, and now, after six wonderful years, you must go see *Godspell* on Broadway.

Dare to Use Similes and Metaphors. The ability to recognize a similarity between two situations that outwardly look quite different is a fundamental strength in human thought and, therefore, in writing as well. Similes state comparisons overtly, as in T. S. Elliot's lines, "The readers of the *Boston Evening Transcript*/Sway in the wind like a field of ripe corn." or Dante's, "The primal age was beautiful as gold." In metaphors the comparisons are implicit, as when Nikos Kazantzakis speaks of "the world, covered by a dense fog of mortality. . . ." Properly used, similes and metaphors can lend enormous vitality and depth to writing. Note the similes and metaphors in these paragraphs by Edmund Wilson:

> On the dreary yellow Michigan waste with its gray stains of frozen water, the old cars wait *like horses at the pound*. Since the spring before last, Henry Ford has been buying them up at twenty dollars apiece, and people drive them in every day. Old, battered, muddy roadsters, sedans, limousines, touring cars and trucks—in strings of two or three they are dragged off to the disassembly building, following foolishly and gruesomely *like corpses shaken up into life*, hoods rickety and wheels turning backwards. Once inside, they are systematically and energetically dismantled: the flat road-ruined tires are stripped away; the rush-flare of an acetylene torch attacks the stems of the steering wheels; the motors are cleaned out *like a bull's tripe* and sent to make scrap iron for the blast furnace; the glass is taken out and kept to replace broken factory panes; the leather from the hoods and seats goes for aprons and handpads for the workers; the hair stuffing of the seats is sold again; even the bronze and babbitt metal are scraped out of the connecting rods and melted up to line new connecting rods. Then the picked and gutted *carcass* of the old car is shoved into a final *death chamber*—crushed flat by a five-ton press, which makes it scrunch *like a stepped-on beetle*.
>
> The home of the open-hearth furnaces *is a vast abode of giants*: groans, a continual ringing, the falling of remote loads. The old automobiles sent in on little cars are *like disemboweled horses at the bull-ring whose legs are buckling under them*. A *fiend* in blue glasses who sits in a *high throne on an enormous blue chariot or float* causes it to move horizontally back and forth before the white-glowing *mouths* of the furnaces, feeding them the flattened cars *like so many metallic soft-shell crabs*. . . .

Each metaphor creates a mental picture, an equation between the subject at hand and an image from another realm. Mixing inconsistent metaphors jumbles the images, like projecting two overlapping slides on a screen. Consider the business executive who said, "You don't *test the waters* with *trial balloons* and then *reverse your field*." Three pictures are mixed together here: *Testing the waters* suggests a bather's dipping in a toe to check the water temperature; a *trial balloon* goes into the air and has nothing to do with water; and to *reverse your field* is drawn from football. To envision all three at once we'd have to imagine a county fair.

Following are some other particularly horrific uses of mixed metaphors, the work not of journalists but of the people they were quoting:

> "The administration has an awful lot of other things *in the pipeline*, and this has more *wiggle room* so they just *moved it down the totem pole*," Baldwin said.

> "What would I do if *Mother Jones* wanted to interview me?" asks an executive at a fairly large corporation. "I would tell them I was out of town, and there's no telling if I'd be coming back. You know those people are coming in *with their cannons smoking*, and you know they'll *shake the closets* until *they've got some scalps*."

> "I intended to stress the experience factor in the primary; that is my *ace in the hole*, so to speak," Cocke said. "I'm not a *bull in the china shop* going in with a *meat ax* and *letting the fur fly* where it may."

When someone asks us to imagine a bull's wielding a meat ax in a china shop, odds are that he or she is using metaphors without realizing it. These phrases have become so shopworn that their original meaning has been forgotten.

QUOTATIONS

Quotations let readers *hear*; they bring immediacy and authenticity to the page. Note how the point of each of the following two paragraphs is enriched and substantiated by the use of a direct quotation:

> Gibran had little sympathy for the cult of leisure. "Work is love made visible," he said. "If you cannot work with love but only with distaste, it is better that you should leave your work and sit at the gate of the temple and take alms of those who work with joy."

> Flynn's acquittal on the rape charge was all but assured when the plaintiff, asked what she had said when the defendant suggested that she remove her clothing, replied, "I didn't have no objections."

Quotations add *flavor*, too. Note how A. J. Liebling quoted Louisiana's Governor Earl Long on the death of his uncle:

> "He got drunk and pulled a man out of bed and got into bed with the man's wife, and the man got mad and shot my poor uncle, and he died."

Or how Gregory Jaynes of *The New York Times* quoted an elderly black farmer:

> Out in his cotton field Sunday morning before church, Perry Patterson dropped to one knee and caressed a blossom, turning it as a jeweler would turn a jewel to the light. He explained that the flower was only temporarily white, that it would be crimson in a day and that in no time at all it would be a boll.
> "It'll get speckled and tougher and then it'll pop open and it'll be that pretty cotton," said Mr. Patterson. "It'll be like one fluffy something all over your hand."

Or how Hunter S. Thompson quoted a member of the Hell's Angels motorcycle gang: "I smashed his face. He got wise. He called me a punk. He must of been stupid."

The idea, of course, is not just to throw quotations into a story, but to select the *best* quotations. Which are the best? One criterion is to look for quotes that convey emotion; as the newsroom adage puts it, "Quote for opinion, not for fact." Another criterion is relevance: Much of the poignancy of Martin Luther King's statement, "We've got some difficult days ahead, but it really doesn't matter now, because I've been to the mountain top," comes from the fact that King said it in his last speech before being assassinated. A third criterion is that the quotation should be meaningful to readers. When science writer Thomas O'Toole of the *Washington Post* covered man's first landing on the moon, on July 20, 1969, he was confronted with tens of thousands of words of radio conversation between the astronauts and the National Aeronautics and Space Administration's mission control center in Houston, Texas. From a transcript crammed with technical jargon, much of which was unintelligible to a general audience, O'Toole selected passages that were evocative and jargon-free. Here is an excerpt:

> In describing the moon, Armstrong told Houston that it was fine and powdery. "I can kick it up loosely with my toe.
> "It adheres like powdered charcoal to the boot," he went on. "But I only go in a small fraction of an inch. I can see my footprint in the moon like fine grainy particles."
> Armstrong found he had such little trouble walking on the moon that he began talking almost as if he didn't want to leave it.
> "It has a stark beauty all its own," Armstrong said. "It's like the desert in the Southwestern United States. It's very pretty out here."

Only in old movies and in the gaffs of amateurs does anybody tell a reporter, "You can quote me on that!" Normally a journalist conducting an interview assumes that anything said may be quoted, and understands that he or she decides which quotes, if any, will go in the story.

Reporters often edit quotes, chiefly to save space. But if you do this, you must take care to preserve both the flavor and the exact meaning of what was said. If you remove words from within a quotation, indicate the deletion by ellipses—three dots if only a few words are omitted and four dots if the deleted material includes the end of one or more sentences. Deletions from the beginning or end of a quotation usually need not be signalled by ellipses—but, again, take care to avoid distorting a quotation in the process of editing it. Don't emulate the paperback publisher who took a review saying that a novel was "a towering heap of trash" and reduced it, on the back cover of the book, to the single word "towering."

The same principles of selection apply to the question of whether to quote bad grammar, slang or profanity. Ask yourself if the quote in question has impact, is relevant and is meaningful. If so, in it goes.

Put quotation marks *only* around direct quotations: what someone actually said or wrote. Never promote a paraphrase into a direct quotation. Suppose, for instance, you're quoting a talk at a meeting of the Classics Club by a professor who says, "Ancient history often must be reconstructed from bits and pieces as fragmentary as the poems of Archilochus." Questioning the professor after the talk, you ascertain that Archilochus was a Greek poet, few of whose poems have survived intact and who, therefore, is known chiefly from fragments of his work. When you quote the professor, you might explain this reference to your readers as follows:

> "Ancient history often must be reconstructed from bits and pieces as fragmentary as the poems of Archilochus," Professor Baxter said. Archilochus was a Greek poet of the seventh century B.C. most of whose work has survived only in fragments.

Or, you could paraphrase part of Baxter's remarks like this:

> Professor Baxter explained that much of ancient history must be painstakingly reconstructed "from bits and pieces as fragmentary as the poems of Archilochus," the ancient Greek poet, few of whose works have survived intact.

Do *not* put your words into someone else's quotation. This quotation is inaccurate:

> Professor Baxter said, "Ancient history often must be reconstructed from bits and pieces as fragmentary as the poems of Archilochus, the ancient Greek poet whose work survives mostly in fragments."

Baxter did not say it that way. Only his exact words belong in the direct quotation.

Attribute all quotations, to clarify who is speaking. Unattributed quotations, known as *orphan* quotes, are maddening. As a rule, each time you introduce a direct quotation you should attribute it to the speaker, even if the context already suggests the speaker's identity. You need not reattribute longer quotations except when they have been interrupted; you only have to remind the reader who is talking when the ongoing quote has been broken.

Quotations that amount to more than a short phrase are usually handled most gracefully by placing the attribution inside the quote. In this way the strongest parts of the sentence—the beginning and the end—can be devoted to the quotation itself and not wasted on the attribution. Put the attribution at the earliest convenient breaking point.

"Said" is a perfectly suitable verb for use in attributions. Employ synonyms for "said" only if they genuinely add something to the meaning of the sentence. "Shouted," "whispered," "gasped" or "screamed" all carry their weight, in that they help us hear the speaker's tone of voice. But avoid using empty synonyms like "stated" or "elucidated," and affected words like "declared" or "opined."

Why not just, "Said"? Pointless synonyms for "said" serve only to draw attention to themselves—and they're usually the least important words in the sentence. (Drawing by C. Barsotti; © 1981 *The New Yorker* Magazine, Inc.)

Take care, too, that the verbs you use to attribute quotations mean just what you mean them to say. "Pointed out," for instance, means to draw attention to something generally agreed to be a fact, as do "revealed" and "confirmed." It's correct to write:

> Professor Abell *pointed out* that "Mars is the fourth planet from the sun."

But avoid using similar language when the facts are in doubt. You would *not*, for instance, want to employ loaded language like this when the facts are in doubt:

> The prosecutor *pointed out* that the defendant was "guilty as sin," and *revealed* that he was "a bloodthirsty murderer."

DESCRIPTION

Description can appeal to any of the senses: It can conjure up the *sound* of an electric guitar, the *smell* of fresh ground coffee, or the *feel* of a mink stole. But because the dominant human sense organ is the eye, the most effective description is visual. "Let me *see* it," editors say. "Paint the picture." Few of us, watching television, would turn off the picture and rely on the sound alone. Yet that is just the effect produced by a writer who neglects to include description in a story. The resulting story may convey the facts, but it is unlikely to appeal to the emotions. In the following examples, note how much livelier are the right-hand columns, where description is employed:

Lacking Description	Including Description
Weather was favorable for the launching of the ship. Music was provided. The First Lady, fashionably dressed, christened the ship. The cruiser slid down into the water while 2000 onlookers voiced their approval.	Bright sunlight and blue skies greeted the launching. A sixteen-piece brass band dressed in scarlet uniforms with blue piping, their bugles and tubas gleaming in the sun, played John Philip Sousa's "Under the Double Eagle" march. The First Lady, wearing a tailored beige suit and matching hat, christened the ship by smashing a bottle of champagne against its gunmetal-grey bow. The cruiser slid gently into the harbor while 2000 onlookers cheered.
The whooping crane, threatened with extinction, is a lovely tall bird. It displays several colors.	The whooping crane, threatened with extinction, is a graceful snow-white bird with long black legs. It stands nearly five feet tall and sports a bright red tuft of plumage at the crown.
Displaying obvious signs of exertion, the lumberjack accepted the congratulations of friends. All around were to be seen signs of his labors.	Panting and bathed in sweat, the lumberjack accepted handshakes and slaps on the back from friends. Wood chips carpeted the ground around his feet.

Description, like good writing in general, should be concrete and specific; the mind's eye cannot see abstractions. Instead of *facial injury*, for example, write *black eye*. A *female retail merchant exhibiting mirth* is better described as *a laughing woman behind a fruit stand*. An *expensive necklace* is more vividly described as a *string of pearls*.

Specific, concrete description deserves a place in even the most momentous stories, where important news crowds the page. Here is how Jack London described the aftermath of the 1906 San Francisco earthquake:

> The streets were humped into ridges and depressions and piled with debris of fallen walls. The steel rails were twisted into perpendicular and horizontal angles. . . . Before the flames, throughout the night, fled tens of thousands of homeless ones. Some were wrapped in blankets. Others carried bundles of bedding and dear household treasures. Sometimes a whole family was harnessed to a carriage of a

delivery wagon that was weighted down with their possessions. Baby buggies, toy wagons, and gocarts were used as trucks, while every other person was dragging a trunk. . . . Everywhere were trunks, with across them lying their exhausted owners, men and women. Before the march of the flames were flung picket lines of soldiers. And a block at a time, as the flames advanced, these pickets retreated. One of their tasks was to keep the trunk pullers moving. The exhausted creatures, stirred on by the menace of bayonets, would arise and struggle up the steep pavements, pausing from weakness every five or ten feet.

A reporter sees much more in the course of covering a story than can normally be described in a news story. The idea is to select the most *relevant* descriptive elements. When Liz Balmaseda of *The Miami Herald* interviewed Ricci Reyes, whose husband, actor Richard Adan, had been stabbed to death only five months after their marriage, she chose to describe a scene that emphasized the tragedy of how young and vital Adan had been, and what his death was to cost his bride:

> On the last night they spent together, they danced in the living room until it was time for him to go. He wore black chino pants and a black T-shirt; she wore a long punk-style T-shirt. Ricci watched Richard from their balcony. She yelled to him, "I love you." He said, "Me, too," and began to dance in the street. She said she didn't like that answer. "All right, I love you. Now get back inside."
> But she wanted to watch him from the window, and she didn't leave until he was just a little figure dancing in the night.

The use of *color* aids effective description; just as we seldom watch TV with the picture turned off, neither do we turn the color control down and watch in black and white. Color helps even when the colors are drab, as is illustrated by these paragraphs from an International News Service dispatch on the 1917 execution of the glamorous spy Mata Hari. As recreated by INS correspond Henry Wales, Mata Hari's last hour was saturated in the color of death:

> Then she drew on her stockings, black, silken, filmy things, grotesque in the circumstances. She placed her high-heeled slippers on her feet and tied the silken ribbons over her insteps.
> She arose and took the long black velvet cloak, edged around the bottom with fur and with a huge square collar hanging down the back, from a hook over the head of her bed. She placed this cloak over the heavy silk kimono which she had been wearing over her nightdress.
> Her wealth of black hair was still coiled about her head in braids. She put on a large, flapping black felt hat with a black silk ribbon and bow. Slowly and indifferently, it seemed, she pulled on a pair of black kid gloves. Then she said calmly: "I am ready."

Description should always serve the interests of accurate reporting. Resist the temptation to exaggerate description in hopes of adding impact to a story. Describing, for example, a convicted murderer who is missing a front tooth, has one glass eye, but is neatly dressed and speaks articulately, a reporter out to exaggerate could make the convict look more threatening than he really is by mentioning the first two characteristics and omitting the latter two. Don't do it. Like every other element of a news story, description should be accurate, fair and objective. As we noted previously, Jack London found plenty of tragedy to report when covering the San Francisco earthquake, but he avoided sensationalizing his description; he was careful to delineate the limits of the tragedy: "Wednesday night, while the whole city crashed and roared into ruin, was a quiet night," London wrote. "There were no crowds. There was no shouting and yelling. There was no hysteria, no disorder. . . . In all those terrible hours I found not one woman who wept, not one man who was excited, not one person who was in the slightest degree panic-stricken."

Description can be woven through a story, but don't try to "smuggle" in descriptive phrases where they bear no relation to the context. Smuggling like this only gets in the way:

> Luther swung the bat *with his tatooed arms* and hit a single to right field. . . .

> My client is innocent," said defense attorney Wetson, *who was dressed in a blue pinstripe suit and windowpane-check shirt.*

Such descriptive phrases work only when they are relevant to what is being reported in the adjoining copy. For example:

> *His neck adorned with heavy gold chains, large diamond rings on the fingers of both hands,* Gleason told reporters, "Baseball has been good to me."

> *Her hands shaking,* she could not fish the food stamps from her purse. *In a quavering voice,* she asked the checkout clerk for help. "I haven't eaten today," she whispered.

Some stories, of course, offer little or no opportunity for description: A press release announcing a change in the federal prime interest rate will not be perked up by describing on what kind of paper the release is printed. But when the opportunity to employ description presents itself, take advantage of it. To do otherwise is to blindfold your readers.

FIVE DEADLY SINS

Improving writing involves eliminating bad habits as well as developing good ones. Some of the most common bad habits are:

Euphemism

A euphemism is a bland or prettified expression substituted for a plain, frank one. Its function is to obscure or veil a harsh truth. Who are among the practitioners of euphemism? The funeral parlor attendant who cannot bring himself to say that someone *died*, but must say that he "passed away" or "is deceased." The weather forecaster who, feeling that she may be caught in an inaccurate forecast if she predicts *rain*, instead predicts that "a rainfall condition will be present." And the CIA, which says "nondiscernible microbionoculator" when it means a *poison dart*.

Euphemism	Straight Talk
Financially deprived	Poor
Inmate	Prisoner
Correction officer	Guard
Indisposed	Sick
Interment	Burial
Liquidated	Killed
Canine control officer	Dog catcher

As their job is to reveal the truth rather than to obscure it, journalists shun euphemism.

Excessive Abstraction

Excessive abstraction refers to the process of taking something simple, puffing it up by using fancy language, then writing as if only the more imposing version correctly represented it. The chronic abstractor cannot write, "Passengers are boarding the aircraft," but instead writes, "The aircraft boarding process is under way." Note that "process" adds nothing to the meaning of the sentence; it is pure inflation. Sufferers from abstractitis write, "The city is entering an expense-reduction mode," rather than simply, "The city is cutting expenses." Employees cannot simply have jobs but must have "job functions." They are not "promoted" but "undergo career advancement."

At its worst, excessive abstraction becomes almost unintelligible. Try translating the following aphorisms, rendered into gobbledygook by English professor Charles Willeford and passed along by humorist John Keasler of *The Miami Herald*. (Hint: You already know the answers.)

Pulchritude possesses solely cutaneous profundity.

It's fruitless to attempt to indoctrinate a superannuated canine with innovative entertainment-oriented maneuvers.

All articles that coruscate with resplendence are not truly autiferous.

Missiles of ligneous or petrous consistency have the potential of fracturing my osseous structure, but appelations will certainly remain innocuous.

A plumber wrote to the National Bureau of Standards saying that he had found hydrochloric acid to be good for cleaning out blocked pipes but wondered whether it might damage the pipes if he continued using it. The plumber got back a letter from Washington reading, "The efficacy of hydrochloric acid is indisputable, but the chlorine residue is incompatible with metallic permanence." Here we have a masterpiece of abstractitis. Note how the plumber's simple remark that hydrochloric acid is good for cleaning pipes has been abstracted into "the efficacy of hydrochloric acid," while the danger to the pipes becomes a matter "incompatible with metallic permanence." The plumber wrote back, thanking the bureau and saying that he would continue to use hydrochloric acid. In reply he received a second letter, warning that "we cannot assume responsibility for the production of toxic and noxious residues with hydrochloric acid, and suggest that you use an alternate procedure." Awed by the high tone of the government letter, the plumber replied with renewed thanks, and said he was ordering forty barrels of hydrochloric acid right away. The bureaucrat, alarmed by the potential damage that could ensue, finally resorted to simple language. In a third letter, he wrote, "Don't use hydrochloric acid! It eats holes in the pipes!"

The journalist's model is the bureaucrat's third letter—simple, informative and to the point.

Cliches

Cliches are words and phrases that have lost their original meaning and flavor through overuse, like an old shirt that has been washed so many times that it fades to grey. The first reporter who described lengthy labor negotiations as *marathon talks*, the first broadcaster at a football game who remarked that *shadows are lengthening across the gridiron*, the first writer who summed up a disturbance with the phrase *violence flared* may have had a good idea at the time, but these phrases have since been exhausted by overuse: They've become cliches.

Some Cliches

Driving rain	Heated exchange
Snow blanketed the city	Freak accident
Coldblooded killer	Uneasy truce
Crushing blow	Stinging rebuke
Light as a feather	Top priority
Smooth as silk	Snuffed out
Violence erupted	Sweeping reforms
Brutal murder	Filthy rich
Coveted trophy	Stubborn as a mule
Ravages of time	Cut and dried
Shoo-in	Point in time
Clean as a whistle	Heavy handed
Tired refrain	The bottom line
Babyfaced	Nook and cranny
Toe the mark	Hurricanes packing winds
Claimed the lives of	Followed in their footsteps
Tragic accident	Miraculous escape

Mudslinging	Torrential rain
Guarded optimism	Confirmed bachelor
Hard-earned wages	Ill-gotten gains
Deafening roar	Rushed to the scene
In the wake of	Categorically denies

Cliches drift through the language, dressed in the rags of their former elegance, and their faded gentility lends them a certain appeal, but professional writers learn to turn them away at the door. *Never* use cliches except in direct quotations, and then only rarely. In the words of Wollcott Gibbs: "Anything that you suspect of being a cliche undoubtedly is one and had better be removed."

Jargon and Vogue Words

Jargon is specialized language, intelligible within a given sect, group or organization, but not to the general public. Vogue words are terms that enjoy a brief period of popularity—sometimes limited to certain circles, sometimes more generally—and then pass out of style, to retire as cliches or simply to disappear. Neither should be used in newswriting unless the terms are explained.

Governments tend to inflate language, as they do currency. In Washington, things are *utilized* (used) or *subjected to situational improvement* (fixed). Books are *accessed* (checked out) from *media resource centers* (libraries). The House of Representatives embarks upon *district work periods* (recesses). One reason for using bureaucratic jargon is to make trivial matters sound important. Another is simply to obscure the facts: An Arkansas legislator serving on an education subcommittee agreed to vote for funds to teach poetry in prison only if the classes were called "Reading and Language Arts" rather than "Poetry." If the classes were called poetry, he explained, his constituents would know what was meant, and might object to using public funds to teach prisoners so impractical a subject.

The National Council of Teachers of English hands out "Doublespeak Awards" for those who use such needless jargon as *combat emplacement evaculator* (shovel), *encore telecast* (rerun) and *personal preservation flotation device* (life preserver.) Russell Baker, the *New York Times* columnist, satirized the jargon rampant in welfare agencies with this description: "She is a female senior citizen and she resides in substandard housing of pedal-containment design. . . . She suffers from inadequate familial relationships resulting from insufficient family-planning skills."[*]

Academic institutions in general—and the social sciences in particular—are cluttered with jargon. One of James Degnan's writing students at the University

---

[*] Translation: "There was an old lady who lived in a shoe. She had so many children that she didn't know what to do."

of Santa Clara wrote, "The choice of exogenous variables in relation to multi-colinearity is contingent upon the derivations of certain multiple correlation coefficients." After extensive discussion, Degnan and his student decided that the sentence meant, "Supply determines demand." A student at another school wrote, "The increased affluence among the children that results from the greater educational opportunities apparently began a process whose results are now being evidenced, as they contribute their financial input to the community." What does this mean? That "children in the community benefitted from good schools, got good jobs and have returned home to spend their money." A book describing the plight of natives in the Amazon jungle employed prose as impenetrable as the jungle itself: "Their viability is already exceptionally parlous, and their societies are teetering on the brink of irrevocable stupration." Translation of this sentence, which for most readers will require a trip to an unabridged dictionary, yields, "The tribes are in trouble and may not survive."

The following samples of jargon were collected by Samuel Williamson and Robert Morseberger:

Jargon	*Plain English*
Substantial	Big or large
Currently	Now
Termination	End
Not impossible	Possible
Not unreasonable to suppose	Probable
To a substantially high degree	Much
In the eventuality that	If
In reference to	Referring to
Devoid of usefulness	Useless
A not inconsiderable number	Many
Restore to operational condition	Repair
Demonstrate a preference for	Prefer
Manifest an antipathy toward	Dislike
Is supportive of	Supports
It is my conclusion that	I conclude
Did not succeed in achieving its objective	Failed
My thinking leads me to the conclusion that	I think

Vogue words can beguile writers and readers for a while, but soon their popularity fades. Writers who used *rip-off, far out, bummer* or *hassle* in the 1960s are as likely to be embarrassed by their choices today as would be their predecessors in the 1920s who resorted to *snockered, bee's knees* or *oh you kid*. Vogue words sprout like weeds in political writing, producing *credibility gap* (something suffered by politicians when people don't believe what they say), *viability* (meaning it can be done) and the cliches *grass-roots appeal* and *on the hustings*. Candidates all too often are referred to as *hopefuls,* a word closely related to the abomination *hopefully*—as in *They said they were hopeful that hopefully they could settle the strike* (meaning, "They said they hoped to settle the strike."). Flashy new words or phrases that give the writer a sense of being particularly clever should be viewed with a very cold eye indeed: When you think you're being clever, watch out.

Redundancy

Redundancy means that two or more words are being used when only one would suffice. Redundancies usually occur when the writer doesn't understand the precise meaning of the word. *Completely unique* and *quite unique* are redundant; unique *means* one of a kind. *True facts* is redundant (if untrue they aren't facts), as are *burning flames* (what other sort of flames are there?) and *died of a fatal injury* (a nonfatal injury couldn't kill). "The other horn of the dilemma is equally unattractive" is redundant; "dilemma" *means* a choice in which the alternatives are equally unappealing; if one is more attractive than the other, the choice may be difficult but it's not a dilemma.

A FINAL WORD

Writing well is hard work. To expect that you will be able to write prose of professional quality without first having put a great many words on paper is no more reasonable than to suppose that you can win the Boston Marathon without first training for it. Don't sit around waiting for inspiration to strike; the issue is not whether *you* are inspired, but whether you can inspire your readers. As economist John Kenneth Galbraith observed:

> All writers know that on some golden mornings they are touched by the wand—are on intimate terms with poetry and cosmic truth. I have experienced those moments myself. Their lesson is simple: it's total illusion. And the danger in the illusion is that you will wait for those moments. . . . Do not wait for the golden moment. It may well be worse.

Deciding whether you have what it takes to write professionally usually involves a process of apprenticeship as lengthy as training to be a physicist or professional basketball player or ballet dancer. And it is best approached in the same earnest and unassuming spirit. The principles of good writing are useful only insofar as they are applied, again and again, until they become as ingrained as a pianist's finding the right notes or a quarterback's taking the snap from center. The way to learn to write is to write—every day, for weeks and months and years.

SUMMARY

Effective writing is characterized by *accuracy*, *clarity*, *economy* and *vitality*. Accuracy, a fundamental principle of journalism in its own right, is also important in promoting a readable style. To achieve a lucid style, get the facts at hand and in mind. Through research and reporting, careful note taking, use of the dictionary and effective self-editing all promote accurate newswriting.

Clarity and simplicity are preferable to an overblown style that calls attention to itself; the journalist's aim is to inform readers, not to impress them. The writer who has something to say should say it in a direct and straightforward manner. Good writing is unpretentious, specific and concrete, natural and easily understood. Also, good writers never use two words when one will do. Remember that every word extracts its price in terms of readers' time. Trim unnecessary words (*deadwood*) during editing.

Vitality in writing is promoted by using strong verbs and the active voice. The relatively weak verb *to be* in its many forms (is, was, were) is overused in writing, and should be replaced where possible with more specific and therefore more informative verbs. The active voice is preferable to the passive. Vitality can also be enhanced by using the positive rather than the negative, and by incorporating similes and metaphors, color and description.

Among the bad habits that beset many beginning writers are: the use of *euphemisms*, polite but indistinct words, when more blunt or direct words would better convey the meaning; the use of *cliches*, words or phrases that have been worn out through overuse; excessive *abstraction*, the process of puffing up something simple with fancy language, and then writing as if only the more imposing version correctly represented it; the use of *jargon* and *vogue words*, language meaningful only to a limited group or within a limited time, without explanation; and *redundancy*, employing two or more words when one would suffice.

6

WRITING BREAKING NEWS: THE LEAD

The *lead* is the beginning of a news story. Its form depends on the nature of the information it conveys. In stories lacking a sense of urgency, or in those intended primarily to convey humor, background information or emotion, the lead may take a relaxed, indirect approach—as in this Associated Press story from the front page of the Omaha *World-Herald*:

DECORAH, IOWA (AP)—Graduates at Luther College's commencement Sunday would have heard a speech on the pursuit of excellence, but speaker Garrison Keillor said God changed those plans.

Keillor, host of National Public Radio's "A Prairie Home Companion," said he was going to give an "excellence" speech but the "Lord laid a message on my heart" when He sent hot and humid temperatures to the area Sunday.

The message was "Be brief," Keillor said. . . .

This kind of lead is generally referred to as a "feature" lead, and we discuss it further in Chapter 9.

In "breaking" or "hard news" stories, the lead should normally convey the essence of the story at the outset, without delay. Readers of these stories will want to know what happened, right away. This breaking news lead, urgent and to the point, ran in the same day's *World-Herald*, just above the Garrison Keillor story:

DHAKA, BANGLADESH (AP)—A hurricane that swept out of the Bay of Bengal killed at least 1464 people throughout Bangladesh, authorities said yesterday.

In this chapter, we explore the classic "five W" breaking news lead. Generally, such a lead consists of a single sentence, no more than thirty-five words in length, that reports the essentials of the story: who, what, where, when, and why or how. Learning to write a tight, accurate lead is good training: It teaches economy, vitality, and news judgment. The five W lead is a fundamentally important tool of the trade, as essential to the newswriter as a hammer is to a carpenter.

To get a feeling for writing a breaking news lead, let's start with a familiar story—the Pied Piper of Hamlin. As legend has it, a village in Austria plagued with rats called in an exterminator, the Pied (meaning "paid") Piper, and promised to pay him to play a magical tune on his pipe and lead the rats out of the village. Agreeing to the deal, the piper played his tune, and the rats rushed headlong into the canal and drowned themselves. Their rat problem solved, the mayor and town council reneged on their promise and refused to pay the piper his fee. In response, the man played another tune, one that enchanted the children of the village. The children followed the piper to the outskirts of town and disappeared with him through a hole in a mountain, never to be seen again.

Telling this story as a fairy tale, the Brothers Grimm begin at the beginning: "Once upon a time, there was a town called Hamlin that was plagued by rats. . . ." We don't learn of the most newsworthy developments—the abduction and disappearance of the town's children—until the end, several pages later.

A newspaper reporter writing a breaking news lead to the Hamlin story would begin quite differently, revealing the news in the very first sentence:

> All the children of Hamlin were abducted today by an exterminator who was angered over the town's refusal to pay him for getting rid of its rats.

Or:

> An exterminator calling himself the "Pied Piper" today abducted the children of Hamlin after the mayor reneged on a promise to pay him for ridding the community of rats.

Or:

> Angered by Hamlin's refusal to pay him for ridding it of rats, an exterminator called the "Pied Piper" today led the town's children through a hole in a nearby mountain to an unknown destination.

Each of these leads approaches the news from a slightly different angle. The first emphasizes *what* happened, the second *who* did it, the third *why* he did it. But each delivers the essence of the story in a tightly wrapped package. That's the idea behind the breaking news lead. We may still have plenty of questions: Who is this Pied Piper? Why did the children go? Why didn't the police try to stop him? But the lead has conveyed the essence of the story.

Central to the art of lead writing is understanding what makes for *news*. To write a breaking news lead, the newswriter builds the lead around the most newsworthy elements of the story. Let's say, as an example, that the mayor of Miami Beach parked his car next to City Hall this morning, bought a copy of *The Miami Herald* at the newsstand on the corner, read it while having scrambled eggs and coffee at Gyro's Diner down the street, then strolled up to his office— just as he does five days a week. That's not news. But let's also suppose that, as the mayor is walking from Gyro's to his office, a coconut falls from a palm tree, strikes him on the head and knocks him out. *That's* news.

The trick is to write a lead that conveys the news, without getting it cluttered by inessential material. We would *not* write:

> The mayor of Miami Beach today *parked his car, bought a newspaper, ate scrambled eggs at Gyro's Diner*, then, while walking toward City Hall, was struck on the head by a falling coconut and knocked unconscious.

The information in italics is not essential to the story; it just gets in the way. It is better to limit the lead to the real news:

> The mayor of Miami Beach was struck on the head by a falling coconut and knocked unconscious today as he was walking to City Hall.

Clean, simple leads are the most readable. If you've done your reporting well enough to know that the mayor was wearing a light blue suit and a Panama hat, that he had three days left in his term of office and that he planned to dedicate a shopping mall in the north side of town, that's fine, and you may want to mention all those facts later in the story. But keep them out of the lead. If, however, it happens that the mayor had proclaimed today Coconut Day, you'll want to place that ironic piece of information in the lead:

> The mayor of Miami Beach, just after having proclaimed today to be "Coconut Day," was struck on the head by a falling coconut and was knocked unconscious as he was walking to City Hall.

THE FIVE Ws

The five Ws of the classic breaking news lead—who, what, when, where and why or how—help both in drafting the lead and in checking it over to see whether anything essential has been left out.

Who

A brief characterization suffices for the lead. Proper names should appear in the lead only when they are likely to be known to readers. If Herbert Klagman, a travelling sales representative from Willow, North Dakota, runs his car into a ditch, don't waste space naming him in the lead. Few readers will have heard of him. Make it "a travelling sales representative" or "a Willow man" in the

"Who? What? Where? Why? And when?"

The "Five Ws" rule, though hardly inviolable, remains a sound guide to constructing straight news leads. (Drawing by Vietor; © 1979 *The New Yorker* Magazine, Inc.)

lead, and name him in the next paragraph. If you are reporting on a meeting of the American Numismatics Association, you would be wise to avoid cluttering your lead with that long, difficult title. Instead, write: "a group of coin collectors." The point is to identify the *who* of the story in a way that will mean something to most readers.

What

This is usually the heart of the lead: What happened? What's the story? Most often this can be expressed in two or three key words—a subject and verb, or a subject, verb and object: *Child drowned. Candidate loses. South Africa declares war.* Boiling the story down to its essence this way helps in composing the lead. Imagine that you see an explosion in a department store that shatters windows and sends injured shoppers reeling into the street. A passer-by rushes up to you and asks, "What happened?" Would you say, "The peaceful routines of downtown life were disturbed today when. . . ."? Probably not. Nor would you lapse into a cliche like, "Violence flared downtown today when. . . ." More likely, you'd say something like, "There was a big explosion in Bay's Department Store! A lot of people got hurt! The windows were blown out! There's broken glass all over the street!" A lead built upon this sense of *what* happened might read:

> At least eight persons were injured today when an explosion rocked Bay's Department Store on Main Street, blowing out windows and spraying shards of glass onto the street.

When

News is timely, so specify *when* it occurred. The exact hour and minute of the when element need not be spelled out in the lead—at 12:53 A.M., say—but enough should be included so that the reader knows whether a robbery took place at night or in daylight, yesterday or last Friday.

In specifying when an event occurred, be mindful of when your audience will read the story. A story written for an afternoon (or PM) newspaper calls for a *today* angle. For example:

> The Cartwheel Bank *today* announced that it will cut interest rates on auto loans from 11 to 10 percent.

The same story written for tomorrow morning's (AM) paper would read:

> The Cartwheel Bank announced *yesterday*. . . .

The wire services (see Chapter 15) transmit news to various time zones and across the international date line, so to avoid confusion they spell out the day of each occurrence:

> A leading bank announced *Monday* that it is cutting auto loan interest rates from 11 to 10 percent. . . .

Where

Anchor your story firmly in space as well as time. Where did the event occur? Did it happen on Main Street here in town? Or in the mountains of Bolivia? Here, too, the key is to use a meaningful phrase that will create a clear picture in the reader's mind, not necessarily to spell out exact addresses. For example, there's no need to write:

> A hit and run driver struck and injured Betty Garnet, of 77 Fulton St., Hapsville, in front of 3311 Beltline Parkway last night. . . .

Instead, make it:

> A hit-and-run driver struck and injured a Hapsville woman last night on a dimly lit stretch of Beltline Parkway adjacent to the Calumet Industrial Park. . . .

Why and How

The final W and the H are meant as a reminder that the lead should round out its account of the story, leaving no loose ends dangling or vital elements missing. Taken together, *why/how* questions remind us to help include *all* the vital elements in the lead—to *explain* the story.

Look for the *why* in stories that involve *motivation*. If, two days after being indicted for fraud, a congressional representative announces that he will not seek reelection, mention the indictment in the lead of your story. It suggests *why* the representative isn't going to run again.

The *how* is important in stories that deal with *action*. *How* did the automobile crash? *How* was the mayor of Miami Beach knocked out? Answering the *how* is another way of painting a *picture* in the reader's mind.

EIGHT TIPS FOR WRITING LEADS

To write leads that create a compact, clear and complete picture of the story, consider these eight rules:

1. Keep it *brief*.
2. Keep it *simple*.
3. Describe people in a *meaningful* way.
4. Start with the *heart* of the matter.
5. Keep it in *focus*.
6. *Round out* the story.
7. Let the *main* verb carry the main news.
8. Use *action* verbs.

Keep It Brief

The shorter the lead, the better, as long as it covers the essential news. Associated Press leads average only twenty-five words in length. We recommend that breaking news leads seldom exceed thirty-five words.

In the more sedate days of the past, leads were longer, as were English sentences generally. This lead appeared in the Chicago *Daily News* in 1921, a day after President Warren G. Harding commemorated the Tomb of the Unknown Soldier in Arlington National Cemetery:

WASHINGTON, D.C., Nov. 11—President Harding, in his address at the bier of the unknown soldier, at Arlington Cemetery, today pledged that the "influence and strength" of the nation shall be exerted against "the cruel arbitrament" of war, against the "horrors of modern conflict" and barring "war's disastrous and depressing tragedies from the stage of righteous civilization" as the highest tribute the nation can pay to its heroic dead.

This sixty-five word sentence tries to cover so many points in the President's speech that the reader might lose track of what was said. Here, it's rewritten for brevity:

WASHINGTON, D.C., Nov. 11—President Harding today urged the country to pay tribute to the Unknown Soldier buried in Arlington Cemetery by using its influence and strength to prevent war from ever happening again.

Two years later, Harding's penchant for prolix speechifying was ended abruptly by a fatal stroke. But as the President lay in state in San Francisco, the long-windedness of the press continued unabated:

SAN FRANCISCO, Aug. 3 (AP)—In a gray draped room far above Market Street, San Francisco's main artery, all that is mortal of the 29th President of the United States of America reposed to-day while the city by the Golden Gate, shocked by the sudden calamity that had occurred in its midst, and hushed with sorrow and grief, paid silent homage to the departed chief executive of the nation.

Today it would read this way:

SAN FRANCISCO, Aug. 3 (AP)— President Warren G. Harding lay in state here today in a gray-draped room high above Market Street, as residents of the city expressed their shock and grief over his sudden death.

Keep It Simple

Almost any story, however momentous, can be conveyed within a single sentence. The more important the story, in fact, the more brevity counts. The end of World War II was a big story; had you been covering it, would you prefer to have written a windy lead like this?

After nearly six years of horror, during which millions perished as the bloody talons of conflict embraced Europe, Asia and Africa, light dawned today upon the conclusion of the greatest conflict in the history of humankind.

Or, would you choose to have written, as did one journalist, this statement?

The war is over.

To write a simple lead, limit it to the essentials—the material the reader needs in order to visualize what happened and to understand the story. Needless specifics only clutter the lead, as the following example illustrates:

Lamont T. Cranford, 57, of 62 Main St., a salesman for the Security Life Insurance Company, Inc., was stabbed and wounded at 8:43 last night in the parking lot of the Son-of-the-Sheik restaurant, 378 Watershed Pkwy., by two men, one described as wearing a green beret and the other as dressed in a Chinese-red suit, when he refused to hand over his wallet, which contained $23.74, and tried to fight off his assailants.

If we move the unnecessary details to their rightful berth—in the body of the story—and restructure the sentence to eliminate its eleven commas, the result is a lead that gets to the point:

A 57-year-old insurance salesman was stabbed and wounded last night when he tried to fight off two muggers in the parking lot of the Son-of-the-Sheik restaurant on Watershed Parkway.

Details about the muggers' colorful dress and the exact amount stolen would appear later in the story, where they enrich the account without getting in the way.

Whenever possible, make the lead a simple declarative sentence that proceeds directly from subject to verb to object. Avoid using unnecessary dependent clauses:

> Last night, the Board of Education, after two hours of raucous debate punctuated by a teacher walk-out and a fist fight between two parents, voted to require a Bible course at Coral Gables High School.

Although the walk-out and the fight do belong in the lead, they should not be placed so that they interrupt the flow of the sentence. It would be better to write this lead as follows:

> The Board of Education last night voted to require a Bible course at Coral Gables High School after a raucous meeting interrupted by a teacher walk-out and a fist fight between two parents.

Keeping your lead simple also means that you should use plain, everyday words that most people understand, not words they will have to look up in a dictionary. The police arrest a *suspect*, not an *alleged perpetrator*, who is charged with *auto theft*, not *grand larceny, auto*, and is *jailed*, not *incarcerated*. The cop who told you about it didn't *apprise* you of the facts, nor has he *stated* or *related* or *declared* them; he simply *said* it.

Describe People in a Meaningful Way

Names that mean nothing to readers should be kept out of the lead. Consider the following lead:

> Joe Jones drove his car into a watermelon truck in a spectacular accident in Hapsville yesterday.

Who ever heard of Joe Jones? Instead of just mentioning his name in the lead, you should identify Jones in a fashion that means something to your readers. Jones may be the father of three children, a hardware salesman, a good bowler, a Vietnam veteran, a former sky-writer and a part-time driving instructor. The final identification bears the most relevance to the story, because driving is at issue, not bowling or hardware sales. You should thus write:

> A part-time driving instructor drove his car into a watermelon truck in a spectacular accident in Hapsville yesterday.

Leads should be written from the heart as well as from the head so they can enlist the readers' sympathy:

A father of three children drowned yesterday when he tried to rescue a dog that had fallen overboard in Biscayne Bay.

Or happiness:

A Maine potato farmer who had lost his crop to the ravaging spud beetle yesterday won $1 million in the State Lottery.

Or simply amazement:

A 93-year-old World War I veteran captured a fleeing bank bandit here yesterday by knocking him on the head with his cane and pinning him to the ground until the police arrived.

Start with the Heart of the Matter

The essence of most breaking news stories, as we said earlier, can be stated in two or three words: *Convict escapes. City sacked. Judge fines banker.* The job of a lead is to focus the reader's attention on this, the heart of the news.

Let's say the State Department of Education issues a report highly critical of the methods the Hapsville schools are using to teach elementary students how to read. What are the key words to this story? *Department issues report*? No. Just issuing a report doesn't make for news. The heart of the story is what the report says: *Department criticizes schools*. A lead built on these words might read as follows:

The State Department of Education today sharply criticized the way Hapsville schools are teaching students how to read.

Suppose that a thief, his hand wrapped in a rag, smashes a jewelry store window, grabs a fistful of watches and runs up the sidewalk. A plain-clothes police officer parked nearby yells for him to stop, then opens fire with his revolver. Struck in the leg, the man falls to the pavement. What is the heart of this story? *Store robbed* doesn't get at the main news. More newsworthy is *man shot*:

A man was shot and wounded by a plain-clothes police officer today on a crowded downtown sidewalk after he allegedly broke a jewelry store window and ran away clutching a handful of watches.

Coming up with the lead is the hardest part of writing a story, because you can't write a good lead until you've thought through the details and grasped the essence of the news. A common failure in writing leads is to "back into" the news:

At a meeting of the Board of Police Commissioners last night, police chief Waldo Heath was suspended for taking his patrol car on a pleasure trip to North Platte, Neb.

The beginning of a sentence is what the readers read first, so why waste it? Start right off by presenting the main news. The heart of this news story is *chief suspended*, so try starting the lead that way:

> Police Chief Waldo Heath was suspended from his job last night for taking his patrol car on a pleasure trip to North Platte, Neb.

Like many of the rules of newswriting, the rule against backing into the lead can be broken. Sometimes newswriters purposefully back into a story when the *why* seems as important as the *what*. This was the case with one of our leads in the Pied Piper story:

> Angered by Hamlin's refusal to pay him for ridding it of rats, an exterminator called the "Pied Piper" today led the town's children through a hole in a nearby mountain to an unknown destination.

This strikingly similar lead, from *The Miami Herald*, also backs into the news in order to emphasize the *why* element of the story:

> Unhappy with what he and his agent decided was an unacceptable renegotiated contract offer from owner Joe Robbie, Dolphins quarterback Dan Marino on Thursday walked out of training camp at St. Thomas University.

Or, backing into the lead by way of an introductory clause can help put a story in perspective:

> ADDIS ABABA, ETHIOPIA (AP)—In a move to cut off a Somalian tank column threatening to sweep their left flank, the Ethiopians set a line of defense south of Suzat yesterday and at last report were fighting desperately to hold the city of Jaca.

But when in doubt, stick to the "no backing in" rule. Avoid writing such slow-starting leads as these:

> In a speech given to Thames College students yesterday, Senator Thomas X. Haverstraw charged . . .

> By a 9 to 4 vote yesterday, the Board of Aldermen decided to . . .

> As she was walking across Route 2 a mile north of town, a 47-year-old mother of seven was suddenly . . .

Keep It in Focus

A good lead says *one* central thing. Leads that try to say two things at once can wind up saying neither very effectively:

> A Hapsville insurance executive was critically injured in an automobile accident on Hurley Road last night, and he was later arrested on a charge of driving while intoxicated.

The "and" in the middle of this lead acts as a "hinge" that joins two distinct bits of news. Is the story primarily about a person who was badly injured, or is it about someone who was arrested for drunken driving? Usually, it's best for the newswriter to keep the lead focused on the *one* most newsworthy aspect of the story. If the injuries are severe, they should dominate the lead:

> A Hapsville insurance executive was critically injured last night when his car went out of control on Hurley Road and crashed into a tree.

If the injuries are minor, then the lead could focus on the arrest:

> A Hapsville insurance executive was arrested on charges of driving while intoxicated last night, after his car went out of control and struck a tree on Hurley Road.

"Laundry list" leads like the following one tend to make readers' eyes glaze over:

> The interstate Commerce Commission today proposed new regulations that would institute additional federal checks of interstate poultry shipments, relax some standards concerning use of recapped tires, mandate the recharting of six southern barge routes and revoke licenses of truckers convicted of speeding.

Here, the best news would seem to be the last item: A law revoking licenses could affect all truck drivers, and that's a lot of working men and women. The lead should thus focus on that one aspect of the story:

> Truckers convicted of speeding would lose their licenses under new regulations proposed today by the Interstate Commerce Commission.

Round Out the Story

Not every lead needs all five Ws, but be alert to the hazards of dropping any of them. Suppose you're writing a piece on an accident involving two young athletes returning from a basketball game. An adequate five W lead might read as follows:

> Two Hampton University basketball players narrowly escaped drowning in a flash flood last night when their car was swept into a culvert off Route 2 in Hapsville.

But watch what happens if one or more of the five Ws are dropped carelessly from this lead. For instance, suppose we omit *who*:

> A car was swept into a culvert off Route 2 in Hapsville by a flash flood last night, almost drowning its occupants.

Who were the occupants? If this lead were broadcast over a radio station by an announcer who cut it after that one sentence, it would bring a spate of phone calls from listeners worried about friends or relatives who were out driving. If we drop the *what*, the lead might read this way:

> Two Hampton University basketball players fell victim to a flash flood last night when their car was swept into a culvert off Route 2 in Hapsville.

What, exactly, happened? Were the players drowned? Were they injured? Similar problems arise if we drop the *where* and *when*:

> Two basketball players narrowly escaped drowning when a flash flood swept their automobile down a culvert.

Did this happen last night in Hapsville, or last Wednesday in Tomato, Kentucky? What would happen if we dropped the *why* or *how*:

> Two Hampton University basketball players narrowly escaped drowning last night in a flash flood near Hapsville.

If the lead reads this way, readers cannot see what happened. Because the story deals not with an issue but with action, the important question is not *why* they nearly drowned, but *how*: The flood swept their car off the road and down a culvert. Remember, an action lead should paint a picture.

In stories about issues, the *why* can be vitally important. Consider this lead:

> A prominent Hapsville business executive plunged twelve stories to his death yesterday from the window of his office on Main Street.

This seems adequate—until we find out *why* he apparently plunged twelve stories.

> A prominent Hapsville business executive plunged twelve stories to his death on Main Street yesterday minutes after learning that he faced indictment on charges of embezzling $250,000 from his company's pension fund.

Let the Main Verb Carry the Main News

A sentence uses one main verb to convey its central action; without that verb the sentence would collapse. In a news lead, this verb should carry the principal burden of the story. A common failing is to write something like this:

> The City Council held a meeting last night, during which it voted to impeach Mayor Henry C. Strongfellow because he "has not done a day's work in three years."

The trouble with this lead is that its main verb, "held," conveys only the fact that the council met, while the heart of the news—the impeachment—has been relegated to a dependent clause: "during which it voted to impeach. . . ." Almost invariably, you should reserve dependent clauses—clauses that depend for their existence on the main part of the sentence—for nonessential information. Let's rewrite the lead so that its main verb conveys the essence of the news:

> Mayor Henry C. Strongfellow *was impeached* by the City Council last night on grounds that he "has not done a day's work in three years."

Use Action Verbs

The verb is the engine that drives the sentence. Dull, lifeless verbs—like the ones in italics in the following lead—slow the lead down:

> An 89-year-old retired accountant was injured yesterday when his car *went* off the Allerton Pike near Swampscott, *proceeded* down a fifty-foot embankment and *encountered* a giant elm.

Action verbs reflect the action they were chosen to describe, and help bring the reader into the story:

> An 89-year-old retired accountant was injured yesterday when his car *veered* off the Allerton Pike near Swampscott, *plunged* down a fifty-foot embankment and *struck* a giant elm.

Action verbs can help readers hear as well as see, as is illustrated by this noisy lead from the Pittsfield, Massachusetts, *Berkshire Eagle*:

> Growling, shouting, wailing, whooping and all the while stepping in time to his pyrotechnic guitar, Bob MacVeety of Bluestars led his group through a gamut of bluesy rock 'n roll yesterday.

Of course, if action verbs are pushed beyond the point of relevance, they may degenerate into journalese or cliche:

> Douglas *ripped into* plans for a proposed waterway . . .

> A federal judge today *blasted* the hopes of environmentalists who . . .

> A Justice Department anticrime probe was *blunted* today, when . . .

Use the strongest verb that's accurate, and no more. A lead that *slams*, *hurtles*, *rages* and *rams* without justification can be pretty disconcerting to readers.

BREAKING THE RULES

Most writing rules are guidelines, not laws, and can be broken when the occasion calls for it. For instance, a breaking lead may have to run to more than one sentence if it raises a pressing question that readers will want answered without delay. Consider this sad story from the Associated Press:

CRYSTAL RIVER, FLA. (AP)—A 20-year-old woman was struck by two cars and killed when she rescued her dog from traffic on U.S. 19, authorities report. The collie dog was not injured.

Two-sentence leads also can serve to present both sides of a debatable assertion. This one is from the Buffalo, New York, *News*:

The shadow of Mayor Griffin looms over what are expected to be the three most competitive Common Council primary races September 10. Nevertheless, most of those running say they'll win or lose on their own merits.

Similarly, the rule limiting leads to thirty-five words may be violated if the writer genuinely needs the extra space. Perhaps additional information is needed to put the story in proper perspective. This forty-three word lead is from the *Los Angeles Times*:

INSTITUTE, W. VA.—A giant cloud of gas derived from the chemical that killed thousands last year in Bhopal, India, escaped Sunday from Union Carbide's plant here, injuring six employees and sending almost 200 nearby residents to hospitals seeking medical treatment for respiratory and skin irritations.

Sometimes, too, more than thirty-five words are required to draw together the elements of a diverse story. Such was the case in this fifty-one word lead, taken from the St. Louis *Post-Dispatch*:

CENTERVILLE, MO.—Mayors of the three largest towns in Reynolds County are entangled in political controversies that have resulted in criminal charges against one of the mayors, an indictment by a grand jury of another and the resignation of the third after he was involved in a fist fight with a local merchant.

And, sometimes, a subject is so complicated that it demands a longer lead. This one has forty-one words.

BOSTON (UPI)—A severe shortage of transplant organs may be due to a deep-seated psychological reluctance by medical personnel to remove organs from bodies that appear alive and to ask grieving families for permission to perform the procedure, a psychiatrist reported today.

The five W formula can be discarded to lend a fresh twist to an otherwise routine story. The reporter who wrote this story for the *Virginia Pilot/The Ledger-Star* relegated the news of petty crime to the second paragraph, and led with a feature-style teaser:

NORFOLK—Pizza lovers are more than welcome in Milton's Pizza at 852 North Military Highway. That is, when the store is open and they are paying customers.

But a police stakeout of the restaurant Thursday night led to the arrests of five people—include the business's cook—for having an after-hours party complete with pizza and beer, the police said. . . .

For more on going beyond the conventions of the five W breaking news lead, see Chapter 9.

COPY FORMAT

Porter & Ferris / hosp., police, clips

Format

NEW YORK—News copy typewritten on paper (sometimes called "hard copy") normally follows this basic format:

Always type your name in the upper left corner of the first page (where we've typed "Porter & Ferris").

Following your name, on the same line, list the sources from which you got the story. If you called the hospital and the police department and consulted clips from the newspaper library, the source line might read: "hosp., police, clips."

A few spaces below your name, type the *slug*, which is a one- or two-word designation of the story. (The slug on this story is *format*.) Normally you should clear the slug with an editor, so that everyone involved can recognize the story by its slug. The slug should also appear at the upper left corner of every subsequent page of copy.

Leave plenty of blank space—at least one-third of a page—at the top of the first page. Editors need headroom to insert instructions, journalism teachers to mark grades and make comments.

Write "(MORE)" at the bottom of the page, to indicate that additional copy follows.

(MORE)

format / 2–2–2–2

Type the slug and the page number at the upper left of every page of copy. This way, editors can tell at a glance which story it is and where each page belongs in it.

Indent the first line of each paragraph. Double or triple space and leave ample margins, to facilitate editing. Avoid hyphenating words at the end of the line; if you hyphenate, the compositor setting the story in type may not know whether the word was hyphenated because you ran out of space or because it's normally spelled that way.

Don't split a paragraph from one page to the next. Finish each paragraph on the page you began it.

Use standard proofreading marks (see page 174) when going over your hard copy.

Type "– 30 –," the old telegrapher's symbol for "the end," to designate the end of the story.

– 30 –

ON THE JOB

Let us suppose that it's your second week at work on the Hapsville *Recall,* an afternoon daily in a New Jersey river town with a population of 100,000. At 11 A.M., an hour before the noon deadline, you hear the city editor call your name. He says to get over to the Holiday Lawn Chair Company, where delivery truck drivers have been on strike. There's been a report of violence at the plant. "Take Judy the photographer and her car and see what's going on over there," he says in a raspy voice. "Gimme a call soon's you get there, now. Don't keep me waiting until the swallows return."

You and the photographer drive to the scene. On the way you see an ambulance screaming by in the opposite direction. When you arrive at the plant, a red brick structure built on a land fill jutting out into a swamp, you find a couple dozen angry-looking pickets milling around the entrance. Nearby stands a knot of police officers. Going up to a cop with a gold bar on his shoulder, you ask what happened.

"Well, it was quite a brawl," he says. "Some scabs tried to take deliveries out of the plant and cross the picket line with their trucks. Some of these guys here pulled them out of their cabs and beat them pretty good. Guess you saw the ambulance. It took three of them to the hospital. Also one of the delivery trucks got turned over—that Econoline van over there."

Thanking him for the information, you call the city desk over your car radio and tell the editor what you've got.

"Good," he says, after hearing about the beatings. "How many arrested?"

"Uh . . . I forgot to ask," you admit sheepishly.

"Well *ask*, for cryin' out loud, then call rewrite. All we got room for is a couple of 'grafs. Make 'em good."

You go back to the lieutenant, who says the police arrived too late to see who did it, and so have as yet made no arrests. He's planning to ask the injured drivers if they can identify their attackers. You return to the car radio and call in to the woman on rewrite duty. She's an ex-UPI reporter who can compose a story nearly as fast as she can type. You dictate a lead to her:

> Striking union truck drivers for the Holiday Lawn Chair Company battled with scabs who crossed . . .

"Hold it, hold it," she interrupts. "What's this 'scabs' stuff? That's like calling someone 'scum.' You're a reporter, not a shop steward. Let's stick to the facts."

You try again:

> Striking union truck drivers of the Holiday Lawn Chair Company battled with *nonunion drivers* who crossed the picket line at the company's plant.

"Fine," she says. "But *when* did it happen, last week?"

"Uh, no, just an hour ago," you reply, trying to overlook the sarcasm.

"Okay," she says. "Now, you mind telling me what happened?"

"I did. I just gave you the lead."

"That doesn't say *what* happened. They had a fight, right? Guys got beat up, right? Anyone hurt?"

"Oh. Yes, as a matter of fact, three were taken to the hospital. I was getting to that in the next 'graf. And a truck was overturned."

Hearing a sigh on the other end, you tell her the rest of the facts, then sign off. You interview people on the scene, talk with the police to let them know you'll be calling later to see if they've arrested anyone, check with Judy to make sure she's got all the photos she wants, then call the city editor and get permission to return to the office. On the way back, you jot down a few practice leads to see how they will stack up against the one the rewrite woman will have written. Your first reads:

> Striking drivers at the Holiday Lawn Chair Company today beat up nonunion drivers and overturned a company truck when they tried to cross the picket line.

This lead delivers more of the story than did your first attempt, all but the hospitalization of the injured drivers. But the English is flawed by the use of colloquialisms like "beat up." Also, the sentence is confusing. Does the "they" refer to the strikers or the nonunion drivers? You try again:

> Three nonunion truck drivers were hospitalized with injuries today and one of their trucks, a green Ford Econoline van, was overturned when the nonunion drivers attempted to drive through a picket line at the Holiday Lawn Chair Company and were attacked by striking drivers who pulled them from their trucks and beat them up with clubs outside the plant.

At fifty-eight words, this lead is clearly too long; it's also cluttered. Do you need to identify the van as a *green Ford Econoline*? Can't you cut some of that verbiage around the picket line? Also, part of the lead is unsubstantiated: Were the men actually "hospitalized"? All you saw was the ambulance taking them to the hospital; perhaps they were simply patched up and sent home.

Back to a fresh sheet of paper.

> Three nonunion truck drivers were injured today and their van overturned when they tried to cross a picket line at the Holiday Lawn Chair Company and were attacked with clubs by striking drivers.

This sentence flows smoothly and paints a picture of what happened without clouding the image with nonessential details.

Back in the city room, you eagerly read the afternoon edition of the paper. The lead constructed by the woman on rewrite seems to move faster than yours. And it has more drama:

> Nonunion truck drivers trying to cross a picket line at the strike-bound Holiday Lawn Chair Company today were pulled from their cabs by striking drivers and beaten with clubs.

But her lead leaves out some elements of the story, such as the fact that the truck was overturned. Privately, you prefer yours.

SUMMARY

The classic breaking news lead is but a single sentence, usually no more than thirty-five words long, that conveys the "five Ws"—*who*, *what*, *where*, *when*, and *why*—and an "H," for *how*. The *why* explains motivation; the *how*, action. This sort of lead often serves best when the news being reported is particularly important, interesting and fresh.

When writing a breaking news lead: Keep it *brief* and *simple*; a simple declarative sentence is ideal. Describe people in a *meaningful* way, keeping your readers' knowledge and interests in mind. Start with the *heart* of the matter: Jump right into the main news. Keep it in *focus*: Don't try to say several different things in the lead. *Round out* the lead, and don't leave any loose ends dangling. Use *action* verbs, and let the *main* verb carry the burden of the main news.

7

WRITING
BREAKING NEWS:
THE BODY OF THE STORY

Newspapers are more often scanned than scrutinized; one survey found that the average reader spends only a half an hour with the daily paper, and finishes reading only a fraction of the stories he or she begins. That's one reason why breaking news stories normally begin with the essence of the news, and convey a brief but well-rounded account of the story within the first few paragraphs.

Fiction is structured quite differently. Literary stories, in fact, often begin with relatively incidental material, then build to a climax. Diagrammed, such a story might look like this:

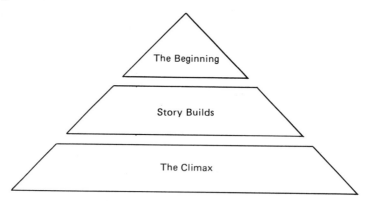

The tale of Little Red Riding Hood is customarily told this way, with the climax near the end:

The beginning	Once upon a time there was a little girl named Red Riding Hood. One morning her mother told her that Granny had become ill, gave her a basket of goodies and told her to foot it to Granny's house on the other side of Big Woods.
Story builds	In the middle of the woods, Red met a wolf. The wolf told her that the fastest way through the woods was by the South Road. This was really the slowest way. The wolf then took a short cut to Granny's house. When he got to the cottage he locked Granny in a linen closet, pulled on her nightie and jumped into bed.
The climax	Red arrived. "Granny," she cried, "what a mammoth pair of canines you've got." At this, the wolf leaped up and chased her around the room. A passing woodsman, hearing the girl's cries, burst into the room and killed the wolf with his ax. Granny was let out of the closet, and they all lived happily ever after.

But in a breaking news story, we put the climax at the beginning. Then the story proceeds in *descending* order of importance, conveying ever less newsworthy material, with the least important detail last. That's why breaking news stories are said to be organized in the form of an *inverted pyramid*. Diagrammed, their structure looks like this:

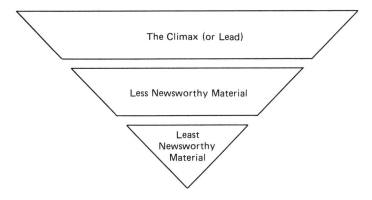

Here's the story of Little Red Riding Hood, rewritten as a breaking news story:

The climax (or *lead*)	A 10-year-old girl and her grandmother were saved from being eaten by a wolf today when a woodsman passing by their cottage near Big Woods killed the wolf with his ax.
Less newsworthy material	The girl, identified as Little Red Riding Hood of 14 Glenwood Drive, and her grandmother, Old Gray Hood, 75, of 39 Road's End, were reported to be shaken but in good condition at Woodland Memorial Hospital.
	Their rescuer was identified as Fred Flanagan, 20, a tree feller for the Big Woods Pulp and Paper Co., who was on his way home from work when he saved the pair. He said the wolf had disguised himself in the old woman's clothes, crawled into her bed and attacked the girl as she entered the bedchamber.

Least newsworthy material

Miss Hood told Flanagan she had encountered the wolf in the woods earlier in the day but that he had not harmed her. Her mother had given her a basket of goodies she was taking to her grandmother, who has been ill.

The inverted pyramid format ensures that readers will learn of the most important news even if they read only the top paragraph or two of the story. It also makes it easy for editors to cut stories to fit available space; all they need do is cut from the bottom, and they don't have to worry unduly about lopping off anything vital: Whatever survives will always be more newsworthy than what has been deleted. Little Red Riding Hood's news story could be cut to as little as the first one or two paragraphs, and it would still communicate the essential news.

When an important element of a story is *not* conveyed up top, editing can wreck the story. This UPI dispatch lost its punchline at the hands of an editor at the Columbia, South Carolina, *Record*:

HANOVER, PA. (UPI)—Robert Beckner is the kind of guy who can sleep anywhere.

Take Wednesday night, for example. Beckner, of Hanover, decided to nestle between the railroad tracks at the Broadway Crossing in this York County community.

After he had fallen fast asleep, a West Maryland Railroad freight train came chugging down the track.

And that was it—no word of Beckner's fate.

LIGHTNING STRIKES FASTER TODAY THAN IN 1838

Before the Civil War, reporters typically wrote leisurely dispatches that read more like letters home than like urgent appeals to the readers' attention. This story, which appeared in the *Long Island Democrat* in August, 1838, was written by poet Walt Whitman, who worked for many years as a reporter and editor. Whitman was a great writer, but his story manages to violate nearly every rule of modern newswriting.

At Northport on Saturday, 28th July, an unfortunate and somewhat singular accident occurred from the lightning. Mr. Abraham Miller of that place had been in the fields, engaged in some farm work, and was returning home as a storm commenced in the afternoon, carrying in his hands a pitchfork. A friend of his who was with him advised him not to carry it, as he considered it dangerous. Mr. Miller, however, did not put down the fork but continued walking with it; he had gone some distance on his way home, and had just put up the bars of a fence he passed through, when a violent clap of thunder occurred, followed by a sharp flash. The acquaintance of Mr. Miller was slightly stunned by the shock and, turning around to look at his companion, he saw him lying on his face motionless. He went to him and found him dead; the lightning having been attracted by the steel tines of the fork, had torn his hand slightly and killed him on the instant.

Today, instead of telling this story in chronological sequence, as Whitman did, we would put the essential news first, and then recount the details:

A Northport farmer was killed by a bolt of lightning Saturday when it struck the tines of a pitchfork he was carrying while walking home from work in his field.

The victim, Abraham Miller, had been warned by an acquaintance just before the incident to leave the tool behind. . . .

STRUCTURING THE STORY

The lead of a breaking news story tells the story quickly, in general; the body fills in the specific. The fundamental principle in structuring the body is to *present the material in the order of its newsworthiness*, with the most newsworthy material at the top. In practice, a good way to do this is to write a sound lead, then "back up" the lead. This means fleshing out the most important elements, often in the *same order* in which they're presented in the lead.

Suppose you've written this lead:

> A newly elected Hapsville city council member today made public his last year's income tax statement and called on other elected officials to do the same.

The most important elements here would seem to be (1) *who* the council member is; (2) *what* he is doing; and (3) *why* he's doing it. So, we promptly back up the lead to fill in this information:

Who	Council member Thornton Weiskoff, who had promised to release the statement during last fall's election campaign, reported a total income last year of $45,750.
What	Included in the total were Weiskoff's $25,000-a-year salary as a social studies teacher at Hapsville High School, $15,000 earned by his wife as a secretary at the same school and $5750 the couple earned from a rental property. Like other council members, Weiskoff receives no salary for holding his council post.
Why	Weiskoff said he released the statement to show that he had no conflict of interest. He urged other elected officials to do likewise. "How else," he asked, "will the people of Hapsville know they can trust those who serve them unless officials come forth as I have to show they don't owe anyone any special favors?"

The same considerations hold for action stories, like this account of a fire rescue, from the *Chicago Tribune*:

> CHICAGO—A Chicago firefighter yesterday crawled through dense smoke to save a person trapped in a burning building, the second time within three and a half months he has made such a rescue.

Here the focus is the hero: the firefighter. The writer quotes him right away, in the second paragraph:

> "Too often you end up with dead people" in fires, said firefighter Guy McGowan, 31. "It's a good feeling when they live."

The other leading character in the story is the person McGowan rescued. We read about him in the next paragraph:

> McGowan saved three-year-old Ronald Ford Jr., of 1636 W. Maypole, who was in critical condition yesterday at Cook County Memorial Hospital, being treated for smoke inhalation.

Next, the story revealed *how* the rescue took place:

> The first firefighters to arrive at the burning building were told by the boy's parents that he was still inside. McGowan and other firefighters dashed in.
>
> "We went into the kitchen and didn't find anybody," McGowan said. "Then I went into the bathroom and I found the boy lying unconscious on the floor.
>
> "I got him out as quick as I could. I started doing CPR (cardio-pulminary resuscitation). There was no heartbeat or breathing. Then the paramedics came and took over. The smoke was real thick in there."

The lead also mentions the rescue McGowan made a few months earlier, so now the writer backs up that aspect of the lead:

> On May 8, McGowan, detailed to Hook and Ladder Company No. 11 for a day, rescued a woman and four children from a sixth-floor apartment at 3833 S. Federal in the Robert Taylor Homes.
>
> The five were trapped in a rear bedroom, the only room in the apartment that had not been gutted by flames. The bedroom had almost burned through when McGowan dashed into the apartment and rescued them. All were unharmed.

The important thing to remember is that the body of the story, like the lead, should emphasize the most important news—and that the way to emphasize it is to put it up high. The lead to this *Miami Herald* story of sunken treasure emphasizes, naturally enough, the chest of sunken treasure:

> KEY WEST—Capping a week of extravagant finds, a team of divers working for treasure hunter Mel Fisher yesterday found eight treasure chests laden with silver coins and gold bars.

The body provides a description of the treasure chests:

> After three and a half centuries on the ocean floor, the wooden boxes were found intact. What's more, the metal hinges still worked on one of them, said Beth McHaley, a vice president of Fisher's Treasure Salvors Inc.
>
> "There has never been a treasure chest found intact on any shipwreck found in modern times," McHaley said. . . .
>
> By noon Friday, Fisher's divers had brought up seven unmarked wooden chests filled with approximately 3000 silver coins each, McHaley said. Each coin is worth from $200 to $12,000, depending on its condition, she said.
>
> By 1:30, the divers had dragged up a smaller box filled with gold bars. McHaley would not disclose the number of bars nor their estimated value.

Only then, after having let us have a good look at the treasure, does the writer fill in background:

> The booty is a part of the mother lode of the Nuestra Senora de Atocha, a seventeenth century treasure galleon that sank in a hurricane in 1622 about 41 miles west of Key West.

Then the writer backed up the part of the lead that referred to the "week of extravagant finds," news of which had already appeared in the papers:

> On Saturday, Fisher's divers found the main ballast with its mounds of silver bars, a treasure Fisher has been pursuing for 16 years.
> Another 140 silver bars were brought up from the deep Friday, bringing the total of the 70-pound bars to 390, McHaley said.

Of course, if the lead is fouled up, the body of a story that backs up the lead will be fouled up, too. Remember the story in the previous chapter about the insurance salesman who was mugged in the parking lot of the Son-of-the-Sheik restaurant? Suppose we had led it with too much emphasis on the "where" element of the story:

> In the parking lot of a local restaurant last night, two muggers robbed a 57-year-old insurance salesman after they stabbed him when he refused to hand over his wallet.

If the body followed the emphasis of this misbegotten lead, it would have looked like this:

> The attack came at the Son-of-the-Sheik restaurant, 378 Watershed Pkwy., at 8:43 P.M.
> The pair, one of whom was wearing a green beret and the other a Chinese-red suit, made off with $23.74, the mugging victim told police.
> The victim, Lamont T. Cranford, of 62 Main St., a salesman for the Security Life Insurance Company, Inc., was stabbed after he refused to give up his wallet and tried to fight off his attackers.
> He was taken to Mercy Hospital and treated for a knife wound in the abdomen. His condition was listed as "stable."

The most important news here is *what* happened—that a man was stabbed and wounded while resisting a mugging—and *who* was involved, not *where* it happened. If we reorganize the lead to stress these elements of the news, the rest of the story falls into place:

> A 57-year-old insurance salesman was stabbed and wounded last night when he tried to fight off two muggers in the parking lot of a local restaurant.
> Lamont T. Cranford, of 62 Main St., a salesman for the Security Life Insurance Company, Inc., was admitted to Mercy Hospital with a stomach wound. He was reported in stable condition.
> Cranford told the police he was attacked at 8:43 at the Son-of-the-Sheik restaurant by two men who approached him and demanded his money.
> Cranford said he refused to hand over his wallet and began to fight the men off. It was then that they stabbed him, he said.
> The pair, one of whom wore a green beret and the other a Chinese-red suit, escaped with $23.74, Cranford said.

KEEPING THE STORY ROLLING

Accomplished newswriters learn to lead their readers through each story, even though it may cover a lot of ground and jump around quite a bit from one topic to another. One key to doing this is to *limit each sentence, and each paragraph, to a single subject*. Think of each sentence and paragraph as a container that holds one kind of information. In the sunken treasure story, the early paragraphs deal with the treasure chests, the later paragraphs with how the treasure was recovered; the writer doesn't mix the two subjects together.

To guide the reader from one topic to another, start each paragraph dealing with a new subject with a few words that indicate what it's going to be about. In the treasure story, the phrases "By noon Friday. . . ." and "By 1:30 . . ." differentiate between the various loads of treasure being described. The phrase, "The booty is part of the mother lode. . ." signals that the next paragraph will tell us from where the treasure came.

Introductory phrases like these serve as *transitions* to help guide readers through the story. In this account of the hysteria touched off by Orson Welles's radio broadcast of H. G. Wells's *The War of the Worlds*, George Mahawinney of the *Philadelphia Inquirer* used transition sentences to stitch together accounts of panic in widely scattered locations. The transition sentences are italicized.

A terrified motorist asked the patrolman the way to Route 24. "All creation's busted loose. I'm getting out of Jersey," he screamed. . . .

At Caldwell, New Jersey, an excited parishioner rushed into the First Baptist Church during evening services and shouted that a tremendous meteor had fallen, causing widespread death, and that North Jersey was threatened with a shower of meteors. The congregation joined in prayer for deliverance.

Reactions as strange, or stranger, occurred in other parts of the country. In San Francisco, a citizen called police, crying: "My God, where can I volunteer my services? We've got to stop this awful thing."

In *Indianapolis, Indiana*, a woman ran screaming into a church. "New York is destroyed; it's the end of the world," she cried. "You might as well go home to die."

Throughout Atlanta was a wide-spread belief that a "planet" had struck New Jersey, killing from 40 to 70,000 persons.

At Pittsburgh one man telephoned a newspaper that he returned to his home in the middle of the broadcast and found his wife in the bathroom, clutching a bottle of poison.

"I'd rather die this way than like that," she screamed before he was able to calm her. . . .

Note that when introducing individuals into a story, you should avoid leading the paragraph with their names, because readers will probably not know who they are. When possible, identify them first, then name them:

"The governor's mother-in-law, Mrs. Helen DiSimone . . ."
"A passenger on the flight, Frank Schickele . . ."
"A spokesperson for the opposition, Charlotte Champlin . . .

ORGANIZING THE LONGER STORY

Longer, more complicated stories can be structured by nesting two or more inverted pyramids within the overall framework. This means, in effect, telling the story twice—each time with fresh information. The entire story is told in a few succinct paragraphs, then the whole thing is covered again, on a finer level of detail. Diagrammed, such a story would look like this:

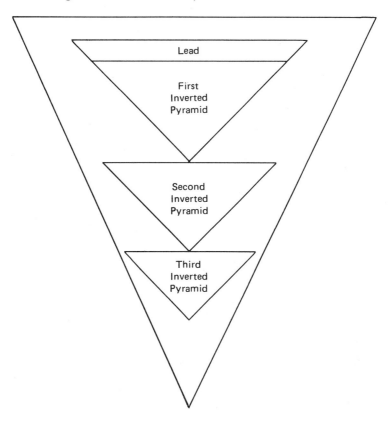

The first three paragraphs of this piece from *The New York Times* is an inverted pyramid story in itself, outlining a court decision in a battle waged by residents of Long Island to keep convicts from being transferred to a local mental hospital:

First
inverted
pyramid

The Appellate Division of State Supreme Court ruled yesterday that the state could transfer 1,000 prisoners to three vacant buildings on the grounds of the Pilgrim Psychiatric Center in West Brentwood, L.I.

The decision

The move is part of a plan to alleviate prison overcrowding.

Reason for it

Officials of the town of Islip, one of the petitioners in the case, said they would appeal the decision today in the

Opposition to it

State Court of Appeals this morning, which they hoped
would be before the state had time to move any prisoners
into the facility.

Then the story is told again, with greater detail, in a second inverted pyramid:

In its 4-to-1 decision, the Appellate Division rejected
arguments by Islip, Suffolk County and several civic associa-   More
tions that the state had failed to consider possible adverse   on the
effects of the transfer plan on neighborhoods surrounding   decision
the facility or on patients at the psychiatric center itself,
which is believed to be the largest mental hospital in the
world.

Second   "We cannot overlook the dangerously overcrowded con-   More on the
inverted   ditions in the state's prisons and the potentially explosive   reasons for
pyramid   situation they create," the justices wrote. "This renders ef-   the decision
forts to alleviate those conditions matters of the highest
public priority."

State officials had wanted to begin moving prisoners into
the new jail this week but were delayed by a preliminary
injunction issued last week by Justice James A. Gowan in
State Supreme Court in Suffolk County.

Yesterday state officials said that they hoped to move
40 prisoners into the jail today and planned to increase
the inmate population to 400 within five days. . . .

Opponents of the inmate transfer were dismayed.   More on the
"There will be an automatic disruption to our lives over   opposition
here," said Diane Lundegaard of Dix Hills, president of
the Four Towns Civic Association, one of the groups that
filed the lawsuit that led to yesterday's ruling.

"Our peaceful community will have to be on the alert
because we will be residents of a prison town."

A news story—even one that "tells it twice"—should never repeat itself. When
recounting aspects of the story, always work in fresh information.

TELLING THE STORY CHRONOLOGICALLY

Complicated events may be easier to follow if they are recounted *chronologically*.
In a short news story the chronological account might start immediately after
the lead, as follows:

Chronology   The 18-year-old son of Mayor Fulton G. Spalding was arrested by
Hapsville police last night on a charge of possession of drugs.

The boy, Herman F. Spalding, a senior at Hapsville High School,
was driving his car north on Sickler Road, the police said, when he
was stopped at about 10 P.M. for a broken taillight.

Police searched the car when Spalding started "acting strangely,"
said Sgt. Thomas Flawson of the traffic squad. In the trunk, he said,

they found four ounces of marijuana and a small quantity of a white powder that they suspect is cocaine.

The boy was released overnight on his own recognizance and was to appear for an arraignment in Hapsville District Court this morning.

Diagrammed, this short story would look like this:

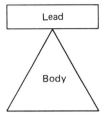

The chronological structure resembles that of traditional tales like the original account of Little Red Riding Hood. Such chronological stories are easy to write—*too* easy, in fact: They can become a crutch. But they work well when the news involves a complex series of events, and they are especially effective in stories that involve a lot of action.

For longer chronology stories, you should summarize the essential news first, in a traditional inverted pyramid, before going into the chronology: First tell readers who won the fight and (generally) how; then go into the blow by blow. Diagrammed, the longer chronological story looks like an hour-glass:

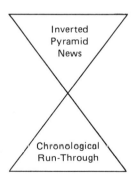

One such story appeared in the Dallas *Morning News*. This was the lead:

A naked man who police said was turned away from the Best Western Hotel "because he had no baggage" was jailed early Thursday after he slashed a police officer with a beer bottle, the police said.

Next the newswriter outlined the whole story in the inverted-pyramid format:

Northwest patrol officer George S. Finley was in good condition at home Thursday after receiving 14 stitches in his head from doctors at Parkland Memorial Hospital, said Sgt. Dwaine Sides.

Gary Lee Macon, 26, of South Dallas, was being held on investigative charges of evading arrest and two counts of aggravated assault on allegations he attacked Finley and threatened another officer, Sides said.

Macon was also treated at Parkland Memorial Hospital, then taken to Lew Sterret Justice Center where he remained late Thursday in lieu of $20,000 bond, jail officials said.

Now the story is recounted in detail, chronologically:

The chase began at about 6:30 P.M. Wednesday after the man had been turned away from the Best Western Hotel "because he had no baggage," Sides said.

"When he didn't receive a warm welcome, he ran out the door and a squad car happened to be driving by."

The squad car chased Macon down Industrial Boulevard and into the 100 block of Irving Boulevard, Sides said, where he climbed over a fence and came at the four officers with a broken beer bottle after he was cornered.

"It was humorous before that, but it got serious then," he said.

Finley tried to knock the bottle from the man's hand with a baton, but could not, Sides said. Instead, the man lunged at Finley and cut his hand, then cut his own chest and throat several times before police were able to subdue him, Sides said.

THE INVERTED INVERTED PYRAMID

The *inverted* inverted-pyramid story, as its name implies, stands the customary breaking news story format on its head: It puts the news not at the top but at the bottom, like the punchline to a joke. This upside-down format works well with light or humorous items, like this Reuters brief:

WASHINGTON, D.C.—The Interior Department issued a press release Thursday saying that because of budget cuts it no longer would deliver its press releases by messenger.

"We can no longer afford to deliver news releases on a regular daily basis to all media outlets in the metropolitan area," Assistant Secretary for Public Affairs Douglas Baldwin said.

The release was delivered by messenger.

INTERPRETATION

In issue-oriented stories it's often not enough for reporters simply to convey the facts. They also need to explain what the facts mean. This means emphasizing the *how* and *why* aspects of the news, well up in the body of the story.

Here is a dispatch by Robert Reinhold of *The New York Times* about a vote by the Organization of American States condemning Britian's role in the 1982 Falkland Islands war. The outcome of the vote had been expected—Britian was fighting Argentina, a member of the OAS—but the vehemence expressed at the meeting came as a surprise. Reinhold's lead thus emphasized the emotions involved:

WASHINGTON, D.C.—After 17 hours of emotional debate ending early this morning, foreign ministers from Latin America today condemned Britain's attack on the Falkland Islands and urged the United States to halt its aid to the British.

The story elaborates on the facts for one paragraph, then concentrates on explaining the significance of the vote and its expected impact:

> More on
> the facts
>   The action came in a 17 to 0 vote with 4 abstentions at the Organization of American States building here. The United States abstained, along with Chile, Columbia and Trinidad and Tobago, calling the resolution one-sided.
>   The action appeared to represent a significant setback to United States relations with Latin America.
>
> What the
> facts mean
>   Sources at the OAS said they had seldom seen such emotion and frustration emerge over an issue. . . .
>   The resolution was softened to avoid a complete break with the United States. Instead of voting to condemn the United States for aiding Britain, the ministers merely urged Washington to halt aid.

THE UNINVERTED PYRAMID

The inverted-pyramid format, though valuable for covering important breaking news, is, of course, only one way of structuring a news story. There are as many other approaches as newswriters can invent. One approach is to uninvert the pyramid, telling the story with the news at the end. This works best with stories that have a strong emotional appeal. Here, an AP reporter handles the tragic tale of a teenager's suicide by *inverting* the inverted pyramid. The breaking news—the suicide itself—isn't reported until the sixth paragraph:

CHICAGO, Nov 13 (AP)—The first great blow to Gary Cohen's young life came three years ago. His mother died of cancer.

Five months ago, his 15-year-old sister, Janice, accidentally shot herself while handling a gun in the family weapons collection. She was paralyzed from her chin down.

His father, Philip, 38, lonely and pained since his wife's death, was plunged into a mood of despair. He went to the hospital every day and often sat by the girl's bedside throughout the night.

Last Friday Gary walked into his father's bedroom and found him dead—shot with one of the weapons from the collection. Nearby was a note telling of his agony since the death of his wife and the accident that crippled his daughter.

Yesterday was Veteran's Day and Gary had the day off from school. He was alone in the basement apartment. The police say he went to the weapons collection, took down a 12-gauge shotgun, aimed the muzzle at his head and hooked a toe up against the trigger.

At the age of 13, he shot himself to death.

Sol Cohen spoke painfully of his grandson: "A child doesn't see that there can be a future. He thinks the world disappears with one tragic act."

Light stories, too, respond well to the inverted inverted-pyramid treatment. While John F. Kennedy was president, the Associated Press Washington bureau got wind that someone had accidently been plugged into the nuclear war hot line at the White House. A hard news lead on the story might have read:

WASHINGTON, D.C.—A private citizen trying to reach an animal hospital in Virginia recently was accidently plugged into the "hot line" used to warn the President in the event of a nuclear attack.

This would have been a serviceable, but rather flat, lead. Instead, the AP treated it this way:

WASHINGTON, D.C. (AP)—The President was awakened recently by the buzzing of his "hot line," the phone hook-up to the Pentagon used to warn him of a nuclear attack.

"Is this the animal hospital?" a voice asked.

"No," said the President.

"Is this South 5–6855?"

"No, this is the White House."

"Is Mr. Wilson there?"

"No, this is the President."

At this, the caller hung up.

According to the White House, which confirmed the story yesterday, the mysterious caller had apparently been trying to reach the Animal Hospital in Alexandria, Virginia, when he was accidentally plugged into the President's hot line.

A switchboard operator at the hospital said she had been having trouble with her phone for the past three weeks. "We've been hearing other conversations," she said. "Apparently there have been some crossed wires somewhere."

The White House said that the Chesapeake and Potomac Telephone Companies had been asked to look into the matter.

Follow-up stories may also lend themselves to a departure from the standard inverted-pyramid format: If the main information involved has already been reported, it's not breaking news, so there is less justification for the immediacy of the standard breaking news approach. The news of a judge's ruling in the case of a sex questionnaire distributed at a New York high school appeared one morning in the New York *Daily News*, with this conventional inverted-pyramid lead:

A Manhattan federal judge ruled yesterday that the Board of Education and the principal at Stuyvesant High School violated the First Amendment rights of the editor of the school newspaper when they prevented him from distributing a sex questionnaire to students.

Later that day, the *New York Post*, an afternoon paper, carried the same story. Rather than beginning with the hard news—the judge's ruling—the *Post* version began a year earlier, with the student's original decision to conduct the sex survey, and got to the fresh news only in the fourth paragraph:

A year ago, Jeff Trachtman, the editor of the Stuyvesant High School newspaper, decided it would be a good idea to take a survey of the sexual attitudes of his schoolmates and publish the results.

School officials, however, did not share his enthusiasm for the project and barred the survey.

But that wasn't the end of it. The 17-year-old senior, supported by his father, Gilbert, a psychologist and professor at N.Y.U., and the New York Civil Liberties Union, sued the Board of Education, charging that the youth's First Amendment rights were being violated.

Manhattan Federal Court Judge Constance Baker Motley, in a 19-page decision, agreed. She ordered school authorities yesterday to allow the survey of 11th and 12th graders and permit the results to be published in the school paper, the Stuyvesant Voice. . . .

The *Post*'s more leisurely approach worked because this story, though newsworthy, had already appeared in the morning papers. A similar situation confronts print journalists covering major stories that have already been broadcast over radio and television. Newspapers reporting the royal wedding of Prince Charles and Lady Diana Spencer in 1981, for instance, tended to emphasize background and color: Most of their readers had watched the wedding on television, and stories written in a standard, breaking news format would merely have recounted what they'd already seen. For the same reason, the news magazines, which generally are nearly a week late with the news, usually lead their stories by recounting the how and why of each news event, and often don't get around to recounting what happened until the second or third paragraph.

News reports written in formats other than the inverted pyramid are often called "feature stories." We discuss features in detail in Chapter 9.

ONGOING STORIES

Ongoing stories present the latest developments in a continuing news event that has made headlines before. Trials, government hearings, election campaigns and corporate scandals can go on for weeks, months or years. In writing ongoing stories, emphasize the *new* news ahead of the old, of course, but don't wait too long before reminding readers of the background. The part of the story that provides the background is called the *tie-back* or *recap*.

The following AP dispatch about an ongoing conflict between Soviet diplomats and the town of Glen Cove, Long Island, leads with fresh material, then recaps the background, then returns to the new. First, it leads with what's new:

GLEN COVE, L.I. (AP)—The State Department has ordered the mayor of Glen Cove to stop meddling in foreign affairs and let local Soviet diplomats use the city's golf courses, beaches and tennis courts.

"Discriminatory actions such as that taken by Glen Cove interfere with conduct of foreign relations of the United States," the State Department said in a letter to Mayor Alan Parente.

THREE RULES OF ATTRIBUTION

Much of the news that journalists relate concerns events that they did not witness themselves, but learned about second- or thirdhand. In such cases, they do all they can to verify the information, and they also take care to *attribute* it to its source. Here are three situations in which attribution is essential:

(1) *Attribute all material if there is any reasonable doubt as to its accuracy.* If you *saw* a man jump from the Golden Gate Bridge, then simply describe what you saw. But if you did not see the man jump, and your story relies upon the words of two or three witnesses who say they saw him jump, *attribute* the description to them. Tomorrow another witness may turn up saying that the man was pushed.

Attribution should be used whenever a conclusion appears to be a matter of opinion: Police "theorize" that the burglar hid in the museum at closing time; the fire marshal "said he believed" that the fire was started by an arsonist. Remember that experts can be wrong.

Attributing opinions also helps reporters guard against inadvertently editorializing. Don't write, "The 'Star Wars' system would help prevent war." Opinions may differ. Write instead, *"The President said* the 'Star Wars' system would help prevent war."

Attribution helps avoid the appearance of mind reading. A reporter cannot know what people really think or feel, only what they *say*, or how they *seem*. Use attribution to make that distinction clear. Don't write, "The President *feels* that new taxes are required." Only the President himself knows what he feels. Write instead, "The President *told reporters* he feels that new taxes will be required," or simply, "The President *proposed* new taxes."

(2) *Attribute any material that tends to damage someone's reputation.* When reporting something bad about someone it's only fair to attribute the material to its source so that readers can judge its validity. If, say, a school principal is described in court as "paranoid," it makes

---

Then, it recaps some background:

In May, Mr. Parente revoked permits for recreational facilities for Soviet citizens living at or visiting the estate, Killenworth, in Glen Cove. The ban came after published reports that the top floor of the 49-room mansion was filled with advanced surveillance equipment used to eavesdrop on telephone calls and other communications related to Long Island's defense and high-technology industries.

The Glen Cove City Council voted 6 to 1 to support Mr. Parente.

Then, it returns to the fresh news:

Today, an adviser to United States Mission to the United Nations, Sol Kuttner, delivered the State Department's letter to Mr. Parente. . . .

The more prominently the story has played in the past, the less background is required. But always provide *some* background, and write it directly, so that the story will make sense even to a reader who's just returned from Bora-Bora and hasn't seen a newspaper in a month.

a lot of difference whether the testimony came from a court-appointed psychiatrist or a student the principal expelled.

Attribution is especially important in matters involving crime. A suspect's guilt or innocence is determined by a judge and jury, not by the police. In the story earlier in this chapter about the mayor's son being arrested on a charge of possession of drugs, the police said they stopped his car because it had a broken taillight, and that they searched the trunk of the car when the young man began "acting strangely." In the trunk, they said, "they found four ounces of marijuana and a small quantity of a white powder that they suspect is cocaine." Don't write:

> . . . The police stopped Spalding's car **because its taillight was broken** and searched it **after Spalding began acting strangely**. In the trunk **they found** four ounces of marijuana and a small quantity of cocaine.

You don't *know* if that was what happened. The police may have stopped the car because of the taillight, or they may have framed the boy to embarrass the mayor, set him up and planted the drugs. What you *do* know is what the police *say* happened. So write the story as follows:

> The 18-year-old son of Mayor Fulton G. Spalding was arrested by Hapsville police last night on a charge of possession of drugs.
>
> Herman F. Spalding, a senior at Hapsville High School, was driving his car north on Sickler Road when he was stopped at about 10 P.M. because of a broken taillight, **the police said.**
>
> Spalding started "acting strangely," **according to Sgt. Thomas Flawson of the traffic squad,** whereupon the police searched his car. In the trunk, **Flawson said,** they found four ounces of marijuana and a small quantity of a white powder that *the police said they suspected* was cocaine.

(3) *Attribute all quotations*. Any copy that appears between quotation marks should be attributed, so that readers know who said it. Quotations lacking attribution are called "blind" or "orphan" quotes, and are to be avoided.

SUMMARY

In literature, stories often begin with the less important details and build to climaxes at the end. Breaking news stories do the opposite: They start with their climaxes and leave the less important details for last. This is known as the *inverted pyramid* style of organization.

To structure the body of a breaking news story, present material in descending order of its newsworthiness, with the most important information highest, the next most important lower down, and so on, to the end. One way to approach this is to think in terms of "backing up" the lead, recounting first the aspects of the news that deserve the strongest emphasis in the lead.

In complicated news—for which the lead cannot tell everything in one sentence—the story may have to be told several times, in a series of miniature inverted pyramids, each delving into more specifics than the one before. There should be no repetition in such stories.

Occasionally, breaking news can be told chronologically, with the details given in the order in which they occurred. This works well in detailing complicated action stories, provided that the chronological section is preceded by an inverted pyramid.

Some breaking news can be told in an *un*inverted pyramid. These *news features*, as they are called, are organized like the feature stories described in Chapter 9. A reporter may choose to "featurize" a breaking story when the news is a little old and readers would be more interested in the background, or when a particular element of the story seems especially sad, funny or interesting, so that it deserves to be emphasized at the expense of other perhaps equally newsworthy aspects of the story.

Ongoing stories should be led with fresh material, but also should recap what's happened before. To lead the readers through the story, limit each sentence and each paragraph to a single subject, and signal changes in subject through the use of topic sentences.

8

GENERAL ASSIGNMENT NEWSWRITING

Most reporters start their careers working on "general assignment"—that is, covering a wide variety of stories rather than specializing in a particular kind of news or "beat." The stories that general assignment reporters are most frequently assigned include obituaries and those about accidents; fires; crimes; speeches; reports; press releases and press conferences; and meetings. In this chapter we discuss how to handle these basic news assignments.

OBITUARIES

An obituary—or "obit"—is an account of someone's life published on the occasion of his or her death. The occurrence of death constitutes breaking news, but most of the obit takes a long view, summing up the accomplishments of a lifetime and serving, as one reporter put it, as a way of "passing along the culture from generation to generation."

Some papers, among them the *Louisville Courier-Journal* and the *Baltimore Sun*, employ specialists who write nothing but obituaries. Others, like the *Los Angeles Times*, have an obit editor who parcels out assignments among the general staff. Not every reporter relishes reporting on the dead, but most, when assigned to a stint on the obit desk, take care to do their very best work. One reason is respect for the dead; it's only fitting that an individual's final, and perhaps only, appearance in print should be accurately and sensitively composed. The

127

other reason is respect for the living; obits are read closely by the friends and family of the deceased.

Most obituaries consist of only a few paragraphs. Much of the information they report comes from undertakers, part of whose job is to gather facts about the deceased and convey them to the press. If further information is needed, the reporter may call the family, who are less likely to resent the intrusion than to be grateful for the journalist's desire to be accurate.

The death of a prominent person calls for a longer obit, sometimes too long to be written on deadline. Reporter Lee Dembart once produced a polished 2000-word obituary of philosopher Bertrand Russell in less than four hours; rather than trust to such virtuoso performances, however, editors prefer to have the lengthy obits of important people prepared in advance. The wire services and larger newspapers write obits of the famous well ahead of time, and keep them on file to await the day of death. Alden Whitman, a highly regarded obit writer for *The New York Times*, interviewed many prominent people to garner material "for use at a future date"—a euphemism for the one story about themselves they would never read: their obituary. This allowed Whitman to include original quotations and firsthand description. His obit of painter Pablo Picasso is a good example:

> Picasso was a short, squat man with broad muscular shoulders and arms. He was most proud of his small hands and feet and of his hairy chest. In old age his body was firm and compact, and his cannonball head, which was almost bald, gleamed like bronze. Set into it were deep black eyes of such penetration and alertness that they became his trademark. . . .

Obituaries are not eulogies; obit writers report the bad along with the good. Whitman called scientist and humanitarian Albert Schweitzer "thin skinned . . . grumpy . . . brusque," and said he had a "formidable sense of his own importance . . . and a do-good paternalism toward Africans." An obit, Whitman said, should be like a well-focused snapshot: "If the snapshot is clear, the viewer gets a quick fix on this subject, his attainments, his shortcomings and his times."

Obits are usually placed on a page of their own, but if the deceased was sufficiently newsworthy, the obit may be tacked on to a straight news account of the death that starts on page one. If the death resulted from a newsworthy story, such as a major accident or a homicide, the obit may run as a sidebar to the news story.

A standard obituary lead can be based on the classic five Ws: *Who* died? Give the name, age and address, along with a brief description of who the person was and what he or she did. *Where* did he or she die? Was it at home, in a hospital, on the street? *When?* Usually this means yesterday or today. Sometimes, though, it was a week earlier—on a trip, for example—and the death is only now being made public. *How* did the person die—of *what* cause? Squeamish about disclosing the cause of death, newspapers used to resort to euphemisms: A "long illness" meant cancer. "Died suddenly" meant a heart attack. Now, most prefer to be blunt.

When identifying the deceased in the lead, first mention the most newsworthy thing he or she accomplished in life. This might, for instance, involve a long-ago brush with fame:

> Albert Polk, 78, *who in 1934 won a flagpole-sitting contest* with a record 56 days aloft, died of a heart attack yesterday at the Alexander Hamilton Home in Hapsville.

> Arnold Turbot, 66, a *retired floor superintendent for the Arkwright Tool Company*, died of cancer yesterday at his home, 45 Wamback Drive.

If the deceased was neither prominent nor newsworthy, the body of the obit can be written chronologically, from cradle to the grave.

> Turbot was born April 16, 1918, in Glasgow, Pa., and moved to Hapsville as a young boy. A graduate of George W. Plunkitt High School, he joined the tool company as a janitor in 1946 and retired last year.
> He was a communicant of Our Lady of the Sacred Heart Church and a member of the Ancient Order of Hibernians and the Superintendents Club of Hapsville.

Always name the "survivors"—the living members of the deceased's immediate family.

> Turbot is survived by his wife, the former Emma Foley; two sons, William, of Roanoke, Virginia, and Thomas, of Utica, New York; a daughter, Mrs. Hazel Lipinsky, of Hapsville; a brother, Samuel, of Ames, Iowa; and eight grandchildren.

Finally, mention the wake, if there is one, and the funeral services, so friends can come to pay their respects.

> Calling hours will be at the Alderson Funeral Home, 20 High St., tomorrow from 9 to 11 A.M. and 3 to 5 P.M.
> The funeral is to be held Thursday at 10 A.M. at Our Lady of the Sacred Heart Church. Burial will be in All Souls Cemetery.

The obituaries of prominent persons usually emphasize their lives over the details of their deaths, as this AP obit of a Marine Corps General illustrates:

WASHINGTON, D.C. (AP)—General David Shoup, 78, a former commandant of the Marine Corps and winner of the Medal of Honor who broke with the military establishment to criticize U.S. involvement in the Vietnam War, died Thursday of a heart ailment in Alexandria, Va., the Pentagon announced today.

The Navy ordered its flags flown at half-staff until his burial Monday at Arlington National Cemetery.

As commander of the November 20, 1943, assault on Japanese-held Beito Island, one of three making up Tarawa in the Gilbert Islands in the Pacific, Shoup brought the Marines through one of the war's bloodiest battles. A colonel, he took over command of a division when its headquarters could not get ashore.

Wounded in the leg, Shoup "fearlessly exposed himself" to rally his men to charge the heavily fortified island and reinforced our hard-pressed, thinly held lines," the citation accompanying his Medal of Honor said.

Shoup served as commandant of the Corps from 1959 to 1963.

In 1967, the retired Shoup broke with the military establishment to criticize United States involvement in the Vietnam War, saying it was "pure unadulterated poppycock" that U.S. security was at stake.

A suggestion about style: Because obits deal with one individual, it's easy to make the mistake of writing repeated sentences that start with the third person.

> . . . *He* came here with his parents as a young man. *He* graduated from Dewey High School and began work as a riveter at the Apex Tool Company. *He* was made a supervisor in 1962 and retired in 1975.
>
> *He* was a member of the First Lutheran Church. *He* was also a member of the Tiptop Bowling Club and the Riveters of America. . . .

Instead, vary the patterns of the sentences so they don't all sound the same.

> . . . Moving here with his parents as a young man, Mr. Munson graduated from Dewey High School and began work as a riveter for the Apex Tool Company. In 1962 he was made a supervisor; he retired in 1975.
>
> Mr. Munson was a member of the First Lutheran Church, the Tiptop Bowling Club and the Riveters of America. . . .

ACCIDENTS

Information about automobile accidents comes either from reports filed by the traffic squad of the local police department or, if the accident is serious and time permits, from the reporter's going out and talking to the police at the scene. Here, too, some of the five Ws come in handy:

Who, if anyone, was injured? Get their names, ages, addresses and, if possible, their occupations. Check the clips to determine if the injured were prominent figures. A fatal car crash on a country road in Westchester County, New York, made the front page of nearly every paper in the country—because the man killed was John D. Rockefeller III.

What are the injuries? This information usually comes from the charge nurse in the hospital's emergency room or admitting office. Ask the nurse for the nature of patients' injuries and for the condition of the victims. The same sort of injury—a concussion, for example—can put one person in satisfactory condition and leave another in critical condition, which means close to death.

How did the accident occur? The police rarely witness an accident. They determine how it happened by interviewing eyewitnesses and those involved. They may also try to reconstruct an auto accident from clues, such as the length and direction of skid marks or the way a guardrail is bent. Reporters generally rely on the most authoritative version, attributing the information to its source.

The standard five W lead and inverted-pyramid format work well for accident stories. Start with the heart of the news—the injuries—rather than damage to the car or manner in which the accident occurred:

A 35-year-old mother was seriously injured in a two-car accident today on Lincoln Street at Mooreland Hill Drive as she was driving her 5-year-old daughter to school.

This lead uses the phrase "in a two-car accident" because in this instance we do not know exactly how the accident occurred, and we do not wish to prejudice the case either way. We also include the daughter in the lead, even though she was unhurt, because many readers drive their children to school and are concerned about highway safety.

The body of the story fills in the details, generally in the same order as the lead.

Mrs. Polly Vibberts, of 35 Shuttle Meadow Ave., was reported to be in critical condition at Memorial Hospital with head injuries. Her daughter, Susan, was unharmed.

Next, discuss *how* the accident occurred:

Mrs. Vibberts's car collided with one driven by Curtis Pease, 56, of 34 Percival Ave., at about 10:30 A.M., the police said.

Pease was quoted by the police as saying the Vibberts car ran through a stop sign on Lincoln Road and crashed into him. Damage to both cars was extensive.

Note that the police don't claim to know just how the accident occurred. They didn't see it. The sole adult witnesses were Mr. Pease and Mrs. Vibberts, if she survives. All we know is what he said happened.

If an accident is sufficiently bizarre, the *how* aspect may outweigh the *who*. The unusual nature of this car crash obliged the Manchester, New Hampshire, *Union Leader* to emphasize the *how* of the crash before going into the nature of the injuries:

DUMMER—A Berlin family of five was hospitalized Saturday after its car went off the side of Route 16 and hit two trees that prevented the vehicle from falling 60 feet into the Androscoggin River.

The Paul Lacroix family was traveling north at about 4:10 P.M. when their 1982 Subaru station wagon veered off the river side of the road about 2.6 miles north of the Milan-Dummer town line.

Dummer Police Chief Norman Roy said the car veered towards the right side of the road, then went off the left side and over the embankment before hitting the trees.

The injuries suffered by Lacroix, 32, were unknown, but his wife Dianne suffered a cracked pelvis and internal injuries. Their children, Jason, 8, had head contusions; Joel, 3, had facial injuries and Justin, 7 months, had a broken leg.

All five were admitted in Androscoggin Valley Hospital.

Roy said the family "was very lucky those two birch trees were there. Otherwise they probably would have been down into the river."

Passers-by saw the car go off the road and went to a nearby house to call Milan Emergency Service. Also responding to the scene were Roy, Deputy Fred Plant, Trooper Dennis Tremblay and two officers of the Milan Police Department.

The accident is under investigation by Dummer police.

FIRES

The scene of a fire may look chaotic, but procedures for fighting fires are generally well organized. Fire departments respond to calls in terms of alarms: the more alarms, the more force is mobilized to put out the fire. In big cities, one alarm normally draws a unit of three vehicles, referred to in fire jargon as "apparatus." These consist of an engine, also known as a pumper, which carries the hose and pumps water from the hydrant; a ladder truck, which has aerial equipment for reaching a building's upper floors; and a car carrying the battalion chief in charge of the unit. Reaching the fire, the chief can decide if the blaze is large enough to warrant calling for additional apparatus. If so, additional alarms may be issued. A "three alarmer," then, might involve six apparatus, twenty-four firefighters and three chiefs, along with ambulance and rescue trucks.

The firefighters riding with the engines usually arrive first. They run a hose into the building. Nozzle handlers direct the spray. "Vent men" head for the roof and open up a hole so heat and smoke can escape. Other firefighters search for people in the building.

Reporters usually direct their questions to the fire marshal for information at the scene. The marshal's job is not to fight the fire but to investigate how it got started, so he may have time to answer questions while the fire is still being brought under control. Make your questions brief and to the point:

Who was hurt? The fire marshal may not have the names of the victims, but he should know how many victims there were and to what hospital they were taken. You can get their names and injuries from the hospital emergency ward.

Who discovered the fire? Because the marshal has to investigate the cause, he's probably going to know who discovered the fire and called in the alarm. Interview that person.

What caused the fire? The marshal may not know for sure, but he should have a pretty good guess—which can go in the story, as long as you label it as such. Is there anything suspicious about the fire? Arson is a serious crime, and if officials think the blaze might have been deliberately set, the angle should probably go in the lead.

How did the fire spread? A complete fire story should describe how the blaze spread from one part of the building to another, and how firefighters tried to contain it. When did it start? When did they get it under control?

Fighting the fire is part of the story, especially if it involved acts of heroism. Firefighters have one of the most dangerous of all jobs; they run twice the risk of getting killed or injured as do the police. When they go to unusual lengths to do their jobs, they deserve credit for it.

Try also to ascertain who owns the building, how much damage it is estimated to have suffered (this can be a dollar figure), and any further consequences of the fire, such as lost personal property, people left homeless who must be given shelter, and whether the cause of the fire warrants warning readers about how to prevent similar fires. During the oil shortages of the mid-1970s, for example, many fires were touched off by exploding cans of gasoline that drivers stored in their homes or in the trunks of their cars for use in emergencies. News accounts of such fires often included warnings by officials to avoid the dangerous practice of hoarding gasoline.

CRIMES

Accurate information about the commission of crimes can be difficult to come by. Crime is an emotional matter; accounts by eyewitnesses and victims often differ. Moreover, as the story goes through several tellings—the victim tells the detective, the detective tells the reporter, the reporter writes it up—it may become further distorted.

With serious crimes, try to check the facts with those involved and with eyewitnesses. Crime victims sometimes hesitate to talk to reporters; they've already been hurt enough and may not wish to have it all recounted in print. When you explain to them, however, that you've already gotten most of the information from the police and you just want to make sure it's accurate, they'll usually cooperate. At the police end, read the incident report on the case and talk to the detective in charge. Writing the story, make sure readers know where the information came from—from the people who saw what happened, or second-hand, from the accounts of police officers who arrived later.

Minor crimes may be written as briefs and gathered together in a column titled "Police Blotter" or the like. An example follows:

> A stuffed bear reported missing from the Red Hand Pub, Skokie, Sunday morning, was returned yesterday by members of the Pi Kappa Alpha fraternity at Northwestern University, said pub owner Lars Beck.

> A red ten-speed bicycle belonging to Fred Franklin, of 34 Ipswitch Lane, was reported stolen yesterday from the rack in front of Tommy's Pizza, 156 Long Acre Drive, between 12 noon and 1 P.M. Its value was estimated at $500.

More serious crimes, like burglaries, assaults and robberies, call for more thorough stories. Usually these are written in the inverted-pyramid format.

Burglary

A burglary consists of breaking into a building or a car for the purpose of stealing something. If the police fail to catch people with the goods, the charge is sometimes reduced to attempted burglary, or perhaps trespassing. A burglary story should answer three basic questions: *How did the burglars get in? What did they do inside? What was taken?* The owner tells the police what was stolen, so attribute that information to the owner. Burglary victims sometimes inflate the size of their loss in hopes of enlarging the insurance settlement; readers should not be left with the impression that the police can vouch for what was stolen.

The following burglary story leads with what was taken:

> Five cases of cigarettes and about $500 in cash were reported stolen during an overnight break-in at Danny's variety store, 141 Seventh Ave.

Then, the story details how the burglars got in and what they did inside:

> Police said the thief or thieves climbed to the roof of a shed in the rear and broke a window. The storeowner, Danny Cohen, said the coin boxes of four video games and a juke box were rifled. The cigarettes amounted to 120 cartons, he said, with a value of about $800.

The lead emphasizes that the burglary was *reported* today, because that is the freshest information, and we don't know just when the break-in occurred. The body refers to "thief or thieves" because we don't know how many were involved.

Because burglaries are among the most common varieties of crime, reporters learn to look for ways to give them a fresh or unusual twist, as in this *Milwaukee Journal* account:

> Milwaukee County Circuit Judge Leah Lampone said Thursday that she felt the same as many of the victims who had appeared in her court.
>
> Police reported Thursday that Lampone and her husband, Kevin O'Donnell, lost $50, a checkbook and identification papers to a burglar who broke into their N. Lake Drive home sometime Tuesday night or early Wednesday, while she, her husband and their child slept upstairs.
>
> Her feelings after the incident reminded her of what many victims have told her, Lampone said.
>
> Lampone told police that the missing items were taken from her purse by a burglar who removed a downstairs storm window, raised an inner window and climbed inside the house. A dentist who lives nearby later recovered the empty purse.

Assault

The criminal charge levied in an assault case depends on the severity of the attack. "Simple" assault is an attack by one person on another, usually with fists. Assault "with a dangerous weapon" involves the use of a gun, knife, club or other instrument. "Aggravated" assault occurs during the commission of another crime, such as when a stick-up man beats up a clerk while robbing a store. In an extremely severe attack the charge may be assault "with attempt to commit murder" or "attempted murder."

The difference between an assault story and one involving murder is very often the bad luck of the victim; murder victims are those who die of their wounds. This *Atlanta Constitution* account of a deadly bar fight begins with the essential news—that a man has been killed—before it goes into the assault that caused the death.

An Atlanta man was killed early Sunday morning when a woman allegedly threw a knife during a fight in a restaurant and he was struck in the chest, police said.

Ricky Askin, 20, of 666 Foundry St. N.W., died at Grady Memorial Hospital after the incident, said Atlanta police spokesperson David R. Yood.

Arrested and charged with murder in the slaying was Helene E. Atkinson, 27, of 2046 Seattle Circle S.E., Yood said. She was being held without bond.

According to Yood, Ms. Atkinson threw a knife during a fight at a restaurant at 196 Vine St. N.W., and the knife struck Askin in the chest. Yood said that when a bottle was thrown during the melee, Ms. Atkinson apparently thought the bottle was thrown at her, and she threw the knife.

Robbery

Robbery is the taking of property by force or by threat of force. The crime differs from theft in that it entails a direct confrontation between the robber and the victim. *Theft* involves stealing when the victim is not around, or at least not looking, as in a shoplifting incident.

The Ws of a major robbery include *who*, if anyone, was hurt? *What* was taken? *How* did the robbery occur? *How* did the victims respond? *What* did the robbers look like? *How* did they make their escape? And *what* are the police doing to catch them?

When covering a robbery, try to talk to the victims, either in person or over the phone. Confronting a robber is a scary experience; readers will want to hear how people reacted. If the incident resulted in someone's getting hurt, that angle would lead the story.

This crime story involved a substantial amount of money and no injuries, so its lead enumerated what was taken:

Nearly $45,000 in cash and jewelry was taken from a Grove Street jeweler's yesterday by two masked bandits who smashed display cases and threatened clerks with pistols, the police said.

Then it discussed *how* the incident happened:

The pair entered the Better Buy Jewelry, 13 Grove St., at about 4:30 P.M. and pulled what the police described as sawed-off shotguns. They told customers in the store and three sales people to lie down on the floor in back of the counter. The thieves scooped cash from the register and display cases to get at watches, necklaces and other jewelry.

The store owner, Arnaud Floridette, said the men told them to keep their heads down for five minutes.

"They said they had someone watching the store, and if anyone moved it would be the last thing we did," he said. "I would have stayed there a week if they'd told me to. By the time we looked up they were gone."

Who the robbers were was the next topic in the story:

The bandits wore baseball caps and women's stockings pulled down over their faces. They were described as about 6 feet tall and wearing dark clothing. No one in the store saw how they got away, the police said.

Then, more was revealed about what was taken:

Floridette said they took about $1000 in cash and $44,000 worth of jewelry, including about a dozen diamonds.

Finally, an important element in most robbery stories was addressed: What are police doing to catch the thieves?

Detective Lt. Anthony C. O'Dougherty of the Hapsville robbery squad said an alarm had been put out for the pair but that he did not have much hope of an arrest. "In these cases," he said, "unless you get them at the scene, nine times out of ten they've gotten away with it."

WARMING UP COLD FACTS

Statistics are like leftovers—more digestible if warmed up. For the newswriter this means turning cold numbers into personal, human terms.

An FBI annual report on crime for a recent year included these statistical summaries:

As in recent years, murder victims were male in approximately 3 of every 4 instances. . . . Firearms predominated as the weapons most often used in the commission of murders. . . . Nationwide, 63 percent of the murders were committed through the use of firearms. Handguns were the weapons used in 50 percent of all murders. A comparative study for the past 5 years showed a decrease in the use of firearms to commit murder. . . . Fifty-two percent of the murder victims were acquainted with their assailants, and 1 of every 5 victims was related to the offender. The greatest percentage of murders (43 percent) resulted from arguments.

Here's how Ronald J. Ostrow of the *Los Angeles Times* warmed these cold figures into a readable lead:

WASHINGTON, D.C.—Portrait of a murder: Odds are that the victim will be male and he and the killer will have known each other and have been arguing before the slaying.

There is a 20 percent chance that the killer and the victim will be related.

Most likely, a firearm will be the death weapon, though somewhat less likely than five years ago. The handgun by far will be the probable instrument of death.

The portrait is sketched by the FBI annual study of crime in the United States. . . .

A newly published almanac might not seem like a promising source for material for a bouncy feature, but an Associated Press reporter who took the trouble to study the almanac's tables of data on American communities came up with this lead:

CHICAGO (AP)—If you are looking for a drink, Eau Claire, Wisconsin, is the best place in the country, with one neighborhood tavern for every 629 residents.

If you are a teetotaller, you might want to move to Florence, Alabama, where the U.S. Census Bureau could not find any taverns to count.

Hay fever sufferers will be sneeze-free in any Alaska city, but Coldwater, Michigan, has the highest ragweed pollen index of any place in the nation.

These tidbits and hundreds of others are found in the new "Places Rated Almanac" published by Rand McNally & Co. . . .

SPEECHES

In the nineteenth century public oratory was a major form of entertainment, and newspapers devoted column after column to notable addresses. Today, there's seldom space for that. Anything less significant than the president's State of the Union Address must be reported in brief, often in only a few hundred words of newspaper copy or a half minute of air time. For the journalist, this means building the speech story strictly on the news. The speaker's main theme is not necessarily the lead; the real news may be something the speaker says at the end of the speech, or even in response to a question after the speech is over.

Reporters covering a formal address by a public figure are often provided with an advance copy of the text. This makes their job easier: They can read the speech ahead of time, underline key phrases, and start thinking about a possible lead. Then they listen carefully to the speech, following along and marking any deviation the speaker makes from the text. If the speaker deletes a passage written by the speechwriters and already included in the prepared text, reporters may choose to report that fact, leaving it to the readers to ponder why the passage was excluded.

A speech story begins, of course, with the *lead*. Then, typically, it backs up the lead with a *foundation quote*, adds *background* to put the speech in context and goes into further detail about the main points of the speech, in the *body*. It may also include any *reaction* the speech may have drawn.

The lead normally concerns the most newsworthy thing that was said. The mere fact that somebody gave a speech is almost never news:

> The President today delivered a thirty-minute address to a conference of Baptist ministers.

Who cares? A President delivers lots of speeches. Ticking off a list of the topics covered is not particularly newsworthy either:

> The President today discussed taxes and freedom of religion in a speech to a conference of Baptist ministers.

The idea, as always, is to work the substance of the *news* into the lead:

> President Reagan today told a conference of Baptist ministers that he will work to restore prayer to the schools and to maintain tax exemptions for churches and church schools.

The circumstances of the speech may deserve mention in the lead, if only to establish the context in which the remarks were made. But avoid cluttering the lead with incidental details, like the italicized material in the lead that follows:

> Governor Henry T. Willard *said in a speech to 150 students and faculty members at a meeting of the Political Science Club of Hapsville University* last night that he favors doubling the state tax on cigarettes, liquor and beauty aids to help support local school systems.

Instead, omit the inessentials and get right to the heart of the news:

> Governor Henry T. Willard told a Hapsville University audience last night that he favors doubling the state tax on cigarettes, liquor and beauty aids to help support local school systems.

When the speaker is the president, the governor or another prominent person, the lead usually begins with the *who* element. But when the speaker is less well known, the lead may emphasize *what* was said, as does this lead to a speech story in the Chicago *Sun-Times*:

> Illinois could face a critical across-the-board shortage of teachers beginning five years from now, the dean of the state's largest teacher education college warned yesterday.

Next can come the *foundation quote*: a strong, lively quotation that backs up the central point of the lead. It belongs high in the story—in the lead or somewhere in the first few paragraphs:

> "The next 24 months are critical for us to recruit students," said William S. Dunifon, education dean at Illinois State University. "If we are not successful, we will face the unhappy and destructive circumstances of a shortage so critical that public policy makers may opt for the 'any warm body in a classroom' approach as they did in the past."
>
> Dunifon forecast the shortage while he and other university officials outlined for reporters an agenda for improving teacher education at ISU and its sister universities in the Board of Regents system.

Now you should add some *background*—information to help readers interpret the meaning and significance of the speech. Background is usually produced by reporters' digging up clips in the newspaper morgue and interviewing the speaker and others:

> Chicago and downstate schools already have a shortage of mathematics and science teachers, something felt throughout the country.
>
> Chicago also is short of substitute teachers and fully qualified bilingual teachers—a problem shared with other urban systems—and fears it won't come up with enough speech therapists, social workers, psychologists and nurses.

The *body* of the speech story spells the details of what the speaker said—all the news that fits:

> Dunifon also recommended higher pay for teachers. Statewide, the average starting salary was $14,780 in the last school year. The starting salary in Chicago's public schools was $15,471.
>
> He called for a starting salary of $20,000, which the General Assembly rejected in June as too costly. Dunifon said top salaries should be "parallel" with administrators', to keep gifted teachers. He suggested a range of between $45,000 and $50,000.
>
> Dunifon predicted that 25 to 28 percent of the state's teaching force, which now numbers about 118,000, will retire between 1990 and 1994.

The *reaction* of the audience and the larger community also belongs in a speech story. The reporter covering the Dunifon speech called around and found that the teacher shortage wasn't quite as universal as Dunifon had said, and that the solution he proposed might make the problem worse:

Suburban school districts generally have not faced shortages, said Supt. Ron Barnes of Palos High School District 23. They have attracted math and science teachers from downstate and parochial schools, he said.

Some educators also predicted that higher standards for teacher education would put a damper on supply.

Dunifon, however, had mentioned in his speech some evidence that rebutted this criticism, so the reporter included that, too:

But Dunifon said that since ISU raised requirements the quality of applications has improved, while the quantity remained stable.

A speech story can report not only what the speaker said, but what the information *means*. This *Washington Post* speech story does just that by emphasizing the why or how element in the lead:

Education Secretary William J. Bennett last night continued the administration's push for public schools to teach civic and moral values, telling an audience that American children must be told that this country is morally superior to the Soviet Union.

In a speech prepared for the Eagle Forum Leadership Conference, the New Right education lobby founded by conservative activist Phyllis Schafly, Bennett defended himself against critics of his assertion that religion belongs in schools as a way to instill children with basic values.

Next came the foundation quote:

"I was accused of trying to promote my own 'brand of Christianity' and of seeing myself as a messenger 'heaven-sent to silence the heathen,' Bennett said. "For supporting the free expression of voluntary prayer in our public schools, I was called an 'ayatollah.' "

He continued, "Clearly, our schools should not attempt to inculcate sectarian beliefs, or support any one religion over another. . . . But just because our public schools do not teach religion does not

mean we wish them to be places devoid of respect for religion, for the Judeo-Christian tradition, or for the values that so clearly emerged from it."

The values he said should be taught are "patriotism, self-discipline, thrift, honesty, and respect for elders." He added: "To be specific, one should know, for example, that there *is* a moral difference between the United States and the Soviet Union. . . ."

In the story's last paragraph, the reporter noted a connection between the speech and the Reagan administration's education policy:

Bennett and his under secretary, Gary Bauer, have made value education a cornerstone of a "fall offensive." Bauer two weeks ago told an Ohio anti-pornography

convention that lack of values in public schools was the principal cause of a breakdown of America's social fabric.

The most readable speech stories alternate paragraphs of direct quotation, interpretation, reaction and description. Several consecutive paragraphs quoting the President on the federal budget might try anyone's patience; so might several paragraphs of background, or of description of the setting of the speech. But weaving all these together can produce a sprightly dispatch, like this one from *The New York Times*:

Lead states the essence of the news	BILLINGS, MONT., Aug. 11—President Reagan warned today that a failure by Congress to approve new taxes would lead to "larger budget deficits, higher rates and higher unemployment."
Background, reaction and color	In his strongest exhortation yet for the three-year, $98.9 billion tax bill, Mr. Reagan told a boisterous, friendly crowd of 12,000 that most of the increase would arise from correcting "unintended tax advantages." These, he said, had accrued from "sloppiness" in past tax bills, including the tax cut measure he pushed through Congress last year.
	Other proposed revisions would improve collection of taxes "legitimately owed" but not paid by Americans, Mr. Reagan said, asserting that only $18 billion of the tax increase would fall on "the average American."
Foundation quote	"The bottom line is this," he said. "Would you rather reduce deficits and interest rates by raising revenue from those who are not now paying their fair share? Or would you rather accept larger budget deficits and interest rates and higher unemployment?"
Background	In Washington, White House officials said Mr. Reagan had made a "pretty firm" decision to give a nationwide televised address Monday, calling for support of the bill. At the same time, political tensions mounted over the White House's "hardball" tactics against Republican opponents of the tax increase.
Audience reaction	For Mr. Reagan, today's speech marked a first for his presidency: an open declaration favoring increases in at least some taxes. Appearing somewhat uncomfortable in this role, Mr. Reagan discussed the tax bill in a flat, somewhat defensive fashion. Most audience applause, in the main speech he gave today, was in response to his customary one-liners and crowd-pleasing jabs at Washington, D.C.
Body of speech	"If I could correct four decades of fiscal irresponsibility in one year, I'd go back to show business as a magician," Mr. Reagan declared as his audience burst into cheers. "You know, it might be more fun pulling rabbits out of a hat than jackasses out of the way in Washington."
	Acknowledging at another point his unhappiness with high federal budget deficits, Mr. Reagan brought laughter when he said: "For a conservative President like me to have to put his arms around a multibillion-dollar deficit—well, it's like holding your nose and embracing a pig. And believe me, that budget deficit is as slippery as a greased pig."
Description	The President's appeal for new taxes was accompanied by a surprising display of presidential pageantry in a Hollywood-style celebration of the 100th anniversary of California

Billings and Yellowstone County replete with singers and dancers in sequins and feathers, Indians in native dress and high school bands.

REPORTS, PRESS RELEASES AND PRESS CONFERENCES

Organizations and individuals issue press releases and reports and hold press conferences to present findings of fact or to express viewpoints on issues in their spheres of interest. In our bureaucratic society, tons of such paper are issued daily. Most of it gets "spiked"—discarded by editors as unnewsworthy—but the remainder still amounts to a substantial portion of the day's news.

The fact that someone held a news conference or released a report is seldom newsworthy in itself. There are, of course, exceptions: President Nixon was so reluctant to meet the press that his merely scheduling a press conference made headlines. The reclusive Howard Hughes also made news merely by agreeing to hold a news conference over the telephone. Normally, however, the real news lies in the content, not the context.

The first rule in handling reports and press releases is to *digest* their contents before trying to write a story. As we discuss in Chapter 11, David Brinkley advises reporters to read the release, then set it aside and *think* about it. What is the essence of this material? The answer to that question is the key to writing the lead.

To digest means to *condense*. Most reports and press releases are much too long-winded by newspaper standards. Following is a typical press release:

NARRATICONG LODGE #9
ORDER OF THE ARROW

THOMAS A. EDISON
COUNCIL #352
Boy Scouts of America   1395 K Oaktree Drive
P.O. Drawer L   North Brunswick, N.J.
Edison, N.J. 08817

The Home News Publishing Company
123 How Lane
New Brunswick, New Jersey

Dear Sirs:

Narraticong Lodge #9, Order of the Arrow, B.S.A., would appreciate your help in publicizing our annual banquet which will take place in December. The banquet will be held on December 20, at the Neilson Dining Hall of Douglass College in New Brunswick. The dinner, which will consist of roast sirloin, will be served at 6:30 P.M. Our guest speaker will be Wally Dallenbach, Indianapolis race car driver and this year's New Jersey Athlete of the Year. Tickets are $6.00 a person and are available to anybody calling banquet chair Doug Weber at 828-1234. The Lodge would be most appreciative of an article or a listing in your Calender of Events. A reply, either negative or positive, would be greatly appreciated. Thank you for your time and support.

Yours in Scouting,

Richard A. Olsen Jr.,
Lodge Vice Chief

The news item written from this release consisted of a single sentence:

Wally Dallenbach, Indianapolis 500 racing car driver and New Jersey "Athlete of the Year," will speak at a Boy Scout banquet Tuesday, December, 20 at 6:30 P.M. in the Neilson Dining Hall of Douglass College.

Generally, the lead should stress *what* the release or report says, rather than who is saying it. There are exceptions, of course. When the United States Surgeon General's Office first issued a report linking cigarette smoking and cancer, for example, news stories often began, "The U.S. Surgeon General warned today that . . ." because the Surgeon General's prestige added considerable weight to the then-controversial thesis that smoking causes disease. But usually, it's preferable to start the lead with the *content* of the report, as did this lead from the Manchester, New Hampshire *Union Leader*:

LONDONERRY—Surface and subsurface waters in the vicinity of a landfill closed two years ago have been contaminated by hazardous wastes and the cost of restoring the area could reach $15 million, according to a report from Goldberg-Zoino Associates, hydrological consultants of Newton, Massachusetts.

Few readers would have gotten far had the lead begun as the report itself did:

Goldberg-Zoino Associates, hydrological consultants of Newton, Massachusetts, reported today that . . .

In this press release from the Rand institute, Rand itself looms large:

NEWS RELEASE
THE
NEW YORK CITY
RAND INSTITUTE   545 MADISON AVENUE NEW YORK 10022
(212) 758-2244

For further information contact:
Ben Martin

FOR RELEASE MONDAY, MAY 8, AMs

EFFECTIVE AND INEFFECTIVE POLICE OFFICERS CAN
BE SPOTTED EARLY, RAND INSTITUTE STUDY FINDS

NEW YORK, N.Y.—A study by the New York-Rand institute
shows that New York City police officers who perform either
effectively or ineffectively can be accurately identified during
their first months on the force.

Rewritten to put the news first—and to brighten the prose style—the lead to
the Rand story read like this:

> Rookie police officers usually demonstrate whether they're going to be good or
> bad cops during their first few months on the force, says a study by the New York
> City Rand Institute.

The news story should *translate* any jargon or technical language into terms
general readers can understand. A report from the Kitt Peak National Observa-
tory announcing that "a QSO redshift of $z = .66$ has been measured," was
translated by a science journalist into a lead reading:

> Astronomers said today that they had located the most distant object yet observed—
> a quasar so far away that its light has been traveling through space since before the
> sun was born.

On major stories, the release or report is often only the start of the reporting
job, the springboard from which the reporter digs up background and reaction
through research and interviews. This business story in *The New York Times*
began with an announcement from the Ford Motor Company headquarters in
Dearborn, Michigan, that it planned to sell control of Ford's Rouge Steel Company to a group of Japanese corporations. To put the sale in perspective, the
reporter added a good deal of background. Indeed, the lead is the only paragraph in the story based on the press release; the reporter dug up all the rest
of the information on his own.

From press
release

Background

DEARBORN, MICH., July 2—The Ford Motor Company said
today that it planned to sell a controlling interest in its Rouge
Steel Company subsidiary to a group of Japanese concerns led by
Nippon Kokan, Japan's second largest steelmaker.

The takeover of Rouge Steel, the nation's eight-largest steel company, would represent the first major investment by a large Japanese steelmaker in the United States.

The sprawling, 1,200-acre River Rouge complex in Dearborn,
just southwest of Detroit, is a legacy of the first Henry Ford, who
decided in the 1920's to build a fully integrated operation, where
raw materials go in one end and cars come out the other. It is the
only one of its kind in the nation.

The company's fleet of Great Lakes freighters brings iron ore
down from the company-owned mines in Minnesota. At Rouge,

the ore comes off the piers to become iron in Ford blast furnaces, then to become steel which goes on to the rolling mill and, ultimately, the auto assembly line. Even the glass for the cars is made on site.

The Japanese presence in this epitome of the American industrial complex has a bitter element in it. In 1977, Henry Ford 2nd defiantly pledged to drive the Japanese car imports that were eating away at his market "back into the sea."

But since then, competitive pressures have forced the company to quietly buy auto components from Japanese companies. With sales sharply down, there is no money to modernize the aging Rouge plant. . . .

Occasionally a news release is so clever that it demands coverage even though it may not be intrinsically very newsworthy. Here's part of one that brought smiles to the faces of New York area reporters:

LEONARD P. STAVISKY

The Assembly
State of New York
Chairman Education Committee
Rules Committee
Ways and Means Committee

Immediately Release

STAVISKY GETS DOG INTO
PH.D. DEGREE-MILL

RIN TIN TIN'S GREAT-GREAT GRANDDAUGHTER
PASSES TEST WITH A WAG AND FEE

It's possible to enroll a dog for a mail-order Ph.D. degree in out-of-town diploma mills procuring customers in New York State, the Chairman of the Assembly Education Committee revealed today.

Shanna, a six-month-old German shepherd, was signed up for a doctoral degree in "Recreation Management and Supervision" by Pacific College in Los Angeles, the Chairman, Assemblyman Leonard P. Stavisky, announced.

The animal is the great-great granddaughter of Rin Tin Tin, a featured player in cowboy movies and early TV serials.

Stavisky managed to arrange for Shanna's matriculation as a candidate for a doctoral degree even though her only previous formal education was at Tri-City Dog Obedience School in Albany—where the animal became a dropout.

The dog, owned by Paul Shiffman, the Assembly Education Committee's executive director, was enrolled in the Ph.D. program as part of Stavisky's investigation into what he termed "unscrupulous degree mills" advertising in New York.

He produced a receipt for a $5 money order as a down payment for Shanna's Ph.D.

The college president, in accepting Shanna's application, said, "Your talent and experience are going to be recognized sooner or later. Welcome, my friend, to Pacific College."

Diploma mills are nothing new, and the release was clearly intended principally to get Assemblyman Stavisky some favorable publicity, but the story was too funny to resist. Reporter Peter Gianotti of *Newsday* fleshed out the story by interviewing Stavisky, contacting California legal authorities and trying to call Pacific "College." His account, which follows, was written as a news feature:

Except for the fact that Shanna Shiffman is a dog, she probably isn't all that different from the other Ph.D candidates at Pacific College.

Shanna, a 6-month-old German shepherd with a classy lineage—traceable to Rin Tin Tin—was formally enrolled in the Los Angeles "degree mill," a New York assemblyman said yesterday. Without regard to sex, color or ancestry, Shanna is now in a program leading toward a doctorate of sorts in recreation management. Assemb. Leonard Stavisky (D., L.-Whitestone), who chairs the body's education committee, said that Shanna's successful enrollment shows that at that particular mail-order mill, the only criterion for admission is $150.

"Now, we have the height of lunacy," he said. And that lunacy, he added, is advertised in such national magazines as *Esquire* and *Psychology Today*. Stavisky said he intended to introduce legislation to stop degree mills here. More serious, Stavisky said, is the potential use of degree mills by educational personnel for recertification to obtain salary increases.

Pacific College hasn't got a phone listing. Robert Raymer, consumer services representative in the California attorney general's office, said an institution there has to only show financial resources for state education department approval. "There seems to be a weakness to California law" he said.

Shanna is owned by Paul Shiffman, the Assembly Education Committee's executive director. Shiffman said his dog did have "field experience" in the backyard, and is interested in being upgraded to supervisor of child recreation, or watchdog.

Shiffman said a series of letters were sent by Shanna—through an interpreter—to degree mills throughout the country. Pacific College's response was the "most blatant." The fees ranged from $50 for an associate degree to $150 for a graduate degree. For $25, Shanna could have received a transcript of courses not taken but passed.

All that, even though she dropped out of obedience school.

Press *conferences* normally begin with prepared statements, copies of which may be distributed as press releases. Then reporters ask questions. The questions may range far astray of the subjects of the press conferences, leaving the reporter with a potpourri of material to be organized into a story.

The task of organization can be handled by structuring a press conference report much like a speech story. Lead with the most newsworthy thing the person had to say, quote him or her saying it, then amplify on the body of the remarks, intermixing background, context and reaction. Marginal notes clarify the structure of the following *Chicago Sun Times* account of an appearance by U.S. Interior Secretary James Watt on NBC's "Meet the Press":

Lead focuses on what he *said*, not the fact that he appeared on the show.

WASHINGTON D.C.—Interior Secretary James G. Watt said Sunday he has always been a champion of wilderness protection, but he stopped short of pledging support to legislation that would permanently bar leases in those pristine areas.

Foundation quote

Background

Body quotes

Reaction

Despite the controversies that have swirled around him since he took office, Watt said he has had "a great two years," and maintained that federal lands "are better managed today than they were two or three years ago."

In an appearance on NBC's "Meet the Press" Watt repeated a promise made last month not to use a loophole in current protection to issue drilling leases at the end of the year.

Congress three times in 1982 voted to budget bills to block the Interior Department from issuing leases. The latest ban expires on Sept. 31, giving Watt three months to issue leases before the areas are closed to development permanently under the 1964 law creating the National Wilderness System.

Watt's voluntary ban was the latest development in an 18-month battle with Congress over 80 million acres of designated wilderness area and another 37 million acres being studied for wilderness.

Watt a year ago proposed a bill that would have withdrawn all wilderness areas from leasing until the year 2000. It would also have allowed the president, without Congressional approval, to open wilderness areas for drilling in times of "urgent national need" and required Congress to make decisions on potential wilderness by certain deadlines.

Congress rejected Watt's proposal. Instead the House passed a measure with a permanent ban that could be lifted only if both Congress and the president decided there was an emergency need for drilling. The measure had 54 Senate sponsors but did not pass the Senate last session.

Asked on the interview program whether he would support this bill, Watt said he couldn't answer because he was "not sure of the specifics" of it. He said he did support the concept of drilling bans.

He also denied he had changed his position on the wilderness issue. Watt in his annual report last year listed as one of his goals extending wilderness exploration for 20 years and he has cited a controversial legal opinion saying he was required to issue leases.

But Sunday, Watt said, "We ought to preserve and protect the wilderness. I have always championed that. The President has always championed it. We think it is good public policy."

But one environmental group said Watt was wrong to claim his position has been consistent.

William Turnage, executive director of the Wilderness Society, said in a prepared statement issued promptly after the television appearance that Watt "broke all his records for lying to the American people. He distorted the answer to virtually every question he was asked. The biggest lie of all was his contention that he has supported protections for wilderness during his time in office."

MEETINGS

Whether it's the village Board of Selectmen hiring a dog warden or the Congress of the United States voting on a defense budget, much of the work of American government is transacted at meetings open to the public. Yet only a few people attend these meetings; most of us rely upon the press to tell us what transpired there. Since the meetings themselves generally deal with more than one topic, so do the stories. The principle challenge to the reporter, consequently, is how to structure the story.

Suppose that the Hapsville City Council at its semi-monthly meeting decides (1) to give a "vote of thanks" to Helga White, the city's assistant librarian who is leaving for another job; (2) to change the drinking age within city limits from 18 to 21, and (3) to hold a 2.5 million bond issue referendum for construction of a city sewer system. A "laundry list" lead that summarized all the council actions would be cluttered:

> The Hapsville City Council last night voted to hold a $2.5 million bond issue referendum for construction of sewer system, raise the drinking age within city limits from 18 to 21 and give a "vote of thanks" to an assistant city librarian who is leaving for another job.

Better to lead with a single piece of news, then work the rest into the body of the story. The bond issue may be important, but it's months away, and it might fail at the polls. The new drinking age is a hot issue. Three teenagers have died in recent auto accidents that the police attributed to drinking at legal bars. The matter is being debated by schools and civic groups. Parents' groups have gotten up petitions and written letters urging action. Of all the items, therefore, the new drinking age would seem to most interest readers. Make it the lead:

> The Hapsville City Council last night raised the legal drinking age within city limits from 18 to 21.

How should you structure the story? You might go on about the new drinking law, but if you do that, you'll take readers to the sixth or seventh paragraph before telling them *what else* happened at the meeting. That would violate the basic rule of writing breaking news: to sum up the essentials of the story before getting into the details. At the other extreme, if you go directly to the other issues, the story will read like an agenda. After all, you chose the drinking law for the lead because it was a hot issue. You should thus compromise: Report the drinking law story in the first few paragraphs, then touch on the other news:

> The measure, which passed by a six-to-three vote after a long debate, imposes a maximum $5000 fine on any bar or liquor store owner whose establishment is convicted of serving minors. It takes effect January 1st.

Backers of the measure pointed out that three teenagers had died in recent auto accidents that the police attributed to drinking at legal bars. "Passing this law," said Councilman Robert Longstreet, who introduced the bill, "shows the public that we refuse to stand idly by while Hapsville youth slaughters itself on the highway for the profit of a few saloon keepers."

The police said that in each accident, the driver of the car had been drinking at local bars before the accident occurred. In each case, the driver was arrested on charges of driving while intoxicated.

First, a transition: In another action, the Council approved a $2.5 million bond issue referendum for construction of a city sewer system. The measure would be put on the ballot in the November election.

Now you should discuss the circumstances surrounding the decision. Did the new law stir up a fervor, or did it pass without a murmur? As the eyes and ears of the reader, you try to recreate the flavor of the session. A "setup" paragraph introduces the debate.

Passage of the law came after a heated one-hour debate, during which council members heard criticism of the proposal from, among others, a pub owner and representatives of Hapsville University student groups.

Larry Cargill, owner of Paddy's Pub, 417 North Main St., said the new law would have an opposite effect from the one intended. Instead of drinking at bars within the city limits, he said, minors would drive to neighboring towns where the law is not in force.

"Then, if they get loaded, they've got a lot farther to travel to get home," said Cargill, whose bar is popular among local college students. "The chances of their having an accident are much greater."

In support of the measure, Hilda Floridette, president of the Hapsvillians for Decency, said that closing bars to teenagers would encourage togetherness in the family.

"When they can't go down and waste time at the local gin mill," she said, "our children will be more likely to stay home and read and play games in the evening, as they did when I was a girl."

Having disposed of the drinking issue, your story can detail the other council business touched upon before. Again, along with telling readers *what* happened, try to give them some feeling about *why*. Sometimes this can be done by quoting part of a council member's argument supporting a measure; sometimes reporters themselves provide the background that helps readers understand the rationale behind a decision.

Commenting on the bond issue, Councilman Angelo DiNicolo said new sewers would cost home owners an average of about $800, depending on how much road frontage they owned. Payments would be spread out over the 20-year life of the bond.

The project, which was passed unanimously by the Council, could get under way three months after its approval by voters and would take about two years to complete, he said.

"You look around and practically every other town our size has sewers," said Councilwoman Agnes Feister. "I just don't see how we can grow and attract industry unless we have a modern waste-disposal system."

The meeting also included a "vote of thanks" to Ms. White, the assistant librarian. This vote also deserves mention somewhere in the story. But its impact and interest value are negligible, so it can go at the bottom.

> Before adjournment, the Council passed a "vote of thanks" to Helga White, assistant librarian at the Hapsville Public Library, who is leaving her job after twenty years of service. Ms. White will spend her time helping her husband run a chinchilla ranch in Sherman, Texas.

SUMMARY

Most reporters begin by working on general assignment, which means they write a wide variety of news. They frequently start by writing obituaries, covering accidents, fires, crimes and speeches; and by writing stories based on reports, press releases, press conferences and public meetings.

An *obituary*, or "obit," is someone's life story published to accompany the news of his or her death. Lead with the most important things the person accomplished in life, then summarize the rest; report the bad along with the good.

In reporting on *accidents* and *crimes*, attribute all information to the sources: Eyewitness accounts of accidents are few and sometimes unreliable. In addition, because reports of crime are often fraught with emotion, they may easily become distorted before the reporter ever hears them. When writing about *fires*, report the human drama along with the fire and smoke.

Most *speech* stories consist of a lead, foundation quote, background, the body of the speech and reaction. Don't forget to also provide color from the scene. *Reports* are issued to educate the public from the viewpoint of a particular organization; here the key is to explain the report clearly and simply, and to provide the context needed to understand it. *Press releases* and *press conferences* generate much of the news, but they should mark the start of reporting a story, not the end of it: Check the facts, get background—in short, try to expand and deepen the story through your own reporting. When covering *meetings*, explain *why* decisions were made as they were.

9

FEATURE WRITING

Not all newspaper stories need be written in the fast-paced style that characterizes breaking news. Some, called *feature* stories, are told in a less hurried and more inventive manner. Features may begin with quotations, descriptions or even funny stories. The heart of the news, which would take up the very beginning of a straight news story, often does not show up for several paragraphs.

The term "feature" originated many years ago, when newspapers were filled with breaking news and any other kind of story stood out as a special feature. Today, nearly half the stories in most papers are features.

Feature stories work best when the news they convey is stronger on interest than urgency, or when the story is not so important as to demand the breathless haste of the inverted-pyramid format. If straight news stories stress *what* happened, features stress *how* and *why*. Stylistically rich, features are strong on description, atmosphere and personality. They showcase a newspaper's best writers.

The dividing line between features and breaking news stories isn't always perfectly clear, but in most cases they can be distinguished from the outset, right in the opening lines. Here, for example, is a straight news story:

> A Traverse City bank has sued a local man to recover some of the nearly $40,000 it gave him by mistake in exchange for worthless and out-of-date German money.
> The man, Stephen Holcomb, 31, spent more than half of the money on stereo equipment, fishing and hunting gear, a new station wagon and a trip to Chicago. According to the police, he had only $18,177 left when apprehended. . . .

Because this story is neither especially fresh nor of earth-shaking importance, it doesn't have to be told as straight news. The following Associated Press account treats it as a feature story, telling it in an indirect fashion. Note that it uses colorful quotations liberally.

> Last September, Stephen Holcomb walked into a bank with a 100,000-mark note that was printed in Germany in 1923 and exchanged it for nearly $40,000. According to a banking expert in Detroit, the note was worth "less than a United States penny" even in 1923, a year of extreme inflation in Germany.
>
> Don Dooley, the International Harvester dealer here, said that the transaction had started when Mr. Holcomb, 31 years old, asked him if he could use the bill to buy a fancy new I-H Scout with an AM-FM radio.
>
> "I told him I couldn't take that thing," Mr. Dooley recalled. But he did call the National Bank and Trust Company to ask what 100,000 German marks was worth, apparently forgetting to mention the date on the bill.
>
> A while later, Mr. Holcomb returned to the dealer with a handful of cash. The bank had exchanged the note for $39,700.
>
> Mr. Holcomb began buying and kept on buying. "I have a lot of good memories," he said later.
>
> He drove his new $7,000 Scout to Chicago and stayed at a hotel where he tipped the elevator operator $900. "I thought he was doing a real good job running that elevator, that's all," he said.
>
> He bought a stereo tape deck, a double-barreled shotgun, a pistol and a new fishing pole. When he got back to Traverse City, his spree was over. A sheriff's detective, Jim Palmer, paid him a visit at his motel room and left with all his new toys.
>
> "They came busting in my room," Mr. Holcomb said, "and they took my truck and about $5,200 cash. The two cops hauled me down to the bank and told me to sign something, so I guess that's where I lost the money I had in the bank."
>
> No criminal charges have been lodged, but the bank, which will not discuss the case, has sued for the $18,177 it has not recovered. . . .

Notice that what occupied the lead of the straight news version—the fact that the bank is suing Holcomb—doesn't even show up until the bottom paragraph of the feature version. That's the sort of freedom the feature approach allows. But freedom from formula also makes feature stories more challenging to write. In this chapter we look at the most popular kinds of feature stories, then discuss how to structure them.

VARIETIES OF FEATURE STORIES

As we discussed in Chapter 7, "Writing Breaking News: The Body of the Story," the feature format is sometimes employed to write breaking news; the resulting story is called a *news feature*. Other kinds of features include *sidebars*, *follow-ups*, *profiles*, *mood stories*, *trend stories*, *human interest stories*, *explainers*, and *service features*.

Sidebars and Follow-Ups

A sidebar accompanies a hard news story. It runs on the same day as the main story, usually alongside it on the same page (hence the name "sidebar"). Its function is to explore one aspect of the main story more closely than the rapid pace of a straight news account permits. When Elvis Presley died, *The New York Times* led its straight news account this way:

> Elvis Presley, the first and greatest American rock-and-roll star, died yesterday at the age of 42.
>
> Mr. Presley, whose throaty baritone and blatant sexuality redefined popular music, was found unconscious in the bedroom of his home, called Graceland, in Memphis yesterday at 2:30 P.M.

Next to this story on the front page the *Times* ran a feature sidebar that stressed the *who* aspect of the story, summing up Presley's stature. It began:

> For most people, Elvis Presley *was* rock-and-roll. And they were right. Bill Haley may have made the first massive rock hit, and people such as Chuck Berry and Little Richard may have had an equally important creative impact on this raucous new American art form. But it was Elvis who defined the style and gave it an indelible image. . . . With his ominous, greasy, swirling locks, his leather jacket and his aggressive undulations, Elvis was a performer whom parents abhorred, young women adored and young men instantly imitated.

Whereas sidebars run on the same day as the main news stories, follow-ups run a day or more later and report on the consequences of the earlier developments. One kind of follow-up is the "reaction" story—like this *Providence Journal* story concerning the response among students at the University of Rhode Island to a threatened investigation by the State Legislature:

> "This is a real serious threat. A lot of us have been trying to stimulate interest in political affairs. I hope something like this doesn't kill it."
>
> Gerald McDowell, newly elected president of the Student Senate at the University of Rhode Island, sat in the crowded student union sipping coffee and commenting on the furor created by the talk by a Communist at the university last night and the threat of a legislative investigation.
>
> His thinking reflected that of other students and campus leaders. A reporter talking to students at random on the campus could find no one who didn't fear that the intellectual life at URI would be stifled if legislators began a campus probe.
>
> On Tuesday Rep. David F. Sweeney introduced a resolution in the Assembly calling for an investigation of conditions at URI that "may be detrimental" to the students, the faculty and the state and federal governments. . . .

When writing sidebars and follow-ups, it's important to indicate their relationship to the main news, and to do so fairly early on—as the reporter covering the college story did in the second and fourth paragraphs, when he mentioned that a speech by a Communist the previous night had led to the threat of a legislative investigation of the campus. Don't assume that readers will know about the main story; they may not. When a disaster sent a bus and several cars plunging into Tampa Bay in 1980, a sidebar by Gene Miller of *The Miami Herald* began:

> Richard Hornbuckle, auto dealer, golfer, Baptist, came within two feet Friday of driving his yellow Buick Skylark off the Sunshine Skyway Bridge into Tampa Bay.

News of the bridge collapse was plastered all over the front page of the *Herald*, but Miller was still careful to specify which bridge he was talking about (the Sunshine Skyway) and when the incident happened (Friday); he thus tied his sidebar to the main news story.

A follow-up that reaches furthest back in time is the "where are they now?" story that concerns someone who once made a splash in the headlines and has since sunk back into obscurity. Note this example:

> John Bradley puffed nervously on a cigarette and looked at his old wristwatch for a second time. He was sitting on the edge of his chair in the electric pose of a runner ready to bolt from a starting block. The subject that had been raised was one he had avoided talking about publicly for more than 20 years, and he didn't want to talk about it now. But decades of professional politeness wouldn't let him walk away.
>
> So the 56-year-old ex-Navy corpsman leaned back woodenly in his chair and stared straight ahead. Then, quickly and mechanically, he told his version of one of the most famous war stories of all time:
>
> "There were several guys on the hill trying to attach a flag to a large pipe. It was a two-inch or a four-inch pipe. I don't know myself how big a pipe it was. But it was a heavy pipe, and when they got the flag attached, they tried to raise it. But you know, the wind started whipping up and they were trying to put it in this rocky ground.
>
> "It sounds ridiculous to have six men trying to raise one flag, but with this wind whipping around, it just became too much for them. So I jumped in and give them a hand. . . .

Had this story in the *Chicago Tribune* been written as hard news, the lead might have read as follows:

> The last surviving figure in the famous flag-raising picture on Iwo Jima during World War II said today that he did not see "too much heroics" in what he had done.

Instead, the *Tribune* reporter only hints at the story in the first two paragraphs, advising that Bradley is going to discuss a subject "he had avoided talking about publicly for more than 20 years" and promising readers "his version of one of the most famous stories of all time." This sort of suspense is almost impossible to obtain in the inverted-pyramid, breaking news format.

Some follow-ups, also called "situationers," bring readers up to date on recent news developments, reporting how a situation now stands. A week after a violent racial clash had occurred in South Boston, a reporter for *The New York Times* returned to the neighborhood to see what was going on after things had quieted down. His update began:

> In the afternoons, the yellow school buses roll out of South Boston in military formation. A phalanx of police motorcycles roars down the overpass into the "staging area"—the parking lot of the boarded-up shell of a shopping center at the black Columbia Point housing project—followed by a bus, more motorcycles, more buses, a command car, drab autos filled with plainclothesmen in sportscoats, another wedge of motorcycles.

Along the bus routes the walls are lined with scrawled messages: "Niggers Go Home," "Boneheads," "This is Klan Country," and "Go home Mayor Black." Boston's Mayor is Kevin H. White. . . .

Profiles

A profile presents a word portrait of an individual. It is one of the most popular kinds of feature stories. The subject may be someone who figures prominently in the news—a movie star, a sports hero, an author—or someone who has not made the news but who is interesting anyway. The important consideration in a successful profile is that it must present a *story*. The following profile of an unknown girl named Marcy, published in *Newsweek* as a sidebar to a long cover story on teenage runaways, begins with a paragraph of description, then, in the second paragraph, outlines the newsworthiness of this particular story:

At 17, Marcy is a gentle girl. Her face tends to plumpness, her streaky blond hair needs retouching, and she uses no make-up. She wears baggy gray workman's pants topped by a floppy green-and-black sweater. She is genuinely pretty. Her blue eyes, however, are glazed and dreamy; she is nearly always high on drugs. Marcy is a runaway living in New York's East Village.

Not every runaway is just like Marcy. She had a deeply disturbed background long before leaving home, while some runaways show a path that is relatively normal. But Marcy is not atypical. Increasingly, the runaway subculture is becoming a poignant skid row for young derelicts like Marcy—an accessible underground where they collect like sediment because there is no farther to fall.

The lead paragraphs of this *New York Post* profile of two heroin addicts combines description with an early sketch of the story behind the action:

Dean Brocke jumped from the roof of the Village Hotel in a single sweeping motion, his hands flung back to avoid the outstretched arms of a police sergeant, his head turned over his left shoulder toward the street five stories below, his long hair fanned outward. A net set up by the police caught him, and the crowd gasped with relief. Dean's twin brother, Dennis, broke into tears; he alone knew the three years of heroin addiction that had led his brother to the ledge. And he had known, he said, that Dean would jump. . . .

Dean and Dennis Brocke were born 11 minutes apart, 23 years ago in Fort Worth, Texas. Their father, a brigadier general in the Marines, died when they were young, and their mother remarried several times. . . .

The lead indicates the story behind the profile: What led this young man, from a respectable family, to attempt suicide? Read on, the lead suggests, and you'll find out.

Mood Stories

Mood stories attempt to report on the state of mind of a group or community. Many of them are written as follow-ups: How are coal miners holding up twelve weeks into a strike? How do diners feel about a new sales tax on restaurant checks? What is the reaction of an Amish community to a court ruling that they must, against their wishes, send their children to public school?

Because the thoughts and opinions of a large group can be pretty abstract, feature writers often lead with a portrait of a single individual who, to some degree, represents the attitudes of the others. Such was the case in this feature in *The New York Times*, which explored the validity of a claim by President Jimmy Carter that Americans were feeling bad about themselves:

> Harry Olson, a tall, soft-spoken man, leaned forward at his desk, frowning as if he were trying to find a flaw in his personal situation. But it was hard.
>
> "Maybe I should worry, but I don't," he said. Not about himself, his children, his community or his country.
>
> "We do take an awful lot for granted in this country," said the 39-year-old owner of Waterloo Implement Inc., a farm-equipment dealer. "A lot of people could live off our scraps. But this is a good town to do business in, in good farming country. I guess I'm fairly successful, and I'm happy at what I'm doing. I guess I don't worry too much about the future."
>
> Mr. Olson is not alone. For Waterloo, straddling the Cedar River in northeastern Iowa, is a city where people generally seem to feel comfortable about themselves, their community and their country. And notably missing, to all outward appearances, in this industrial city where employers take pride in their employees' work ethic, is what President Carter and others have described as a general malaise among Americans. . . .

The structure of the Waterloo story is classic for a mood piece. Like the report on the University of Rhode Island students presented earlier, it leads off with a statement of one man's opinion. This means not that he is the only man the reporter interviewed, but that his opinions are sufficiently typical so that he can represent views shared by many of his townspeople. In the fourth paragraph—the key paragraph of the story—the writer switches from the specific to the general, previews what other people are going to say in the story and tells readers why they should read on: because the mood the reporter has found among the American people is not the "malaise" the President had claimed.

Obviously it's no simple matter to determine what is going on in the minds and hearts of a group of people. At the very least, a reporter doing a mood piece should try to interview as many and as wide a variety of people as possible. A reporter covering a proposed restaurant tax would talk to diners at coffee shops as well as those at more elegant eateries; another, writing a piece on how a community feels about teenagers and drugs, would talk not only to teenagers but also to their parents, as well as to police, school authorities and religious leaders.

Even with plenty of legwork, mood pieces can suffer from bias and distortion. For this reason, newspapers and broadcast news organizations sample the public mood more scientifically, by commissioning public opinion polls. The box on "Precision Journalism" in Chapter 12 discusses this approach in more detail.

Trend Stories

Trend stories are designed to report on changes that occur gradually—like the rising number of households headed by single mothers, or the "gentrification" of a poor neighborhood by young professionals who improve the properties but drive old residents out. The feature format works well for such stories because they often do not involve immediate breaking news. Moreover, they evolve too slowly to warrant their being handled in the breaking news format.

As with mood pieces, a useful approach to writing trend features is to *personalize* the trends by depicting the lives of individuals who are affected by the changes. *The Wall Street Journal* personalized a trend story about a growing shortage of hotel rooms this way:

> When Norman Hildes-Heim, a New York architect, visited Minneapolis a month ago to work with executives of Radisson Hotel Corp. on plans for a new hotel, he ran into a problem that he hadn't planned on: He couldn't find a hotel room.

This feature from the *Washington Post* on a growing trend toward seeking government aid for the victims of violent crime opens with a startling, personal image of what crime can do even to a survivor:

> Theresa Maybury still flashes back to that Labor Day two years ago when a Culpepper, Va., stonemason rammed a rusty shotgun into her son's stomach and pulled the trigger.
> "I still see him," Maybury said of the bearded man convicted of murdering her son. "He'll be laughing and joking five feet from me, just as he did during the trial."
> Maybury said she was totally unprepared for the trauma that awaited her after the death of her 18-year-old son, Joseph, including being told to wait in the same witness room as the suspect in the slaying and listening to the defense portray her son as a hoodlum who was begging for trouble.
> Determined that the families of other victims should not have to go through what she did, Maybury became a volunteer counselor in Alexandria's new Victims Assistance Program, one of a growing number of local aid programs. . . .

Just be sure the trend you cover *is* a trend. In 1981 a clever public relations man managed to convince several reporters and editors that the hula hoop—manufactured by his client—was about to make a comeback. Stories appeared predicting that the hula hoop fad would sweep the nation, as it had in the 1950s. But it didn't.

Human Interest Stories

Human interest stories rely for their appeal almost *entirely* on their interest value rather than on their importance. They entertain, amuse and help readers reflect on the human condition. In the hands of a sensitive writer, a human interest feature can sound depths normally untouched by the news. Perhaps no one is better at accomplishing this than Jimmy Breslin, the New York columnist. The following column, written for the *Daily News*, describes a retarded girl at a YMCA swimming pool. Breslin builds an astonishing depth of emotion almost entirely through the use of simple and straightforward—though astutely selected—description and dialogue:

> She sat on the edge of the pool with her heavy legs drawn up. She kept looking at her feet to make sure that they were on the tile; she felt that if one foot went off the tile and hung over the side of the pool that her body would follow the foot and she would disappear forever into the frightening water.
>
> It did not matter that she was at the shallow end of the pool and that the swimmers at this end of the pool, including her two friends, and the young man and woman who had come to help them, stood in water that was only waist-deep. In the world in which Betty lives, she has been betrayed so many times that she could see no reason why the water for her suddenly would not become very deep and close over her head and begin drowning her the moment she fell into it.
>
> "Come on, Betty," the young man, Steve Golden, said. He stood in the water with his big arms held out to her.
>
> "You can't make me go in there," Betty said. She is about 35, but she speaks in the quick high tones of a child of perhaps 10.
>
> "It's fun, Betty," Steve said.
>
> "You can't make me go in there," Betty said.
>
> Steve turned to make sure that Betty's two friends did not get out of his reach: Betty's friends were men with distorted faces. One of them made a garbled sound, a call for attention, and then, knowing that Steve was watching, he made an attempt at swimming. His chin came up, rather than go into the water, and uncoordinated arms thrashed at the water. One hand came down and went into the water almost cleanly. But the other hand missed and the body began to sink. "That's good," Steve said.
>
> A few feet away, the young woman, Denise Hannon, had the other man floating on his back. His body stiffened and she kept telling him not to worry.
>
> They stayed in one corner of the pool, the two retarded men and the two helping them. Betty sat on the edge of the pool and she watched them and said nothing. For weeks she had been saying that she wanted to go swimming at the YMCA when the others were taken. She had built it into a dream. Now that she was finally here, she found she was too afraid to move. . . .
>
> "If you go in, then we'll all clap for you," Steve Golden said.
>
> "Clap?" Betty said. She began to clap her hands.
>
> A young guy who had been swimming laps stopped and called over to her, "Come on in with me, Betty."
>
> "How do you know my name?" she said quickly.
>
> "Everyone is saying your name," the young guy said.
>
> Betty looked and now she saw that everyone in the pool had stopped swimming so they could watch her. Suddenly, none of the swimmers was uncomfortable any more. Betty covered her eyes again.
>
> At 9:30, the young woman who was the lifeguard stood up to blow her whistle and clear the pool for the night.
>
> "Betty, we've got to go home," Steve said. "Come on, you've got to do it now or you'll just have to go home."
>
> Betty's little hands came off the side of the pool and went around Steve's neck. Her eyes widened and began to roll. Her mouth opened. She hesitated. Then she pushed herself off the side of the pool. Her heavy legs turned the water white as she dropped in.
>
> Everybody in the YMCA pool clapped. Betty turned around and smiled out of

happiness and clapped with them. Then they helped her out of the water and had her pose for a picture. Betty waved furiously at the camera as the young woman, Denise Hannon, took her picture.

Explainers

An explainer is a story that interprets an issue of public importance. Explainers are especially helpful in illuminating highly controversial questions, like abortion or gay rights, about which emotions run high so those involved may be tempted to distort the facts. They are also employed to set forth the basics of complex questions, like nuclear power or the arms race, because the average reader has a hard time simply understanding the vocabulary involved.

The opening paragraphs of this explainer on capital punishment (which ran in *The New York Times* as a sidebar to a breaking news story announcing the execution of convicted murderer Charles Brooks, Jr.) summarizes four main points of contention: whether capital punishment is moral, whether anyone can be executed "humanely," whether the circumstances surrounding an execution would "quicken the pace" of others and whether doctors' aiding in executions is medically ethical:

> HUNTSVILLE, TEX.—The execution early this morning of a convicted murderer by injection of a lethal dose of anesthetics, the first such execution in the United States, today sharpened the debate over the moral validity of the death penalty and over whether it can be administered in a "humane" manner.
>
> At the same time, there were growing fears among opponents of the death penalty that the means by which the Supreme Court spurned the condemned man's 11th-hour appeal Monday would quicken the pace of executions among the 1150 death row inmates across the nation. There was debate, too, among doctors about the ethics of using medical procedures and medical technicians to end a life. . . .

Service Features

Service features convey practical information and advice. They suggest, for instance, how to find a bargain stereo receiver, fight crabgrass, repair a broken front step, aid someone choking on a piece of food, quit smoking, or win unclaimed scholarship funds. Feature writers try to make such service information immediate and concrete by putting it in terms of individuals. This service feature about home security systems, which appeared in the *Los Angeles Times*, begins with an anecdote:

> When the bars on her windows failed to deter a burglar from making off with her stereo and jewelry, Diana Barnwell decided it was time to protect her home with a burglar alarm system.
>
> To scare off intruders, heavy bars were fitted to the Los Angeles woman's back door and her windows were wired with electronic detectors that, when tampered with, would trip an alarm. The bill came to $2200.
>
> But in a matter of seconds one morning last February, a burglar foiled the expensive

system with an ordinary screwdriver and a pair of wire snippers. The new stereo she had just bought to replace the stolen one was carted off in the box it came in. . . .

Like Barnwell, thousands of consumers are learning the hard way that security systems are not always secure. . . .

Service features may not be page one news, but they must be reported and written just as carefully. Readers who know little about Mideast oil may know a lot about motorcycles, and you'll hear from them if your piece on motorcycle repairs is inaccurate. And although leisure-time athletes may forgive you for misspelling the name of a Soviet ambassador, tout the wrong pair of running shoes and they'll blame you for their blisters.

THE STRAIGHT NEWS—FEATURE SPECTRUM

The choice of whether to employ a straight news format or to write the story as a feature depends on the nature of the news. The realms of straight news and feature news are not mutually exclusive, and, within the broad areas where they overlap, either format might work. The following chart illustrates the realms of features and hard news stories plotted in terms of the immediacy and importance of the news development at hand.

Inverted-pyramid preferred	Either format OK	Feature format preferred
Immediate, breaking news	News important or fresh but not necessarily both	News interesting but not necessarily timely
	Examples:	
Scott elected mayor	How Scott won	Profile of Scott
Imperial Hotel burns down	Hotel had colorful past	Fire a hazard in many old hotels
Boy scout post gets big federal grant	Post booming under new leadership	What it's like to be a scout today
Tornado hits Iowa town	Tornado victims dig out the next day	How to survive a tornado

---

STRUCTURING THE STORY

Feature writing offers the newswriter greater opportunity to flex his or her style—to explore color, texture, detail, to quote at length, to give the reader the feel of the story. But with this freedom comes greater responsibility. People will read a bare-bones breaking news story more or less without regard for its style, if they feel that they *need* to know its contents. But in a feature, whose facts may be less urgent or less important, it's up to the writer to demonstrate why the reader should keep reading.

With that in mind, let's take a look at the anatomy of a feature story. For convenience we divide the feature into four parts.

The first is the *lead*. Unlike a hard news lead, a feature lead may run for several sentences, even several paragraphs. But as with hard news, the lead is the most important part of the story; it must arouse readers' interest, and it must "lead" them into the story. Next comes a section that summarizes what the story is going to say and indicates why it is of interest. Because this section resembles an advertisement for the story, it is sometimes called the *billboard*. The third section is the *body* of the story. And finally comes the *conclusion*, known in newsmagazine parlance as the "kicker."

The Feature Lead

The lead to a feature story serves to arouse the reader's curiosity, as if the writer were saying: "Come over here and listen; I have something interesting to tell you." Writing the lead is a creative matter; no formula can substitute for the writer's individual skill. But, for the purpose of illustration, feature leads can be organized into categories.

The *topical lead* lays out the gist of the story right away. As the following example illustrates, it resembles the lead on a breaking news story:

> Propelled by visions of clean air, warm skies and a new start, Americans are moving into this city and its environs at a rate of more than 400 a day. And many, when they arrive, are finding some of the same problems they thought they had left behind in places like Buffalo, Chicago and Los Angeles.

As this lead from *The New York Times* indicates, topical leads work well on issue-oriented stories. The idea is to condense the essence of the issue into a clear, well-turned statement, the shorter the better. This brief lead to a feature in the *Los Angeles Times* concerns the refusal of Americans to start thinking in terms of liters and kilometers instead of gallons and miles:

> The metric system appears to be an idea whose time has gone.

A witty lead, moreover, can rescue an otherwise dull story. This lead, by George Lardner Jr. of the *Washington Post*, enlivened a grey tale of special-interest law making:

> The worms crawled out of H. R. 11409 this week with barely a squiggle.
> Wholesale bait companies that import some $8 million a year worth of Canadian night-crawlers will no doubt be disappointed. The bill would have lifted the import duties they have to pay.
> But H. R. 11409 is far from dead. The worms have been replaced by opera glasses, binoculars and the like. . . . The worms . . . seem to be one of the few special-interest items that aren't still wiggling around, looking for a niche in the nation's tax or tariff laws, as the 95th Congress lumbers toward adjournment.

Marty Tolchin of *The New York Times* demonstrates in this topical lead that brevity is the soul of wit:

"Why us?"
This was the message in thousands of words and reams of paper offered today by 62 state and local government officials at the conference on inflation.

Another way to begin a feature is with an *anecdotal lead*: a short account (or anecdote) of an interesting or humorous event that illustrates the thrust of the story that follows:

> A breathless American traveler dashed up to a counter at the Toronto airport one day not long ago holding a letter that bore an 8-cent United States stamp.
> "Is this the right amount of postage for a letter to New York?" he asked the Air Canada clerk. She replied that it was the right amount but the wrong kind. "You have to use a Canadian stamp here," she said.
> Perplexed, then exasperated, the man exclaimed, "Well, where do I get one of those?" Then, shaking his head, he stormed away without waiting for an answer. The airline clerk turned to the next passenger in line and muttered: "They just really think we're their bloody 51st state!"

The feature that followed had nothing to do with postage stamps; it concerned the growing irritation Canadians were feeling toward America's tendency to treat Canada as a poor relation. In devising a way to get into the story, the *New York Times* reporter used the incident at the Air Canada ticket counter as a story in miniature to illustrate the point of the piece.

In their ideal form, anecdotal leads have a beginning, a middle, and a punchline at the end, like a good story told by a raconteur after dinner. Here is one from *Newsweek*:

> A bull elephant grazes idly near a clump of trees. Moving in on him are three ABC-TV cameramen, a soundman, three professional hunters, a producer, a director and Texas Gov. John Connally, clutching a formidable .458 Browning magnum. "Can I take him?" Connally whispers to the guide. "No," replies the guide, "I think we'll wait a bit." Connally inches closer, his heart pounding against the wireless microphone under his shirt. Finally, the guide gives the word and Connally cuts loose. BLAM! A brain shot rocks the 5-ton monster back on his haunches, his trunk raised in a mighty, plaintive roar as he crumples to the earth, dead. The party rushes forward, "Gee, they're tremendous," says Connally, eyeing its feet. "It'll make a nice briefcase," says the guide, fingering its hide. "Governor, I congratulate you. It was a fine shot."

The story that followed provided an account of the television show, "American Sportsman," which sought to follow famous personalities as they caught fish and shot wild animals. By the way the anecdote is told, readers can readily tell that the writer does not exactly applaud ABC's attempt to wring entertainment from the act of killing an elephant.

Scene-setting leads are composed primarily of description. Like movies, they use images to tell a story, as in this lead to a *Rolling Stone* account of the landing of an unmanned space probe on Mars:

> The Viking One lander, a grey spider with the bulk of a big motorcycle, detaches from its orbiter and drops down between the outstretched crescent arms of Mars. It

cuts into the upper atmosphere, a metal surfer holding its own poise and counsel—the humans are too far away to help now. As the air grows thicker, the lander casts off a protective shell, spreads a parachute, descends toward the red landscape. At 4,000 feet three engines ignite. The parachute falls away; the winds of Mars will tear it into a girdle of bright threads, ornaments from Goodyear.

The lander slows, steadies itself and touches down on Chyrse Planitia, the broad delta of a dead Martian river, late on a summer afternoon. . . .

When the description is evocative and the reporting thorough, a scene-setting lead can enliven even a seemingly routine story. This *Wall Street Journal* story about a short-order cook starts with a description of where he works. The cook then makes his entrance, almost like a star's moving to center stage:

It is 7 A.M. on a weekday morning at the Flair Coffee Shop on Seventh Avenue near 40th Street, in the heart of the Garment District. The first customers of the day groggily file in, take their usual seats and grumble their customary orders. Waitresses scribble down the grumblings and lumber over to the kitchen counters to pass them on.

Poised behind one of the kitchen counters is Sam Hadden, short-order cook. He has been at work a half-hour and he already has a headache. As the orders come rushing in—two up, scramble two, a buttered English—his hands whisk back and forth and his head bobs like a pneumatic drill as he grinds out a steady procession of food.

The name of the game is hurry. Sam can make scrambled eggs in 45 seconds, a hamburger in two minutes, most sandwiches in four seconds. It isn't how good the food is that counts, but how fast it is made, though the best of the short-order cooks insist they make it good, too.

"I guess I'm not being very modest, but I rank myself as one of the best. I can really move that food," says 38-year-old Sam, a chunky man with a goatee and mustache. Mel Nudelman, Sam's boss at Flair, says, "He's a top man. He knows what it's all about, and he produces."

Quotations can make sound leads, especially for profiles. What better way to start a profile of a comedian than with a joke? The following example is from *The New York Times*:

"A woman went to her neighbor's. They're drinking tea," says Myron Cohen, lapsing into his utterly perfect conception of what a New York garment center accent should be, lowering his right eyelid and staring owlishly out with his other eye. "They're drinking tea and she says: 'Tell me the truth. If you found a million dollars, what would you do with it?' Her friend thinks, then she says: 'I'll tell you. If it belonged to a poor person I'd give it back.'"

The Cohen mouth curves into a sly and quiet satisfied smile while his audience of one snickers, giggles and then laughs outright as this joke, delivered quietly and conversationally, sinks in.

Pure Myron Cohen. Dialect and diversion. A punch line to think on. Myron Cohen doesn't shout. He doesn't ask outright that you laugh, because he knows that you will, because his jokes are about you, your marriage, your children, your business, your vacation, your daily life. . . .

To quote two or more people in conversation is to use *dialogue*. This dialogue lead, from an *Esquire* profile of the boxer Joe Louis by Gay Talese, goes to the heart of what will follow: the story of a youthful spirit in an aging body:

> "Hi, Sweetheart!" Joe Louis called to his wife, spotting her waiting for him at the Los Angeles Airport.
> She smiled, walked toward him, and was about to stretch up on her toes and kiss him—but suddenly stopped.
> "Joe," she snapped, "where's your tie?"
> "Aw, sweetie," Joe Louis said, shrugging, "I stayed out all night in New York and didn't have time."
> "All night!" she cut in. "When you're out here with me all you do is sleep, sleep, sleep."
> "Sweetie," Joe Louis said with a tired grin, "I'm an ole man."
> "Yes," she agreed, "but when you go to New York you try to be young again."

Contrast leads emphasize the unexpected:

> Like many another tranquil neighborhood of comfortable middle-class white people, the Laurelton section of Queens in 1964 began to change.
> Middle-income blacks in increasing numbers were buying some of the distinguished Tudor and Colonial homes that line Laurelton's streets under canopies of maple, oak and evergreen.
> Some of the white residents, many of whom had lived in the neighborhood for 20 years or more, began to get nervous. Panic simmered just beneath the surface. Real estate brokers stepped up their activities in the area.
> By all the laws of social change that are believed to govern such situations, Laurelton should have become largely a black community by now.
> But it has not. White flight appears to have been arrested. With a balance estimated at 60 percent white to 40 percent black, Laurelton appears to many who live there to have become a stable, genuinely integrated community. . . .

In this piece from *The New York Times*, at first we are led toward the conclusion that this neighborhood, too, went the way of all the others and had become completely black. The contrast comes at the start of the fifth paragraph: "But it has not."

THE HANGING GUN

Feature leads can be longer than straight news leads, but they shouldn't be ramshackle. Avoid "throat clearing," the cluttering of opening paragraphs with irrelevant material. Chekhov's advice to fiction writers works for feature writers too: "In general," he wrote, "there ought to be nothing unnecessary. Everything that has no direct relation to the story must be ruthlessly thrown out. If you write in the first chapter that a rifle hangs on the wall it must without fail fire in the second or third chapter. And if it isn't going to fire, it mustn't hang."

The Billboard

Once the lead has got the reader interested in the story, the next step is to indicate what the story *is*—that is, what it's going to say. This function is served by what we call the *billboard* paragraph. The billboard should appear high in the story, preferably right under the lead. And, like its namesake on the highway, it should be brief and to the point.

This feature from *The Wall Street Journal*, on unfair foreign competition, begins with a descriptive lead:

> In the black sand in front of his bare feet, a shirtless man named Jaidev is tidying up a capital P, as in Phoenix. Squatting on his heels, he carefully removes what looks like a giant aluminum cookie cutter, then flicks away stray bits of sand with a stick.
>
> Next he dusts the sand with graphite powder and covers it with a box made of molded clay and sand. Molten pig iron is poured in through a hole. When the iron cools, the box comes off, revealing a 200-pound masterpiece entitled "Phoenix Sanitary Sewer."
>
> Mr. Jaidev makes manhole covers for America. Around him in a gritty, tin-roofed foundry, hundreds of other workers are molding, chipping, grinding, brushing, polishing and painting manhole covers labeled "City of Dallas," "Fresno County Sewer," "Hartford County," "City of L.A.," "Newport News Va. Water Dept.," and "Austin Texas Sanitary Sewer."

Then the billboard encapsulated the story to follow:

> To his government, Mr. Jaidev is a small but vital part of India's drive to increase exports and earn foreign exchange. To some of his competitors in the U.S., however, he is part of a network engaged in unfair competition. U.S. foundries claim India is dumping manhole covers. . . .

More complicated stories call for somewhat longer billboards. This trend piece from *Newsweek* begins with an anecdotal lead:

> When Nancy Kelly married Ed Kleinman, they weren't sure who would show up for the wedding. Neither family was pleased: Nancy had spent three years as a novice in a Roman Catholic convent, and Ed had once dreamed of becoming a rabbi. Over the next 10 years, Nancy went to synagogue on Friday night and mass on Sunday—alone—but finally grew weary "of standing between two doors and wearing out the rug between them." Although she still believes strongly that intermarriages can work, this week in Boston Nancy will immerse herself three times in a mikvah—the bath of ritual purification—pronounce herself "a daughter of Abraham and Sarah" and become a Jew.

Then comes the billboard:

> Nancy represents a new strand of American Judaism: "Jews-by-choice," most of whom probably would not have converted except for interfaith marriages. Mixed

marriages are on the rise—between 30 and 40 percent of American Jews now take vows with gentiles, compared with only 7 percent in the 1950s—and in 3 out of every 10 of these unions, the gentile spouse converts. But even after conversion, Jews-by-choice often experience painful problems—strained relations with parents, lack of full acceptance by "born Jews" and rejection by strict constructionists of Jewish law, or Halakha. Only last week Orthodox legislators in the Knesset, the Israeli Parliament, tried to amend the Law of Return to exclude all Jews-by-choice except those converted by Orthodox rabbis. The motion was defeated, but not before emotional public arguments—in the United States as well as in Israel—over the central question: "Who is a Jew?" . . .

The Body

There's no such thing as a story that "tells itself." Every story rests upon an underlying structure that functions like the frame of a house or the skeleton of a vertebrate. When writing a feature you can choose from a number of possible ways to organize your piece, but the structure must be there, and you should be clearly aware of it even if the readers aren't.

The principles of sound organization most useful in feature writing include:

Keep related material together. If your subject in one paragraph is apples, save oranges for the next paragraph.

Use topic sentences to denote your subject. A feature is divided up into several areas, each introduced with a topic sentence. In journalism you won't be doing this for every paragraph, but it's a good idea to begin each *section*, whatever its length, with a topic sentence.

Use transitions to signal changes in subject. Transition sentences and phrases should always contain *information*. Avoid empty transitions. Never write, for example, "Having considered apples, we now turn our attention to oranges."

A feature by Paul Nussbaum of the *Los Angeles Times* illustrates these organizational precepts in action. The story opens with a scene-setting lead:

> They talk with their hands.
> One hand follows the other, swooping, diving, climbing, turning—the fingertips of one constantly seeking a kill shot on the other wrist.
> Reliving the day's flights in the officers club at Miramar Naval Air Station, fighter pilots are conspicuous—less for their olive drab fight suits or khaki uniforms than for their restless hands.
> "If you take him up like this and he can't stay with you"—one hand drops out of a climb—"then you've got him"—the other hand noses over.
> The nearly naked dancer on the stage at the front of the club doesn't have a chance. . . . Even when they are not in their airplanes, these men are flying, recreating the day's air combat maneuvers in endless variation, improving and embellishing reality with each pass of their hands.

Then comes the billboard, in three paragraphs, concluding with a news peg:

> These are Navy fighter pilots, an elite group even in the select military aviation community, an aggressive, egocentric, intelligent, voluble, competitive, cocky, venturesome breed that is trained to do one thing: shoot down enemy airplanes.

They don't drop bombs, they don't ferry passengers, they don't hunt submarines. In a mission that in many ways is little changed since aerial combat was born over the trenches of France in World War I, they fight their battles in isolation, airplane against airplane and pilot against pilot, quick, intense battles that are decided by one's ability to see better and move faster and shoot first.

It is a breed that has attracted national attention recently, since two Navy crews flying F-14 Tomcats shot down a pair of inferior Soviet built Libyan jets over the Gulf of Sidra on August 19.

The body of the story comes next. Any story about fighter pilots must describe what it's like to fly, so Nussbaum first describes the pilots' world aloft:

From the cockpit, an aerial dogfight is not the smooth, almost slow-motion dance it appears to be from a distance. It is a brief (engagements of three minutes are considered unusually long), stomach-churning swirl of confusion. . . . As the sky and earth change places on the horizon with unsettling frequency, the pilots work the stick and throttle with all their attention focused outside the cockpit. The right index finger is poised on the trigger on the control stick, because the opportunity for a good shot flashes before the canopy in a fraction of a second. . . .

Sounds dangerous. Is it? Nussbaum uses this question in the readers' minds as an *unstated* transition, and moves on to take a look at the hazards:

Despite the statistics that show that flying a Navy fighter jet is dangerous business, even in peacetime (a 1970 study showed that 25% of the fighter pilots did not survive a 20-year career—Navy officials say the mortality rate is much lower now, although they have no current figures), pilots consider themselves invincible.

Death is something that will always happen to the other pilot, and the standard line is, "If he's dead, he must have done something wrong."

The essential subject of the story follows: What sort of men choose this dangerous profession? Nussbaum profiles them, leading readers along with clear *topic sentences* that preview the contents of the paragraph. They are italicized here:

For the fighter pilot, flying is everything. The raw joy of strapping on a jet-engined airplane that can fly more than twice the speed of sound, climb like a rocket and perform maneuvers that would make a roller-coaster aficionado blanch is almost impossible for him to describe to less worthy, land-bound wretches.

"Next to sex, it's the best," says Lt. Ben Hymen. Others don't even make that qualification. . . .

Even pilots refer to themselves sometimes as arrested adolescents. . . .

"I don't have to grow up . . . it's just like being a professional athlete," Lt. Cmdr. Tom Dussman acknowledges cheerfully. . . .

It is the emotional and psychological makeup that sets fighter pilots apart, that makes them of one mold.

"You can spot them," says Rishelle Knutson, whose husband has been flying for the Navy since 1963. . . .

But all of the traits that make them good pilots can make these men hard to live with. They are very good at screening out their feelings, at emotionally ejecting when things get too hot, too personal. . . . The women in the lives of Navy fighter pilots soon learn they are sharing their men with an airplane, with a ship and with a squadron. . . .

"They're very outgoing, but they're hard to get to know beyond a certain level," says Rishelle Knutson. . . . Chucki, the female bartender at the Miramar officers club who has been serving drinks to pilots for four years, says that "if it doesn't have rivets, they don't know how to deal with it. I like 'em, but they can't deal with women.". . .

The italicized sentences illustrate what we mean by writing transitions that convey information. Nussbaum's fast-moving feature would be stopped in its tracks by such an empty transition sentence as "Having considered the pilots' bold acceptance of danger, we now consider whether their emotional development may have been arrested." Instead, he kept the story moving by writing, "Even pilots refer to themselves sometimes as arrested adolescents. . . ."

The Conclusion

A hard news story can end abruptly, when the reporter runs out of time, space or facts. But feature writers usually try to end their pieces with a bit of a flourish. For example, an ending might sum up the basic point of the story with a quotation. The story mentioned earlier about the unhappy Canadians ended with a quote:

"How many former Prime Ministers can the average American name?" an irritated Montreal lawyer asked. "In fact, how many Canadians of any type can he name?"

Or, the conclusion might make a final point. Nussbaum of the *Los Angeles Times* concluded his fighter pilot feature by reminding readers that the pilots, if boyish, nonetheless are taken quite seriously by their colleagues.

For all their bravado and self-confidence and cliquish loyalty, or perhaps because of it, fighter pilots are the most envied group in the military, a breed that is protected and pampered and almost universally respected.

"They're a lot more fun than line officers," says Lt. Cmdr. John Stabb, the highest ranking non-aviator on the aircraft carrier Ranger.

"And I envy them. They put it on the line every day."

The conclusion, however, need not pretend to "wrap up" a story if the story isn't over yet. Indeed, one of the advantages of the feature approach is that it can deal with ongoing stories in which nothing has happened lately that would qualify as breaking news. Selwyn Raab of *The New York Times* began a follow-up feature about a child who had been missing for two months with this lead:

Every day Detective William Butler retraces the route that six-year-old Etan Patz should have taken on that Friday morning two months ago when he disappeared.

And he wound it up with an open-ended conclusion:

"This is the toughest of crimes to solve," said Lieut. Earl J. Campazzi, commander of the squad. "There are virtually no clues. Whoever took Etan probably did it in a matter of seconds. But we've got to keep looking for Etan and we have no intention of stopping."

SUMMARY

The term *feature* applies loosely to several sorts of stories written in other than the classic inverted-pyramid breaking news format. Features typically are concerned with "softer" or less timely news. They tend to be more ruminative and descriptive than breaking news stories, and they permit the writer greater freedom of organization and latitude of style.

Sidebars are features written to accompany breaking news. *Follow-ups* report on later developments in previous news. *Profiles* present word portraits of people who may have been in the news or who may simply be of interest. *Mood stories* seek to report on the state of mind of a group or community. At the least, they require that a reporter interview a wide variety of people. At their most ambitious, they may employ public opinion polls and other sociological devices to determine public attitudes. *Trend* stories chronicle important changes that occur too slowly to qualify as breaking news. *Human interest* is a term used to designate features likely to interest readers even though they may have little news value. *Explainers* present the arguments on all sides of an issue, as free as possible from the biases and rhetoric of the parties to the dispute. *Service features* provide readers with information and advice to help with their daily lives; consumer items and tips on getting action from government and business are characteristic service features.

The structure of a feature story can be divided into four parts: the lead, the billboard, the body and the conclusion. The *lead* to a feature must attract and hold the readers' interest. This can be done in many ways. Some of the more popular are the *topical lead*, which goes right to the point; the *anecdotal lead*, a microcosm of the overall story; the *scene-setting lead*, a passage of description that serves to set the stage for the story; leads based on *quotations* or *dialogue*; and the *contrast lead*, a turnabout.

The *billboard* should come soon after the lead, reasonably high in the copy. It outlines the subject of the feature and indicates why it may be of interest. Depending on the nature of the story, the billboard may be as short as a single sentence or as long as several paragraphs.

The *body* of the feature requires intelligent organization. As the writer, you must determine what are to be the main elements of the story, arrange them in a workable order, and lump most of the subordinate material into the appropriate parts of the piece. The fact that features are not as formally constrained as straight news stories does not mean they should be any less carefully structured.

The *conclusion* offers a chance to wind up the story in a way that reminds readers of its central point. Quotations make good conclusions, if one can be found that succinctly makes its point.

10

EDITING YOUR COPY

The big league outfielder who drops a fly ball must live with the hoots of the crowd. So must the cellist who falters in a recital, or the actress who forgets her lines.

But writers get another chance. Having written something, they get to edit it—to tighten its organization, simplify complex sentences, improve word choice, cut verbiage, check for inaccuracies and make dozens of other improvements, all before anyone else sees a word of it.

Even the finest writers can write bad drafts. Their flowing, seemingly spontaneous styles are usually the result of extensive rewriting and self-editing. If their finished works look as effortless as Fred Astaire's dancing, it's for the same reason: They were the products of lots of hard work. There's no shame in discovering shortcomings in your work; finding problems is the first step toward solving them. If you think a piece is perfect, *that's* the time to worry. Chances are you're kidding yourself.

IMPROVING SELF-EDITING

The following sections pose some useful questions to ask yourself when editing your copy.

Can the Organization Be Improved?

Organizational problems are much easier to solve once you can see a particular piece on a page or display screen. Perhaps you have been guilty of *throat clearing*—that is, of putting unessential material at the top of the story. Now is the time to delete the irrelevant material, so the readers get quickly to the meat of the matter. Perhaps the piece *rambles* in places; now that you can perceive the thrust of the narrative, you can prune such digressions. Excessive *seesawing* from one side of an issue to the other—signalled by too many sentences beginning with "But" or "Although"—can be corrected by pulling related elements together. Improving organization means putting less strain on the language; this, in turn, means that you can cut *needless words*.

When organizational problems are severe, don't be afraid to tear the story up by its roots and start again from scratch. There's nothing sacred about a draft. Some magazine writers go through as many as a dozen or more drafts before arriving at a finished article. Newspaper deadlines seldom permit that much reworking, but there's usually enough time to edit and rewrite at least once or twice. Use the time available to improve the structure of your copy.

Are You Saying What You Mean?

Words are the writer's tools. Using the wrong word is like using a hammer to tune a motorcycle. When editing your copy, be sure that each word means what you suppose it means. When in doubt, check the dictionary. Be especially sure to check the definitions of technical terms. A hurricane, for instance, is a circular storm with high winds; it is known as a typhoon in the western Pacific. A violent storm is not a hurricane only unless its winds circulate. A rifle has a grooved barrel that spins the bullet; a gun does not. The bullet or slug is what is fired from the barrel; the shell stays behind. A suspect may be charged by the district attorney, but can be indicted only by a grand jury.

Beware, too, of such frequently misused words as:

In his talk, Toller *inferred* that he might not seek a second term. (A speaker *implies*; a listener *infers*.)

The school opened with far *less* students than in previous years. (For numbers of individuals, it is *fewer*, not *less*. Refer to *less* water in a bucket, but *fewer* drops from a faucet.)

The police said two masked men *robbed* the jewels shortly before dawn. (The owners of the jewels can be *robbed*, but the jewels themselves are *stolen*.)

Prune hyperbole. Do you really want to say that the owner of the yacht basin is "fabulously" wealthy? What will you write next week, if your subject is a Rockefeller?

Is Your Copy Factually Accurate?

Even the most careful writers sometimes make mistakes. The important thing is to discover and correct mistakes before they are published. Accuracy is primarily the writer's responsibility; never rely on editors to catch errors for you. They may catch the mistakes, but if they don't the results can be embarrassing. This correction appeared in *The New York Times*:

> In Tuesday's *Times*, Joseph W. Barr, chairman of the Franklin National Bank, was inadvertently misquoted on the condition of the bank. His actual statement was that the bank is solvent.

Watch for hard-to-spot errors like ages, addresses and the exact spellings of unusual names. Check to see that all quotations are reproduced accurately,

Careful checking of the facts before publishing a story can save the effort of making a correction afterward. Drawing by Booth; © 1980 *The New Yorker* Magazine, Inc.

"*Correction: The obituary for 'Ta Ta' Bottorff appearing in the November 12th edition of the Post-News and Gazette-Telegram incorrectly listed 'Ebbie' Bottorff, of Spickert, as the son of 'Ta Ta' Bottorff. 'Ebbie' Bottorff is the brother of 'Ta Ta' Bottorff, and also we are pleased to say that both 'Ta Ta' Bottorff and 'Ebbie' Bottorff are living and in good health. The Post-News and Gazette-Telegram regrets the error.*"

and that each is attributed to the right person; attributions get mixed up more often than you might expect. Make sure, for instance, that you haven't transformed the prosecutor into the defense attorney, the right cross into a left hook, innocence into guilt, day into night.

Be alert for internal contradictions; a self-contradictory story cannot be accurate. A story headlined "Allal el-Fassi, 82, Dead" said, a few paragraphs later, "His age was 65." A profile of a comedian said he had been in show business "for six decades," and a few paragraphs later listed his age as 58. A publisher's dustjacket copy on a book expressed regret that its author had "delivered the manuscript only three months after his untimely death." An obituary of a man lost at sea reported that he would be "buried" at a local cemetery on Saturday. A reporter wrote, "A court-appointed psychiatrist said that Mr. Kearney had complained of being small for his size until he was about twelve years old."

Does the Copy Answer Readers' Questions?

Copy editors urge newswriters to "be a mind reader." By this, they mean that newswriters should anticipate questions that might reasonably occur to readers, and should answer them in advance.

The copy editors of *The New York Times* publish an in-house newsletter, *Winners & Sinners*, devoted to applauding good *Times* editing and writing and lampooning the bad. "Try to imagine in each story what questions are likely to arise in a reader's mind," they advise:

> It's our business to furnish information, not raise questions and leave them unanswered. . . . When a dispatch says that the King of Bhutan "spoke in English with a trace of a British accent," it would be a good idea to tell our customers what language the king normally speaks. Be a mind reader. Think of the questions that might tantalize a reader. Then bang your fist on the desk (quietly of course) and demand the answers.

One way to answer questions in advance is to be specific. Just *where* on the river did the boat strike a submerged rock and sink? Other boaters in the area will want to know. *When* did the knifing on the bus occur? Readers who ride that route will react to the news differently depending on whether the knifing took place at 6 A.M., when buses are empty, or at 6 P.M., during the rush hour. *Which* hand did the pitcher injure, and with which, by the way, does he pitch? *What*, exactly, did the demonstrator shout when he broke up the meeting: "Point of parliamentary procedure"? "You're a bunch of bigots"? "Help, I'm covered with ants"? It makes a difference.

If a hard-to-see traffic light is being blamed for an accident that killed a pedestrian, be precise about the location of the accident; motorists living in the area will want to know. If food and clothing are being collected to assist flood victims in a nearby county, make sure readers know just where and when the gifts are being collected, so they can help out if they care to. If police warn that pickpockets plague the downtown shopping area, spell out how the pickpockets operate, and pass along advice from the police about how shoppers can protect themselves.

When updating an ongoing story, don't assume that your readers will remember what appeared in yesterday's papers. Give them at least a sketch of the background information they need if they are to understand the news. Avoid the mistake of the network television reporter who filed a three-minute report on a referendum being held to recall the mayor of Cleveland without recounting why Clevelanders were displeased with their mayor in the first place.

Explain unfamiliar terms:

The White House physician, Myron Crane, said the President "sustained a mild contusion" when he struck his head. *"Contusion" is the medical term for a bruise.*

The spacecraft would take 30,000 years to reach the distance of the nearest star, Alpha Centauri, 4.2 light years away. *A light year is the distance light travels in one year, about 6000 billion miles.*

When you discover that you have unanswered questions of your own when writing a story, get on the phone and try to get the answers. Don't be shy, for instance, about calling back the police to check whether the truck that jumped a curb on Main Street was going north or south. Rather than describe the woman who poured red paint over the steps of the nuclear missile plant as "unidentified," call a few more people involved in the demonstration to see if they can identify her. If you're unable to learn the answer to an obvious question, admit it, and explain why you don't know:

Navy surgeons could not immediately account for how the pilot survived a 5000-foot plunge to the sea without a parachute.

Police were searching for Wilcox. *They said he checked out of the Criterion Hotel Wednesday leaving no forwarding address.*

Names of the victims *were withheld* pending notification of next of kin.

Attribute information whenever readers might have cause to wonder about its source. Most such cases are covered by two rules: (1) attribute all quotations; (2) attribute information whenever there is any reasonable doubt about its accuracy.

Let's look at these two rules in detail:

1. *Attribute all quotations.* When quotation marks appear it should be made clear who is talking. If an unattributed quotation appears in the lead . . .

The new Senate office building, branded a "boondoggle" and a "mausoleum" by critics, was dedicated yesterday in Washington.

. . . tell your readers, within the next few sentences, who spoke those words.

. . . Senator Wilcox Baine, Republican of California, described the office building as a "boondoggle and a waste of money."

COPY EDITING SYMBOLS

Although electronic editing on word processors is becoming widespread, old-fashioned editing on paper is likely to remain part of journalism for some time. The important point to remember is that pencil editing is normally a form of *communication*. Reporters and editors use it to convey the changes they would like to see made in copy. As with all communication, line editing should be clear and easy to understand. This requires familiarity with standard copy editing marks like those illustrated here:

Words to be added to copy should be inserted as should letters and punctuation marks intended to stand above the line, such as these "quotation marks." Commas are inserted from below to prevent their being confused with apostrophes or single quotation marks. Words transposed are in this fashion, and for letters and phrases the same applies. Single letters and punctuation marks are best eliminated by using deletion symbols. Words and phrases are deleted by drawing a line through them a line through them. A period when inserted should be circled to avoid its getting lost. Indicate new paragraphs with a paragraph mark.

To join two paragraphs, or to lead an editor's eye down through deleted copy, use a line like the one that ties the beginning of this sentence to the end of the previous one. A slash drawn through a capital letter makes it lower case. Three lines under a lower-case letter promote it to a capital. Changing a numeral into a spelled-out number calls for a circle, as in 9, and the opposite is true, as for sixty-four. Do the same to regularize abbreviations: Avenue Ave.

Use a mark like this to make a space between two words that have been run together; close up spaces in this manner. If copy was correct to begin with and has been marked inadvertantly, use stet, a Latin abbreviation for "Let it stand." If corrections Become too extensive to be read easily, retype them to make life easier on editors, copyreaders Typesetters and.

There were skeptics on the Democratic side of the aisle as well, among them Senator Herbert Cramdon of Ohio, who called the building "a mausoleum, more suitable to ancient Egypt than to modern America."

Occasionally, sources of quotations are characterized without revealing their names. The result is known as a "blind" quotation. Blind quotations should be employed only when necessary, because they tend to arouse suspicion—why are we not being told who is talking?—and can lend news stories an insubstantial quality, like that of spirit voices at a seance. A blind quotation is permissible, however, when it's impossible to determine the name of the speaker:

As the fighters awaited the decision a spectator called out, "Ali, you'll always be the champ."

A blind quotation may also be used when the reporter has agreed not to identify the speaker:

"The President is in hot water over this one," said a State Department official who asked not to be identified.

2. *Attribute information whenever there is any reasonable doubt about its accuracy.* Suppose a warehouse on the corner of Main and Criterion Streets burns to the ground. A witness says she saw a man fleeing the scene carrying a gasoline can. Nobody else saw the man. The detail is too important to leave out of the story, but it cannot be related as fact, because it is the account of only one person, who may have been mistaken. How should you write this story? Include the material, but attribute it to its source, so that readers may judge for themselves:

Rosemary Baird, a clerk in a stationary store a block from the warehouse, said that at about the time the fire broke out she saw a man dressed in a black raincoat run from the warehouse carrying what appeared to be a gasoline can.

The rule of attributing when in doubt is especially important if the information involved is *potentially damaging* to anyone. Newspapers often carry stories that damage people's reputations—about an assembly line worker said to have shot his wife while drunk, an architect fired on grounds of incompetence, a motorist confesses to a fatal hit-and-run. The appearance of such news items can be painful to the persons named as well as to their families and friends. Especially if there is any reasonable doubt about the accuracy of damaging information, a sense of fairness requires that the source of the news be clearly cited, so that readers know where the information originated:

Prosecuting attorney Wilbur Evans said in his opening statement on the first day of trial that he would prove that the defendant, Roy Zane, shot and killed his wife on the night of February 11th after taking part in *what Evans called* a "drinking bout" at a local tavern.

Mrs. Williams was dismissed as architect on the Hapsville Mall project on grounds of incompetence, *School Board President Alicia Meyers told the Town Council.*

The police said Sykes admitted driving the car involved in the hit-and-run death of a 9-year-old girl on an Atlantic Street two nights ago.

Note that attributing damaging information does *not* protect a newspaper against libel suits. The press is responsible for what it reports, regardless of whether it obtained the information from a third party. (For more on libel, see Chapter 17.)

Is the Style Clear, Succinct and Evocative?

Vague words should be replaced with precise words, weak verbs with strong verbs. Cliches, tired language and jargon can be eliminated, and wordy constructions tightened: The fewer words, the better. Some of the problems most frequently corrected during editing are:

Redundancy. There is no more obvious way to waste words than to say the same thing twice, yet it is surprising how often redundancy crops up in newswriting. These examples caught the eye of editors at *The New York Times*:

> Nino Martina . . . died of a heart attack Thursday in his native Verona, Italy, where he was born. ("Native" *means* he was born there.)

> Thomas Glynn is a New York writer who frequently camps in the outdoors. (After this story appeared, a reader wrote in to ask, "When did you last camp indoors?")

> The Ford Foundation's loan . . . is separate and apart from the Foundation's $10 million terminal grant. . . . (If "separate," it is also "apart.")

Other common redundancies include such phrases as "consensus of opinion" ("consensus" always refers to "opinion"); "revert back" ("reversion" *is* backward); "her first and only St. Louis appearance in two years" (if it's the first, it has to be the only one so far); "advance planning" (you can't plan something unless it lies in the future); and "self-confessed" (who else can make a confession?).

Mixed Metaphors. Metaphors enliven writing by creating pictures in the readers' minds: The "*sunset* of the Roman Empire" is more evocative than the "*end* of the Roman Empire." But writers sometimes confuse matters by crowding several metaphors, creating a jumbled image. This happens most often in first drafts, and can be corrected during editing by choosing the single metaphor that works best and discarding the others. Following are some especially painful mixed metaphors:

> The Assembly members also were miffed at their Senate counterparts because they have refused to *bite the bullet* that now seems to have grown to the size of a *millstone* to the Assembly members whose *necks are on the line*. (If the bullet is as big as a millstone, no wonder the Senators would risk having their heads chopped off rather than bite it.)

"In this recession, at least so far, many of the millions of unemployed are discovering that *the wolf is not at the door*, that society has given them a *cushion* that enables them to *tighten their belts* a bit and live pretty much as they did when they were working." (If the wolf does show up, perhaps they can fight him off with the belt and cushion.)

Misplaced Words. Misplacing words can produce unintentional hilarity in print:

". . . The elephant belonged to her grandfather whose tusks were studded with diamonds. . . ."

"In the 1972 training camp, the Jets waited one week for Namath to show up and during the next week he signed a contract in the dining hall at Hofstra University in Hempstead, Long Island, which expired last May 1st."

"The Assembly passed and sent to the Senate a bill requiring dog owners in New York City to clean up after their pets, on penalty of $100 fine. The bill also applies to Buffalo."

Long, confusing sentences are breeding grounds for misplaced words and phrases. Whenever possible, edit them down into simple declarative sentences.

Slang. Slang tends to be ambiguous, and its currency is usually restricted to a relatively narrow audience. This is not to say that you ought never to employ slang or popular language. But if, during self-editing, you are in doubt

---

WHAT'S WRONG WITH THIS COPY?

Sometimes the most glaring errors are the most difficult for an editor to catch. Can you spot the mistake in this paragraph from *The Wall Street Journal*?

WASHINGTON, D.C.—The Senate approved 49–41 legislation to extend the federal government's borrowing authority through Sept. 31.

Or in this publisher's promotional letter?

The contents of *ENCYCLOPEDIA* of Michigan includes an Introduction, Pre-History and Archaeology, History, Geographic Configuration, Biographies, Picture Tour, State Gazetteer, Historical Places, State Constitution, Bibliography and Index.

We believe this is the most comprehensive reference to the state of Illinois ever published. You may send for an approval copy to examine for 30 days before deciding whether or not to purchase.

Or in this *Baltimore Sun* feature?

Doug Jones stood poised atop a construction crane yesterday afternoon, ready to leap 182 feet into the Inner Harbor in an attempt to set a world's high-diving record at the Baltimore City Fair.

Sixteen stories below, on Constellation Dock, a little girl turned to her father and asked, "What if he misses?"

"He gets killed," her father answered quietly.

In a few minutes, the suspense was over. At 3:40 P.M., while thousands of City Fair visitors held their collective breath, Mr. Jones jumped, made two somersaults and landed in 25 feet of water in the Inner Harbor.

His audience, crowded along the harbor promenade and squeezed into the deck of the Constellation burst into cheers as Mr. Brown, 26, bobbed to the surface of the water and climbed onto the dock to face television cameras.

(*Stumped? See answers on page 182.*)

WRITING AND EDITING ON A COMPUTER

In ever-increasing numbers, journalists today do their writing not on typewriters but at the softly glowing screens of VDTs—video display terminals hooked up to computers. Computers dedicated to use in writing are called *word processors*. Because many different sorts of computers (or *hardware*) and programs (*software*) are being used in journalism, and electronic technology continues to evolve rapidly, we won't try to describe in detail how to operate each computer. But following are a few general tips about writing and editing electronically:

The first thing to keep in mind is that computers are not "smart." They are dumb. All they can do is exactly what they have been told. The long list of commands that has to be entered into a computer in order to tell it what to do is called a *program*. If a computer seems smart, that's because it's running an efficient program. Computers are fast, and accurate, but they aren't smart.

Running a computer is like driving an ox. It's no use getting angry at the ox if it won't do what you want; instead, you have to learn the commands it knows how to obey. The computer will *not* learn to speak your language. You must learn to speak its language.

The VDT, which is the means by which journalists normally converse with their computers, consists of three parts: a typewriterlike keyboard for writing copy, a set of keys used to manipulate the copy and a screen on which to monitor the results. A square of light on the screen, called the *cursor*, tells you where you are in the copy. Its position can be changed by using the appropriate manipulation keys, through such commands as *forward sentence* or *back paragraph*. To move steadily forward or back through your copy, use the *scroll up* and *scroll down* keys. Many systems also offer a *find* (or *go-to*) key, useful for locating a word or phrase; if you've just drafted a lengthy music feature and need to locate the paragraphs dealing with Miles Davis, you can order the computer to *find* "Davis," and it will stop with the cursor located at the first place in your piece where that name appears.

Most systems also offer *global* commands. These automatically find every place where a given bit of copy appears, and change it as instructed. Suppose you've written "gun" all through a story about an antique Browning Automatic, only to have an acid-tongued editor inform you that the Browning is a "rifle." You can correct your mistake throughout the copy by using a global command—but remember, the computer doesn't know what you want; it only does what it's told. If you've written that a victim was "gunned down," a global command to change "gun" to "rifle" will change the phrase "gunned down" to "riflened down."

To *insert* words in copy, move the cursor to the appropriate spot and type the insertion. To *delete* copy, use the keys marked for that purpose; most systems will, on command, delete

about whether to use slang or vogue words, you'll probably be better off without them.

REFERENCE WORKS

Editing copy calls first of all for using a dictionary. To expect editors to "fix" your spelling or replace misused words is to ask them to do your work for you. A short paperback edition is handy for checking spelling. "Collegiate" dictionaries provide adequate definitions of most commonly used words. Unabridged editions are indispensable for looking up unusual words and for investigating subtleties of definition.

Able references for grammar include *The Random House Handbook*, E. L. Calli-

anything from a single character up to a paragraph or more. Blocks of copy can also be *transposed*—moved to a new spot in the story—by using the cursor to mark them off and to indicate where they are to go. Delineate the copy to be transposed by using keys marked *define block*.

Once the piece has been written and self-edited, it goes into the computer's memory. The computer adds it to a *directory*, also called a *menu* or an *index*, listing all the copy *on-line*, or accessible through the system. Editors can then *call up* the copy—that is, make it appear on their screens—at any time. Once they have edited and cleared it, again electronically, the piece is available to the copy desk, then to the production people. The computer sets it in type, so there is no need to worry about typographical errors introduced by a human typesetter. In many operations the newspaper can even be laid out page by page, electronically, without individuals' resorting to paper and paste.

In order to keep track of who has edited and approved a piece of copy, each person who works on it may be asked to *log* his or her name or initials on the copy. Thus, each story carries with it a record of how it made its way through the editorial process. Some systems even permit editing to be superimposed so that it looks like handwritten editing on a page, which allows the writer and other editors to review how the edited version compares to the original. When the changes have been agreed upon, a single command integrates the edits into a finished manuscript.

To obtain *hard copy* of your story, order a *printout*. A story may go through the entire editorial process without being generated as hard copy, because the electronic system is so efficient that it all but eliminates the need for paper and ink, but hard copy is handy for reference when you're away from the computer terminals.

Some day, when most homes have computers, newspapers may cease to be printed on paper. Instead, they might take the form of electronic data transmitted to home computers, and then read on a screen or printed out, whole or in part, by those who want hard copy to read over breakfast or on the train to work.

Computers can be maddening—especially if you hit the wrong key and accidently erase a story you've been working on for hours and have forgotten to *back up* (duplicate). But they're here to stay. Years ago, reporters protested when the first typewriters were introduced; they preferred to go on writing longhand, at standup desks. But nobody today writes longhand at a standup desk, and the day has just about arrived when nobody will bother with a typewriter, either; computers are more efficient. A *Publishers Weekly* survey found that writers who switched to word processing reported gains of 30 to 40 percent in their productivity.

han's *Grammar for Journalists* and the *Harbrace College Handbook*. For guidelines on overcoming common writing problems, see *The Elements of Style* by William Strunk Jr. and E. B. White; *The Careful Writer* and *Watch Your Language* by Theodore Bernstein; and *Words on Words* by John Bremner. Valuable short essays explaining word usage can be found in Fowler's *Modern American Usage* and its companion volume, *Modern English Usage*.

Roget's *Thesaurus* has both advocates and detractors. Advocates say it helps them achieve greater variety of usage by leading the way from habitual words and phrases toward fresher, less predictable language. Detractors call the *Thesaurus* a crutch, and they say that writers can develop better "mental muscles" by arriving at fresh synonyms and original phrasing for themselves.

The style books of the Associated Press and United Press International address many of the questions that come up frequently in daily newswriting. Larger

MISTAKES SELF-EDITING COULD HAVE PREVENTED

The ancient Romans had an expression, "Sometimes even Homer nods," meaning that anyone can make a mistake. If you catch mistakes like the following examples by vigilant self-editing, you can laugh over them with your friends instead of bearing the brunt of the laughter of thousands of readers.

HARRISBURG—Over in Pennsylvania, there's a new state program designed to transform hundreds of Pennsylvanians into miniature, subsidized farmers. But some farm groups are a little edgy.

—AP radio wire

No wonder they're edgy. The farms are to be miniature, not the farmers.

MISSOURI DEER KILL NEAR 50,000

—Kansas City, Mo., Star

Is "kill" a noun or a verb here?

JUVENILE COURT TO TRY SHOOTING DEFENDANT

—Salt Lake City, Utah, Deseret News

Is "shooting" a verb or an adjective?

STOLEN PAINTING FOUND BY TREE

—Philadelphia Evening Bulletin

"By" fits, "Beside" doesn't: Such are the headaches of headline writers.

AUGUSTA, MAINE—The president of Bangor's student teacher association has told the legislative education committee a questionnaire distributed to Bangor teachers showed that many used capital punishment in maintaining order in their classrooms.

—UPI radio wire

Keeps down class size.

DEATH CAUSES LONELINESS, FEELINGS OF ISOLATION

—Meriden, Conn., Morning Record

Yes, and it's rough on the survivors, too.

ROSEMARY HALL GETS NEW HEAD

—Hartford, Conn., Courant

Rosemary's a residence hall, not a woman.

"East is east, and west is west, and never the twain shall meet." Shakespeare may not have been a sports writer, but he sure knew what he was talking about with that remark. . . .

—Albany, N.Y., Times-Union

Shakespeare wasn't a sports writer, and he wasn't the author of that line, either. Bartlett's Quotations could have set this writer right.

ILL HEALTH SUSPECTED

POMPIDOU DIES

Morgantown, W. Va., Dominion-Post

Suspicions confirmed!

DR. TACKETT GIVES TALK ON MOON

—Indiana Evening Gazette

BILL WOULD PERMIT ADS ON EYEGLASSES

—Tulsa, Okla., Daily World

Unheralded astronaut and ad man remind us of the ambiguity of the word "on."

COLD WAVE LINKED TO TEMPERATURES

—San Clemente, Calif., Daily Sun-Post

With the exception of victimless crimes (which need not concern us here), every single crime committed in this nation of ours involves a victim.

—San Francisco Chronicle

And except for tautologies, there are no tautologies.

DEAD EXPECTED TO RISE

—Macon, Ga., News

Yes, and there may be more of them, too.

IMPORTANT NOTICE. If you are one of the hundreds of parachuting enthusiasts who bought our "Easy Sky Diving" book, please make the following correction: On page 8, line 7, the words "state zip code" should have read "pull rip cord."

—Warrenton, Va., Fauquier Democrat

Corrections can be funnier—and more embarrassing—than the errors that prompted them. As a journalist, you should learn to scrutinize your copy while it is still in the first draft, so that you can catch and correct your mistakes before they are published.

newspapers supplement them with style books of their own that help guide their staffs toward consistent usage, spelling and punctuation.

SUMMARY

Self-editing is an integral part of the process of newswriting. Use that time to double-check that your copy is accurate, that each word means what it is intended to mean, that it is consistent and that it either answers every reasonable question readers might have or else explains why it has failed to do so. Work to ensure that the language is clear, succinct and evocative.

Attribute information to its source whenever readers might wish to know the source. Specifically, this means you should attribute all direct quotations and any controversial or dubious information, especially if it is likely to be damaging to someone's reputation. Replace redundancy, mixed metaphors, misplaced words and inappropriate language or slang. Use the dictionary to be sure that every word is spelled and used correctly; do not expect editors to correct errors for you. Using reference works on grammar and usage can also help you answer questions that arise during editing.

Answers to editing problems on page 177: The Senate approved 49–41 legislation to extend the federal government's borrowing authority through *Sept. 31: Thirty days hath September*. . . .
The contents of ENCYCLOPEDIA of *Michigan* . . . is the most comprehensive reference to the state of *Illinois* ever published. . . .
Doug *Jones* stood poised atop a construction crane yesterday afternoon, ready to leap 182 feet. . . . His audience . . . burst into cheers as Mr. *Brown*, 26, bobbed to the surface of the water and climbed onto the dock to face television cameras.

11

WRITING FOR BROADCAST

Broadcast newswriting calls for simplicity and clarity even more than does writing for print. A reader who is confused by a sentence in a newspaper can reread it, but someone listening to broadcast copy hears it only once, and must understand it at once. "If I were teaching a class of young writers," says television writer Andy Rooney, "I'd advise them to keep in mind what something sounds like when they read it aloud, even if what they are writing is for print. Anyone should be suspicious of a sentence he's written that can't be read aloud easily."

BASICS OF BROADCAST WRITING

Like all good writing, broadcast writing is a creative process, and can't be done by formula alone. But there are some helpful guidelines:

Keep it *short*. In television and radio, the news must usually be conveyed in even fewer words than in print. A twenty-second radio news item amounts to only about one-third of a page of double-spaced copy—fewer than 100 words— in which to report the entire story. A twenty-second television report fits on a single page, and that's using oversized type, with the copy restricted to the right half of the page. So make every word count.

Keep it *simple*. Remember, listeners either understand what you've written on first hearing, or they won't understand it at all. A perfectly respectable print lead may be too complex for broadcast. Try reading this one aloud:

Warning the government of El Salvador not to abandon major land-reform measures, the Senate Foreign Relations Committee on Wednesday cut $100 million from the administration's military aid requests for the Central American country.

A broadcast writer would simplify this lead, getting rid of the long dependent clause and emphasizing the basics:

The U.S. Senate Foreign Relations Committee sent a warning to El Salvador today that it doesn't want that country to abandon its major land-reform measures. It cut 100 million dollars from the administration's military aid requests for El Salvador.

Simple declarative sentences are what the ear understands best. Stick with one fact to a sentence, then build. Read aloud, this newspaper lead is difficult to comprehend:

Beginning a short holiday at his fog-shrouded ranch on a mountain top near Santa Barbara, President Reagan today lobbied congressional representatives by telephone on the budget Wednesday and also studied for his European summit trip.

Here, the lead is rewritten into simple declarative sentences:

President Reagan began a short holiday at his ranch today by telephoning congressional representatives and asking them to support his budget proposal. It was a good day for it. A dense fog covered the Santa Barbara area, and the President had to stay indoors anyway.

Write *conversationally*, the way people—*articulate* people—talk. Remember that someone is going to have to *say* the words, so write for the speaker as well as for the listener.

The following lead . . .

Israeli Prime Minister Menachem Begin today reiterated that the United States is paying "lip service" to Israel's security, in that it is still continuing to supply sophisticated weapons to his country's Arab adversaries.

. . . isn't bad in print, but it's quite an earful when heard over the air. Let's rewrite it into a more conversational form, making it easier to understand:

The Israeli Prime Minister today once again accused the United States of paying "lip service" to Israel's security. His complaint? That the U.S. is still supplying sophisticated weapons to the Arab nations.

Prefer the *present tense*. Newspapers and magazines prefer the past tense, but television and radio newswriters normally use the present tense: Guatemala *is* asking the United States for military aid for the first time in five years. Medical researchers *say* interferon may bring relief to herpes sufferers.

Of course, it would be silly to try to force every story into the present tense:

An unidentified man *is falling* to his death from the George Washington Bridge today. . . ."

But you could write:

"Harbor police *are searching* for the body of an unidentified man who fell to his death from the George Washington Bridge today. . . ."

Use *simple* English. As in all newswriting, short words are preferable to long words, the commonplace to the arcane: They did it *now* . . . not *at this time*. The City Council *acted* . . . rather than *took action*. Also beware of weak words like *resided* for lived, *according to* for said, or *is of the opinion that* for maintains. Nobody *succumbs* or *passes on*; they *die* or are *killed*.

Keep the subject close to the verb. Start with the subject, then employ an active verb to describe what happened to the subject.

The *gunman* (subject) *shot* (verb) the owner. . . .

Avoid the passive voice. It complicates sentences and costs extra words:

Two hostages were grabbed by the gunman . . . one of them was hit over the head. . . .

The active voice, in contrast, keeps your sentences lean and clean and gives your writing more pace and punch:

The gunman grabbed two hostages . . . hit one of them over the head . . . , shot and wounded a man who tried to stop him . . . then ran from the store, escaping with more than five-thousand-dollars.

Use adjectives and adverbs *sparingly*. Focus on the essentials. Colorful, descriptive language is fine, but it should drive the story, not merely ornament it. Irrelevant description can be maddening in broadcast newswriting. Imagine that you heard this ludicrous lead over the radio:

The President, wearing a dark blue suit, told reporters he feels war is inevitable. Running his fingers through his tousled red hair, he went on to say that. . . .

Description does work well, however, if it is relevant:

The President's voice trembled as he told reporters he feels war is inevitable.

Write your copy *promptly*. Don't make the mistake of thinking you can knock it out later, as air time approaches; later there may be new stories, new deadlines. If you're waiting for the lead—for example, if the robbers are holed up in the bank with their hostages, and you don't know if they'll surrender in time for the 6 o'clock news—don't just sit around waiting. Write "B" copy—background information to go below the lead—and put together file film and other visuals to go with it. Then, when the news breaks (and you can bet it will break moments before air time), you can write a lead, pick up the "B" copy and go on the air immediately.

BROADCAST COPY FORMAT

The "talent" (the person who reads copy during the broadcast; the term has nothing to do with ability) shouldn't have to squint or stumble on the air. For high visibility, broadcast copy should be typed and double or triple spaced. For radio, leave at least an inch of margins. For television, divide the page vertically into two columns. Audio copy goes on the right half of the page. Videotape, film, visual effects, graphics, voice-over, who's speaking and other instructions go on the left.

In the upper left-hand corner of the page, use a slug (one or two words to specify the story), your name or initials and the date. For radio, you may add the time as well. Use separate pages for each story. Write (MORE) at the bottom of the page if the story continues.

Never split words or sentences from one page to another. The best way to remember *not* to do this is to imagine that the talent is reading your story and says, "A fire in downtown Chicago killed. . . ." Now suppose that the talent looks for the next page, and there isn't one. That's called egg on the anchor's face, and it may mean goodbye to the newswriter.

Deliver neat, clean copy. Retype it rather than hand in pages marred by corrections. If last-minute corrections are unavoidable, make them easy to read, *not* like this:

Robert Radford won 6th award.

This is too hard to read. Instead, make corrections like this:

Robert ~~Radford~~ REDFORD won ~~6th~~ THE award.

Avoid proofreading marks. They're fine for print, but not for broadcast copy. But do employ punctuation to help the talent. Periods, commas, question marks and dashes (two hyphens) are used frequently; semicolons and exclamation marks, hardly ever. Three periods (. . .) cue the talent to pause. (In broadcasting, unlike print, the dots don't mean something is missing.) Pauses can be effective, but use them sparingly.

Never use abbreviations, with the possible exceptions of *Dr.*, *Ms.*, *Mrs.* and *Mr.* Spell out almost everything else, from states and countries to days and months. Punctuate the way the words should sound—for example, F-B-I if the letters are emphasized; NATO if they are read as one word.

Spell out any number under 10 (some prefer that ten be written out too).

Then use 11 through 999. Write out any number above 999—thousand, million, billion. In broadcasting, never write $5.5 million. Always write five-point-five-million dollars or five-and-a-half-million dollars. Write out all fractions. Add *st*, *nd*, *rd* and *th* to dates: October 28th or October seventh. Never use symbols: Write *dollar*, not $; *percent* not %; *number* not No. or #.

Use people's names in the first sentence only if they are well known, or if you identify them promptly thereafter. Otherwise save the names for later in the story. Omit middle initials unless they are part of the person's name (W. C. Fields, for instance). With someone who is very well-known, you may even omit the first name, as in Secretary of State Schultz or Prime Minister Thatcher. Avoid false titles like *receptionist* Jean Clark or *teacher* Jane Jones.

Use quotations, but use them carefully. Because listeners cannot see quotation marks, you must tell them when you're using a direct quote. Quotes can be indicated through an inflexion of the talent's voice, or, more traditionally, by your writing "quote" and "unquote."

As in print journalism, all quotations should be attributed, so that there's no doubt about who said what. *Unlike* print journalism, in broadcasting the attribution usually *precedes* the quotation. This quotation looks fine to the eye, but try reading it aloud:

> "The days of cheap gasoline are over," Paul Broede, the Secretary of Energy, told members of the American Automobile Association. "Gas-guzzlers are becoming as rare as dinosaurs."

With the attribution first, the same quotation is much easier to understand:

> Secretary of Energy Paul Broede told the American Automobile Association . . . "The days of cheap gasoline are over. Gas-guzzlers are becoming as rare as dinosaurs."

Indicate the correct pronunciation of hard-to-pronounce names and words as shown here:

(EEVE) (SAN-LARAH)
Clothing designer Yves Saint-Laurent
(COUR-AHN)
The Koran, the Muslem holy book . . .

Don't rely upon the talent to check pronunciation: You do it. For people's names, check a biographical dictionary or the list of common given names at the back of a collegiate dictionary. You can also simply call the person you're naming. For the pronunciation of unfamiliar words, consult the dictionary. For the names of unfamiliar cities and towns, call the information operator in that region. Watch for wire service advisories on pronunciation of names and words recently in the news.

Most of the rules of broadcast newswriting boil down to this: The simpler and cleaner the copy, the easier it will be for the talent to read it clearly and for the audience to understand it. As Andy Rooney says, "To be spoken aloud,

IN TELEVISION NEWS, WRITE FOR "A SMALL AUDIENCE," SAYS DAVID BRINKLEY

David Brinkley, a veteran reporter and anchorman for NBC and ABC News, has long been regarded as among television's most adept newswriters. His spare, lucid prose, which sounds natural and spontaneous, actually results from rigorous rewriting and self-editing. Often Brinkley is still editing one of his heavily inked scripts in the last moments before the red camera light glows and he goes on the air.

What characterizes good broadcast news writing?
Brinkley: The first thing to remember about broadcast writing is that it resembles *conversation*. The audience for television or radio news is *not* a mass audience. It's a small audience—normally one, two or three people in a room.

Therefore, the form and structure of each broadcast news story should be conversational—carefully written, but written as conversation. Never write a sentence to be broadcast that you would not speak if you were talking to someone else. I don't mean that the writing can be sloppy or precise, but that it needs to be conversational in tone.

A useful approach is to read the copy aloud as you write. I've been doing it for 30 years, and I *still* try out sentences aloud to see if they are easy to say and if they come out right. When I work at home writing a script, guests in the house who are not accustomed to my working habits think I'm crazy, downstairs talking to myself.

Clarity is another important quality of good broadcast writing. The viewers get to hear broadcast news only once. They cannot go back and reread it if they miss something. So you must make yourself clearly understood, the *first time*.

Brevity is important. Take out every word you don't need. Replace long words with short words if you can.

And try not to use the most obvious word in every case. Try to use language that has an *edge* to it. In too many newspaper stories, after you've read the first three words of a sentence you know what the rest is going to be, because you've read that sentence before, in almost the same words, year after year. Try to avoid that. The mind moves *faster* than speech. Every intelligent listener is always a little *ahead* of you. If you write in such a tired and predictable way that your audience knows what you are going to say before you say it, you are being a bore. People will listen if you use fresh, slightly surprising words and phrases.

You make it sound easy. Why do so many writers find it difficult to be clear, succinct and original?
I think it's a psychological problem. A person who has worked hard at writing something tends to treasure every word of it. He finds it difficult to admit that a word he has put on paper may not need to

the sentences have to be shorter and the writing simpler. You can't turn a clever phrase, because if the audience doesn't catch it the first time, they can't go back and read it over again."

Broadcast newswriting is not oratory; it reaches people in relatively private circumstances, alone behind the wheel or at home with their families. It calls for directness and understatement. Says broadcast newswriter Nate Kaplan, "When writing for broadcast, visualize the person you are talking to. Make that person become you. You're asking the screen: Tell me what happened, how it happened, why it happened. Talk directly to me."

As in print, there are plenty of ways to lead a broadcast news story. You can summarize the story with a lead that covers the principal facts:

The Voyager One space probe is taking its first photographs of the distant planet Uranus.

be there. I wouldn't attempt to say *how* this tendency should be overcome. I would say only that it *must* be overcome, because otherwise you'll be boring. A bore is someone who takes too long to say too little.

Clearing away the verbal undergrowth can be tiresome and time-consuming, but if you work at it, you can raise your average level pretty high. Writing trains and disciplines the mind, and the same discipline that applies to writing must be applied to film and to television. You can't structure a story with a camera unless you can structure it with a typewriter.

How good is the newswriting on most local television newscasts?

I don't really see nor hear very much of it, but I would say that its level is not as high as it ought to be. A lot of it sounds canned, almost as if the newsperson himself or herself was hearing it for the first time. I gather that often they have taken a story off the wire service, may have touched it up a little, but have done little more than that.

A better rule—whenever you are working from wire service copy, from a handout or other printed source material—is to use it as a source of *information*, not as a source of *prose*. Read it. See what it means. *Think* about it, for as long as it takes. Then set it aside and write the story yourself, in your own words. Don't pick up phrases or sentences from the source material. Write your *own* sentences.

Should students aiming for a broadcast news career go into newspaper work first?

It's not *essential* to work on a newspaper first, but I would say it's helpful. It's a good way to learn the nuts and bolts of our business. Newspapers, particularly the better ones, are better equipped to train young people than we are. They have assignment editors and copy desks and so on. We are not really structured that way.

What other principles should broadcast newswriters keep in mind?

A couple of mechanical considerations: Some combinations of syllables are difficult to pronounce—a word ending in "s" followed by another one beginning in "s," for example. You have to learn to avoid them. The way I do this is, as I say, to read each sentence aloud.

Beyond that, it's important that the right word or words in each sentence be *emphasized*. I may be inclined to stress this more than most, and it may seem obvious, but if you listen to people on the air you will see that you can change the entire meaning of a sentence by emphasizing the wrong word. You'll have said the right words but have delivered the wrong message. I go over the copy after I've written it, and *underline* the words I think need to be emphasized to make certain that the meaning is clear. I would recommend this practice to everyone. After a while, after you have underlined the phrases you want to stress, you won't have to pay much further attention to the punctuation, because you will in effect have memorized the copy.

Other than these mechanical considerations, there are no absolute, rigid rules in journalism except for fairness and accuracy. Everything in journalism begins with "it depends." Each story is different. How you handle it depends upon *who* is involved and *where* it happened, *how* and *why* it happened, and what happened *before*, what is likely to happen in the *future* and how often it has happen in the *past*. There is more variety in journalism than in any other field on Earth.

Or, you can generalize in that first sentence, then get down to specifics:

> New concerns were voiced today for what we are doing to our atmosphere. A federal government report warns of rising levels of toxic metals in the air.

You can paint a picture:

> Ten-year-old Betty Johnson . . . smeared with mud, wet and crying for her mother . . . is glad to be home. That's what she told police after surviving a fall into a stream bed as rain-swollen waters swept her six miles under bridges and through a tunnel.

You can be clever, but guard against getting too cute:

> Dear Santa: You better watch out. A new medical report says you're a prime candidate for a heart attack.

Also, don't overload the first sentence with details. If the Metro Commission has declared that a new tax rate is to go into effect next month, your lead might begin:

> Taxes are going up . . .

Shun verbless sentence like, "An earthquake in Alaska today." Verbless leads work occasionally, but nobody talks that way.

The lead should capture the listener's attention and set the tone of the story. It can be the most important point in your story, like the lead in a breaking newspaper story, but it doesn't have to be. The main purpose of the lead is to alert the audience to what's coming, and to make them want to hear more.

THE BROADCAST STORY

The broadcast story is typically short—twenty, thirty perhaps sixty seconds. It's a form of *storytelling* in which *compression* counts. *Think* about the story before you start writing: What about this news *matters* the most? Write *that*. Then go back and check your notes and other original material to ensure that you've left out none of the essentials.

Compressing a story means condensing it without distorting it. Think of the story as a jigsaw puzzle: If you exclude facts that lie toward the periphery of the puzzle they won't be missed, but if you leave out something central, the result will be an obvious gap.

A handy way to structure a broadcast story is to lead with a sentence or two summarizing the news, then cover each point in greater detail, a sentence at a time. Each sentence should *move* the story and add something new to it. Here, a complicated financial story has been boiled down to twenty seconds for broadcast:

> The Federal Reserve's Paul Volcker is still talking about "hanging tough," but he and his Board are walking a tightrope between two dangers. Too tight a policy . . . and there's a liquidity crisis—nobody has any money to lend or use. Not tight enough . . . and inflation returns, wiping out hard-won gains of the last couple of years.

Broadcast stories should cover all five Ws, but the fact that they are so compressed tends to make the *why* element especially important:

> The tide is turning against California's Peripheral Canal.
> Why? Because of overwhelming opposition in northern California and significant doubts about its cost in southern California.

How do we know? The next two sentences deliver the facts:

If the June eighth primary election were held today, the Peripheral Canal Proposition would be rejected. In a new public opinion poll, eight out of ten northern Californians say they will vote against the Canal. A substantial number of Republican voters in the south also have reservations about it . . . primarily because of its cost.

Finally a sentence of background is included, for the benefit of listeners who haven't been following the story:

The Peripheral Canal, 43 miles long, would deliver water from the northern part of the state to southern California by way of the California Aqueduct.

A breaking news story in print delivers the essential news at the outset. Newspaper features reveal their most newsworthy elements in the billboard, usually within the first several paragraphs. But the broadcast story, because it is so short, can withhold the major news until the end. A straight news lead for the following story might have begun; "The world's ninth heart transplant patient survives . . . ," but NBC correspondent Bob Flick wrote it this way:

18-year-old Charles Martin sat in the Houston police station this morning with his head in his hands, speaking softly about his wife. "She was upset because of the wind blowing her hair and it being too hot," he said. "I guess we were both pretty upset about our financial condition. Our car had broken down on us and things like that."

Martin said he and his 15-year-old wife Kathleen argued and he left the house. When he returned Kathleen had a gun pressed against her head. He grabbed for the gun and she pulled the trigger. Kathleen Martin's life, haunted since childhood by illness . . . and filled with despair about the future, ended in violence.

Tonight her heart beats in the chest of Everett Thomas Junior, a 47-year-old accountant from Phoenix, Arizona.

Thomas, the world's ninth heart transplant patient, is pronounced in excellent condition.

On what would have been a routine story about an Indiana election, Flick looked for the significance behind the voting figures, recalled the candidates' campaign rhetoric and came up with this:

The Indiana Primary turned out to be one of those nice elections.
Nobody lost and everybody threw a victory part.
Richard Nixon *won* because he was the only Republican on the ballot.
Senator Kennedy *won* because he got more votes than any of the Democrats.
Senator McCarthy *won* because he got more votes than he had expected.
And Indiana Governor Roger Branigin *won* because he had nothing to lose.

Jim Vinson of CBS-KNXT-TV advises young newswriters not to squander all their good material at the beginning of each story, but to save something for the end—as does this story about a bank robber:

They caught a burglar last night inside a Bank of America up in Alameda.
Caught him red-handed.
He had broken into the bank by climbing through a roof air vent, then lowering himself on a rope to the floor.
He was carrying wire cutters, a flashlight, gloves and three empty pillowcases.
Someone spotted him and called police before he could fill the pillowcases.
It was midnight. At that time of night, the burglar should have been at home asleep on the pillowcases.
He was an eight-year-old boy.

WRITING TO SOUND AND PICTURES

Broadcast newswriters handle images and sound as well as words. The audio and video inserts they use most often are called *voicers* or *stand-ups, interviews, actualities, lead-ins, lead-outs* and *teases.*

In *voicers,* as they are known in radio, or *stand-ups,* as they're known in television, the reporter on the scene talks into a microphone. The content of voicers or stand-ups can be anything from an on-the-scene description to a news analysis prepared by a reporter in the studio.

Interviews involve reporters's questioning people who are involved in some way in the story. Sometimes the reporter's questions are included in the broadcast, but more often only the answers go on the air. Film or tape excerpts of interviews are referred to as "sound cuts," "segments" or "bites." Their role in the story resembles that of direct quotations in print stories.

Actualities may be defined as anything that happens at the scene that is captured on audiotape, videotape, film or a live camera or microphone—from volleyball players at the beach to scientists monitoring the first photographs from the surface of Mars. Actualities are the heart of radio and television news.

Lead-ins are copy that sets up an audio or video report by preparing listeners for what they are about to hear or see. The lead-in sets the scene, identifies the reporter and outlines the story:

> The Voyager aircraft is enjoying smooth sailing on the third day of its intended flight around the world without stopping or refueling. Here is a report from NBC News correspondent Roy Neal.

An above-average lead-in also arouses listeners' interest. This was the lead-in to a story about the incinerator room at the Treasury:

> Here's a story that is guaranteed to bring tears into the eyes of anyone who enjoys the feel and smell of freshly minted money. Joe Jones has the sad details.

Lead-ins should be short, and should neither give away the story nor merely preview what the reporter has to say. Avoid making the reporter repeat the lead-in. For example, don't say, "And now here's Joe Jones with a report on the night the lights went out on Broadway," if Jones begins by saying "This was the night the lights went out on Broadway."

Because there may be many lead-ins in the course of a broadcast, newswriters try to vary their language and style. This lead-in is rather detailed, but clear enough to hold audience interest:

> The U.S. Consumer Product Safety Commission has banned the use of urea-formaldehyde foam to insulate homes and school buildings after the middle of this year. But what about those homeowners who already have this kind of insulation? David Horowitz looks at the possible hazard those people face . . . and what they can do about it . . . in this evening's closeup report.

Humorous leads can also brighten a broadcast:

> It was all right for William Shakespeare to say "All the world's a stage" . . . he didn't have to meet building codes. As far as city bureaucrats are concerned, it's not the play that's the thing. It's the rules. And for at least one theater, the rules are a problem. Susan Hahn reports.

Lead-outs immediately follow each audiotape or videotape-film segment. On radio, the lead-out—or *tag*—is essential: It reminds the listener who the speaker or reporter was. A good lead-out adds something to the story as well. A lead-out about Israeli bombing of Beirut might note that the bombing ended at sundown. A lead-out to an account of a fire might update the number and condition of the injured. When possible, the lead-out should also build a bridge to the next item.

Anyone who has written for newspapers has employed lead-in and lead-out paragraphs, in the form of topic sentences and transitions. One paragraph sets up the speaker or the subject. A paragraph or two of direct quotes follows (in broadcasting, these direct quotes are on audiotape or videotape-film). After the direct quote, a sentence or two make the transition to another part of the story. The lead-in and lead-out in broadcasting may bracket as little as a single film clip or as much as a complete reporter package that includes a stand-up or voicer, interviews and actualities.

Teases are bits of copy that hint at what is coming up later. They should be snappy but informative. If too vague or coy, they become ludicrous, like the parody tease "Film at Eleven!"

Here are some typical teases:

> When we continue, Pat with the top-of-the-week weather outlook . . . and the story of a big surprise discovered by house wreckers in Wilmington.

> When Kelly and I come back, Entertainment Editor Jim Brown will be here with a report on how they peddle the movies.

> We'll have more news and a look at today's developments in business . . . when we continue here in Newscenter Four.

The point of the tease is to keep listeners tuned in. With remote-control devices making it easy for viewers to change channels instantly, a good tease can be worth a couple of Nielsen rating points. Here's a classic tease, written in the 1960s and still remembered today:

> The odds tonight are 10 to 1 in Vietnam . . . 25 to 1 in London . . . and in Las Vegas, 5 to 2. The games? War, politics and baseball. Joseph Benti here. Details next on the 11 O'Clock Report.

The stories concerned a Green Beret outpost where GIs were outnumbered 10 to 1, an election in London, and a World Series game with one team favored to win at 5 to 2 odds.

The following newscast employs a variety of lead-ins, lead-outs and a tease into the commercial. It was broadcast by KNBC in Los Angeles. First, the lead-in sets up reporter John Marshall's two-minute story, without duplicating any of its essential information.

Kelly (TALENT ON CAMERA)	A University of California professor told Congress today that the Earth's temperature is starting to rise as a result of atmospheric pollution. Melvin Calvin . . . a Nobel Prize winning scientist . . . said the South Pole Ice Cap already has started to melt . . . and that human life could be threatened within 50 years. More on the problem from Newscenter 4 Reporter John Marshall.

—TO CASS SOUND—

CASS SOUND FOR 2:00

("*CASS SOUND FOR 2:00*" refers to a video cassette containing a self-contained report that runs for two minutes.)

MATTES:

At :34	Santa Monica Bay
At 1:19	Speaking Dr. Ingersoll
At 1:33	Dr. Ingersoll
At 1:49	Marshall

ENDS: ". . . NEWSCENTER 4."

("*MATTES*," *also called IDs or Supers or Lower Thirds, are lettering superimposed on the screen. The four Mattes listed in this script tell the director when to put certain information on the screen:* "Santa Monica Bay" *at 34 seconds into the package; whose voice the audience is hearing at one minute and 19 seconds; who is speaking at 1 minute and 33 seconds; and the reporter's name at one minute and 49 seconds into the two-minute package.*)

TALENT ON CAMERA	There was more bad news on the environment today. A professor at U-C Irvine, who first warned of the dangers of fluorocarbons in 1974, says the build-up of the chemical in the upper atmosphere has tripled since then, despite efforts to curb its use.
	Dr. Sherwood Rowland said that fluorocarbons decrease the amount of ozone in the stratosphere . . . making it more easily penetrable by ultra-violet light.

FLUOROCARBONS
CASSETTE   —TO CASSETTE SOUND—
                                  CASS SOUND FOR :34

MATTE: F. SHERWOOD
ROWLAND
                                  ENDS: ". . . END RESULT OF THAT
                                  WILL BE."

(Now the newswriter uses a lead-out to round out Bob Navarro's in-the-field report and to bridge to another environmental report, this one on the air quality of California.)

TOM   Dr. Rowland told Reporter Bob Navarro that fluoro-
(TALENT ON CAMERA)   carbons are still being used in aerosol containers in Eu-
                         rope . . . and that U-S sources include refrigerants
                         and the manufacture of such items as seat cushions
                         and surfboards. His findings are disputed by U-S
                         Chemical Manufacturers Association, which says there
                         has been a *de*crease in upper atmosphere fluorocar-
                         bons. Kelly?

KELLY   The State Air Resources Board concluded a two-day
                         seminar at Cal Tech, Pasadena, today on the impact of
                         diesel cars on air quality in California.

DIESEL CASSETTE   —TO CASS V/O BG—
V/O BG :13

("V/O BG" means the talent will continue reading copy "V/O"—voice-over—while the video cassette's picture and sound are played.)

                         One scientist predicted that if the growth in popularity
                         of the diesel autos continues, by the year 1990, Los
                         Angeles smog will be twice as bad as it is now . . . and
                         the problem won't be confined to just L-A.

MATTE: Pasadena
SOT   CASS SOUND FOR :34

("SOT" means sound on tape.)

MATTE: JOHN TIRJONIS
                         ENDS: ". . . THAN IT IS TODAY."

KELLY   The State Air Resources Board is considering stricter
                         emission regulations on diesel engines . . . even
                         though the technology for making effective improve-
                         ments is at least two years away . . . according to in-
                         dustry sources. Tom?

(Now a tease to the news segment that will follow the commercial.)

TOM   When we continue . . . Pat Sajak with the Weekend
(TALENT ON CAMERA)   Weather Preview . . .
                         —TO COMMERCIAL—

Had this environmental package aired on radio, the newswriter would have identified the speakers not by graphics but in the copy. The stories would have sounded much the same.

WRITING FOR AUDIO

In radio, as in television, news copy should be accurate, concise, conversational, colorful and easy to understand. Radio is *only* sound—the only pictures it lets the listeners *see* are mental pictures created by the spoken word—but mental pictures can be quite vivid. Some of the most innovative of all newscasting is done on radio—from creative local newscasts like those of WFMT-FM in Chicago, which vary in length according to the importance of the news, to in-depth, issue-oriented network programming like National Public Radio's "All Things Considered." Many network correspondents who have gained fame on television say nonetheless that they are proudest of their radio spots.

Radio stations rely largely on the wire services for information, although network affiliates get network feeds, and major big-city stations, particularly the all-news stations, field reporters of their own. The AP and UPI broadcast wires offer brief news summaries, special reports, sports news, financial news, occasional in-depth summaries and reports on people, trends and places in the news—all in broadcast style. The "A" wire contains major newspaper stories giving the broadcast newswriter the complete details. These stories, containing many paragraphs, are usually cut by radio newswriters; radio news stories seldom run more than thirty seconds each. The "B" wire contains newspaper stories of lesser importance; many stations omit it. The state and local wires are of great importance to the many radio stations that emphasize local news.

Audio news services offer live and taped news reports around the clock, along with actualities of major news events to be integrated into the local radio news broadcasts. UPI Audio and AP Radio are the two principal services.

Ideally, every professional radio station news department should write its own copy, air each story once and rewrite the story to give it a fresh angle if the news is important enough to be included in the next newscast. In practice, many stations merely "rip and read," meaning that they edit and read raw wire copy with little or no rewriting. Their justification for this practice is that they lack time and money, but its consequence is to deprive listeners of an independent voice answerable to the community. Still, many fine radio stations have impressive news operations, and even the laziest stations will rewrite major stories during "drive time"—7 to 9 A.M. and 5 to 7 P.M.—when the size of the radio audience swells with people driving to and from work. The important thing for the newswriter is to get a job in a station that wants newswriting and isn't satisfied with "rip and read."

Don't just rewrite the wires. *Absorb* the facts from every available source before you compose the story. Beware of the temptation to borrow phrases from the wire copy. A memorable wire service lead may seem hard to beat, but remember that every other wire subscriber in town has access to the same copy, and some may read it on the air. Anyway, you'll never know if you can do better unless you try.

Following is a typical wire story lead:

> Argentina lost six warplanes Sunday in a large-scale air attack on British ships off the beachhead on East Falkland Island, a defense spokesman said today.
> The attack left a British frigate in flames. Five Argentine Mirage jets and a Skyhawk fighter-bomber were shot down, the spokesman said, and one Mirage and two Sky-hawks were listed as probable kills.

Although this is not a bad lead, any newswriter could rewrite it a dozen different ways to make it more adaptable to radio. For example:

> British forces shot down six Argentine warplanes today during a large-scale attack on British ships in the Falkland Islands. A British Defense spokesman said the attack left a British frigate in flames. But five Argentine Mirage jets and a Skyhawk fighter-bomber paid the price. They were shot down during the attack, and three other planes were listed as probable kills. The fighting took place off the beachhead on East Falkland Island.

The radio story is more active, uses shorter sentences, leaves out unnecessary details. And it is well rounded. It had better be: In this instance, the wire story *lead*, rewritten, became the complete radio news *story*.

The more wire services your radio station subscribes to, the more wire copy you have to work from. The first problem is organization. Rip each story with a ruler and discard the stories you know you won't be broadcasting. Make these decisions promptly, and don't fret about them afterwards. File other stories for future reference: backgrounders, special features, analyses. Label (slug) each story that's left. Make the slugs short and specific. Group related stories together. Read each carefully, with a skeptical eye. If the accuracy of an item seems questionable, confirm it yourself, or, if this isn't possible, check it against the version supplied by the other wire service.

Watch for *corrections*, *advisories* and *kills*. When a correction comes in, correct the original copy immediately. Advisories tell you which stories may be updated; keep an eye out for the update, so you don't inadvertently air stale copy. A *kill* is like an alarm bell. It means that the story should be disregarded; it may contain errors, often serious or libelous ones. Locate the copy and throw it out at once, to avoid its being aired by a colleague who may not have seen the kill.

Radio news stories rarely run more than thirty seconds. Each should have a two- or three-word slug, the date, the time and your last name or initials:

DOWNTOWN FIRE
5/30
12:35 P.M.
Jones

Some of the best radio news stations are all-news stations, but as radio newswriter Al Downs says, "24-hour radio news is like stoking a gigantic furnace. It's a maw, always wanting more stories." There is less time to polish copy in a twenty-four hour news format than there is in a five to fifteen minute radio news show that one writer can organize.

Radio is something of a writer's medium, in that it emphasizes words, but it puts great demands on the newswriter's ability to write for the ear. "You're much more aware of sound when you write for radio," Downs says. "If you do it long enough, you develop a lilt and a swing. The copy might read like hell just looking at it visually, but on the air it sings." Some radio newswriters read their draft copies aloud to themselves. Others write with a particular announcer's voice in mind. Some team up with talent for years, and eventually produce copy so smooth and initial that it sounds as if the talent thought it up spontaneously.

The audio tape recorder is the essential tool of radio news today. It captures the sounds of events—including natural, or "wild," sound. The newswriter listens to the tape, selects a usable section, finds the in cue (the first few words of the audio to be used) and then the out cue (the last few words of the audio to be used). Then the writer cues up the tape by returning to the beginning of the audio cut. The audio cut is edited or dubbed (recorded onto another tape) into a complete audio news package: the cartridge or CART. A good newswriter will edit out anything on the tape that is irrelevant or distracting: awkward pauses, irritating background noise, unclear or rambling statements and unnecessary questions.

The most common edit involves culling direct quotations from interviews and actualities. These sound cuts (bites) should be no shorter than ten seconds and seldom longer than thirty seconds. The average is twenty seconds. Bites function like direct quotations in a newspaper or a magazine story. The sounds of people involved give pace, substance and immediacy to the story. But they should be brief, to the point, dramatic, punchy. If you can say the same thing better or faster, do so. As with quotations in print, a good sound cut normally emphasizes emotion or opinion. The newswriter takes care of conveying the facts.

Often the newswriter works with audio tape filed by a reporter. When a reporter or newswriter conducts an interview over the phone, it is called a "phoner." Reports from the field are called "voicers," or ROSRs (radio on scene reports). The newswriter takes all the available material—phoners, voicers, interviews, actualities, studio-read copy—and edits it onto a tape cartridge (CART) for playback over the air. If it is the reporter's self-contained story (voicer or ROSR) the newswriter simply writes a lead-in that sums up the latest news development, and then adds something like: "Reporter Janet Jones tells us about it." If it's an interview with the reporter's asking questions on the tape, the newswriter's lead-in might say: "Fire Commissioner John Smith told reporter Janet Jones how the fire started." If the reporter is not going to be heard, the lead-in copy could say: "Fire Commissioner John Smith described what happened."

Each tape cartridge (CART) is numbered and timed. The newswriter makes sure he or she lists the number of the CART, how long the CART runs, sometimes the in cue (the first two or three words of the audio) and *always* the out cue (the final two or three words of the audio).

Suppose you're writing an account of a major downtown fire, to air on the 6 P.M. newscast. The harried reporter on the scene has called in to fill you in on the facts, and while on the phone filed a piece of raw tape from his cassette recorder by clipping wires leading from its audio output directly to the contacts inside the transmitter on the phone handset. Listening to the tape, you hear this:

It's hard to say exactly what happened, but we're pretty sure it must have been, or probably was, no . . . I'm sure it was a smoldering cigarette . . . [truck noise . . . mike noise . . . muffled question from reporter]: How many were killed . . . Commissioner? Four persons, no . . . maybe three . . . or three . . . or . . . [long pause] . . . here . . . I have the official death total right . . . just a second . . . I have it here somewhere . . . oh, here it is . . . four persons dead . . . 20, no, make that 23; no, 24 . . . that's it. 24 people injured. [Question] Who . . . [noise] . . . started the fire . . . [off-mike question is hard to hear]. The fire was started by a careless smoker . . . I don't know if it was a man or a woman . . . we haven't figured that out . . . but a smoker was smoking in a room on the 22nd floor . . . when . . . [pause] . . . [Question off-mike, garbled, impossible to understand] . . . I think probably fell asleep . . . I'm . . . [loud noise] . . . What was that? [Question:] describe what: [obscured by noise]. Well . . . it was a classic mattress fire. It started in Room 2219 and burned there for about an hour before flashing over into the hallway just before 9 A.M. . . . What? We put it out just a few minutes ago . . . 11:15 A.M. I guess . . . yes . . . 11:15 A.M. [Question:] How many . . . saved . . . how many? We've been saving people all morning . . . hundreds . . . from the upper floors . . . our guys went up there to get many of them. Some people ran down a fire escape to the top of that [loud noise] marquee up there . . . can you see that? Yeah, up there . . . Hundreds evacuated. We were lucky, I guess . . . yeah . . . the hotel marquee . . . we rescued them: [Question muffled:] . . . Two of the dead were found in a room . . . what? I can't answer you now, I'm talking to these reporters here . . . go see Don . . . I'll be with you in a second . . . let's see . . . two found in a room next to, adjacent to the smoker . . . we found another in a room across the hallway . . . [garbled question] . . . What? I don't know . . . What was that? Oh . . . one was in the corridor. I guess overcome by smoke. That happens a lot . . . trying to reach the fire escape. [Question:] Who . . . firefighters? . . . How many guys did we have fighting this? I don't know. Let me check . . . oh yes . . . about 130 . . . more than 130 men. They fought the fire and extinguished it at 11:15 A.M. I'm talking with Jane Brown, who was staying in the hotel . . . where were you? [Brown]: On the twenty-second floor. [Question]: Tell me what happened. [Brown]: I heard a man screaming and my husband went to the door and saw there was a fire. I stepped out of my room and saw the water and started screaming. The elevators weren't working. By the time we got to the ground everyone was screaming and panicking. I was . . . what? [Voice] You folks, get back . . . [garbled] . . . end tape.]

It's pretty rough, but you do manage to dub a couple of usable quotes—the commissioner saying it was a "a classic mattress fire," for example, and Jane Brown's eyewitness account. Using wire service copy, your notes from talking with the reporter and the tape, you put together the story this way:

DOWNTOWN FIRE
5/24
4:35 P.M.
Bly

A fire touched off by a smoldering cigarette swept through the Conrad Hilton Hotel this morning, killing four persons and injuring at least 24 others. Fire officials said the blaze was started by a careless smoker in a room on the 22nd floor. Fire Commissioner John Smith described what happened.

CART: 34
RUNS: 15 seconds
OUT: ". . . BEFORE 9 A.M."

(On the CART, the Fire Commissioner says: "It was a classic mattress fire. It started in Room 2219 and burned there for about an hour before flashing over into the hallway just before 9 A.M." Then you write a copy bridge that leads to the next piece of on-the-spot audio, an interview with survivor.)

Hundreds were evacuated from upper floors before the fire was extinguished about 11:15 A.M. Jane Brown was staying on the 22nd floor when the fire broke out

CART: 34
RUNS: 15 seconds
OUT: ". . . SCREAMING AND PANICKING

(On the CART, Brown says: "I heard a man screaming and my husband went to the door and saw there was a fire. I stepped out of my room and saw the water and started screaming. The elevators weren't working. By the time we got to the ground everyone was screaming and panicking." Now for a lead-out)

Two of the four dead were found in one room . . . another in a room across the hallway . . . and one in the corridor by the fire escape where he was overcome by smoke. More than 130 firefighters put out the flames. Several guests ran down a fire escape to the top of a hotel marquee where they were rescued by the firefighters.

WRITING FOR VIDEO

Television is a visual medium, as everybody knows, but like all news media it relies upon words. As Eric Sevareid, one of the deans of network television news, put it, "One good word is worth a thousand pictures."

Some important stories have no visual element; you can't very well shoot film of a change in the prime interest rate. Others take place beyond the reach of the cameras. But even when good film is available, television news stories are structured around the words of a script, not around the pictures. "Pictures, when they are available, are matched to words," says Ruven Frank, twice president of NBC news. "The words come first—not words to pictures." Surveys show that viewers listen to television more than they look at it. TV news editors work in much the same way. "I rarely look at the pictures when I'm editing a piece," says Don Hewitt of "60 Minutes." "I just listen."

The goal in television newswriting is to *blend* words and pictures into a coherent whole. The newswriter usually begins by looking at tape or film shot at the scene, writes a script and then edits the visuals according to the script. Only if time is short or the visuals especially compelling do newswriters edit the visuals first and then write the script to suit the pictures.

As we saw earlier in this chapter, a television news script includes words to be spoken by the talent, information on the audio and visual material to be aired and instructions to help the director of technicians air it smoothly. The script is divided vertically: Audio goes on the right. Everything else goes on the left—all the instructions concerning videotape and film, graphics and special effects, who's speaking and how.

If the left column reads TALENT ON CAMERA, the right will contain copy to be read by the talent while he or she is on the air. If the talent is to read but not be seen, as when doing a voice-over (V/O), the left column might read

"Happy Talk" local news shows make for good ratings, but do they make for news? (Drawing by S. Harris; © 1980 *The New Yorker* Magazine, Inc.)

VIDEOTAPE CASSETTE, and the right would have the V/O copy. VIDEO-TAPE CASSETTE SOT means sound on tape; the talent is silent at this point, so on the right we have only the IN CUE and OUT CUE from the tape; the talent, hearing the out cue, is alerted to await a cue from the floor director to resume reading aloud. VISUAL on the left means a picture, usually a still, that may fill the scene or, more often, appear in a portion of the screen behind the talent; the copy on the right is read by the talent while the visual is up.

The instructions on the left include timings—for example, when this information will help the director. VIDEOTAPE CASSETTE SOT :25 means the cassette runs twenty-five seconds. AT :23 SOUND UNDER alerts the sound engineer to lower the volume on the videotape's natural sounds so the talent can be heard more clearly while doing a voice-over. AT :30 SOUND UP FULL designates when the V/O will end and the tape sound will again predominate.

The simplest task for a newswriter is writing lead-in copy that sets up a piece of film or videotape. A graphic (map, illustration, photograph) might be used during the lead-in copy. Then, while the talent continues to read the copy, the viewer sees an actuality on videotape or film, with natural sound under or no sound at all. Then the picture goes back to the talent for the lead-out, and on to the next story.

Sometimes a writer may let an actuality play the natural sound full so the viewer gets a sense of the event, the players and the situation. The talent pauses while viewers hear a bit of newsworthy natural sound. In addition, newswriters often use a piece of an interview that has been produced in the field. Such segments can be used as pieces of direct quotes on camera or as voice-overs for other visuals.

Here's how television coverage of the hotel fire discussed earlier might read. First comes the lead-in:

VIZ HOTEL FIRE
TALENT ON CAMERA
(*Graphic behind talent is the photograph of the Hotel in flames.*)

A fire touched off by a smoldering cigarette swept through the Conrad Hilton Hotel this morning, killing four persons and injuring at least 24 others.

(*Start video cassette, natural sound under :08 with V/O from talent in studio.*)

—TO CASSETTE—

Fire officials said the blaze was started by a careless smoker in a room on the 22nd floor. Fire Commissioner John Smith described what happened:

AT :08 SOUND UP FULL

IN CUE: "IT WAS A CLASSIC . . ."

(*Picture of Fire Commissioner talking into the camera; runs 15 seconds.*)

MATTE: FIRE COMMISSIONER
JOHN SMITH
(*Identifies the speaker.*)

AT :23 SOUND UNDER
CUE TALENT V/O COPY

(Talent in studio reads copy over visuals of fire.)

AT :30 SOUND UP FULL
(Picture of Jane Brown talking about the camera; runs 15 seconds. Visuals continue, using her voice-over.)

AT :45 CUT TO BROWN ON
CAMERA

MATTE: JANE BROWN
AT :35 SOUND UNDER

CUE TALENT V/O COPY
(Visuals of fire as talent reads written narration.)

(Firefighters fighting the blaze; rescue attempts.)

AT 1:05 NATURAL SOUND FULL—NATURAL SOUND FULL—

OUT CUE: ". . . JUST BEFORE 9 A.M."

Hundreds were evacuated from upper floors before the fire was extinguished about 11 A.M.: Jane Brown was staying on the 22nd floor when the fire broke out:

IN CUE: "I HEARD A MAN SCREAMING"

OUT CUE: ". . . SCREAMING AND PANICKING."

Two of the four dead were found in one room . . . another in a room across the hallway . . . and one in the corridor by the fire escape where he was overcome by smoke.
(MORE)
More than 130 firefighters battled to put out the fire. Several guests ran down a fire escape to the top of a hotel marquee where they were rescued by firefighters

One of the television newswriter's regular duties is to write voice-over narration to go with visuals. There are a few tricks to doing this right. First of all, don't write too many words. Voice-overs call for plenty of pauses, few words and good pacing. Let the visuals play; give them room to breathe. If the film shows people waving American flags, don't waste time explaining what kind of flags they are; the viewers can see that.

Try to *coordinate* words and pictures, so that they reinforce each other. Avoid the sort of word-picture disjunction that plagued the early days of TV advertising, when the film might show a car racing down the highway while the V/O discussed its luxurious interior.

Occasionally, however, juxtaposing words and visuals that don't match can be effective. A mayor's saying there is no poverty in his city could be the voice-over of an actuality showing beggars on Main Street. Obviously such a technique can be abused. In this case it implies that the mayor is either a liar or is ignorant of the facts. Use this approach sparingly, and only when the facts warrant it.

The following report on the killing of American Nazi leader George Lincoln Rockwell, put together under deadline pressure, employs nearly all the elements available to the newswriter: videotape and film, in-studio graphics and still photographs, voice-overs and on-camera narration. Yet its structure remains a matter of straightforward storytelling. Ultimately, what counts is the script, and what makes a good script is able nonfiction storytelling.

TALENT ON CAMERA	George Lincoln Rockwell . . . the commander of the American Nazi party who talked of
STILL: ROCKWELL WITH SWASTIKA	hate and dreamed of being president of the United States . . . was shot to death today. And the man charged with his murder is a former member of Rockwell's party. The dreams of the 49-year-old Rockwell were punctured by the sniper's bullet as Rockwell drove from a parking place in an Arlington-Virginia shopping center near his home.
DISSOLVE TO B&W SLIDE: SUSPECT AND DETECTIVES	Within an hour . . . police arrested John Patler, a former captain in the American Nazi party.
DISSOLVE TO B&W SLIDE: PATLER AND ROCKWELL	Patler was a 29-year-old, married, unemployed student who had spent three years in the party. He was kicked out in April because party officials said he was having "considerable disagreement" with Rockwell. They said Rockwell had noticed "Communist thought creeping into Patler's work."
DISSOLVE to STILL: ROCKWELL'S COVERED BODY IN THE PARKING LOT	Patler was arrested three-quarters of a mile from the parking lot ambush where Rockwell was shot in the head and the chest. CBS News Correspondent John Hart was at the scene.
VIDEOTAPE SOT :46	
(*"SOT" means sound on videotape.*)	
—CUT TO VIDEOTAPE— IN CUE: "ROCKWELL WAS . . ."	
(*These forty-six seconds of videotape comprise the self-contained report by Correspondent Hart.*)	
	OUT CUE: ". . . JOHN HART, CBS NEWS, WASHINGTON."
AT :46 CUT DIRECTLY TO FILM FILM 1:00 MAG POSITIVE :32 INITIAL SOUND UNDER	Everywhere Rockwell and his men went— there was trouble.
(*Positive color film with magnetic sound, consisting of historical footage from the files showing Rockwell in action.*)	
SUPER: SAN FRANCISCO OCTOBER 22, 1966	This 1966 demonstration in San Francisco found Rockwell and the American Nazi party in its usual role—trying to talk to a crowd of people who didn't want to listen to them.

As eggs splattered around him: Rockwell—a Navy Fighter pilot in World War Two who recognized Hitler as a prophet—got up to talk to the large crowd.

Rockwell's prepared speech told about deporting Negroes to Africa and hanging Jewish and Communist traitors. But the crowd was not ready to listen to him.

AT :32 SOUND UP   IN CUE: "MY FELLOW AMERICANS . . ."

(*Rockwell shouts his appeal to the angry audience.*)

DISSOLVE OUT OF FILM TO
STILL: MATT KOEHL   In Arlington today . . . Matt Koehl—national secretary of the American Nazi party and its number-two man—said he would take over the leadership of the party immediately. Asked by reporters who appointed him, Koehl said: "Commander Rockwell ordered it long ago. I can't replace him. No one can. But I will lead the party from now on."

(*The in-studio camera slowly zooms in on the still of Koehl's face while the voice-over copy is read by the talent in the studio.*)

Followers of Rockwell gathered in the barrack headquarters to mourn the death of the man they called "the American Fuehrer." Ralph Forbes . . . who says he is the western division commander of the party . . . then met with reporters. He said Rockwell told him a month ago that he, Rockwell, was a marked man. News reporter Jere Laird asked Forbes if *he* was afraid of being killed.

AT :29 SOUND UP SUPER: IN CUE: "NO SIR, I MEAN . . ."
FORBES

                                    OUT CUE: ". . . GOING TO HELP OUR PEOPLE WIN."

AT 1:15 V/O NARRATION
BRIDGE   Forbes was asked, "What if Rockwell—a World War Two veteran—is denied burial in Arlington National Cemetery?"

AT 1:23 SOUND UP   IN CUE: "THEY BETTER NOT . . ."
                                    OUT CUE: ". . . THAT WOULD BE A DISGRACE."

AT 1:46 GO OUT FAST   (VERY, VERY FAST OUT)

(*This means the film ends and the director immediately leaves the film to cut to . . .*)
B&W SLIDE: DALLAS   Meanwhile in Dallas . . . Texas . . . in the plaza area where President Kennedy was assassinated . . . members of the American Nazi party picketed an anti-Vietnam War demonstration. There was no fighting and no arrests.

(*Lead-out copy completes the report.*)

SUMMARY

Writing for broadcast should be at least as succinct and simple as writing for print. In broadcast news, the listener gets but one chance to hear a story, so write for the ear and make sure your words can be understood the first time around. Try to write conversationally, the way articulate people talk. Television and radio are more immediate than print, so whenever possible use the present tense. Write simple, direct English, in short declarative sentences. Make your copy clean, fresh and current. Use short words instead of long, the active voice instead of the passive.

What matters in writing a broadcast news story is that it fit into the time available, and that it be accurate, fair, clear, lucid, colorful and easy to understand. The lead should capture the listeners' attention and set the tone of the story. Build the story logically, often chronologically. Condense skillfully so that the story is complete, yet be as concise as possible. Digest the facts, then write a *story* that speaks directly to each listener as an individual.

Broadcast newswriters make frequent use of *voicers* or *stand-ups*, *interviews*, *actualities*, *lead-ins*, *lead-outs* and *teases*. Lead-in copy sets up the audio or video report, explaining to the listeners what they are about to hear or see. Lead-outs consist of copy that comes immediately after the audio tape or videotape-film. Teases are bits of copy that tell listeners what is coming up.

Radio stations rely heavily on wire services, and the newswriter's job is often to rewrite those stories into original broadcast stories. A good sound cut usually conveys emotion or opinion; factual material is better handled in written copy.

In television, the words and pictures work together to tell the story. The more complex the story, the more important the words become. Most television writing takes place after the videotape or film is shot.

One frequent use of sound with visuals is voice-over (V/O) narration. There is no need to add intrusive copy to a series of self-explanatory visuals, but don't hesitate to add words when visuals alone give an incomplete or misleading sense of a story. In a complicated video package, the newswriter uses all the elements available: graphics, actualities, interviews, reporter accounts. The newswriter's job is to tell the story accurately, concisely, simply, colorfully and quickly.

PART IV Reporting

Truths that are kept silent become poisonous.
Nietzsche

In politics, never deny anything unless it's true.
Lincoln Steffens

12

AN INTRODUCTION TO REPORTING

Reporters gather the news in three principal ways: through *research*, *interviews*, and *observation*. Often, all three techniques are employed in covering a story: A reporter assigned to a murder trial, for example, would check in at the court clerk's office to go over depositions and affidavits filed in the case, interview attorneys on both sides to learn what strategies they planned to use in court, then observe the trial, quoting the testimony and describing what went on in the courtroom and finally interview the jurors to see how they arrived at their verdict.

RESEARCH

Documents are vitally important to reporters. Reporters have the right to examine nearly all public records, and these materials can yield black and white evidence that supplements or contradicts accounts based on human recollection.

Knowing how to lay hands on the right paper is especially useful when following the trail of graft and corruption. Jerry Landauer, an investigative reporter for *The Wall Street Journal*, exposed a major pension fund scandal involving coal companies and the United Mine Workers union by comparing two innocent-looking sets of documents filed with government agencies. One set, at the United States Department of Labor, contained the names of coal companies that had agreed to contribute 40 cents to their workers' pension funds for every ton of coal mined in a year. Another set, filed with the states where the companies did business, showed how many tons they had actually mined. Comparing the two sets of figures, Landauer found that the companies—with the acquiescence of crooked union officials—had contributed only a fraction of what they owed the workers' pension funds.

Government bureaucracies keep records of almost everything. Payroll records show who works for the city and how much they earn. Expense reports reveal where the mayor stayed on his trip to Washington and how much he spent for dinner. Purchasing vouchers record what materials an agency bought from suppliers, from the long distance phone calls made by the police chief to the amount of chalk used by the high school English department.

Government departments keep timesheets showing how employees spend their work days; these can be used to assess worker productivity. The public works department keeps copies of plans for municipal building projects that specify the materials to be used in each construction project; a newspaper can get a copy of the "specs," then hire an engineer for a day and go down and see if the taxpayers are getting the quality of building they've paid for.

Government agencies are fountainheads of documentary information. Call the state welfare agency to learn whether the cost of administrative overhead has been cut, as the governor promised it would be when she took office two years ago. County health and hospital officials should have figures on whether drug-related cases involving teenagers have decreased now that a new drug education program has taken effect in the schools. The Government Printing Office in Washington, D.C., offers a vast array of books and pamphlets that can provide background for feature stories or ongoing coverage of anything from geophysics to hoof and mouth disease.

Most municipalities have a useful volume called the *City Directory* that lists people living in the city—not alphabetically, as the telephone directory does, but by address. If the police radio says there's a fire at 56 Jones Street, you can look up the address in the directory, see who lives across the street, call them and get a description of the blaze. The *City Directory* lists people's occupations and the names of their family members as well—though the listings are usually at least a year or two out of date, and should be employed with caution.

Background information can be gathered from private organizations and research institutes as well: Whatever the topic, a group can usually be found that studies it, from real estate associations that monitor home mortgage rates to labor organizations that study whether employees who work at computer monitors all day suffer from exposure to radiation. Does your town suffer more or fewer heart attacks and cancer deaths than other places? Call the American Cancer Society or Heart Association in Washington and look into it. Does the local library carry enough books for the population it serves? Call the American Library Association for comparison figures.

The faculties of colleges and universities spend as much time learning as they do teaching, and professors are usually happy to share their knowledge with journalists. A political scientist can analyze election returns; a biology professor can help a reporter understand the controversy over genetic engineering; an art historian can reveal what art scholars think of the Magritte oil just acquired by the local museum.

Private individuals and businesspeople, too, can help with research. One of the advantages a veteran reporter has over a newcomer is that the veteran has had more time to cultivate reliable sources. A retired state comptroller can help a reporter make sense of a complicated budget proposal. A real estate agent may act as a guide to the economic health of a neighborhood. A talk over coffee with a group of truckers can be as revealing as a dozen Interstate Commerce Commission reports.

The newspaper's library, also called the "morgue," is an important research source. To check the background of important people, see *Who's Who* or the *Dictionary of American Biography*. To find magazine articles in a given field, look up subject categories in the *Reader's Guide to Periodical Literature*. Relevant books can be located through the subject edition to *Books in Print*. Many newspaper libraries carry microfilmed copies of *The New York Times*, and stories in the *Times* are indexed. National crime statistics are published annually in the FBI's *Uniform Crime Reports*. The newspaper librarian can help you with additional research tools.

The clip file in the newspaper library contains the stories that have appeared in the paper in the past. They are catalogued in three basic ways: by the name of each person who appears in the story, by the title of each institution mentioned and by general topic. Reporters assigned to cover a meeting or conduct an interview routinely read through the clips right away, making notes on what to watch out for and which questions to ask. The research can help ensure accuracy, aid in achieving a balanced perspective and add flavor and depth to a story. Note the improvement that research brings to these stories:

The assignment	The Mayor, up for reelection, announces a crackdown on prostitution and pornography.
Research	Four-year-old newspaper clips report that the Mayor inaugurated a similar crackdown when he originally took office, but never followed up on it.
The story	Quotes the Mayor's strong proclamation against vice but also relates his earlier promises on the same issue; lets readers decide for themselves whether he means it this time.
The assignment	A proposal by the phone company to increase telephone rates passes the state Public Service Commission.
Research	A longtime opponent of rate hikes—who, the clips reveal, used to show up religiously at PSC hearings to rail against the telephone company—was absent from this year's hearings. Reached by telephone, she says she has been hired as a "community relations consultant" by the telephone company at a hefty salary.
The story	Is the telephone company buying off its opposition?

INTERVIEWS

The next step after research is usually to talk to people. How to conduct an interview is the subject of Chapter 13, *Interviewing*. Suffice it here to say that young reporters need to guard against two common interviewing problems. The first is exhibiting excessive timidity: the "uh, . . . er" syndrome. The second is failing to push to get all the information needed from each interview: the "Gee, I forgot to ask" syndrome.

Both problems can be minimized through preparation and practice. Prepare a list of questions or topic headings that are aimed at getting the material your story will need, not vague, all-purpose questions of the "So, how did you get started in show business?" variety. Having adequately researched the story and knowing what to ask will do a lot to bolster your confidence during the interview.

If you feel timid when approaching people, remember that those you interview are often just as afraid of you as you are of them. If you ask questions in a clear, confident manner, you'll be surprised at how readily most people will answer. The journalists' job, after all, is an honorable one, and there's no need to be hesitant or apologetic about doing it. At the outset of an interview, identify yourself, explain what you are doing, and get to the point: "Hello, I'm Sue Wells of the Hapsville *Recall*, and we're doing a story about noise from the airport. You live a half mile from the main runway. Does noise from the planes bother you?"

Clear, positive phrasing of questions sets the stage for clear, positive answers. A vague or hesitant question invites a vague or hesitant answer:

Ask, "Where were you standing when the explosion took place, Mrs. Wilcox? What did you see?"

not

"Can you tell me anything about the explosion, Mrs. Wilcox?"

Ask, "Lieutenant, I need the ages on those boys arrested in the Treelawn burglary."

not

"Lieutenant, could I possibly get the ages of those boys arrested in the Treelawn burglary?"

Ask, "What's your name? How is that spelled?"

not

"Do you mind if I get your name?"

Ask, "Frank, I have to talk to the Mayor this afternoon. I know she's busy, but this is an important story."

not

"Frank, is there any chance of my getting to talk to the Mayor this afternoon?"

As much as they may try to prepare themselves, reporters sometimes are assigned to cover stories in fields about which they know nothing. A reporter who can't balance a checkbook may be required to explain the city's new budget, a lifetime urbanite assigned to cover a hogcalling contest, a felinophobe dispatched to cover a cat show. When caught in such a situation, it's best to admit your ignorance to the people you're interviewing:

"You referred a moment ago to the 'Barrett Report,' Commissioner. I'm afraid I'm not familiar with that report. Can you fill me in?"

"Officer, the boy is charged with possession of a 'zing gun'? What *is* a zing gun?"

"Professor, the press release describes your invention as a breakthrough in 'ambient temperature superconductivity.' Would you explain what that means in nontechnical language?"

"My, but this is a pretty . . . uh . . . cat, Mrs. Patterson. Now what exactly makes a cat like this a champion?"

The goal of reporting is comprehension. Write only what you understand. If you don't grasp the news, your readers won't, either.

OBSERVATION

Reporters are observers by profession; they learn to look for details that add to the immediacy and impact of the story. The reader should be permitted to *see* what happens and to *hear* what people say. In this story from *The New York Times Magazine* about hang gliding, the reporter uses quotations and description to draw the reader into the scene:

> Clad in sneakers, cut-off jeans and an orange crash helmet, Jim Aronson stood calmly about *4 feet* from the edge of the *790-foot cliff* that overlooks the Catskill resort town of Ellenville, N.Y. A *harness under his shoulders and around his stomach* attached him to his Pacific Gull Alpine, a high performance kite whose *34 ½-foot Dacron sail luffed impatiently in the 5-knot breeze*. Directly below him, a *pile of jagged rocks ran down into a forest of pine and hardwood stretching as far as his intended landing site, a young cornfield, about a half mile away*. Aronson took hold of the *aluminum trapeze* bar connected to the kite frame, walked *two and a half steps* on the *balls of his feet*—and dropped off the edge.
> "Oh, God!" shrieked a middle-aged woman who was watching.
> "God bless him," intoned her companion.
> Once in the air, the craft *dived sharply down the cliffside* before Aronson moved his control bar forward to lift its nose and level the *shivering sail*; then he banked to the northeast along the mountain face in a vain search for rising winds. A few minutes later, *sinking steadily in the neutral air, he headed for the cornfield and descended in a series of slow spiral turns*. Finally, nose up into the wind, vast sail swept back toward the

ground, he settled gently on his feet; from the cliff high above, he *looked like an orange moth that had landed on a piece of green baize.*

Don't count on memory to recall the color of a ballerina's costume or the way riot cops were armed. Make *notes* on what you observe. Meyer Berger, the Pulitzer Prize winning reporter for *The New York Times*, scribbled constantly while working a story, noting details like the kinds of trees lining the streets, the sort of clouds overhead, the types of clothes people were wearing. He then incorporated the most pertinent and evocative pieces of description into his stories.

Description is especially useful in presenting portraits of people. Behavioral studies have found that people communicate only part of what they want to say through words themselves. The rest comes across through inflection, facial expression and body language. To provide readers with a complete picture, *show* the people talking as well as those quoting them.

Description strengthens the impression made by the quotations in the following paragraph from a story about the excitable mayor of Utica, New York, who in his first term made so many changes in the city that he soon had half the town on his back:

> Regularly, at press conferences, council meetings, and almost daily in his office, Hanna would rant against the "Big Boys" who kept thwarting his plans to save the city. "Where were the chamber of non-commerce and the newspapers and all the smart guys in this town who say they don't like my way of doing things when that urban renewal disgrace of a mudhole just sat there for 15 years?" He *shouted* at a public hearing, his *eyes watering* and a *vein pulsating in his forehead.* "With all the brains in this town, what did they start that I stopped? What ideas did they ever give me? This lousy town was falling apart when I became Mayor, and I tell you now that in two years we'll lose another 3,000 or 4,000 people and pretty soon Utica will be a ghost town."

In this passage from an *Esquire* article, the reporter uses description to call attention to the contrast between the grandiosity of what the speaker is saying and the lack of discipline evidenced by his mannerisms as he says it:

> "Our object will be to design a spaceship to take ten thousand to one hundred thousand people on a journey to the stars," he said. *He leaned back in his chair, belly straining against his shirt, and grabbed another beer from the six-pack.*
>
> "I'd be quite willing to have my brain transplanted into a star probe," he said, *gulping the beer. He belched loudly.*

THE RULES OF REPORTING

The cardinal rules of reporting are enterprise and energy. Good news stories are sought out by reporters prepared to ask persistent questions, to follow up each promising lead, to do the necessary research and fact checking. And reporters need to balance their zeal to get a story with a scrupulous concern that they report it accurately and fairly. Among the characteristics of the most effective reporters, then, are *promptness*, *persistence*, *thoroughness*, *skepticism*, *caution*, and *enthusiasm*.

Promptness

Promptness means beginning to work on an assignment when the editor assigns it, not after reading the rest of the paper or having a second cup of coffee. News is a rushed, competitive business; dawdling can mean missing a news source, getting caught in traffic on the way to a press conference or lacking time to read the clips.

Editors appreciate early advisories on how a story is shaping up. If a reporter's preliminary digging turns up something particularly interesting, the editor will want time to arrange for extra space in the paper; if the story falls through, the space will have to be allotted to another story. Because editors don't like being surprised, especially close to deadline, you should keep them abreast of what's happening.

Persistence

Persistence means continuing to dig. Don't settle for the run-around, the brush-off, the superficial or evasive answer. If you telephone someone and are told he or she is out, find out where he or she is and call him or her there. When leaving a message, establish when you may expect the call to be returned; if it isn't returned on time, call back. If a question is not answered responsively, rephrase it and ask it again.

A clear understanding of the laws relating to the public's right to know is of great help to a persistent reporter. In states that have a "Sunshine Law" requiring public access to most public records, some investigative reporters carry a copy of the law with them every day. This way, when bureaucrats tell them they can't reveal something, they can produce a copy of the "Sunshine Law" and say, "According to this, I have a right to know."

Beginning reporters sometimes shy away from pursuing a story for fear that their perseverance may displease people. But as long as they are polite, sensible and candid about it, hard-digging reporters earn more respect in the long run than do those whose timidity induces them to back off before reaching the heart of the story.

Thoroughness

"There is no substitute for hard work," Thomas Edison said. "Genius is one percent inspiration and ninety-nine percent perspiration." The object of reporting is to get not just some of the story, but *all* of the story, or as much of it as possible. Seek people out. At a fire, talk not only to the officials and firefighters, but to bystanders and evacuees as well. Don't settle for two witnesses to a shooting if you can interview three or four.

In stories involving controversy, thoroughness demands that reporters represent all sides of the issue. This promotes fairness and objectivity, and it also helps the reporters themselves understand the story better, by having viewed it from more than one perspective.

Skepticism

An old Russian proverb says, "Not everyone who snores is sleeping." Reporters learn to always check for the truth behind appearances. The trick is to maintain an active skepticism without lapsing into cynicism.

A skeptic reserves judgment until all the facts are in and refuses to take things at face value or on first impression. A cynic believes people act solely from base motives, and looks sourly on human affairs. Healthy skepticism aids reporters when perennial candidates insist that they're not going to run in the upcoming election, when scientists announce "positive proof" of extrasensory perception or when theatrical promoters plead poverty following sellout concerts. Skepticism is the journalist's first line of defense against distortion, exaggeration and deception.

Cynicism amounts to thinking the worst of everyone. Reporters can easily fall victim to cynicism, if only because, like social workers and police officers, they see so much of the sad and seamy side of life. The danger of cynicism is that it can blind you to the most exciting sorts of news stories, those that contain a substantial dose of the new and unexpected. It is not true, for instance, that all politicians are corrupt, all lawyers venal or all merchants greedy. Life is more subtle and various than that. As Alexey Tolstoy said, "All the beauty of life is made up of light *and* shadow."

Caution

A reporter who jumps to conclusions lands in trouble. Suppose a businessperson beset by financial difficulties plunges to his death from the window of his office on the twenty-fifth floor. Can we call the death a suicide? No. The circumstances may suggest suicide, but without conclusive evidence we can't *assume* it was suicide. A press release from the local American Legion post lists new officers to be installed at 7 P.M. It's now 9 P.M. Can we assume the installation has taken place, and write a story for tomorrow morning's paper? No. The installation may have been postponed, the new president may have fallen ill or the post may have burned down. Call and check before writing the story.

It is to guard against reporting assumption as fact that in wedding stories society reporters say the couple "is to" be wed, not that they "will" be wed, and that they routinely call the church or synagogue to see if the ceremony actually took place. More than one couple has been "married" in Sunday's paper even though one of them failed to show up at the altar.

Enthusiasm

In show business, the mark of a star is that he or she works just as hard performing for a meager crowd as for a packed house. Similarly, the mark of a star reporter is energetic performance on humdrum assignments. Top reporters bring the same intense curiosity and care to covering a tenement fire as to covering a war, and they seldom complain about the news value of their assignments. The major newspapers routinely test their brightest young correspondents for enthusiasm by assigning them to stints on unpromising beats: Those who do well in Canada go on to Paris; those who can find news in New Zealand are rewarded with the Tokyo beat.

POLITICIANS RESPECT REPORTERS' PERSISTENCE, SAYS GOVERNOR'S AIDE

Elisabeth Coleman has seen journalism from several perspectives: as a researcher for *Newsweek* magazine, as a television news reporter in Los Angeles, as press secretary for Governor Jerry Brown of California and as a media critic on the Public Broadcasting series "Inside Story."

You've had a chance to observe political reporting, both asking questions as a reporter and fielding questions when you worked with Governor Brown. What was your impression of how politicians and journalists relate to one another?
Journalists and politicians are much more alike than either would want to admit. Both tend to be egoists. They want to get their names in the papers, whether as the subject of a front page story or as its byline. Politicians generally are more honest than reporters suspect, but you can't expect them to volunteer news unless it puts them in a good light. You have to ask the right question if you want to get the right answer. The more competent reporters ask tough questions. They're persistent, and they're willing to accept the truth when they arrive at it. The less competent reporters ask fewer questions, are less persistent, and they tend to decide what their story is in advance.

So you would advise novice reporters to keep an open mind but to persist in asking questions that are likely to bring the news to light?
Yes. Don't be afraid to ask a useful question, even if it seems dumb. Even the simplest question may open doors. There's no excuse for rudeness, but there's also no excuse for not being persistent when you're not getting a direct answer. Politicians, being human, may tend to equate tough questions with a personal dislike of them. For instance, the governor may hold a press conference and a reporter get up and say, "How can you go against the will of two-thirds of the people in this state by opposing the death penalty?" And the governor might naturally think, "This guy's really on my case." Actually, the reporter asking the question may be the strongest opponent of the death penalty in the room. But he's a professional doing his job.

How would you compare political coverage in television as opposed to print journalism?
Local television pays far less attention to politics than do the newspapers. The reason is that studies show that when a political story comes on the air, especially if it's a local story, people turn the dial. And on television, you're limited by time constraints. It's far more difficult to do a good job in a minute thirty seconds on the air than in ten pages written for print.

How do they compare in terms of their influence?
Television is by far the more important influence on the public, on voters. But print is more influential among the politicians themselves. They're often too busy to watch TV when the news show comes on, but the newspapers are always around, and they read the newspapers.

BEAT REPORTING

Beat reporters are specialists in covering particular areas of news. They specialize in education, politics, science, medicine, labor relations, the cultural scene, police stories—any fields that they and their editors feel deserve reporters' undivided attention. The value of beat reporters lies mainly in their expertise: They're expected to know more about the field they cover than anyone else does on the paper. Consequently, editors look to them not only to carry out assignments, but also to come up with stories on their own.

Large news organizations can afford to hire beat reporters trained to cover rather narrow specialties. *Newsweek* hired a reporter with a doctorate in physics to cover space exploration; *The New York Times* employed a reporter with an MD to cover medical matters. Beat reporters working for smaller newspapers tend to be less highly trained in their specialties, and they may be called upon to cover more than one beat at a time.

Most reporters start out on general assignment and qualify for beats only after learning how to write and report general news. At the introductory level, therefore, the important thing is to have a general sense of how to acquire and cover a beat, rather than to delve permanently into the specifics of each area of specialization. An exception is the police beat: Many newspapers put starting reporters on the police desk, to help them gain a grounding in covering breaking news.

To be considered for an established beat, let the editors know that you're interested in a particular field. Familiarize yourself with it, and with the reporters who cover it. Keep up to date with news in the beat, so you'll be able to step in immediately if called upon. Without being a pest, offer to help out on beat stories. If, for instance, the education reporter is tied up covering a school board meeting, you might volunteer to write an account of the report on reading scores that's sitting on his or her desk. The idea is to serve as an apprentice, without stepping on anyone's toes.

Another way to become a beat reporter is to seek out a field of specialization that interests you and deserves coverage, but has not yet been assigned to anyone. In one such instance, a reporter interested in health care got himself off the obit desk by spending his weekends and spare time digging up stories on organ transplants and the rising cost of hospitalization; soon he was covering the health care beat full time.

Sometimes a reporter is the first to perceive that a new field is becoming newsworthy enough to deserve beat coverage. This is called "carving out a beat." In the early days of the civil rights movement of the 1960s, a young reporter on his first job out of journalism school, working for *The Providence Journal* in Rhode Island, used his vacation to travel to Birmingham, Alabama, to cover the violence surrounding anti-segregation demonstrations led by Martin Luther King, Jr. His page one stories, written on his own time, convinced his editors that the civil rights movement was important enough to their readers to demand specialized coverage. They gave the young reporter the beat.

Once assigned to a beat, resolve at the outset to learn all you can about it. Don't start slowly, or you may be pulled off the beat before you get another chance. Get to work at once, *researching* the beat, *outlining* it and *cultivating sources*. Later, once you know your way around, you'll be ready to report the beat from the "inside out."

Researching a Beat

Researching during the first weeks after learning that you've been assigned a new beat should be a matter of total immersion. This is the time to read books and magazines, to learn about the subject, its lingo and the people involved.

A reporter hired to cover television started by watching the full prime-time schedule on every network, seven days a week. He read Erik Barnouw's classic book, *The History of Broadcasting*, along with other books about the technical, legal, ethical and economic aspects of the television industry. He studied a year's back issues of *Broadcast Magazine*, *Television Age* and *Variety*, looking for story ideas, making note of the principal people in television and learning the difference between a rating point and an audience share. Then he interviewed people—the top executives in the advertising, entertainment and news divisions of the major networks; program producers, news correspondents and the assistant emcees who warm up audiences at quiz shows; soap opera actresses, ratings specialists and press agents; Wall Street brokers who follow the TV business; even the bartender at Hurley's in Rockefeller Center who served Johnny Carson and Ed McMann when the "Tonight Show" played in New York.

A young reporter assigned to the police beat read basic books on police science like *The Police and Society* by James Q. Wilson of Harvard University, and magazines like *Police Chief*, which concentrates on weaponry and hardware, and *Police Magazine*, put out by the Ford Foundation, which takes a more sociological approach. He started keeping a list of police terminology in the back of his notebook. Before going to introduce himself to the police chief, he read back clips on the chief.

A science reporter given a chance to cover stories on astronomy and space exploration surveyed back issues of *Scientific American*, *Nature* and *Science*; the more specialized *Aviation Week* and *Sky and Telescope*; and the rigorous *Astrophysical Review*. He also consulted the *Glossary of Astronomy and Astrophysics* to check on the meanings of unfamiliar terms.

Studying the literature as a beat journalist calls for *active* research, as well as passive reading. Think of the books and periodicals as professional resources. If you're covering business news and you come across a profile in *Electronics Age* of a systems analyst who says fascinating things, don't just gape at the piece and wish you'd written it yourself. Clip the article, save it and keep the analyst's name on record as someone to call when you next do a piece that concerns computer systems. If you're covering sports and a press release announcing an NBA rules change has you baffled, see if you can work up a story clarifying the new rule—which otherwise will baffle many fans too. *Exploit* the information; don't just absorb it.

Outlining a Beat

Every organized form of human activity has a structure, and learning that structure is fundamental to beat news reporting. A good exercise for a reporter starting out on a beat is to sit down and outline the field on paper, sketching in the names of the basic units of organization and of the major figures in each. Make a flow chart showing who is responsible for what. The idea is to see how the entire system works.

A new labor reporter, for instance, would list the specific unions in the area along with the crafts they represent, the companies and state agencies with whom they bargain, the legislative bodies concerned with labor law, interested federal agencies, such as the United States Department of Labor and the National Labor Relations Board, and those who are involved in labor-management relations. To see how these elements function, the reporter might look up past stories that covered a major strike. These might reveal that the union membership votes to authorize its executive committee to call a strike if it deems it necessary—but that the vote itself doesn't mean there will be a strike. Contract negotiations are often influenced by the negotiators' self-interests as much as by the issues they are negotiating. The union leaders want to win enough to satisfy their members that they deserve to continue holding high union positions, while management negotiators must answer to their bosses and to the stockholders. Where public employees are prohibited by law from striking, they may stage such job actions as "rule booking" (slowing down work by invoking needless technicalities) or "sick-outs," like the "blue flu" that strikes when police officers stay home from work in droves. Part of the key to understanding how such matters work today is researching how they worked in the recent past.

The reporter's chart should include not only the organization but the principal characters: The individual who runs the truckers' union local and the one who's trying to organize the bottlers; the union lobbyists and the local representatives of the National Association of Manufacturers; the crackerjack arbitrator and the legislators who serve on the labor committees.

Such an outline is a valuable aid in learning the general context of a beat, but it's only a start. A good beat reporter can find fresh stories both inside and outside the traditional area covered by the beat. For instance, a labor reporter needn't be limited to work that is classified as a 9 to 5 job. How does a philosophy professor at a university work at the business of teaching and researching philosophy? What is a housewife's time worth on the labor market, once we add up her functions as chauffeur, nurse, cook, teacher, psychiatrist, accountant and housekeeper? *The Wall Street Journal* once ran a series of profiles of people who don't work at all: an alcoholic derelict on skid row, a "sportsman" who travelled around the world playing polo on inherited wealth and an unhappy retiree who, in the words of the article, "had found out the difference between not having to do anything and not having anything to do."

Good stories can be found in telling what work means to people. In a film aired by the Public Broadcasting System, a Seattle filmmaker named Fred Wardenburg contrasted the life of an auto worker on a Detroit assembly line with that of a mechanic in a custom auto body shop. The assembly line worker was paid twice as much as the other man and had job security for life, but he found the work repetitive and frustrating. The mechanic had a less secure future but looked forward to coming to work each day, knowing that he would be doing something creative in his job.

Like filmmaker Wardenburg, a beat journalist can make use of his or her expertise by digging beneath the superficial events of the day. This sort of probing, reflective journalism is becoming increasingly popular in newspapers, because it can be developed more adequately in print than by print's broadcasting competitors.

Consider the court beat: For years, many court reporters limited their beat to trial stories, covering only what happened within the walls of county courthouses. But with time, the court beat expanded to embrace the overall concept of *justice*. Now the beat takes in everything that happens between the time suspects are arrested, tried, convicted and imprisoned and when they have served their sentences and return to society. Court reporters today are concerned not just with breaking news, but with the issues behind the news: Is the bail system fair to defendants? Are criminals getting off lightly through the practice of plea bargaining? Is it really possible to "rehabilitate" anyone, as conventional wisdom in the American penal system avows? What about the victims of crime: How were they affected, weeks or years later?

Reporters covering the police beat have learned to dig beneath "cops 'n robbers" stories and to report how effectively the department is combatting crime. The police chief might talk a lot about needing more people, but one study in St. Louis found that merely adding police officers to a high crime area did nothing to lower the overall rate of violence. The department may be proud of its glamorous SWAT (special weapons and tactics) team and its heavy firepower, but the evidence suggests that when a gunman is holed up with hostages, good talkers get better results than sharpshooters. Probing coverage like this is what editors expect from beat reporters.

Cultivating Sources

Cultivating sources is a staple of beat reporting. It doesn't mean that you're expected to show up with a box of candy in one hand and a bouquet of flowers in the other. Mostly it's just a matter of getting to know people, asking questions, letting them get to know and to trust you. The reporter's greatest asset in this process isn't necessarily a matter of personality at all; it often consists of the reputation built through the stories he or she writes. A business reporter wrote an exposé of "redlining"—the practice of banks' denying mortgages to an entire lower-income neighborhood, thus stifling neighborhood improvement by making it impossible for anyone living there to obtain a mortgage. The story infuriated many bankers, but they had to admit (at least to themselves) that it was accurate and fair. Once tempers had cooled, the reporter found that his contacts with bankers had been improved, rather than damaged, by the story.

Some sources talk to reporters without expecting anything in return. A National Public Radio reporter putting together an obituary of FDR "brain trust" reformer Benjamin Cohen talked with a prominent Washington attorney who was Cohen's lifelong friend; the lawyer obviously wanted nothing more from the exchange than to say a few well-chosen words on Cohen's behalf.

But often the handiest sources are the ones that expect to benefit from news coverage—public relations people, for instance. In different walks of life they have various titles. Those who work for political candidates or public officials are called *press secretaries*. In the armed forces or at federal agencies they are *public information officers* or "PIOs." Corporations have vice presidents in charge of public relations or directors of communications. Hollywood stars have *press agents*, who sometimes refer to themselves as *publicists*.

Whatever they are called, PR people can be helpful in securing background facts and figures and also in getting interviews with top officials or company executives. Remember, though, they work for those who pay them, not for you. Their job is to promote the interests of their clients. Don't expect PR people to volunteer information that reflects negatively on their bosses. In beat reporting, as in all reporting, getting the whole story means digging everywhere—not just where the digging is easiest.

A freelancer working for a neighborhood weekly in Los Angeles was assigned to write a story based on a self-congratulatory press release from the community recreation center. The release said that the center was installing ramps for the convenience of those confined to wheelchairs, and it quoted the center's director as saying he was "happy to take this step to serve the physically handicapped." Rather than take the release at face value, the reporter telephoned an attorney who, as she knew from covering an earlier story, specialized in representing people in wheelchairs. The lawyer told her that the state legislature had passed a law two years ago mandating access ramps on all public buildings. The deadline for compliance was only a month away. The community center was acting not voluntarily, but in order to comply with the law. The resulting story was far more balanced than the press release. The moral? Distortions produced by consulting biased sources can be neutralized by checking with other sources whose bias runs in different directions.

Toughest to deal with are those who most distrust reporters. Police officers tend to distrust civilians—"unsworn personnel," in police jargon—in general and reporters in particular. "It may sound paranoid to you," a police detective in Ann Arbor, Michigan, told a reporter, "but outside of my fellow officers I don't trust anyone except members of my family. And sometimes I'm not too sure about all of them." Police officers and journalists perform almost opposite

---

PRECISION JOURNALISM EFFECTIVE TOOL, REPORTERS FIND

When the editors of the *Chicago Tribune* looked into complaints that the city's parking meters were shortchanging motorists, they went beyond traditional techniques like interviewing meter readers and disgruntled drivers and looking up city records of parking meter repairs. Instead, a team of reporters was dispatched, stop watches in hand and pockets bulging with change. Their assignment? To pump change into a random sample of meters and measure how much time elapsed before each meter expired.

The reporters' survey revealed that many of Chicago's parking meters were, indeed, short-change artists. But whereas some meters provided less than the time paid for, others returned too much time for the money. Armed with these data, the reporters then conducted interviews. The result was a front page story that combined opinions and reactions with a solid statistical foundation of facts that the *Tribune* had adduced for itself.

The *Tribune's* coverage was part of a growing national movement to bring scientific sampling and information-gathering techniques—the staples of social science—into journalism. Dubbed *precision journalism* in a 1973 book of the same title by Philip Meyer, then a national correspondent for Knight Newspapers, the new approach promised to improve the accuracy and objectivity of news coverage involving public opinion and social trends—any field where the information to be gathered comes from many sources or has accumulated over a long period of time. "Social science has suddenly leaped beyond armchair philosophizing," Meyer wrote. "It is doing what we journalists like to think of ourselves as best at: finding facts, inferring causes, pointing ways to correct social problems and evaluating the efforts of such correction."

Precision journalism offers editors a new way of investigating public attitudes and trends—and it gives them exclusive coverage of the results. The *Los Angeles Times* conducted a scientific analysis to see whether politicians' voting patterns reflected a bias favoring the interests of their major campaign contributors. *USA Today* commissioned a national poll to learn how people felt about pressing political issues, and ran the results on the day of the President's State of the Union Address.

Sometimes the results of a scientific survey can make an entire story in themselves—as when the *Times* tracked changes in the nature of crime in Los Angeles simply by studying a decade's worth of felony probation reports. More often, the statistics serve as the basis for a fuller story. "Some people think a poll is a story," says I. A. ("Bud") Lewis, director of the *Los Angeles Times* Poll. "I maintain it is not. You need to weave it into a story as part of a major issue."

Precision journalism has its limitations. The scientific research it requires takes too much time to be useful in covering most breaking news, and the resulting statistics, like all data, can be misinterpreted. (Warns Lewis, "It's a mistake to think that because it's a poll, it's right.") But when alloyed by common sense and combined with more traditional reporting methods, precision journalism can bring unprecedented reliability to fields of reporting that used to rely on little better than educated guesswork.

---

functions in society. Journalists tend to be skeptical of authority and alert for abuses of power. The police serve as agents of the powers that be, imposing authority upon others; they are expected to enforce even unjust laws. Journalists look after the rights of the individual, whereas the police look after the rights of society. A police officer conducting an investigation craves secrecy; a journalist's job is to make information public.

Police officers see much of the dark side of life, and cynicism and resentment are their occupational hazards. A New York City police officer told a reporter about his job in the South Bronx:

> When I became a police officer I thought my job was to help the community; I really mean that. But all I deal with are criminals. Here the people don't like police officers because all we do is arrest their brothers and fathers. I'm tired of getting dirty looks from them. You get a call and catch a burglar in their apartment, and even then they say you're doing them an injustice . . . all the commotion—I'm seeing a doctor because I've started having stomach troubles.

Bridging a gap like the one separating the life of a reporter from that of the cop in the South Bronx calls for sympathy and learning. But no amount of sympathy should blind the police reporter to stories that put the police in a bad light. When police resentment boils over into laziness or brutality, that story must be reported, too. Tell it straight.

Beat reporters can try to immerse themselves in the lives of the people they write about, and to report the news as it looks from their perspective—from the "inside out," so to speak. Jack London learned about the impoverished East End section of London in 1902 by moving there. As he wrote in his classic journalistic work, *The People of the Abyss*: "I wish to know how the people are living there, and why they are living there, and what they are living for. In short, I am going to live there myself." Social scientists call this method "participant observation." Sociologist Herbert Gans was being a participant observer when he studied suburbanites by buying a house in Levittown, Long Island, and moving in.

Newspaper journalists usually can't immerse themselves in their fields to quite the depths that London or Gans did, but they can take steps in the same direction. A reporter on the welfare beat can arrange to live for a week on a welfare budget, or a feature writer on the "modern living" beat can spend several days with a divorced working mother to see how she runs her house and cares for her children. In 1981 John Hurst of the *Los Angeles Times* investigated life in prison by spending four days behind bars. His lead:

> My hands have been cuffed and locked to a chain around my waist. I peer out a screened rear window of the State Department of Corrections van and watch the gentle green landscape roll by on a beautiful spring afternoon.
> The van winds its way along a pleasant country road in the foothills east of Sacramento, through an oak grove, up an easy slope, and suddenly, there it is.
> It looms, impenetrable, like the Great Wall of China, somber, gray granite, rising in terraces across the countryside.
> The cons call it the End of the World.
> It is Folsom Prison. . . .

Of course, the reporter, unlike the subjects of the story, is only visiting. In the 1970s the president of Haverford College took a leave from his job to work alongside manual laborers. But did this really teach him to see life as they did? After the year was over, he wrote a book about his experiences, then returned to academic life. The laborers kept digging ditches. Like the president of Haverford, reporters cannot pretend to really comprehend someone else's life. But while admitting their limitations, they can nonetheless bring fresh perspectives to the news by reporting their beats "from the inside out."

THE EDUCATION BEAT: ON THE JOB

Beat reporters learn to keep track of several stories at the same time—looking for fresh news while finishing deadline stories due that day, cultivating contacts that may pay off in the future, checking on stories covered in the past for follow-up pieces. Kristin Nord is a University of Missouri journalism graduate and an education reporter for the *News-Times* in Danbury, Connecticut. She works out of the paper's newsroom in Danbury, a large carpeted space filled with desks and word processors. The following excerpts are taken from her diary of one day on the job:

8 A.M.—My first call is to June Goodman, the local representative to the state Board of Education. I want her to pick up information at the board meeting in Hartford tonight. The board is adopting regulations for racially balancing the state's schools—I'll do a story on what's going to happen locally. No answer. I call the public relations person in the education department to send the information back with June tonight.

8:05 A.M.—Start making calls on the main story I'll be doing this morning. Have already placed three calls yesterday; none has been returned. The story is on a Kathy Stewart, a student the Danbury school board wants to expel. She participated in the Danbury High School fighting last fall and is charged with unprovoked assault of several administrators and students. It's the school's first expulsion case. The board has been slapped with a lawsuit by Legal Services, the agent representing the girl in the case, charging that by expelling her the board is violating the new special education laws by failing to provide her with an "individual education plan" and a "suitable education" as mandated by state and federal statutes. It's the first time the new federal Aid to All Handicapped Law has been used in a suit like this.

8:15 A.M.—June Goodman at the Board of Education calls back. We chat about racial imbalance regulations and how she thinks they'll wind up, how the education commissioner feels about the law—he doesn't like it—and how she'll relay the information to me after the meeting tonight.

8:20 A.M.—Call to Danbury High School on expulsion case, leave message to speak with the special education supervisor.

8:22 A.M.—Call school superintendent's office, leave message for him to call about expulsion hearing.

8:45 A.M.—School superintendent's office returns call. We chat about how the lawyer's arguments went.

9 A.M.—Start writing story. Also place call to plaintiff's attorney. He can't talk. I explain I'm on deadline and need a return call as soon as possible.

9 A.M.—Speak with the lawyer and with chairman of the school teacher's association grievance committee about the case. I ask about a tip I had that the school administration may be "selectively substituting" again. This means replacing only regular classroom teachers who are out sick, not specialty teachers, like those for music, art or gym, because it costs more money.

10:30 A.M.—Hand in story on expulsion, rewritten twice. Not as happy with it as I'd hoped I'd be, primarily because I couldn't get to the special education supervisor for the background information I'd wanted.

10:45 A.M.—Lyn Taborsak, an active member of National Organization for Women, calls to alert me that the Parks & Recreation Department is violating Title XIV of the federal guidelines prohibiting sex discrimination. It's offering 14 hours of sports activities for men and only 2 hours for women each week. These programs are offered in the school gyms throughout the city. She will be meeting with Danbury school board members tonight to alert them to the problem and also with the new Parks & Recreation director. We agree that she'll call me tomorrow with information on the meetings.

11 A.M.—Start revising plans for Sunday story. Had wanted to do analysis piece on a state advisory panel's work on school finance reform, but realize I don't have enough time with the way stories are breaking to do an adequate job on it this week.

11:30 A.M.—Call the Danbury school superintendent again, this time to find out about a high school evaluation report prepared by the New England Association of Schools and Colleges. I want a copy, but he says it's not ready and won't be until the end of the week. His delay coincides with a hearing on two former high school housemasters who are trying to get back jobs they lost in last year's reorganization. The evaluation report may not help their case. He may be stalling.

11:50 A.M.—Start organizing story on grievance that the teachers association has just lost in the arbitration, the first of two grievances filed against the Board and superintendent of schools this year. Speak with head of grievance committee for the teachers to get her version of the ruling. She's disenchanted with the local teacher association's representative, who was ill-equipped to handle the case against the board's lawyer. She's unwilling to go "on the record" with these views, but is considering going to the state association with her complaints about the representative. We agree to talk later.

1 P.M.—I go out to lunch—a toasted cheese sandwich at the Portuguese diner down the street.

2 P.M.—Drive out to a split level house in a development on the outskirts of Danbury for an interview with 10-year-old Karen Spram and her parents. She's a sixth grader with severe learning disabilities, garbled speech, limited vision. This year she was placed in a normal class at the Great Plains elementary school under the new federal law that assures handicapped children that they will be educated in the "least restrictive environment."

Testifying before a school board meeting recently Karen stressed the positive aspects of her move, but now as we sit with her parents at her home she speaks about the cruelty she's encountering. The other children do not really understand her handicap, she says, and insist the special number-counting device on her desk that helps her in math is there because she's stupid. Some children on the bus kick her and mimic her speech. Karen's parents try to soft peddle her remarks. "I tell her she's as good as anyone else," her father says. But I don't think Karen believes it.

She shows me her stuffed animal collection and gives me a present of an elephant molded from clay.

4:00 P.M.—End of workday. Drive home thinking of Karen. Feel I have the beginnings of a more complicated story. Originally, I'd thought she would offer an example of a success story. Instead, I've gotten a glimpse of what happens to a family with a "problem" child and of what happens when a "normal" school is not prepared to handle these children.

Tomorrow I'll raise that issue with Karen's teacher. I wonder what she'll have to say.

THE POLICE BEAT: ON THE JOB

Let's say you've been covering the police beat for the Hapsville *Recall*. You started by *researching* the beat. You went to the police chief's office and got a department or organizational chart. It showed the police commissioner at the top, then the top professional, the police chief, then the heads of the divisions: the uniformed division, handling normal patrol, police emergencies and traffic problems; the detective division, divided into squads according to the kinds of crime the detectives investigate. Larger police departments have detectives who specialize in burglary, robbery, narcotics, fraud, vice and homicide, but on this relatively small force, the detectives specialize little. The police get help from backup units such as the country crime laboratory and the medical examiner's office, or "M. E.," a civilian office that establishes cause of death in sudden or violent cases and figures prominently in homicide investigations.

You read textbooks on the fundamentals of criminal law. You learned that although the police arrest people every day, there is considerable doubt as a matter of law just when someone is actually "under arrest," and that they must have "probable cause" to think that they will find something illegal before they're permitted to search the trunk of an automobile, but that the courts differ on just what "probable cause" means. You obtained a copy of the department "search and seizure instructions" handed out to the police advising them on how to comply with these changing elements of the law.

You found that some crime information is part of the public record and

REPORTING CALLS FOR BRASHNESS, SAYS UPI VETERAN

Jack V. Fox worked for United Press International for nearly forty years, starting as a copyboy in their Kansas City bureau, where his boss was Walter Cronkite. He rose through the ranks as an editor in the New York bureau, then London bureau chief, features editor and ultimately a roving correspondent "assigned to travel anywhere in the U.S. where a big story was breaking." Cronkite called him "the king of the generalist reporters."

What has a career in journalism meant to you?
It's a luxury. It can take you around the world, let you meet people you'd never have met otherwise, give you a status in life you'd never enjoy in most jobs. Journalism may not pay much money, but you can get a tremendous charge out of reporting and writing. Something clicks in me the moment I see a big story starting to break. Part of it is the competition. It's a game in a way, and you know that somebody over at the AP is playing the same game. In a sense I'm still a juvenile after all these years.

To me, being a journalist is as important as being a doctor, lawyer, professor, scientist, politician or anything else. It's an opportunity to educate people, to stand in the midst of what's happening in the world. There's a tremendous satisfaction in knowing you've done a good job as a journalist, helped in the betterment of the society, if you will.

What was the most memorable story you covered?
I think it must have been the assassination of John F. Kennedy, which I covered as a rewrite man in New York. The story was so overwhelming that our Dallas bureau simply opened a direct line to the New York bureau and fed us chunks of information without any attempt to put them into story form, as they normally would have done. Everything broke loose. I moved into the rewrite slot and for eleven hours I wrote the Kennedy story with a Dallas dateline and a Merriman Smith byline. Writing under the gun like that for eleven hours was the most dramatic, tension-filled thing I've ever done. Smith won the Pulitzer Prize for his reportage on that story.

I felt icy calm all the while. When I finally got up from behind the typewriter I felt numb. I went to a bar and had a drink. And suddenly I started crying and couldn't stop.

What sort of stories have meant the most to you?
I've become, by happenstance, something of an expert in covering trials. I've covered the Sirhan Sirhan trial, Charles Manson, Ellsberg, Alger Hiss, the Hughes estate, Angela Davis, Patty Hearst. I've almost become an attorney through journalism.

Any advice on covering trials?
Some reporters think trials are dull, but they aren't at all dull if you get wrapped up in them. A trial is like a play. You've got the action right in front of you, a little world in itself. To get into the drama, take notes constantly. Don't wait until you hear something that sounds important, because later on what seemed like an inconsequential detail may loom as a crucial piece of information. Pay close attention to the picking of jurors; you can anticipate a lot about the line the prosecutor and the defense attorney plan to take by listening to the questions they ask of potential jurors. Third, use plenty of direct quotations in trial stories, as in all stories. Finally, describe the scene, how the witnesses looked, how they reacted. Description and quotations are always important.

What makes for a good reporter?
The main requirement is brashness. You've got to be well informed about the story, got to have done your homework, but the main thing then is that you're forever poking your nose into somebody else's business. Reporters do things on the job they'd never dream of doing as private citizens. Often the people you're investigating don't like reporters nosing around. *I* wouldn't like it, if I were them, would you? I was very shy at first, but I learned how to dig for the news. I must have covered 20,000 stories in my life.

police have to release it to the press, whereas other information isn't, and they don't. The information that must be released about a crime consists of little more than the bare bones of the story. The police usually are required to disclose where and when it took place and the identity of any victims—once their families have been notified, and with certain exceptions, such as in rape cases. They also must divulge the extent of loss, damage or injury, and the name, age and address of anyone arrested. You could have written accurate news stories from these skeletons alone, but to put flesh on those bones, you knew you would have to get the police to tell you about each case. You've therefore made it a point to take a personal interest in each of the officers, to get to know them and to let them get to know you.

Each day when you arrive at police headquarters you check the *log*, also called the *blotter*: a list of incidents and arrests so named because in the old days they were so splotched with ink they resembled real blotters. Nowadays, the blotter is a computer printout. Its entries, listed chronologically, record what the police did during each tour of duty.

When you find a blotter item that looks interesting, you ask the desk officer about it. If there's nobody around who knows the details, you look for a more complete report in the relevant department. Details about accidents can be found in reports stored in the traffic squad; reports about such crimes as burglaries and assaults are located in the detective squad office. You look up the report by its blotter number.

Some of your most popular feature stories on the police beat have been accounts of how detectives go about their work. You reported that detectives sometimes turn off the water before entering a tenement on a narcotics raid, so that the suspects can't flush contraband down the toilet, and you explained how one detective investigates bookmakers by disguising himself as a telephone repairperson.

Today it's 3:30 P.M. when you arrive at the yellow brick headquarters of the Hapsville Police Department. Sergeant Frank Dereskevitch is on the desk. You hand him a copy of the afternoon paper, something you do for all the cops on your rounds as a public relations gesture. Dereskevitch acknowledges receipt with a vague nod and hands you the blotter.

Looks like a slow day. At 2:09 P.M. there was a report of a stabbing at the Surf Bar in the North End. There was also one arrest, a Martha Lundigren, 34, 23 Fox Avenue, for assault with attempt to murder, and a woman was taken to the hospital—no other details. Blotter items are fairly cryptic; you have to fill in the story by talking to the detective handling the case upstairs. You note down the case number for reference. (*Jot it down*; *don't trust to memory*.) At 2:30 P.M. a stickup occurred at Raintree Liquors on Raintree Avenue. No details are given. Three accidents happened, two of them fender benders in the downtown area, the third with injuries out on Route 17. You know it involved injuries because the blotter says the traffic cop called for an "amb," or ambulance. One entry concerns a cat up a tree. A man was locked out of his car.

"What's this item here, sergeant?" you ask. "A 10–21 at Ephram's Landing. Never heard of 'code 10–21.' Must be new."

"Water," Dereskevitch says. "A 10–21 is for accidents on the water."

You thank Dereksevitch, go to the pay phone, call up Ephram's Landing and ask for Ephram. He turns out to be Ephram Cooper, owner of the marina on Lake Waramaug. He says a green aluminum skiff floated into the dock empty at about 3 P.M.

"Know who owns it?" you ask.

"Yeah. By the registration number it belongs to a David Rangecroft on Weymouth Drive, about a block off the Lake." You get him to spell "R-a-n-g-e-c-r-o-f-t," thank him and hang up. You look up Rangecroft's number and give it a call. Mrs. Rangecroft answers. Introducing yourself, you say you're down at police headquarters and they've found a boat registered to her family. There's a pause on the line; you sense something's happened and she doesn't want to talk.

"Mrs. Rangecroft, is the police officer there? Would you please let me talk to him?"

The police officer comes on. Warren Musgrave. You know him. (*Knowing the participants is one way covering a beat pays off*.) Last month you did a little feature about his making the semifinals in the state pistol matches. "What's happening there, Warren?" you ask. "That boat they found, someone missing?"

"Yeah, it's these people's son, Tommy. He's 12."

"When was he last seen?"

"He left the house at about noon to go fishing. Never returned."

"You looking for him?"

"I think he might be drowned. The Rescue Squad is coming out to drag the lake."

Thanking him, you hang up and quickly call the city desk at the *Recall*. The other blotter stuff was cold, but this story is still happening. The desk will want the chance to send out a photographer to cover the search. The city editor tells you to check with Rescue and keep her informed.

Before calling Rescue you go up to the detectives' office on the third floor to get details on the crimes you got from the blotter. It is a large room divided into chest-high cubicles in which the detectives have their desks. The man who handled the stabbing at the bar is Carmine DePietro, a detective sergeant. You remember him from a couple of weeks ago when two burglars stole a 500-pound safe from the Pick-a-Wing chicken joint over on Fairfax and were still wheeling it down the street when the police showed up.

"Hey Carmine, what ever happened to those two guys and the safe?" you ask.

Follow-Up on Back Stories

"You wouldn't believe it," he says, eyes wide. "They told the judge they'd just found it on the sidewalk and were wheeling it to the police station like good citizens. They *walked*! The judge set them free! We couldn't prove they'd actually been in the Pick-a-Wing. But don't worry, we'll get them for something else. Guys that dumb don't stay out of the joint too long."

"That stabbing this afternoon, what have you got on it?" you ask.

"Pretty routine sticking. No one really hurt bad. What we got is that this woman Lundigren had been in the bar since early morning soaking up booze with a boyfriend. This other lady comes over and starts making up to the boyfriend and the first lady takes objection to this. She reaches over the bar and grabs one of those little knives the bartender peels lemons with and deposits the knife in the lady's right shoulder. Didn't hit anything important, but the bar erupted in a little melée during which the boyfriend takes off. He may have some reason not to want to see us—I don't know. Anyway, the bartender calls the cops. The Lundigren lady stayed around helping the lady she'd stabbed."

"The charge on the blotter says attempted murder," you say. "That's pretty serious."

"Nah, it's been knocked down already to assault with a dangerous weapon. The lady was sorry the moment she did it; now they're both friends."

The detective handling the other case, the holdup at Raintree Liquors, is not in. You look up the incident report and get the specifics from that: Two men wearing ski masks came in at 2:30 holding a sawed-off shotgun. No customers were in the store; they made off with $750 in cash. The clerk, Claude Spooley, 25, says he doesn't know if they had a car or not. He was told to lie on the floor for five minutes with his nose in the carpet, and that's what he did. (*When the participants aren't around, check the records.*)

"Raintree Liquors," you say, half to yourself. "Hey, Carmine, hasn't that place been held up before?"

"Just a little," says DePietro, relighting the black piece of rope in his mouth he insists on calling a cigar. "This is the sixth time so far this year, and if you ask me it's getting little obvious."

What does he mean, "obvious?" (*What's behind the obvious facts?*)

"We think the clerk is making a little cash transfer to his buddies. Same M. O. each time. Two guys, ski masks, shotgun, come in during a quiet time, 2 or 3 o'clock. No trouble. Clerk never sees anything. Always about the same time in the month. Next month we're staking the place out. When we catch the two guys, we'll get the clerk, too."

"Huh. That's pretty interesting," you say.

"Hey, none of this in the story," he cautions.

"Of course not. But how about if I went along with you guys on the stakeout when it happens?" You think it would make a good story on how the cops catch crooks. DePietro says it's okay with him; he'll ask the captain. (*Plan ahead; as a beat reporter, you'll be back tomorrow.*)

On your way out, you stop by the office of Detective Lieutenant Anthony C. O'Dougherty, who's in charge of the day watch. He's about to leave. "Hey, I heard about your grandson," you tell him. Yesterday a cop told you O'Dougherty's grandson had just graduated from the police academy as a rookie patrol officer. O'Dougherty also has a son on the force, a sergeant on the vice squad. O'Dougherty is scheduled to retire later this month after forty years of service.

You tell him you'd like to get the whole family together for a feature. Lots of pictures, too. O'Dougherty seems pleased. (*It never hurts to be friendly.*)

"By the way," you ask, "what's doing on the Arnaud investigation?" Two months ago, burglars with blowtorches cut through three inches of carbon steel, gained entry to a safe at Arnaud Jewelers and escaped with $150,000 in stones.

"Close. We're very close," O'Dougherty says. "I'll let you know."

"Just make sure you arrest the guys after lunch, okay? I want the story for the *Recall*."

On the way out of the building, you pick up the three accident reports from the traffic squad. You see that the one with injuries resulted in an arrest of a teenage girl for DWI, or driving while intoxicated. "This is the sixth case this month of kids drinking and getting into accidents," the sergeant tells you. "I hate to see it; it's scary. I've got a kid about to take his driver's test. I know *he's* all right, but what about some other donkey on the road?"

You tell him you'll come by tomorrow to get the statistics. There's a proposed ordinance you read about coming up before the City Council to raise the local drinking age to 21. A rash of recent accidents could be a good angle for a story.

It's now 5:30 P.M. You stop in at the Fire Department next door to check the fire log. Nothing. Then you hit the Rescue Squad, which is part of the Fire Department and located in the same building, to ask if anything's turned up yet on the little boy. A Rescue Lieutenant, Nell Fairchild, says there's nothing yet. Two divers went out to the lake, along with a Rescue skiff and grappling hooks. You say you'll check back later. "I hope they don't find anything," Fairchild says. You say you do, too.

Getting back to the news room, you fill in the city editor, a small, owlish woman, on the stories you're working. Nothing earth shaking, except possibly the little boy. You also tell her about the liquor store stakeout idea. She likes it. You check the clips in the newspaper morgue for all the names that surfaced in the blotter items. If anyone is well known, you'll want to mention their background in your story. This time, there's nothing. You check the hospital for the conditions of the accident and stabbing victims, then write a brief on each. Your final deadline isn't until 11:30 at night, but the watchwords on the police beat are "do it now." Later in the evening you may have your hands full covering something else. You also look up Rangecroft, the missing boy's father, in the City Directory and find that he's the owner of Rangecroft Auto Body on Lancaster Pike.

At 7:30 P.M. you pause to eat the sandwich you bought for supper: sardines and onions on rye. Reporters at the other desks sniff the air, like deer getting wind of an intruder.

At 9:00 P.M. your phone rings. It's Lieutenant Fairchild over at Rescue. She says they found the boy. "He walked into the house ten minutes ago. No one was there, so he wandered down to the lake to see what all the commotion was about. Asked one of the fireman what was going on. The fireman told him, 'They're looking for a boy named Tommy Rangecroft.' The kid says, '*I'm* Tommy Rangecroft.' The fireman almost fell over."

"Where'd the boy been?" you ask.

"Apparently he jumped off the boat for a swim, then spotted a friend on shore. The two of them took off and played in the woods all afternoon. Forgot about the boat. When it started getting dark he came home."

You thank the lieutenant for calling, and tell the city editor that the kid's okay. She says to do a story anyway. "I can just imagine what the parents went through," she says. "And a lot of readers will too. Give them a call. Tell them I'm sending a photographer back out to get a picture of them."

You call the house. No answer. Again you turn to the City Directory. In one section it's got a numerical listing of street addresses along with telephone numbers. You look up the houses on both sides of the Rangecroft place on Weymouth Drive. At one there's no answer. At the other, the people say, yes, they know the Rangecrofts. Mrs. Rangecroft is in their front yard right now. (*Don't take "no answer" for an answer.*) You get the mother on the phone and reintroduce yourself. This time she's more talkative.

"I'm glad he's okay," you say. "You must be very relieved."

"Oh, heavens yes," she says. "We were beside ourselves. All the neighbors were just wonderful. But it was awful. Just awful. When he came walking over with that fireman we were speechless. Then I started to cry, and my husband got angry. Tommy was so shocked by all the ruckus I don't think he'll ever stay out again."

You thank her and tell her the photographer's on the way. After hanging up you think about how to write the story. One way would be to make it into a news feature. The angle of Tommy's walking up to the fireman is pretty good—sort of like Tom Sawyer's attending his own funeral. But you decide that approach is a little too flippant. For a while there the family had been terribly worried. You play it straight:

> An evening that began on a scary note for a Hapsville family ended happily last night when the son they feared had drowned turned up unhurt.
> The boy, Tommy Rangecroft, 12, son of Mr. and Mrs. David Rangecroft, of 34 Weymouth Dr., had been reported missing yesterday afternoon when the boat he had taken fishing floated empty into a marina on Lake Waramaug.
> Divers and other firefighters from the Rescue Squad spent more than five hours looking for the lad without success. Lt. Nell Fairchild of the Rescue Squad said the boy turned up at about 8:45 P.M. while the men were still dragging the lake. He and a friend had been playing in the woods, he said.
> Fairchild said young Rangecroft walked up to a fireman and asked what was going on:
> "The fireman said, 'They're looking for a boy named Tommy Rangecroft.' "
> "The kid said, 'I'm Tommy Rangecroft.' "
> "The fireman almost fell over."
> Lieutenant Fairchild said the boy had jumped off the boat after spotting a friend and swam ashore. The pair spent the day playing in the woods.
> "When he came walking over with that fireman we were speechless," said his mother.

"Then what happened is I started to cry, and my husband got angry. Tommy was so shocked at all the ruckus I don't think he'll ever stay out late again."

By the time you hand in your story it's 11 P.M. A half hour until final deadline. You make your last checks at the hospital emergency room for accidents, and at police headquarters. You call the state police barracks that handles accidents on the state highways in the region. All quiet. (*You're responsible for covering your beat; keep checking what's new.*)

At 11:30 you put on your coat and get a "good night" from the city editor. "See you tomorrow," she says. "We'll talk about the stakeout story."

SUMMARY

Reporters gather the news in three principal ways: through *research, interviews,* and *observation.* Research resources include government records, most of which are open to public scrutiny; public and private research organizations; academic institutions; and individuals who have held jobs in responsible positions. One of the reporter's most useful tools is the newspaper library, with its clip file of past stories that have appeared in print.

A reporter's cardinal rules include *promptness, persistence, thoroughness, skepticism, caution,* and *enthusiasm.*

Beat reporters are specialists in covering particular areas of news. Some are experts with advanced degrees in their specialties; others are self-educated.

13

INTERVIEWING

Interviewing is so much a part of journalism today that one of the first images that pop into our minds when we hear the word "journalist" is likely to be that of a reporter with a microphone or pencil and pad in hand, asking someone a question.

Some interviews are intended simply to garner information, as when a reporter covering a visit by the Queen of England asks her press secretary why she always carries a handbag, or a reporter on the nightside city desk calls a hospital intensive care unit to check on the condition of a burn victim. Here, the tactics consist mainly of brisk, simple questions, aimed at obtaining facts.

Other interviews are more adversarial in nature. These range from hard questioning at press conferences to interviews conducted at the end of an investigation in which the reporter is confronting someone with evidence of criminal activity. The chief tactic in adversarial interviews is to know as much as possible about the story, to minimize the chances of being mislead by false or evasive answers.

Interviews can be employed to gather anecdotes or quotations that add color and texture to a story. A *Newsweek* reporter covering the eruption of a volcano in Hawaii made the story seem more immediate by including a quote that readers themselves might have heard had they been standing on the mountainside, watching the lava flow:

> "See that smoke on the ridge?" said an evacuee. "That's just about where my house is."

A specialized but growing type of interview is aimed at producing a Q&A: an edited transcript to run in a newspaper or magazine. Unlike news stories and profiles, which usually present quotations reporting only the answers to interview questions, Q&As include the questions, too—hence, their name. First made popular by *Playboy* magazine, Q&As are now featured in dozens of magazines and a number of newspapers.

PREPARING FOR AN INTERVIEW

The best way to learn something is to *know something*. As television interviewer Mike Wallace says, "You can talk to anybody, I mean *anybody*, if you've done a little preparation. Partly it's a matter of the subject's ego; they respect the fact that you've taken the time to learn about them. But it also alerts them that they'd better not try to pull the wool over your eyes or they're likely to be found out."

Preparation means research, and the loftier the goal, the more exhaustive should be the research. One journalist, preparing for a *Playboy* interview that would expose the shaky foundations of Erich von Daniken's "ancient astronauts" theories, spent months reading not only all of von Daniken's books but also all other relevant books and articles in the field. But the same journalist, rushing to interview the inventor of an electric car in order to write a short article for an afternoon newspaper, contented himself with reading a press release and perusing morgue clips filed under "automobiles, electric," in a taxi on the way to cover the story.

Try never to walk into an interview totally unprepared. One young radio reporter opened a live on-the-air interview with the author of an astronomy book by asking, "Tell me, what are stars, and why do they fall?" Stars don't fall, but the interview went straight through the floor.

ARRANGING AN INTERVIEW

Most formal interviews—meaning anything more ambitious than a fast phone call under deadline—are arranged in advance. Sometimes an editor schedules the interview and dispatches a staff reporter. Often, an enterprising reporter out to develop stories does the arranging for him- or herself—after clearing the assignment with an editor, of course.

The most successful interviewers are those who seek out rewarding people to interview. If, while covering a forest fire, you talk with a forest ranger who seems articulate and perceptive, get his or her telephone number and note that he or she might make for a good profile. When you overhear the owners of Gyro's Diner complaining about their rising gas bill, make a note to call them when you get around to writing a piece on what energy costs are doing to small businesses. If you read a good new novel and learn from the flap copy that the novelist lives nearby, propose to your editor that you schedule a profile.

Celebrities are in demand as interview subjects—too much so, perhaps—because stories about celebrities draw readers. To get in touch with celebrities, use the reference works. Television and motion picture actors are listed in the *Hollywood Reporter Bluebook* and the *Academy Players Directory*, along with their

---

RESEARCH PAYS IN INTERVIEWING

Fact counts for more than opinion in journalism, and in preparing for an interview, as for other assignments, the first step is to research the facts. In the following excerpt from a *Playboy* interview, the subject is Erich von Daniken, whose "ancient astronaut" books, proclaiming that Earth has been visited by aliens from other planets, have sold millions of copies worldwide. The interviewer seeks to pin down the accuracy—or lack of it—in von Daniken's claims not by voicing opinions, but by persistently steering the interview back to the ascertainable facts.

Playboy: . . . In your book *The Gold of the Gods*, you describe taking a voyage through enormous caves in Ecuador where you claim to have seen ancient furniture made of plastic, a menagerie of gold animals, a library of imprinted metal plates and other evidence of a great early civilization. You call this "the most incredible, fantastic story of the century" and say you were guided through the caves by a South American adventurer named Juan Moricz. But Moricz says he never took you into any such caves. Which of you is telling the truth?

von Daniken: I guess we both are telling half the truth.

Playboy: Which half is yours?

von Daniken: I have been in Ecuador several times. I have met Moricz several times and we have been together at the side entrance to those tunnels. But before we went in that entrance, Moricz made it a condition that I would not be allowed to give the location or to take photographs inside. I could understand that, because he didn't want people going in there. So I agreed, we shook hands and we left. And, as a matter of fact, in my book I have not told the truth concerning the geographic location of the place, nor about some various other little things. In German we say a writer, if he is not writing pure science, is allowed to use some *dramaturgisch Effekte*—some theatrical effects. And that's what I have done. But finally, the whole controversy over whether I have been down there in those caves or not seems ridiculous. The main question should be: Does the library of gold plates exist or not? This should be the main question, not whether Mr. von Daniken has seen them or not.

Playboy: Are you saying you have never been inside the caves?

von Daniken: I *have* been inside the caves, but not at the place where the photographs in the book were taken, not at the main entrance. I was at a side entrance. And we were down there for six hours.

Playboy: Did you, in fact, see the things you describe? Seven chairs made of a plastic-like material, a zoo of solid-gold animals, a library of gold plates?

von Daniken: Definitely. No doubt. Though I must say I am not at all sure, anymore, if the so-called zoo is made of gold. It could be something different.

Playboy: In the book you say Moricz led you in darkness, then gave the command, "Switch on your torches!" You write, "We are standing dumbfounded and amazed in the middle of a gigantic hall." Is that what really happened?

von Daniken: No, that is not true. It is what I call theatrical effect.

Playboy: Were you and Moricz even in the caves?

von Daniken: Yeah, sure. He saw everything.

Playboy: Moricz says, "Von Daniken was *never* in the caves; when he states he has seen the library and the other things himself, he is lying. We never showed him these things."

von Daniken: I know those statements, because he has written to me the same thing, and I can well understand it. In 1969, Moricz organized an expedition down there. All the crew members signed documents promising to say nothing about whatever they might find. This was reported in the Ecuadorian press. So when *The Gold of the Gods* appeared, I think members of the 1969 expedition must have told Moricz, "Listen, this isn't fair. Von Daniken has made the thing public. We could have made money with it, but we were pledged to silence." I feel this was the main reason, though there were others, why Moricz now says the whole thing is a hoax. But again, to me the main point is not if I have seen these things or not. I just don't care. The question is, do they exist?

agents' telephone numbers. The agents, in turn, are listed in the *International Motion Picture Almanac*. Authors can be contacted through their publishers. Leaders in the professions can be located through biographical entries in any of a wide variety of specialty directories. Ask a librarian for help.

Those who feel reticent about being interviewed may be approached through an intermediary they trust. A white reporter working on a book about the 1980 Miami riot needed to talk to rioters, all of whom were black and, he suspected, had little inclination to talk to him. He sought the help of an organization of black ex-convicts who worked regularly with ghetto youths and knew many of the rioters. After spending an afternoon talking to members of the group and showing them some writing he had done about other riots, he asked if they would help him line up youngsters to be interviewed. The ex-convicts readily agreed, and soon the reporter had more interviews than he could handle.

If you know *what* you're looking for but not exactly *who*, try canvassing. To research a feature piece on London's notoriously skillful burglars, Pulitzer Prize-winning journalist Thomas Powers ran an advertisement in the *Times* of London headlined: WANTED: BURGLARS. Scotland Yard responded to the ad—they were curious about just what Powers had in mind—but so did a number of burglars, some of whom agreed to be interviewed in return for a pledge of anonymity. Never underestimate people's desire to tell their stories.

When calling for an interview, explain clearly and forthrightly who you are and what you have in mind. Identify yourself, whether you're a staff reporter for the *Chicago Tribune* or a freelancer on assignment for the Northridge Mall *Gazette*. Briefly explain why the interview would make for a publishable story. If you've published similar stories in the past, say so. Explain what *kind* of story you contemplate writing: Is it to be a profile, or will the interview constitute part of a larger story? Where, and approximately when, is it to appear? Why are you writing it?

Problems can arise at this stage if the story you're working on threatens to anger the person, or damage his or her reputation. When such is the case, journalists sometimes fudge their intentions a bit. A political reporter on the trail of corruption in a congressional representative's campaign might say that she's doing a piece on "the growth of Political Action Committees." The statement isn't exactly untrue, but it's far enough out of focus as to render the truth indistinct. Fudging may be unavoidable in some sensitive situations, but the frank truth is often just as effective. The person implicated may regard the interview as a challenge. And, of course, those who don't grant interviews don't get to air their side—a point a reporter can always mention.

Be sure to specify how much time the interview will require, and where you would prefer to conduct it. More effective description can be written into a profile if the interview is conducted in the relaxed atmosphere of the subject's home; interviews conducted with straight news in mind can take place in the subject's office; and informal talks for background might be held over lunch or dinner.

PREPARING INTERVIEW QUESTIONS

"Judge a man, not by his answers, but by his questions," wrote Voltaire, and that is just how journalists are judged in interview situations.

The quality of the questions you ask depends on sound preparation. Walk into an interview with a list of promising questions. During an actual interview, you'll most likely ask new questions that occur to you as the interview proceeds, and end up discarding some of your prepared questions. But having the list will help you remember to hit the main points that need be covered, and will minimize the danger of running dry. Nothing is more embarrassing in an interview than a long silence while you try to remember—or think up—your next question. If properly prepared, you should have sufficient questions to sustain the interview throughout its scheduled length, even if no spontaneous questions suggest themselves.

Concrete questions demand specific answers that are usually easy to provide. Ask a baseball umpire what kind of mud he rubs into the baseball; ask a boat builder what's the best wood for constructing a sternpost.

More general, *open-ended* questions allow the interviewee greater freedom of response. They are best put once the subject is at ease: What did the umpire think of umpires back when he was still playing ball?

Some questions delve into the interviewee's *motivation*: How does the umpire feel when he blows a call and the crowd boos?

Questions rooted in facts are the strongest of all. They're difficult to evade, and, because they're specific, they promote specific answers. They also make for an effective way to pose a harsh or controversial query, because by pointing to the facts they stress that the opinion implied in the question is not necessarily your own. Some samples follow:

Questions Lacking Facts	*Fact-Oriented Questions*
How do you respond to critics who say your book on American history is inaccurate?	One reviewer called your book on American history "sloppy and inaccurate," in that you write, for instance, that Washington was present at the Battle of Yorktown. How do you respond?
What are your plans if things don't go well in the campaign?	The polls indicate that you have no chance of winning as a third-party candidate. What's the point of staying in the race if you cannot possibly win?
Mr. Mayor, there are people saying your administration is rife with nepotism. What do you say to that?	Mr. Mayor, the Ajax Insurance Company just won the contract to provide insurance for City Hall. Does that have anything to do with the fact that your mother-in-law is vice president of the firm?

Fact-oriented questions, moreover, promote candor. Thomas Powers describes this phenomenon in the preface to his book *The Man Who Kept the Secrets*, about CIA Director Richard Helms:

> With a half-dozen exceptions, the former CIA officers I talked to were still loyal to the Agency and simply wanted to set the record straight. Most began by telling me what they wouldn't talk about: The names of agents and fellow CIA officers, the details of operations which had not already been exposed by the press, and so on. As we talked, however, the force of these prohibitions seemed to erode. A name that popped up in one conversation would serve as a useful wedge in another. An operation alluded to by one former official would be elaborated on by a second, corrected by a third, amended by a fourth, and finally rounded off by the first, now that I had most of it anyway. If one keeps on asking questions, the answers will gradually begin to fit together.

THE TOOLS OF THE TRADE

Tape Recording

Use a decent recorder—preferably one with an end-of-tape alarm—and high-quality tape. Inexpensive cassettes are no bargain; they can jam the recorder. Use sixty- or ninety-minute cassettes, not 120s, which are prone to stretch or break. Immediately after making a tape, punch out the tabs in back so you can't inadvertently record over it; if you later want to rerecord on the cassette, you can always put tape over the knockouts. Use long-life batteries, and carry extras. When rewinding and transcribing tapes use an AC converter, to prevent draining the batteries.

A broadcast-quality microphone makes the recording easier to hear, and picks up less incidental noise than a built-in mike. Its presence reminds the interviewee that you're taping, but that's not necessarily a liability. For every person who is shy about tape recorders, another needs the trappings of a formal interview—like the presence of a microphone—to get the adrenalin flowing. And in mob scenes, where a bunch of reporters is crowded around, print reporters who feel upstaged by their broadcast colleagues can wield a broadcast-quality microphone and bark out questions with the best of them.

Clean the recording head after every dozen or so tapes, using a cleaning cassette or a cotton swab dipped in solvent. You'll be surprised how much clearer that makes the sound. In addition, demagnetize the heads regularly, to prevent whistling and squealing; demagnetizing cassettes are available that do this job in seconds.

The wonderful thing about tape is that it gets every word—more or less—so that you can use as many quotations as you like, and at any length. And you can improve your interview technique by playing back the tape and hearing where you could have done better. The trouble is that you *have* to listen to it, to transcribe the quotes. In effect, you're going through the interview twice, and that takes time.

Using the Telephone

The telephone is a powerful tool for conducting short interviews, especially for roundup stories that require interviewing a number of people in a short time. If you're trying to get doctors' reactions to an announcement that a drug they've been prescribing for twenty years causes cancer, you can reach more of them around the country by telephone in one afternoon than you could visit personally in a week. And, if necessary, you *can* do longer interviews by phone. Jonathan Cott of *Rolling Stone* published an extensive and incisive Q & A with Glenn Gould, the pianist, although Gould, a recluse, would talk to Cott only by phone.

Clear recordings of both sides of a telephone interview can be made by attaching a little suction-cup microphone to the handset. Be sure to *tell* the interviewee that you're taping the conversation. To do otherwise may be not only unethical but illegal; in many states, the law forbids covert taping of telephone conversations.

Taking Notes

A 7¾ inch × 5 inch spiral-bound notebook is small enough to fit in a purse or jacket pocket, yet large enough to hold plenty of writing—usually enough to contain all the notes for a feature of up to several thousand words. Its stiff boards make it rugged and permanent. That's important: Never capriciously discard your notes. They may come in handy one day, as they did for the reporter who was called before Congress in 1983 to testify about an unpublished interview years earlier with a man who had then called arms control a "sham," yet was now being nominated to be the nation's arms control administrator.

Write your name, address and telephone number inside the front cover. Some reporters add the words REWARD FOR RETURN in big block letters—a line that has helped recover many a lost notebook.

List your prepared interview questions on the last pages of the notebook. That way, you can find them quickly when you need them. Often the pace of a successful interview depends on your asking questions *promptly*. Head each set of notes with the name of the person being interviewed, the location and the date. Don't trust to memory. Carry several pens. It makes a reporter feel silly to have a pen run dry and have to ask to borrow another; it's like a tennis player's asking the opponent in a tournament for a racket.

The most efficient way to take notes is in shorthand. Some journalists, especially those in England and Australia, are trained in formal systems of shorthand. Others develop speedwriting systems of their own, characterized by abbreviations like these:

t	the
sd	said
cd	could
w	with
tmw	tomorrow
hpd	happened
blv	believe

But not even shorthand enthusiasts take down *everything* that people say. That's a stenographer's job. For the reporter, whether covering a press conference, a speech or a personal interview, the trick is to discriminate between the routine and the potentially newsworthy, and to note only those quotations that have a chance of appearing in the story.

What if a quotation sounds newsworthy, but the speaker is going too fast for you to keep up? A useful technique is to jot down key phrases, then return a few moments later to fill in the conjunctions and other material between. Suppose you're interviewing City Council member Burt Wax, and he's holding forth on one of his favorite subjects, federal school regulations. Wax says:

> I'm tired of bureaucrats' telling us every little thing, from what color blackboards to use to whether teachers can spank kids who get out of line. I've been living in this community all my life, 44 years, and we've got a pretty good town here, in my opinion. But it's getting messed up by these clowns in big government. If students act sassy, teachers should whale the daylights out of them, like they did in my day. I don't know. I hate to see this happen. Things used to be so simple. These bureaucrats ought to be run out of town on a rusty rail, if you ask me.

Rushing to take notes, you skip the parts of Wax's remarks that clearly aren't news—such as how many years Wax has lived in town, and that he likes it there—and jot down the key phrases of the rest. Your notes might look like this:

> Tired—b'cts tlng us evry ltl thng—color bk-bds to whthr tchrs cn spnk kids who gt ot f ln—Town—gtng msd up by ths clowns in big gvt—stdnts act sassy—whale daylights ot f thm—did in my day—b'cats ought to be rn ot f tn on a rusty rail.

Once Wax stops for breath, you can quickly review the notes, adding the necessary connections. Excess verbiage ("I don't know . . . Things used to be so simple," and so forth) can be ignored. Your notes then might look like this:

> Wax: "I'm tired f b'cts tlng us evry ltl thng, frm wht color bk-bds to use to whthr tchrs cn spnk kids who gt ot f ln. . . ." Town is "gtng msd up by ths clowns in big gvt. F stdnts act sassy, th tchr shd whale th daylights ot f thm, like thy did in my day. . . . Ths b'cats ought to be rn ot f tn on a rusty rail."

When writing the story, you can then select the most pertinent quotations from the notes. The relevant paragraphs might read:

Council member Burt Wax railed against federal bureaucrats whose guidelines for public schools, he charged, seek to dictate "every little thing, from what color blackboards to use to whether teachers can spank kids who get out of line."

"If students act sassy, the teachers should whale the daylights out of them, like they did in my day," Wax said. He said federal bureaucrats "ought to be run out of town on a rusty rail."

CONDUCTING THE INTERVIEW

Whether an interview is dynamic or dull depends chiefly on the journalist conducting it. If the interviewer is energetic, well-prepared and to the point, the interviewee will tend to respond on a similar level. If the interviewer is lackadaisical, ill-prepared or confused, the interview will tend to deteriorate, and fast. Following are a few suggestions.

Attitude and Decorum

An attitude of enthusiastic curiosity works wonders. "Reporting, by and large, is being interested in everyone you meet," said A. J. Liebling, and nowhere does his injunction apply more forcefully than in interviewing. Set a sprightly, energetic tone, and don't be shy about asking direct questions; that's what you're there for. If you've done your homework, you need not feel intimidated by the fear of appearing ignorant or naive; learning is part of the job. Avoid lapsing into a cynical or world-weary tone, as if you already knew what you were going to hear; the interviewee may be all too ready to oblige, by acting cynical in return.

Appearance counts; many an interview has gone awry the moment the reporter walked through the door. What appearance is appropriate? It depends on the circumstances. A youthful UPI reporter who went to interview Senator Eugene McCarthy dressed in boots, jeans and a leather vest found that his appearance irritated the Senator, who was trying to get volunteers in his presidential campaign to be "clean for Gene" to avoid the public's identifying him with bearded radicals. The same reporter, assigned to interview folk singer Pete Seeger aboard the sloop *Clearwater* in the Hudson River, wore a suit and tie and found that Seeger eyed him with suspicion. A good general rule is to avoid wearing clothes that call attention to yourself.

Decorum counts, too. Many people put a premium on good manners, and will freeze as solid as an arctic lake at the sight of reporters who chew gum, smoke without asking permission, put their feet up on the furniture or handle objects that don't belong to them. Some journalists try to "break the ice" by acting overly familiar—addressing someone they've just met by his or her first name or adopting an excessively warm tone. Don't do it. The way to break the ice with, say, an eminent judge is to show that you've studied his or her decisions, not by strolling into the chambers and saying, "Hi, how're ya' doin'?" Formality and restraint pay off more often.

EVEN THE SILENT CAN "SPEAK": INTERVIEWER SOMETIMES MUST GO BEYOND WORDS

Even some of the most unapproachable people are prepared to communicate with reporters—on their own terms. Race driver Danny Ongais was known for his taciturnity and patent hostility toward the press—and was disliked by sportswriters in return. When Ongais was badly injured in a horrifying crash at Indianapolis in 1981, a reporter looking down from the press box said sarcastically, "It couldn't have happened to a nicer guy."

Ongais survived, and returned to racing after months in the hospital. Sportswriter Tracy Dodds of the *Los Angeles Times* was wary of Ongais's reputation for unapproachability, but when she encountered Ongais at Riverside International Raceway in California, she decided to try once again to pierce Ongais's seemingly invincible shell of reserve. The interview was not encouraging. But notice Dodds's growing comprehension of what Ongais is trying to say, and—in the second half of the piece—Ongais's way of "saying" it:

I join him on the pit wall, introduce myself and say, "Can we talk?"

He says, "We can try."

That's the nicest thing I've ever heard him say. We're off to a great start.

So I start talking. I tell him that I saw his crash. I tell him how much it scared me. I ask him what he remembers of the crash. But he doesn't answer. He just stares down at the track, shaking his head.

Then I realize that he didn't see the crash. And he was unconscious all that time.

So I ask if he's seen the pictures. He nods. I ask if he doesn't consider himself pretty lucky to have lived through that. He shrugs.

OK. I can see that he's not going to talk about the crash itself. So I ask about the long rehabilitation, the way the doctors saved his leg.

"I'm fine," he says.

But how long did the recovery take? Did he expect to be well enough to race again?

"I'm OK, really."

Well, maybe he'll talk about his decision to continue racing. What made him want to race again? What kind of thinking went into that decision?

"There was no decision to be made," he says.

A long silence follows while I try to decide whether he's being difficult, or whether that's really the answer.

I think that maybe my questions are missing the point somehow, so I just wait. Maybe he'll volunteer a story that tells how he really feels about the whole thing. So I wait.

Finally I ask, "Am I wrong to even ask you about that accident and about the danger out there? Is that a taboo subject? Does it bother you?"

Looking up and smiling, he says, "No, it doesn't bother me. You have the right to ask anything you want."

And he adds, "I'm sorry that I can't help you. I'm sorry that I don't have the answers you want."

"But there is no answer I want," I say. "I just want to know how you feel about what you went through, what it means to you to drive again, what goes through your mind when you see a wall coming up at 200 mph, what you thought about all those months while you were lying in the hospital."

Again he shrugs.

Breaking the Ice

Having prepared, you'll know more about the interviewee than he or she will know about you. The person may be nervous, understandably so: You want information, and he or she will have no control over how you use it. So take matters slowly at first. Indulge briefly in small talk, to let the interviewee settle down and size you up. One communications researcher found that most interviews succeed or fail during the *first four minutes*, based on the sort of impression the reporter makes.

This is a good time to remind your subject of the purpose of the interview, how you intend to use it, and when and where the finished story is to appear.

Now, bewildered, I just sit there beside him and try to sort through what he said. He has said that he's willing to talk, but he won't say anything.

Once again I try. I ask him about the ever-present danger in racing. Does he just not think about it? Or does he just not like to talk about it? Or does he deny that it's there? Surely he has some opinion on a life-and-death subject that is so real to him.

"I'm indifferent to it," he says.

I start to say, "You can't be indifferent to it . . ."

He raises his eyebrows and smiles.

And I finally get it. He's right. He's giving me answers, but not the answers I want. Or can deal with.

I'm expecting stories of gripping fear, recurring nightmares, determination to conquer the track after long suffering and pain.

He's saying not so, not so. He's saying it doesn't bother him. That there is no melodrama. An accident is something you recover from to race again.

"You really never even considered giving up racing?"

"I like what I do," he said. "I enjoy it."

So I say, "Thank you." And he says, "Have a nice day."

"It's you!" he says as I climb into the passenger seat of his 935 Porsche Turbo.

"Yeah, it's me."

"Are you ready?"

Before I decide how to answer that, he roars out of the pits and onto the course.

Out of curiosity I have climbed into a superpowered Porsche with Danny Ongais on a road course full of esses and 180-degree turns. It occurs to me that curiosity killed the cat.

I had planned to pay attention, to notice whether he downshifts going into turn five and what it looks

like to go over a blind hill into seven. But it was no good. All I could do was grip the roll bars and brace myself as hard as I could. I was trying not to flop around in the turns, but I realized that even the helmet strapped tightly to my head was shifting on every turn.

Which turn? Who knows? Who cares?

I knew when we hit the backstretch, though, because the force of the acceleration had me pinned back against the seat.

I became aware, then, of Ongais watching me and laughing. Trying to be casual, I shouted, "How fast are we going?" He shrugged.

When I screamed through the next turn, he reached over to give me a reassuring pat and a smile, and I was thinking, how nice—oh, my God, he's driving with one hand and he's not watching the road!

He was loving it.

I tried to smile, but I'm afraid my smile had some grimace in it.

He asked me another question, but I couldn't hear him, so I smiled and nodded, and he roared past the entrance to the pit.

He must have asked me if I wanted to go around again.

If I had heard him, I would have said yes. It was great. It was exhilarating.

I was marveling at how he could downshift, take those turns so fast without sliding off the road and then get back up to speed again. I was wondering how close to racing speed we were going. I was wondering what it would be like with other cars on the track.

I wasn't wondering why he was driving.

As he slowed into the pit area, he turned and asked another question. "Did you enjoy it?" He knew what my answer would be.

And I was reminded of Brer Rabbit's saying, "I can't tell you, I gots to show you."

What was Ongais "saying" to Dodds? And what does Dodds's story tell us about the role of preconceptions in a journalist's getting a story?

If you ask Jane Fonda, for example, "How did you react to your parents' divorce?" you may elicit a different answer depending on whether you've said you're writing a profile of her, a recollection of her father or a survey piece about the children of divorced parents.

This, too, is the time to review any ground rules. If the interviewee has indicated that he or she wants to talk on a given subject only "off the record" or "for background," review just what these terms mean, so that there can be no confusion. (See the box on pages 252–253.)

A little small talk at the outset can help break the ice. A magazine writer arriving to interview a reputedly grumpy criminologist in Davis, California, encountered the man's wife in her vegetable garden before entering the house and the two fell into an involved conversation over the raising of strawberries. When they went inside the woman told her husband: "Now, this is a wonderful young man; I want you to treat him right." With that, the interview was off to a good start.

But watch for hints that the icebreaking has gone on long enough. An imminent physicist, reached by telephone at a proton decay test site in a 2000-foot-deep Utah mine, interrupted the reporter's opening small talk with a quiet, "Yes, yes." The reporter got the message—that the scientist was busy and had little time—and so moved immediately to the questions at hand. The physicist brightened up considerably, and answered at length.

"Steering" the Interview

Veteran interviewer Pete Martin once told comedian Danny Kaye, at the outset of an interview, "If this interview is any good it'll be your doing, not mine."

"Don't give me that," Kaye replied. "If this thing is any good it's going to be you that's doing it. Don't try to hang your burden on me." Kaye was right. It's up to the journalist to steer the interview in a rewarding direction.

Most interviews, as journalist Ken Metzler remarks in his book *Creative Interviewing*, are "inherently uncomfortable." Oriana Fallaci, one of the world's most respected interviewers, concurs. "I've noticed that when a person goes to interview someone, he often sees himself in a position of inferiority," she says. "And this feeling increases when this someone being interviewed is a person of power." Fallaci advises that journalists fight this feeling, and approach each interview as a potential meeting of equals.

A lot depends on the first questions. Factual questions demonstrate that you're prepared, and they lend themselves to straightforward answers. Interviewing journalist Walter Lippmann, Eric Sevareid began by reviewing several of Lippmann's opinions—thus flattering Lippmann by letting him know that Sevareid had been reading his work—then built his questions on that foundation. More general, open-ended questions can come later, when the interviewee has had a chance to loosen up.

Adept interviewers develop a style something like a physician's "bedside manner" that keeps the interviewee talking once he or she is going in a useful direction. Interviewer Studs Terkel mutters encouraging phrases, like "Yeah, right," "Really?" or "Terrific"—what psychologists call "verbal lubricants"—to keep his interviews moving. People talk more readily if they feel their words are winning approval or sympathy, or attention.

Interviewer Denis Brian used encouraging questions to draw out Alex Haley, the author of *Roots* and *The Autobiography of Malcolm X* and no mean interviewer himself:

HALEY: Without question the best of the interviews I ever did in *Playboy* was with the late Nazi, George Lincoln Rockwell. . . . Of course, obviously,

I didn't agree with Rockwell. But the point was, we had a most exhilarating experience. . . .

BRIAN: When you originally arranged to interview Rockwell did you contact him by phone?

HALEY: Originally by phone. In fact it was very funny. When I called him and told him we were interested in interviewing him he went into a big thing about: "Well, you know, I can't be sure . . . you can't trust these magazines," and so forth. . . . He said, "Will you be doing the interview?" And I said, "That's right." And he said, "I have to ask you a very personal question." And I said, "Go right ahead." And he said "Are you a Jew?" And I said, "No." And I didn't go on. And then we set up the logistics for me coming there and all that and they had no dream when I arrived that I was Black. . . .

BRIAN: What was his first emotional reaction when he saw you?

HALEY: He jerked open the door and jerked it open sort of with his finger in my face. And he was very upset. And he said: "I see you're Black, and I'm going to be very honest with you right now, that we call your kind 'niggers' and we think you should all be shipped back to Africa." And I said "Well, sir, I've been called 'nigger' before. But this time I'm being paid very well for it, so now you go right ahead and say what you've got against us niggers." And that was the way the interview started. And we had no illusions from the beginning, from the get-go, as the saying goes, started right off from first base, you know. And it worked out to be a very, very interesting experience, working with him over a period of time.

With particularly reticent subjects, it sometimes helps to "prime the pump" by telling them some of your own thoughts and feelings in hopes of relaxing their inhibitions. Truman Capote got Marlon Brando to open up by telling him about his—Capote's—troubles. ("The oldest trick in the book," sighed Brando's press agent.) A magazine reporter interviewing a taciturn old man who fished for scallops on the Chesapeake Bay interrupted a long silence by blurting out that he had been afraid of the water ever since childhood. Suddenly the old man said he had been too! And this was the first time he'd ever admitted it to anyone! From then on the interview went swimmingly.

Don't Talk Too Much. "The biggest trap most reporters fall into is not asking questions, but making statements," says investigative reporter Don Barlett of the *Philadelphia Inquirer*. Ask pointed questions, then *listen*. Even dead silence is preferable to verbosity. If an answer seems inadequate, it may help just to look on expectantly—a technique Mike Wallace uses with devastating effect.

Ask Simple, Direct Questions. Long, involved questions are difficult to understand and easy to evade. Keep interviewing questions simple and to the point.

If you ask a simple question and fail to get a responsive answer, you're not obligated just to shrug your shoulders. Ask a *follow-up* question. If the answer is evasive, persist in your questioning until you get a direct response. Notice the simplicity and persistence of Frank McGee's questions, on NBC's "Meet the Press," to an evasive Robert Welch, president of the John Birch Society:

McGEE: Mr. Welch, you or the [John Birch] organization have suggested that the last four presidents of the United States have, to one degree or another, been controlled by what you called the Communist conspiracy in this country. Do you believe that President Lyndon Johnson is controlled by the Communist conspiracy?

WELCH: I think that the influences in Washington working for the Communist conspiracy are very heavy, as I think they have been all the time.

McGEE: Do you believe the President is controlled by them, sir?

WELCH: That would be a definition, again, of controlled. I think that a lot that our government does is controlled, not necessarily Lyndon Johnson, any more than some of the other people, but the total.

McGEE: Do you think he is controlled to the same extent that you felt former President Eisenhower was?

WELCH: I wouldn't even try to form an opinion in my own mind on that, Mr. McGee, for this reason: If you go back and study our stuff, we look, usually, from quite a distance.

McGEE: Does it take a long time to tell if a man is controlled by Communists?

WELCH: We take no position on what is happening until we can get back and look at it from a distance as history, and this is too close.

This sort of approach, persistently honing in on a single important point, can be effective at illuminating the truth behind a smokescreen of rhetoric. When Lester Maddox was governor of Georgia, he proclaimed himself a friend to the working people but did little to elevate the standard of living of working people in Georgia, which at the time was among the lowest in the nation. Interviewing Maddox on "Meet the Press," reporter Claude Sitton put his first question too generally:

SITTON: Governor, what steps are you taking on the state level to alleviate poverty in Georgia?

A question this open-ended invites a campaign speech, which is exactly what Maddox delivered:

MADDOX: Promoting the free enterprise system, states' rights, property rights, an educational program. . . . We have $500,000 increase in our educational budget. We have a crash program in our mental health work, highway construction, the city and county assistance. . . .

So Sitton rephrased his question, making it more specific and concrete:

SITTON: To be specific, would you favor some step by the state to guarantee a living wage in Georgia, a state minimum wage?
MADDOX: To those who cannot help themselves we must provide for them. We are going to do that in Georgia.

Another evasion. Sitton, unperturbed, put the question even more concretely:

SITTON: Are you going to advocate a state minimum wage law?

This time he got a straight answer:

MADDOX: No, sir, not a state minimum wage. That is not necessary . . .

Don't Accept Empty Generalities.   Left on their own, people may prefer to speak in generalities rather than in specifics. Generalities require less effort, but they also make for an extremely dull story. Discussing his interviewing techniques, psychiatrist Harry Stack Sullivan says: "When a patient tells me the obvious, I ask him what he means." Journalists can do the same. If you catch someone talking in generalities, ask him or her to illustrate the point with specifics.

GENERALITY: I like the opera.
SPECIFIC QUESTION: Really? What's your favorite scene?
SPECIFIC ANSWER: I guess it would have to be when Mimi dies in *La Bohéme*. Sometimes it so stuns me that I can hardly get out of my seat to applaud at the curtain.

GENERALITY: The teachers in this school don't like the kids.
SPECIFIC QUESTION: Oh, come on! How do you know that?
SPECIFIC ANSWER: In my history class last week the teacher told us that studying for the test was a waste of time because we were all too stupid to pass anyway.

People sometimes try to present themselves as flawless and dispassionate—which makes them neither truthful nor particularly interesting to read about. Getting subjects to say what they really feel often requires that the interviewer act like a goad, or a devil's advocate. When a high school guidance counselor tells you he's never met a student he didn't like, give him an "aw-come-off-it" look and make him search his memory to find at least one he couldn't stand. When a legislator tells you she went into politics to "serve the people," tell her the same thing could be said of a waiter in a restaurant: Why, *really*, did she first run for office?

PREPAREDNESS KEY TO INTERVIEWING, SAYS NORA EPHRON

Widely known for her thorough reporting and her witty, perceptive style, Nora Ephron has been a newspaper reporter, magazine journalist, columnist for *Esquire* and *New York* magazines and the author of the award-winning screenplays of the motion pictures *Heartburn* and *Silkwood*. Her work has been collected in two bestselling anthologies, *Crazy Salad* and *Scribble, Scribble*. She talked with us in her apartment in Manhattan.

How did you first become interested in journalism?

Ephron: I was 13 years old and in my first year of high school. On vocations day a woman sports reporter for *The Los Angeles Times* spoke. She told us rollicking stories about being thrown out of locker rooms and so forth—this was years ago—and I thought it sounded like fun. I started paying more attention to Lois Lane, and I saw *His Girl Friday*, still my favorite newspaper movie ever.

Then I took a course in journalism from a wonderful teacher. On the first day of class he outlined how to write a lead, told us about the five Ws, then dictated a set of facts and told us to write a lead for tomorrow's high school newspaper. The "facts" were something like, "Kenneth L. Peters, principal of Beverly Hills High School, announced today that the faculty will travel to Sacramento Thursday for a symposium on teaching methods. Speaking at the symposium will be, oh, Dr. Harold Taylor, Haile Selassie, and Wilt Chamberlain"—in any case, three prominent people. We all wrote leads that essentially turned the order of the facts around: "Doctor Harold Taylor, Emperor Haile Selassie, and Wilt 'The Stilt' Chamberlain are to address our faculty Thursday at a symposium in Sacramento."

The teacher read our leads, looked at us with a twinkle in his eye and said, "The lead should be, 'There will be no school Thursday.'" It was a magical moment. The cartoon light bulb went on over my head. Suddenly I understood that the most important question to ask when writing a lead is not "Who, what, where, when and how?" but "What's the *point*? What is the *news* here?" He really hooked me.

What attracted you to journalism as a career?

Part of it was the chance to generalize, the idea that you'd move from one story to the next, not staying with any one thing even should you be covering a beat. And the romance of it, I guess. The movies are always being accused of romanticizing the newspaper business, but I think they're fairly accurate. The newspaper business *can* be romantic, at least in that you're at the White House, or meeting a movie star, doing things you wouldn't normally. Now that's not that big a deal, as it turns out, any of it, but it certainly is more interesting work than most people have. Even on a small-town newspaper, you have a more interesting job than most other people in the town.

How did you land your first reporting job, with the New York Post?

During the 1962 newspaper strike, some friends put out satirical editions of the papers. I wrote part of a parody of the *Post*. The editors of the *Post* were angry with it and wanted to sue. The publisher said, "Don't be silly, if she can parody the paper she can write for it. Hire her." So I was offered a tryout at the *Post*.

The *Post* in those days wasn't very good, but it was a feature writer's dream. During my first week there I did an interview with a movie star, an interview with a film director, a piece about two hooded seals in the Coney Island Aquarium who had been brought together to make a third hooded seal but

Ask One Question at a Time. Multiple-part questions have their place in a big press conference, where reporters may get only one chance to ask everything they want to know, but in a one-on-one interview, ask one question at a time. Otherwise, the interviewee will tend to answer only the easier one. (Q: "Where did you get that pretty green tie? Is that the one you strangled your wife with?" A: "Brooks Brothers.")

Look and Listen. One of the most difficult interviewing skills to master is to keep your eyes and ears open. Yet it's also one of the most valuable. The interviewer can learn a lot by watching the interviewee's expressions and "body language." Hands on knees usually signals openness and a readiness to talk; arms folded in front, Mussolini fashion, suggests defensiveness and a desire to ward off questions.

weren't cooperating, and I spent two days on a murder—my first murder. It was like "Lou Grant" or something.

Tell us about covering the murder.

It was exciting. A man had killed an opera singer in Italy. We didn't care about the opera singer—after all, she was Italian—but the murderer lived in New York, so we cared about him. Who was he? Nobody seemed to know. The other papers were reporting that he was somehow involved in opera.

I went to the guy's apartment building, talked to the doorman, but all I could find out was that he drove a Cadillac. So I went around to all the neighborhood garages, figuring that he had to park his Cadillac somewhere around there. I found his garage. I asked about him, told the man at the garage about the murder. He was thrilled at the information, because the guy owed two months back rent on the garage and now he wouldn't let him have his car until he paid up. He gave me the guy's calling card. It turned out he worked for an optical instrument business in Brooklyn, and had nothing to do with opera.

So I went to the optical supply company. At first, they denied that he worked there. I took the calling card out and put it on the table. It was like, "I see your ten and raise you twenty"—a glorious moment in that poker game journalists play when they've got part of a story and they're trying to get more. That was reporting.

You've interviewed some of the most famous people in the world. What do you find makes an interview a success?

I've always prepared as much as possible. Working for a newspaper, I would pull the clips, read them, make a few telephone calls, learn as much as I could about the person so I didn't have to go in unprepared. Writing for magazines, I did much more preparation. I would spend weeks interviewing perhaps thirty or forty people connected with the subject of the article before doing the interview itself. Until you've done a huge amount of research, you really don't know what the right questions are.

Nothing is more flattering to someone being interviewed than for the interviewer to have done sufficient research. And nothing is more of a turnoff than when the interviewer comes in and says, "Where did you grow up?" All they had to do to learn that was to look it up in *Who's Who*.

Do you find that interviews often go off in quite unexpected directions?

Sometimes. When I was interviewing Helen Gurley Brown [the editor of *Cosmopolitan*] she cried. That was great. She cries all the time, but it was wonderful that she cried in the course of the article.

Many people not in journalism imagine that when you go to interview somebody—say, Burt Reynolds—you're basically trying to get him to say something he didn't mean to reveal. That he once had an abortion. Killed his cat. Actually, that's a very, very small part of the art. Most of the art of interviewing has to do with coming up with an interesting point of view about the person. If you understand that, and write it well, it doesn't matter whether any dark secrets have been revealed.

Often the interview that counts isn't the interview with Burt Reynolds anyway, but the interview with his stepmother's manicurist, who tells you something about his childhood that may end up as only three sentences in the profile, but that helps weave the tapestry. A two-hour interview may produce only one sentence, but even if you come out of it with a single misconception corrected, that can be terribly important. The ordinary, run-of-the-mill interview is much more important than the glitzy, "I talk to the stars" sort of thing. So much of journalism involves talking to ordinary people, trying to get them to tell you the truth.

Pay attention to the surroundings. A *Newsweek* reporter interviewing the director of a drug treatment program became suspicious of the inordinate number of testimonials lining his office walls; they came from the President of the United States, heads of foreign countries, even the Pope. Questioning staff members of the program afterward, the reporter discovered that the documents were fake. The testimonials and signed pictures had been bought at a local novelty shop, and the director's "doctoral degree" came from a college in Canada that sells degrees through the mail.

More often, of course, describing a person's surroundings simply makes the story more interesting. Readers will be interested to know that the author of a book on word processors does her typing on an ancient Royal portable typewriter, or that a brilliant logician keeps such a cluttered desk that he has to call in his secretary to help him locate his pipe.

Don't be afraid to ask tough questions. If they're *really* tough, they probably should be saved for the end of the interview—what some reporters call, "First the warm-up, then the fastball." In his *The Craft of Interviewing* John Brady speaks of "funneling" the interview from the general to the specific. Others say, "You've got to be kind to be cruel."

However you approach it, try not to leave the tough question unasked. It's the one your readers want answered, and, surprisingly, it's often just the one the interviewee *wants* to answer. A young reporter interviewing a narcotics program chief in New York chatted about more pleasant matters for a while, then screwed down his courage and asked the man about the events leading up to his conviction for selling heroin. To the reporter's astonishment, the man brightened visibly and launched into a lengthy recitation of his crimes, ranging from assault and narcotics trafficking to auto theft and selling bogus airline tickets. He *wanted* to confess. To repeat: Never underestimate people's desire to talk. It never hurts to ask.

THE GOALS OF INTERVIEWING

An interview succeeds or fails insofar as it serves the *story*. This is obviously true of interviews conducted for straight news stories: If you call the emergency ward to learn the condition of a burn victim and don't get it, the interview has failed. It's also true of profiles; as we discussed in Chapter 9, a profile should not be a random collection of quotes and impressions, but should be built upon a central story. While preparing for and conducting interviews, keep the story in mind, and guide the interview to meet its requirements.

Interviews can be employed to gather not only facts and quotations, but also material that might be described as *transmutable*, meaning that it can be used in forms much different from quotes and facts. The *Los Angeles Times* began a profile of an executive by describing her arising at 5 A.M., exercising and reading three newspapers before going to work. Had the reporter been there at dawn to watch all this? No. She had a hunch that the *story* here involved the long hours the executive devoted to her job, so during the interview she asked her about her morning routine. Ken Metzler describes a story about a police officer entering a darkened house, answering a call about a prowler. Creeping through the gloom, her gun drawn, the reporter writes, the police officer was thinking, "If I got a bullet between the eyes, I'd never even hear the shot." "And where did you get *that* information?" Metzler asked the writer. "By asking, of course."

Tom Wolfe opened a profile of rock producer Phil Spector with a description of Spector slumped in a seat on an airliner as it sat on the runway waiting to take off. Spector watches raindrops roll down the window. He is seized by a conviction that the plane is doomed to crash. He summons a stewardess and tells her they aren't going to make it. The stewardess tells the pilot, who taxis back to the terminal, where Spector is taken off the plane. Reading the passage, you'd think Wolfe had been sitting in the seat next to Spector. But it all came from an interview. Wolfe says that he makes it a practice to ask people about their thoughts and feelings, and questions them about the details of anecdotes (like the raindrops on the window) to gather material that will be used as part of the detailed description and stream-of-consciousness intimacy that gives his work its novelistic texture.

Transmuting interview quotations into the raw material of a narrative poses the danger that, if the material all comes from just one source, it may not be accurate. To guard against error, check anecdotes with independent sources whenever possible, attribute them to their sources and maintain a professional skepticism about what people say are their deepest thoughts and feelings.

PROBLEMS IN INTERVIEWING

The course of true interviewing never does run smooth. Every interviewer has run into problems like the following.

Boredom

It may sound as if we're blaming everything that goes wrong on the interviewer, but it really is usually the journalist's fault if an interview is dull. Almost anyone will become animated if asked well-posed questions about something that interests him or her or that he or she can be made to see *should* interest him or her. Sigmund Freud discovered oceanic passions hidden beneath the starched appearances of his most straight-laced Victorian patients. James Joyce, an astutely observant and curious novelist, said, "I never met a bore." The reason, of course, was that *Joyce* wasn't boring. Don't be too quick to decide that the interviewee is boring; instead, search for the question that will make him or her come alive.

Gobbledygook

When confronted with someone who talks in jargon, euphemism, or excessive abstraction, simply explain that you don't understand. Keep it up until you— and your readers—*can* understand. Ted Koppel of ABC News is a master of this technique; the instant that an interviewee becomes obscure, he politely interrupts and asks that the answer be rephrased in plain English.

Evasion. Evasion is a common problem, especially when interviewing bureaucrats who fear that they'll get into trouble by saying the wrong thing. Confronting the interviewee with hard facts usually elicits a straight answer. So does *persistence*. If you don't get a straight answer the first time, rephrase your question, honing it to a sharp point. If all else fails, try the *end run*: Ask to speak to a superior who can answer.

OFF THE RECORD

Reporters conduct most of their interviews "on the record." This means that everything someone says can be used in the story and attributed directly to the person who said it.

Sometimes, people don't wish to talk on the record. Having their names appear in the story could in some way cause them embarrassment, even place thier jobs, or their lives, in jeopardy. In these instances, reporters may conduct interviews under one of three varieties of ground rules that assure the sources they will not be identified in the subsequent story. The three are: *not for attribution, for background only*, and *off the record.*

Not-for-attribution means that the information gained can be quoted, but that the identity of the source will be masked in such a way as to prevent readers from telling exactly who it is: "A source close to the police commissioner said today. . . ." or "According to a high official in the company. . . ."

A *for-background-only* arrangement means the reporter can use the content of what a person says, but cannot quote statements directly or attribute them to anyone specific, even if the source were quoted anonymously. Instead, the reporter must use the material on his or her "own hook," that is, relate the story with no attribution, based simply on the reporter's knowledge that it is true. After a not-for-attribution interview, for instance, the reporter could write this: "*A source close to the police commissioner said the department does not favor* using anti-loitering statutes as grounds for rounding up prostitutes." Had the same interview been done on a for-background-only basis, it would have to have been written something like: "*The police commissioner is known to oppose* using anti-loitering statutes. . . ." In the latter instance, the reporter is disguising the fact that he or she got the information from someone close to the chief, perhaps because only one person is so privy to the chief's inner thoughts, and any attribution at all would indicate to those familiar with the department who the reporter must have talked to.

An *off-the-record* agreement binds the reporter most restrictively of all; it means the information gained *cannot be used in the story at all*, on any basis whatsoever. If the district attorney tells you, off the record, that the president of the city council is going to be arrested tomorrow on charges of soliciting bribes from local business people, this agreement prevents you from publishing the information—at least until the arrest occurs.

One advantage of getting material off the record is that knowing what's going to happen in advance allows journalists time to research the background and do a more complete story

---

Stonewalling

President Calvin Coolidge was asked at a press conference if he would comment on an upcoming presidential campaign. "No," he said. Would he comment on the world situation? "No." Had he an opinion on Prohibition? "No," Coolidge said, and added: "Now remember—don't quote me." *That's* stonewalling. A UPI reporter waited for an hour in the cold outside Richard Nixon's Fifth Avenue apartment; then, when Nixon arrived, the reporter asked him a question. Nixon mouthed the word, "No," *but didn't speak*, thus depriving the reporter of even a one-word quote. When stonewalled, it may help to remind the stonewaller that without his or her comments, you'll be able to report only the other side of the story, which may mean presenting him or her in an unfavorable light. But sometimes, alas, there's just no way around the wall.

when the news finally breaks. Another is that, in an investigative story, off-the-record material can often be used to pry information out of other people involved in the story. A reporter knowing about the imminent arrest of the city council president could use that tip to convince some of the business people involved to tell how they had been forced to make the illegal pay-offs.

The disadvantages of an off-the-record agreement, however, can be more than offsetting, since promising a confidential source not to print what he or she tells you prevents you from using the information even if you learn about it from someone else. In the instance of the tip on the pending bribery arrest, should you find out the same information on a background-only basis from, say, a detective assigned to the case, you could still not use it without the district attorney's feeling certain you had welched on your agreement.

What's more, agreeing to off-the-record interviews can create serious ethical problems, as a reporter for *The Washington Post* found out after an interview with the Rev. Jesse Jackson during the 1986 presidential election campaign. As part of an interview he had been assured was going to be kept off the record, Jackson used what he later said he considered an innocent slang word for Jews. He called them "Hymies," and he referred to New York City, which has a large Jewish population, as "Hymietown." Regardless of how Jackson saw the term, however, Jews generally regard it as an ethnic slur. A subsequent *Washington Post* newspaper story that presented details about the interview embarrassed Jackson and seriously marred his campaign. The story, as it turned out, was not written by the reporter who had actually conducted the interview but by a fellow journalist on the *Post*, to whom the reporter had repeated Jackson's remarks. Jackson nevertheless felt himself badly used.

A further ethical question raised by the Jackson interview, of course, is whether a reporter should abide by his promise to keep information off the record if the news he discovers thereby is of crucial value to the public. Some, for instance, would argue that when a politician runs for the presidency of the United States, the public has a right to know about his important inner thoughts and that a reporter who becomes privy to them has an obligation to divulge them, even if it means betraying a confidence.

To avoid putting their staffers in such ethical predicaments, many editors counsel young reporters simply never to agree to take part in off-the-record interviews. "You tell them, 'If I can't print it, then I don't want to know about it,'" goes a common piece of advice. Faced with such a firm stand, news sources can usually be talked into letting you use what they have to say in exchange for their merely not being named. If not, then get busy trying to dig it out of somewhere else.

Limitations are sometimes imposed by interviewees, who agree to an interview on the condition that no questions are asked about certain subjects. If the off-limits material seems newsworthy—and often that's exactly why it's been declared off-limits—most good reporters will try to bring it up, limitations or no. President Nixon once agreed to talk with Barbara Walters only if they stuck to the subject of his wife. "I couldn't talk about her for forty minutes," Walters said later, "so I had to figure out how I would go from that to Vietnam to marijuana and some other things. After a while, as we sat there on the couch, I said, 'We've talked about your family, Mr. President, now let's talk about the problems besetting the American family.'" And so they did.

Hostility should be taken seriously, but not met with anger in return. Remember, it's an interview, not a debate. Adept interviewers learn to keep their temper when provoked. Some use the "as if" ploy: "You're acting as if you think I'm trying to trap you into saying something you don't mean. Is that what you think?" Candor of this sort can ease anxieties.

Out of Time?

Some of the best answers come after the end of a formal interview, while the reporter is packing up and the pressure is off. Television reporter Jessica Savitch said that while working for radio as a college student, she "learned to keep holding the microphone out a few seconds after the person first finished talking, because that's when he's liable to really open up." Another journalist employs what he called "the Colombo technique," named after the TV detective: When he's at the door with his coat on, ready to leave, he says, "Oh, yes, just one more thing. . . ." The answer to this final question, he says, is often the most newsworthy of the interview.

SUMMARY

Interviews may be conducted to gather facts, to garner quotations and anecdotes or as an adversarial matter, to confront someone with information he or she may not care to hear. Reporters approaching interviews think in terms of their *goals*—what purpose the interviews are to serve—and the *tactics* that will best accomplish those goals.

Preparation is fundamentally important to the success of an interview. Prepare enough questions to sustain the interview on their own, should that prove necessary. Concrete, *fact-oriented* questions work best for openers; they demand specific answers. General, *open-ended* questions permit more freedom of response, and may work better once the interview has been under way for a while.

Try to keep the questions *simple*, and ask them one at a time. If you fail to get a satisfactory answer, follow up on the question until you succeed.

A reporter's proper decorum and enthusiastic, curious attitude count for a lot in keeping the ball rolling during an interview. Start by "breaking the ice," then proceed to steer the interview in a worthwhile direction, encouraging the subject when he or she is producing usable material.

The material may go beyond quotations and facts; interviews may also be used to gather anecdotes and information about the subject's thoughts and feelings—material that can be *transmuted* into passages in which the interview context all but disappears.

14

REPORTING PUBLIC AFFAIRS

Covering public affairs means covering the workings of government and politics. Because governments wield considerable power, public affairs stories make news every day, often the top news, and able reporters in the field are ranked at the top of their profession. In this chapter we discuss how governments collect and disburse money, and offer suggestions on covering state and local government, election campaigns and the courts.

American government has grown to the point that it is involved in nearly every aspect of human life. New York State alone has 1400 separate governments within its borders, from county and municipal governments that inspect buildings, manage public education, regulate employment conditions, control weapons and explosives, license trades and professions, preserve historical buildings, operate museums and zoos, manage zoning and urban planning, control rents, collect and dispose of the garbage, maintain the streets and bridges, run transportation systems, provide gas and electricity and administer public welfare, to the state government that issues drivers and liquor licenses, administers parks and game preserves, maintains highways and finds summer jobs for teenagers. And the federal government, the biggest of them all, is into everything from building pipelines and aircraft carriers to minting money to studying the origin of the universe.

The functions of state, local and federal governments can overlap, making matters confusing. When Orange County, California, proposed to convert Upper Newport Bay into a marina, reporters covering the story had to sort out the positions taken by four different concerned agencies: the United States Fish and Wildlife Service; the State Department of Fish and Game; the County Harbors, Beaches and Parks Department; and the planning departments of the several cities involved. Reports filed by all the agencies and environmental groups involved grew to a stack two feet high.

The tangled and unpredictable nature of American government makes it look inefficient and chaotic, but by and large it works, and it's fertile territory for journalists. For one thing, the people involved in government generally are free to speak out; the public affairs reporter doesn't have to rely solely upon official spokespeople, but can interview a variety of people with widely varying points of view. And, plenty of documents are available. American government activity is better documented today than ever before, and most government records are open to scrutiny by the press. Office holders are asked to declare their financial interests; government agencies must estimate the environmental and economic impact of pending decisions; and reporters can look up public records of everything from who owns a porno movie theater to what the Secretary of the Interior told the House Ways and Means Committee about killing wolves in national parks.

THE STRUCTURE OF GOVERNMENT

Every able reporter covering public affairs is a student of the politics and economics of the region, and a good way to study is by reading. For an introduction to government structure, see Neal R. Peirce's *People, Politics and Power* (published by W. W. Norton & Co.). For more detail, consult state and county histories, and read the pamphlets on state and local government published by the state press association and by Sigma Delta Chi, the society of professional journalists. For a list of municipal officials, and for statistics about local government, see *The Municipal Year Book* (International City Management Association, Washington, D.C.). For a guide on state government, see *The National Directory of State Agencies* (Information Resources Press, Arlington, Virginia). Useful references on federal government include *The United States Government Manual* (National Archives), *The Official Congressional Directory* (Government Printing Office) and *The Federal Regulatory Directory* (Congressional Quarterly). See also *Environment Reporter* (Bureau of National Affairs), *A Building Code Primer* (McGraw-Hill), *Zoning and Planning Law Handbook* (Clark Boardman Co.) and *Working on the System* (Basic Books.)

Communities govern themselves in ways as distinctive as Rhode Island clam chowder and Louisiana gumbo. A few American towns, principally in New England, still function as direct democracies; citizens gather at Town Meetings to write their own laws, make policy and choose selectmen to carry them out. But most communities find this system too cumbersome. Instead, they elect representatives who conduct municipal affairs. Some elect a *council* of three to nine or more members, which then picks one of its members to serve as mayor. A *city manager* may be hired to run the city on a day-to-day basis. Another popular approach is the *commission* form of government; commission members are often elected at large—that is, by the city as whole—and can serve both as legislators and as administrators, each running one or more city departments. Large cities favor some form of the *strong mayor and council* system. Here members of the legislative body—which may be called the City Council, Board of Directors, Board of Aldermen, Board of Selectmen or Commission—are elected at large, and form individual districts or wards as well. The "strong mayor" is elected separately, by the people rather than by the council.

The political climate of each community reflects its system of government. Journalists soon learn that the independently elected mayors of big cities like Chicago and Los Angeles are more likely to come into conflict with their city councils than are mayors who are chosen by the councils. In some cities, political parties still count for a lot, and elected officials vote along party lines; journalists covering these communities can predict the outcomes of upcoming votes by consulting with party leaders and counting heads. In many other cities the government is nonpartisan, which means that representatives are neither elected, nor do they vote, along party lines. In such cases the situation confronting journalists is more volatile. Political alliances tend to be transitory and unpredictable, and often are hammered together around specific issues or ascendant personalities.

News is made not only in the clash of conflicting interests, but in the less glamorous but equally important business of simply maintaining and running municipal government. The *special district* is an example. A hybrid form of government found most frequently at the local level, a special district is either *dependent* or *independent*. Dependent districts have jurisdiction within a city or county, and they depend on the city or county government for their mandates and funding. They may run libraries, install and maintain street lights, control mosquitoes or clean the sewers. Independent districts are created by the electorate, and usually cover more than one city or county. In rural areas, for instance, school districts educate children from many little towns, each of which is too small to maintain a school of its own. Fire protection districts and sanitation districts cross city and county lines where this approach provides an efficient way to maintain vital services.

Much of the news of special districts simply involves how they are spending public funds. Many districts have their own tax bases, meaning that they are assigned a piece of the overall tax revenue and don't have to compete with other local agencies for tax money. They may also have the right to sell bonds, incur debts and seek federal funds. Given this autonomy, it's not surprising that special district operations can degenerate into boondoggles. An education writer in Kentucky counted buses in a school district parking lot and found that they totalled only a fraction of the buses carried on the district's books. Digging deeper, the reporter found that school officials were enriching themselves by "buying" nonexistent buses from a Florida corporation in which they had a financial interest.

Special districts can grow to become big and powerful. Robert Moses built up New York's Triborough Bridge and Tunnel Authority and its Parks Department until he was using them to create a vast network of highways, bridges, tunnels and terminals. In California, the Municipal Water District has generated newsworthy controversies as pungent as those surrounding the fights between cattle barons and sheepherders in the Old West.

As towns grow they run into one another, creating a seamless sprawl of the sort that surrounds many American cities today. Some cities have dealt with the problem of multiple townships by expanding their cities to embrace the surrounding towns. Jacksonville, Florida, expanded so dramatically that it swallowed up surrounding Duval County, making Jacksonville, at 841 square miles, the nation's largest city in terms of land area. Another approach is to consolidate the services provided by several cities and towns under an expanded "metro" government. Dade County, Florida, voters approved a metropolitan Dade County system that took over many police, fire, water and other functions for Miami, Miami Beach, and twenty-one surrounding communities. The "metro" Dade County system wields centralized power and gets most of the news coverage, but the individual cities and towns in Dade County retain their own governments, too; reporters face a tapestry of overlapping and interacting public affairs.

How do journalists cover the news of these many little towns, while also covering the municipality as a whole? One way is by establishing special sections of the paper that report the news of surrounding localities, like the *Los Angeles Time's* "West Side" and the New York *Daily News's* suburban editions. Another approach is to employ roundup stories that gather together comparable stories from several towns, like this one, which appeared in *The Miami Herald*:

For nearly two months, they've held workshops, staff meetings and think tanks to mull over mill levies, dabble in debt schedules, tinker with abstract tax figures.

Now, at last, city officials in South Dade are going public with their final budget proposals.

Nearly every municipality, from South Miami to Sweetwater to Florida City, has scheduled final budget hearings either this week or next.

Although the tax rates and revenue figures vary greatly, a common thread links the various spending packages: Just about all of them require a tax hike. . . .

At the state level, government begins to resemble that of nations, at least in its structure. State governing bodies usually are called legislatures, and, like the United States Congress, are divided into upper and lower houses. The division of houses was derived from the English Parliament, where the House of Lords embodies the concept of inherited power while the House of Commons is meant more nearly to represent the majority will of the average citizen. In most states the upper body is called the Senate. Its members usually have larger constituencies and serve longer terms than do members of the House of Representatives—also known as the Assembly or House of Delegates—whose members run for reelection every two years.

One of the ongoing stories covered by public affairs reporters is the struggle between state and local government for control of local affairs. State governments exercise considerable power over the cities. Because states typically pass along a quarter to a third of their tax revenues to local government, they can keep a grip on city purse strings—the state superintendent of education, for example, can tell local school boards which textbooks they are permitted to adopt—and the very forms of government that municipalities choose are subject to state regulation and control. Responding to the complaints of localities that state government exercises too much power, legislatures sometimes adopt *local option*, or *home rule*, provisions that give localities more control over their affairs. The state legislature might, for instance, vote that anyone over 18 can drink alcoholic beverages, but a local option would permit individual counties and townships within the state to enact a 21-year-old standard, or to prohibit the sale of alcohol altogether.

TAXES

When a government needs more money, it has two ways of increasing its tax revenues. One is to expand its tax base: If a state collects tobacco taxes on cigarettes only, the legislature might pass a law extending the tax to cigars and chewing tobacco as well. The other way is to maintain the same base, but to increase the *rate* of taxation: The legislature might retain the cigarettes-only tax base, but increase the rate by a nickel a pack.

But taxes come out of people's pockets, and people will pay taxes only so far. During the 1960s and 1970s, many American cities increased their various business taxes until they drove small businesses out of town, which eroded the municipal tax base. When property taxes soared because of inflation, outraged voters passed referenda limiting property tax rates. Readers pay attention to news stories about taxes because they want to know what's being done with their hard-earned dollars.

Most people are willing to pay taxes as long as they feel that the tax system is fair. Much of the tax news concerns just who is paying taxes, and how much. Taxes that are based on a fixed percentage or charge a fixed amount, regardless of an individual's ability to pay, are said to be *regressive*. Property taxes are regressive, because any property owner, whether poor or wealthy, has to pay the same rate of tax on a given piece of real estate. Sales taxes on candy and soft drinks are regressive, because millionaires and welfare recipients all pay the same tax for chewing gum. A tax that varies according to the taxpayer's income is called a *progressive* tax. Federal income taxes are progressive, inasmuch as people with large incomes pay a higher percentage of income tax than do those with modest incomes.

The most common forms of taxes are *income, sales, value added* and *property taxes*, as well as *excise taxes, license taxes* and *special assessments*.

The *income tax* generates by far the most revenues. Personal and corporate income tax, the mainstay of the federal government, amounts to 60 percent of all federal tax collections. Most states, and some municipalities, collect income taxes, but their unpopularity among the electorate tends to keep local income tax rates relatively low—typically under 10 percent for state income taxes, and only 1 or 2 percent for the cities.

The *sales tax* is a major source of revenue for states, counties and most cities. It is called an *ad valorem* ("according to the value") tax, meaning that it is charged as a percentage of the sales price of each item. State sales taxes typically amount to 3 to 5 percent of the retail price, and city sales taxes may add 1 to 3 percent more. Residents of Denver, Colorado, for instance, pay a 6 percent sales tax: 3 percent to the city, 3 percent to the state.

Property taxes are calculated on the basis of *assessed value* and *tax rate*. In theory, the assessed value represents the fair market value of the property; a house that would sell for $100,000 ought to be assessed at $100,000. But, due to pressure from homeowners to keep their property taxes down, assessments usually undervalue the property. A major news story surfaced when California voters approved Proposition 13, a state constitutional amendment that reacted to soaring property taxes by freezing the assessed value of property at what it had been in 1978. Proposition 13 was popular at first, and it sparked passage of similar measures in other states. But within a few years government services began to deteriorate as a result of the loss of property tax revenues, and disenchantment set in. A newspaper survey conducted in the early 1980s found that California residents who had voted for the measure now had deeply mixed feelings about whether it had been a good idea.

The *tax rate* is the percentage of the assessed value that is charged as property tax. It can be expressed in dollars and cents (for example, $4 per $1000 of assessed value) or in *mills*. A mill is one-tenth of one cent ($4 = 4000 mills). To calculate property tax, multiply the rate times the assessed value. The annual property tax on a house with an assessed value of $85,000 being taxed at a rate of 4 mills is: $85,000 (the assessed value) × .04 (the rate) = $340 property tax.

Both the property tax rate and the assessed value of property vary considerably from county to county. A lot at the corner of Park Avenue and 67th Street in Manhattan is worth much more, and is taxed at a much higher rate, than is a lot the same size in a subdivision on the outskirts of Jackson, Mississippi. Property owners in Louisiana and West Virginia pay only about a quarter as much property tax as do residents of Massachusetts.

Part of the journalist's job is to call attention to inequities in the society, and this can take the form of pointing out how unequal taxation produces unequal public services. Rural counties in the South, where property values are low, spend a fraction as much per pupil in public schools as do wealthy or urban counties, where property values are high. Journalists often monitor the tug of war between middle-class homeowners, who want their property taxes spent on better education for the children in their communities, and residents of poorer areas, who think the tax money should be spread around so that it benefits their children as well.

Excise taxes are sales tax on products. The excise tax differs from the ad valorem sales tax in that its base is the *quantity* of the product sold rather than its value. The federal government, for instance, charges an excise tax per gallon of gasoline, and it uses the proceeds to build and maintain federal highways. One of the ongoing news stories in the days of the energy crisis concerned whether federal gasoline taxes should be increased to pay for measures needed to make the United States independent of Middle East oil supplies.

License taxes and *fees* bring in revenue at all levels of government. States and municipalities charge license fees—a state liquor license, for example, can run to many thousands of dollars—and may also impose a business license tax, usually a percentage of gross sales. Local governments charge fees for a variety of services, from inspecting buildings to reserving tennis courts at the public parks.

Local newspapers in smaller communities report on *special assessments*. These are taxes levied for extra services, like renewing a neighborhood park or paying back money to the town borrowed to construct shelters at bus stops. The services are paid for by fixed fees charged to each residential and commercial units, and the funds are *earmarked* to be spent only for these purposes.

BUDGETS

Governments dispense their revenues according to an agreed-upon plan, the budget. Journalists are not expected to understand every detail of every budget— the budget for a major city like New York can be as thick as a telephone book and as indecipherable as hieroglyphics. But they are expected to be familiar with at least the major features of each federal, state and municipal budget they are called upon to cover.

The process of making up a budget goes on year round, and generates plenty of news, much of it concerning how competing interests in the society struggle to control how public money is spent. The finished budget is an indicator of how those struggles came out—that is, of who won and lost. It also outlines the financial health of the government, and suggests in which directions it is evolving. The many newspaper accounts of the Reagan administration's dramatic increases in military spending did more than tell voters where their money was going; they also promoted a public debate over whether the military build-up was enhancing or degrading national security.

A budget is a forecast: It predicts the revenues the government expects to receive, and how it plans to spend them, during the upcoming *fiscal year*. In most localities the fiscal year begins on July 1 and ends the following June 30, but some date their fiscal year November 1 to October 31, or use a fiscal year identical to the calendar year.

The budget process begins with each government department's drawing up a *budget request* that predicts its income and expenditures for the upcoming fiscal year. The government agencies most involved in community services— those operating the schools and municipal hospitals—hold public *budget hearings*, or *workshops*. The budget requests are sent up from the various agencies to the chief executive (for example, the mayor) who has the unenviable task of cutting here, adding there and trying somehow to put together a proposed budget that is socially defensible, economically viable and politically survivable. Then the proposed budget is submitted to the legislative body (for example, the city council).

Because much of the budget process is open to the public, newspapers not only report on budget proceedings, but also alert readers to upcoming budget meetings—as did this precede in *The Miami Herald*:

During a session Tuesday that the mayor predicted would last from morn 'til night, Coral Gables commissioners will decide on matters ranging from a law that would prohibit picketing in residential neighborhoods to the proposed $34 million budget.

The meeting begins at 9 A.M., with the budget hearing at 5:01 P.M. at City Hall, 405 Biltmore Way. Mayor William Chapman joked Friday that people attending should bring supper, because the meeting would probably last until 10 P.M. . . . .

The cold figures of a budget can be made more meaningful by putting them in personal terms. A *Miami Herald* story reporting a plan under which "the county tax rate would increase by 9.5 percent" personalized the plan this way: "For the owner of an average, $68,000 home claiming a $25,000 homestead exemption in unincorporated Dade, that increase would mean paying about $661 in taxes and garbage fees, $50 more in taxes than last year." The magnitude of a $30 billion weapons system can be personalized by noting that its cost amounts to over $100 for every man, woman and child in the county.

Another useful approach is to compare the current year's with the previous year's budget. It doesn't mean much to report that the city's new budget allocates $50,000 to the summer jobs program, unless readers are also told that $50,000 is only one-quarter of what was spent the year before. Compare projected revenues, too. Are they up substantially over last year's, and, if so, are they realistic? Officials up for reelection sometimes try to delay facing a budget crunch by making rosy forecasts of tax windfalls that never materialize. If reporters or others don't call their bluff, the government is left having to raise taxes or borrow money to make up the difference.

When comparing budget items for different years, watch also for changes in the *structure* of the budget. Officials may reorganize or reassign government functions. They might, for instance, decide that it is inefficient to have both the police and fire departments performing paramedical duties, and assign all future paramedical operations to the fire department alone. Or an agency may change its method of accounting, and thus produce a temporary paper surplus or deficit that has little real significance. This can make it treacherous to compare items in successive budgets, and it's one reason why the best-informed public affairs reporters are those who have followed the budgetary process each step of the way. When in doubt about the meaning of a budget item, don't be afraid to ask for help. Current and former finance officials, attorneys who specialize in public finance cases, and the economics and social science professors at universities are among the experts to whom a bewildered reporter can turn.

There are two sorts of budgets. The *expense budget* covers the day-to-day costs of running a city, state or nation: paying salaries and interest on debt, painting road signs and buying paper clips. The *capital budget* covers major improvements like building new schools and bridges. Expense and capital budgets may be submitted separately or combined into a single document.

Expense items should be financed out of revenues; the government may borrow money in the short term to tide it over while it is waiting for revenues to come in, but it should, by the end of the fiscal year, have collected as much as it has spent. Some of the biggest budget stories of recent years came to light when governments failed to observe this principle. Residents of New York City didn't really awaken to the serious financial plight facing the city until newspapers reported that the city's finances had degenerated to the point that it was using money from its capital budget to pay for immediate expenses—which was like putting out a fire with gasoline.

Governments can borrow in the short term to pay for expense items by issuing *revenues anticipation notes*, also called *tax anticipation notes*. Capital items typically are financed by selling *bonds*. Voters decide on bond issues by voting in *referendums* or *special ballots*. *General obligation bonds* are to be repaid out of future tax revenues. A county might issue general obligation bonds to install storm sewers in a newly developed housing tract; if all goes well, the storm sewers will add to property values in the area, which in turn will generate higher property tax revenues to pay the stipulated interest to purchasers of the bonds. *Revenue bonds* are repaid from the direct proceeds of the capital project. The county might build a public golf course, for example, to be paid back by greens fees and the profits of the restaurant and pro shop.

Bond issues may be touted by those who stand to profit from the work they would finance; reporters should look behind the glowing promises and try to assess what the real impact of an issue will be. When the State of Washington Public Power Supply System borrowed billions of dollars during the 1970s to build five nuclear power plants, a few journalists studied the capital budget closely, then warned that the project looked like a financial disaster. Their warnings went unheeded. When the plants were built, they turned out to be so uneconomical that construction of two of them had to be cancelled, and the electricity produced by the remaining three generated too little money to pay back bondholders. The agency that built the plant had to declare bankruptcy, and hundreds of investors faced losing their life's savings.

State, county and municipal budgets include not only the revenue that the localities plan to raise for themselves, but also money from the federal government. Most of this federal money comes with strings attached. "Earmarked" federal money (for example, the federal gasoline tax) must be spent in a specific way (for example, on highways). *Grants-in-aid*, also called *categorical grants*, generally require that the local government come up with *matching funds*. The federal government might promise a state $2 million to run drug treatment seminars in its mental hospitals, provided that the state matches the grant with another $2 million of its own. *Revenue sharing*, set up by the federal government in 1972, is distributed one-third to local governments, which must use it for capital expenditures or for projects designated as being of national concern, such as public safety, health care, transportation and environmental protection. *Block grants* come with lots of strings attached. In 1974, the Federal Housing and Community Development Act consolidated ten forms of grants-in-aid into a single block grant that provided housing and urban renewal funds to local governments that were willing to conform to a variety of federal regulations. A city applying for a federal block grant to build a senior citizens center must offer proof that 75 percent or more of the center will be used by the elderly. The city must also permit citizens to contribute to the planning of the center, and hold public hearings to enable them to do so.

Reporters have worked up interesting stories by studying the minutia of budget *line-items*. These list expenditures for each department, down to the smallest detail. A journalist studying a budget line-item labelled "fuel supplies" divided the number of gallons of fuel oil used to heat municipal buildings by the total amount spent for the fuel oil, and learned that the city was spending far too much for fuel. A check of public records revealed that the fuel oil supplier was also a heavy contributor to the campaigns of the mayor and the other city officials.

CITY HALL

City Hall is both a training ground for the young reporter and a mainstay for the veteran reporter. Here government works on a human scale, with results that are felt close to home. To find your way around, stop first at the City Clerk's office. The clerk will have a copy of all *ordinances*, *resolutions* and *motions* passed by the city's governing body.

Ordinances are laws; people can be punished for violating them. Violation of a municipal ordinance usually constitutes a *misdemeanor* or an *infraction*, rather than a far more serious *felony*, but fines and jail sentences can be imposed for violating some ordinances. The limit of the punishment the municipality can impose is defined by state law.

Resolutions are not laws, but expressions of policy. They cover a wide range of government activity, from adopting a budget to advising the police department to administer breathalyzer tests to drunk drivers. Municipal governments sometimes vote resolutions simply to express a community sentiment: When World War II broke out, some California cities passed resolutions declaring that Japanese-Americans should be confined to detention camps; decades later, the same municipalities passed resolutions rescinding the detention-camp resolutions, as a gesture of friendship to their Japanese-American friends. A resolution can be changed only by another resolution and an ordinance only by another ordinance.

Simple *motions*, also known as *minute orders*, are employed by municipal governments to direct the administration to take specific actions. A city council might, for instance, vote a minute order giving the city manager authority to buy a new fire truck. Most minute orders are routine, but city officials sometimes try to conceal potentially controversial actions by handling them as minute orders. Public affairs reporters reviewing the minutes of council meetings learn not to assume that everything of importance was labelled as an ordinance or a resolution; they check the minute orders too.

City Hall is a repository of information on the economic power structure of the community—which is just as important to the public affairs reporter as the political power structure. The County Clerk maintains files on all formally organized corporations doing business within the county. These list the directors of each corporation. In some cases the directors are merely figureheads, and the officers and principal stockholders who really control the enterprise may not be listed at all. State law frequently requires more complete disclosure of corporate information, so a reporter who runs into a dead end in trying to learn who controls what can check further with the Secretary of State and the nearest State Tax Office. If the corporation is large and publicly owned (that is, if its stock is available to the public for purchase), the Federal Securities and Exchange Commission will have its quarterly and yearly financial disclosure statements, known as 10K Forms. Large brokerage houses also may be able to supply information on the internal structures of big corporations.

The County Clerk's Offices in many areas maintain a *grantor-grantee index*, a mine of information on deeds, liens, partnerships and the transfer of real estate. The County Clerk's staff or a file clerk at a local title company can help translate the legalese in these documents.

The Finance Department has records of the ownership and assessed value of each piece of property in the community, as well as information on business licenses. A reporter examining these records can learn who are the principal property owners and businesspeople in the community and can also find aggregate statistics that reveal what type of businesses do the most business and hire the most employees.

The County Assessor's office has *assessed property roles* that list property owners. By consulting maps and cross referencing, reporters can determine who owns particular parcels of land. See the Tax Collector's files to determine who is paying the taxes on a given piece of property.

Digging through stacks of computer print-outs and record books may seem unappetizing at first, but the paper chase can become exciting once you learn the ropes. Even an innocuous-looking document can be full of information— attorneys' names, notary public sales, mailing addresses—that help reveal patterns of economic and political power. Two California reporters, suspecting that a city manager was using inside information acquired in the course of his duties to make a personal profit, spent two full weeks checking files of property ownerships. Finally, a record with the city manager's name on it popped up on the microfilm screen. Further checks of municipal and county records showed that the city manager belonged to obscured partnerships that owned land that had soared in value, thanks to city improvements in which the city manager himself had taken a hand. The resulting story led page one of the *Los Angeles Times*.

THE LEGISLATURES

The doings of legislatures—from a Senate hearing on the defense budget to a meeting of the city council—make up the stable diet of public affairs reporting. Indeed, legislatures do so much that reporters may find it difficult to cover everything. At the same time that the State House of Representatives is debating a sales tax increase and the State Senate is voting on whether to acquire a new park, a half-dozen public hearings may be in progress in which more *real* work is getting done than on the floor of either house. Covering the legislature on any given day can be like trying to watch eight different television shows at once. Here are a few suggestions.

Prepare for each day's reporting. Verify the time and place for scheduled hearings and meetings; even veteran reporters sheepishly admit that they have blown stories by getting lost or arriving an hour late. If an agenda is available, study it in advance. Check every item, not just the obviously important ones. When the legislature is pressed for time, as in the last hours before adjourning for the holidays, legislators sometimes put important business on the *consent calendar*: a category intended for the routine items that normally get gaveled through without discussion.

Look for opportunities to write *advance* stories, to be published or broadcast before the hearing or floor debate takes place. To work up an advance, call the principal figures in the matter (often they will be identified in the agenda) and ask for a copy of their prepared remarks or for a summary of what they intend to say. Then call other interested parties to get their reactions.

Consult with your editor to map out a *strategy* for covering the day's legislative events. Make sure you and the editor agree on which stories deserve top priority. Checking with contacts can help here. The agenda may say that the House is going to vote on the off-track betting bill tomorrow, but if the representative sponsoring the bill tells you privately that he or she has worked out an arrangement to have it continued (that is, postponed) until next week, that information will save you from wasting your time on the floor when you could be covering more important matters in the hearing rooms.

Learn the procedures used at legislative meetings. The bible of parliamentary procedures is *Roberts Rules of Order Revised* (Scott, Foresman and Company, Glenview, Illinois). It spells out how legislators make and amend motions, and how they debate and dispose of questions. If you get confused by the parliamentary procedure employed in a particular session or hearing, buttonhole the principals immediately afterwards and ask them to explain what happened.

When possible, arrive early, before the hearings and sessions get under way.

Drop in at legislators' offices, chat with them and their secretaries, try to get a sense of what is coming up. Interview those who are to testify at hearings and get the gist of what they plan to say. That way, when each testifies during the hearing, you have a better idea whether you must stay and listen or whether you can use the time to better advantage.

Keeping on top of the day's legislative business requires staying on the move; experienced public affairs reporters can cover the Hydra-headed activities of the statehouse with acrobatic agility. They will claim a place at the press table in one hearing room, leave a tape recorder running, then move on to cover another hearing. They will follow a witness into a corridor to ask follow-up questions on his or her testimony, peek into another hearing to see if the committee meeting there has gotten to the important part of its business yet and listen to a Senate floor debate over a "squawk box" in the press room while going over clips for a Sunday feature.

Think ahead. If a given hearing seems to be going nowhere, use the time to circulate, introduce yourself and collect business cards and phone numbers. Such contacts can come in handy in the future.

The three-ring circus approach should be employed only as a matter of necessity. Ultimately, there's no substitute for being there. The lead paragraphs of the following public affairs story by *The Miami Herald*'s Casey Frank could have been obtained through telephone calls and a look at prepared statements:

Plans by the Old Cutler Presbyterian Church to open a parish house, preschool, parking area and kindergarten were killed Wednesday by the Metro Zoning Appeals Board (ZAB).

By a 3–2 vote, the ZAB deemed the expansion plans inappropriate. "I respect churches and I love churches. I am a deacon in a Catholic church. But there are too many unanswered questions in this application," said board member Jose Lasa. . . .

But the paragraphs that soon followed could have been obtained firsthand:

Even as they spilled into the lobby after the hearing, the two sides continued to quarrel.

"If I wasn't wearing a pacemaker, I'd take you on right now, buddy," one property owner told Davis. There was no fight.

THE COURTS

The drama of legal confrontation makes the courts a constant source of news, but it also creates headaches for court reporters. Seldom do all the parties to a heated legal conflict feel satisfied with the way the case is reported by the press. Lawyers have been known to cajole and threaten reporters, even to sue them. Judges can be autocratic when dealing with the press: A Kentucky judge, angered over newspaper stories that had quoted remarks made by a prosecutor outside of court, summoned the reporter responsible into his chambers at the end of a week-long bribery trial and told him, "Son, I wouldn't run any stop signs on my way out of town. If you get arrested, I am going to jack up a corner of this courthouse, put you under it and personally kick out the jack." The reporter drove home carefully.

Court reporters learn to live with the pressures of the beat; some even relish them. Says Myrna Oliver, who covers civil courts for the *Los Angeles Times*, "When I find both sides and the judge mad at me, or possibly praising me, I figure I've done a fine job."

Court Structure

American courts deal with two types of cases: *criminal* and *civil*. *Criminal law* concerns conduct thought to be harmful to the state or to society. The proceedings center on a defendant, who is accused of having violated the law. If the prosecution can prove beyond a reasonable doubt that the defendant is guilty, the court then passes a sentence, which might include a fine, jail term or both. A judge who wishes to be lenient may suspend the sentence. This means that the defendant bears the stigma of having been found guilty of committing a crime, but is spared further punishment. Some judges administer conditional discharges; this sets the defendant free, but permits the judge to impose sentence at a later date, should the defendant be convicted of another crime.

Civil law deals with conduct thought to have harmed an individual or organization rather than the society as a whole. The alleged harm may be physical, as when an individual who eats a poisoned oyster sues the restaurant that served it, claiming that the chef acted negligently. The harm can also be financial, as when Walt Disney sued a T-shirt company for unauthorized sale of shirts bearing Mickey Mouse's picture. In addition, the harm can involve someone's reputation; see Chapter 17 on libel.

In a civil case, a plaintiff files the suit, requesting relief at the expense of the defendant. The form of relief can be money—"damages"—or action, as when an environmental group asks the court to order a chemical plant to stop polluting a lake. No allegation of criminal conduct need be involved in a civil case, though civil suits do sometimes spring from criminal actions.

Criminal proceedings are open to the public and therefore to the press, but civil proceedings, because they involve private parties and often concern issues of little or no public concern, tend to be more private. If plaintiff and defendant agree, the proceedings may take place largely beyond the purview of the public and the press.

Each state has its own system of courts, as does the federal government, and each system is organized in the form of a pyramid. Cases start at the broad base of the pyramid, in the *trial* courts, also known as *municipal* or *police* courts. Decisions made at this level may be appealed to an intermediate court, sometimes called a *superior* or *district* or *circuit* court. ("Circuit" comes from the days when judges on horseback would "ride circuit" through their districts, deciding cases as they went.) At the tip of the pyramid stands a *supreme* court. Cases decided by state supreme courts may be appealed to the United States Supreme Court.

A case involving national jurisdiction can be appealed from the state supreme court directly to Washington, and need not wind its way up through the federal pyramid.

Most legal actions, however, never reach court. Criminal prosecutors often "plea bargain," offering defendants the chance to plead guilty to reduced charges in order to save the state the expense of trying the cases. Civil suits may be dismissed for lack of merit, or they may be settled out of court. Fewer than 10 percent of all court business ever reaches trial, and of the cases that *do* reach trial, over 90 percent are disposed of without reaching the ultimate courts of appeal. The Supreme Court of the United States decides only some 150 cases a year, though it is asked to hear many more.

Efforts are being made to simplify legal terminology, but there are still many rather arcane terms for the court reporter to learn. Reference books like *Black's Law Dictionary*, *Ballentine's Law Dictionary* and the pocket-sized *Ready Reference Dictionaries* can help in conquering legal lingo. See the *Legal Secretary's Handbook* for a précis of legal procedures in each state. The local chapter of the American Bar Association has publications useful to reporters.

Covering Court Cases

Court coverage starts with numbers. When assigned to cover a specific of case, first note its *case* or *docket number*. Note also the *department* or court it has been assigned to, and the *calendar number* it has been issued within the court.

To find these numbers, look up the case in the alphabetical *Index of Plaintiffs and Defendants*, available at the courthouse. These provide the case or docket number. Separate listings are kept for criminal and civil cases.

The next step is to look up the case file. Request it from the *clerk's* office. In most courts, this system works like a library. The reporter fills out a card with the case or docket number, passes the card to a clerk, then waits until the file can be found. If the case is inactive, the file may be stored in the basement or on microfilm. And it may take hours to unearth. If the case is active, its file may be in the courtroom where the case is under consideration. In that event, go to that particular court and ask the clerk there for the file. If the judge has the file in chambers but is not working on it at the moment, you may be able to persuade the clerk to bring it out so that you can read it.

Courts have strict rules against removing files from file rooms and courtrooms. This means that the reporter often has to review the file and make notes on the spot, surrounded by the hubbub of court activity. The idea is to read behind the legalese, grasp the essentials of the case and decide what in it will make news.

In civil suits, pay attention to the line down toward the last page of the filing that starts "WHEREFORE." That is where the plaintiffs declare what they are after. They will be seeking one of two types of relief. One form of relief is an *action at law*, meaning that they are seeking property or monetary *damages*. The greater the amounts sought, the greater might be the magnitude of the suit, but keep in mind that attorneys sometimes wildly exaggerate the damages they seek in hopes of inspiring newspaper headlines. The other form of relief is a *court order*, usually an *injunction* or *restraining order*. Both have the effect of ordering the defendant to desist. Such orders are often sought *ex parte*, meaning that only one party appears in court to state its case. If the plaintiff's cause seems to have some merit, the judge may issue a *preliminary* injunction or a *temporary* restraining order (TRO), the intent of which is usually to prevent matters from getting worse until both sides have had a chance to air their views in court. If a developer is bulldozing an American Indian burial ground to build an apartment house and the Indians can get the court to issue an injunction or a TRO, the bulldozing stops until the case can be argued further.

There are many ways for a case to be disposed of without ever coming to trial. The court may issue a default judgment. A divorce, for instance, may be granted by default if the respondent does nothing to contest it. The case may be *dismissed*, on grounds that the plaintiff or prosecution has failed to make a sufficient case. Or, it may be decided by *summary judgment*—a decision made strictly on the legal issues and without considering the evidence. Summary judgments save court time in cases in which all parties agree on the facts, and differ only on the interpretation of the law. In a *consent decree*, both sides voluntarily agree on a solution, which is then approved by the court. The result is not a court decision, but a contract made binding by the court. To reduce the burden of cases crowding the docket, judges sometimes submit a civil case for *arbitration*, if both sides are willing to abide by the decision of a professional arbiter.

The most dramatic cases to cover are those that come to trial, but even here the proceedings seldom have the melodrama of a Perry Mason set. Most courts are crowded. Some handle several cases at once, interrupting the proceedings of one trial to hear motions in another, halting the hearing while the judge issues an order in yet another case. Lawyers, clients and witnesses come and go in an atmosphere more like a railway station than a court of law.

The key to making sense of this swirl of events is the *clerk* of the court. He or she can usually be found at a desk to one side of the judge's bench, buried in paperwork. A sign may read, "Please do not approach the clerk while court is in session." If you heed the sign and sit waiting for a break in the proceedings, however, rival reporters may breeze in, approach the clerk, say a few words, receive an answer or pick up a file and be on their way. The reason is that the other reporters took the trouble, before court was in session, to introduce themselves to the clerk and present the calendar number of the case in which they were interested. Clerks work primarily from calendar numbers. All the reporters had to do was say something like, "What was the disposition of number 3?" To which all the clerk had to reply was something like, "Denied." or "TRO granted, except paragraph three."

The ideal courtroom assignment is to cover a major trial full time. But in practice, reporters seldom get to sit through an entire trial. Instead, like legislative reporters, they normally cover several stories at once. To stay up to date on all the cases, they make the rounds of the courtrooms and judges' chambers, chatting with the clerks and attorneys and bailiffs, interviewing judges, collecting calendar and docket numbers and, when possible, cooperating with other reporters to make sure that nobody misses anything essential that goes on in a court. Some befriend the court stenographers, hoping that if they do miss an important piece of testimony, the stenographer may be willing to read it back to them when the court is in recess.

When covering a trial, keep your head up. Don't get so involved in taking notes that you aren't looking when the defendant flushes with anger at a prosecuting witness's testimony, or the judge rolls his or her eyes in exasperation at an attorney's ineptitude. Flag your notes so that you can locate important passages quickly. Keep thinking in terms of what will be the lead. Advise your editor frequently on the direction the story is taking.

A case can take years getting to trial, and years longer going through the process of appeals. James Thompson, a criminal lawyer who later became governor of Illinois, used to argue against capital punishment by pointing out that he could keep a condemned murderer from the electric chair for ten years or more, at great expense to the state, just by filing various appeals. To keep track of such cases over the years, reporters covering the courts keep extensive files, on index cards or in computer memory, listing newsworthy cases and noting when action on each is next due. In addition, many keep a personal calendar, or "tickler file," that they update daily. Postponed trial dates and other changes in the court calendar are immediately entered in the tickler file, and the information promptly transferred to the newspaper's main file to ensure that it is covered. The rule of thumb is that if a case was important enough to report in the past, its ultimate outcome should be reported as well, so that interested readers won't wait forever for the other shoe to drop.

POLITICAL CAMPAIGNS

Many young journalists feel about politics much as Queen Victoria thought about sex—that it's nasty, but essential to life. The quickest way to lose your political virginity is to cover an election campaign.

The first step—in politics, if not sex—is research. Read the newspapers and watch news broadcasts, of course, but also keep up on political analysis by reading books on politics and politically sophisticated periodicals like *The Atlantic*, *Harper's*, *The New Republic*, *The Nation*, *National Review* and the *National Journal*, which provides detailed coverage of Congressional affairs.

When assigned to cover a politician running for election, call his or her campaign organization and speak with the candidate's press secretary, sometimes called the "media coordinator." Obtain a packet of campaign literature and policy statements, and study it until you understand the position the candidate takes on the major issues. Promptly start interviewing people around the candidate. Even if some of the interviews provide little news, they will serve to introduce you to the campaign staff and establish contacts that may prove useful later on. To interview the candidate, prepare a mix of timely questions, the kind that can produce a newsworthy story, as well as more searching questions aimed at garnering background information for later use.

Build a set of campaign files. Clip relevant newspaper stories, save every useful piece of campaign literature and, of course, retain your notes. The files become increasingly useful as the campaign progresses. Using them, you can check what the candidate says today against what he or she said six weeks ago, identify changes in campaign strategy and develop a clearer picture of whose support the candidate has gained or lost.

Writing campaign stories, like covering the Pentagon or the Budget Office, means translating jargon into clear, simple language that everyone can understand. Politicians naturally try to couch their views in terms that sound broadly acceptable. "The right to life" sounds like a good thing. So does "A woman's right to choose." Yet these two slogans represent opposite positions on the abortion issue. It's the reporter's job to discuss the issues in simple terms that will help readers grasp the substance behind the rhetoric.

When you're not sure what the candidate means, ask direct, hard-nosed questions aimed at clearing up confusion. When Governor Jerry Brown of California was running for president in 1980, he promised to sharply reduce federal expenditures. Reporters pressed him on just what expenditures he would slash: welfare, veterans' benefits, farm subsidies, foreign aid, the defense budget, environmental protection? Brown hedged, and said he would decide that when elected. Not surprisingly, voters soon dismissed Brown's cost-cutting promises as mere rhetoric.

Look for trends in the campaign. Most campaigns represent a dialogue between the expected and the unexpected. Candidates and their campaign managers try to follow predetermined strategies, and it is part of the reporter's job to discern and report on these strategies. It was owing to strategic planning that John F. Kennedy kicked off his 1960 presidential campaign by shaking hands outside factories, to help dispel what polls suggested was an unfavorable public image of him as a rich man's son who never had to work. On the other hand, the campaign must respond to changing circumstances, and journalists watch changing trends in strategy. During George Wallace's 1982 bid for reelection as governor of Alabama, his pollsters discovered, to their surprise, that black voters regarded Wallace as the less objectionable of the two candidates. Wallace promptly started having his picture taken shaking hands with blacks—unexpected behavior that alerted reporters to a shift in his campaign strategy.

The most important trend to watch for is how the candidate is doing at gaining support. This means support among the voters, of course, which may be revealed in public opinion polls, but it also means financial support. The Federal Elections Commission requires candidates for federal office to file periodic statements listing the major donors to their campaigns; many states and counties have similar campaign reporting procedures. Study these documents to learn who cares enough about the outcome of the campaign to have invested in it. Most campaigns are supported by backers who want something in return. This quid pro quo is not necessarily disreputable—there are, after all, millionaires who donate to political campaigns for no worse reason than that they want to see the best candidate elected—but whatever the motives involved, no campaign can be understood without understanding its finances. When George Dukmajian was elected governor of California in 1982, he appointed, as director of the state agency that regulates insurance, an insurance man who had been among his top campaign contributors. This did not mean that the appointment was necessarily a bad one, but the story was interesting, to say the least, and it made the front page of the *Los Angeles Times*.

Support comes from the endorsements of organizations as well. Democratic candidates for president are in trouble if they fail to get the endorsement of the AFL-CIO, as are Republicans who lack backing from the National Association of Manufacturers. Recent years have seen growing influence by public interest groups like the Environmental Defense Fund, Common Cause, and the Natural Resources Defense Council. Some of these public interest groups endorse candidates. Others "rate" candidates. Some seek to create a political climate in which candidates must declare on one side or the other of an issue. The campaign for a bilateral nuclear arms freeze in the 1980s garnered the support of millions of voters, leaving presidential candidates for the 1984 election with little choice but to declare themselves for or against the freeze.

When election day approaches, the candidates involved in a close race may unleash unfair charges, smears, dubious revelations—a whole arsenal of material designed to capture headlines or to discredit the opposition at the last moment, when there's little time left to reply. Journalists learn to view such final-hour stories skeptically, to avoid their being used as a campaign tool.

Election night presents special problems. Morning newspapers may have to go to press before the winners can be declared. They learn not to jump to conclusions; the *Chicago Tribune* headline that erroneously declared that Dewey had beaten Truman in the 1948 presidential election looms large in their memories. It is far safer to report that a candidate was "leading" or "appeared to have won based on earlier returns." To avoid making newspaper copy seem outdated, report election returns as a percentage of precincts rather than by the time on the clock:

> With 47 percent of precincts reporting, the results were:
>   Carpenter (D)-------89,335 (55%)
>   Smithers (R)--------73,092 (45%)

You can write *B* copy and background election stories in advance of learning the results from the polls. Typically, the *B* copy will recap the high points of the campaign. You can then add the lead and various inserts as the results come in.

SUMMARY

Reporting public affairs means covering the workings of government and politics. American government is a complex of overlapping and competing systems—New York State alone harbors 1400 separate governments—and the public affairs reporter must understand its structure in order to report its activities. The most popular forms of municipal government are the *council* system, the *commission* system and the *strong mayor and council* system. *Special districts* may be found on the local level, handling such functions as education and sanitation. As cities grow, some expand to take over various governmental functions from surrounding communities, whereas others hand these functions up to the county government, in a *metropolitan* system. States exercise powerful control over the revenues and policies of the communities, whose influence is sometimes moderated by *local option* plans.

Government collects revenues chiefly through taxation. The main forms of taxation are the *income tax*, *sales tax*, *property tax*, *excise tax* and *license taxes* and *fees*.

Revenues are dispersed in accordance with a *budget*, which serves not only as an accounting of monies spent but also as an indicator of which interests are gaining and losing political influence, and of how the flow of power in the community as a whole is changing. The budget process can be as revealing in this regard as the finished budget itself. To report budgetary matters, try to translate the cold figures into meaningful human terms. One approach is to compare the current year's budget with budgets from previous years.

When covering City Hall, start with the City Clerk's office. Here are kept copies of all *ordinances*, *resolutions* and *motions* passed by the city's governing body. The city Finance Department, the County Clerk's office and the County Assessor's office can supply information vital to understanding the economic power structure of the community, which is every bit as important as the political power structure.

Covering legislative proceedings involves preparation, constant contact with editors and enough flexibility to handle several developing stories at once. Developing contacts helps. Advance stories can be written to "cover" legislative hearings before they take place. A knowledge of parliamentary procedure is imperative.

Covering the courts seldom means witnessing a dramatic trial, because most cases are settled without going to trial. It does mean mastering court structure and learning how to track down legal files by means of their *case*, *docket* and *calendar* numbers. Here a familiarity with legal terminology is essential.

Reporters covering political campaigns present the candidates as individuals, clarify the issues and report on trends in the campaign. The most important trend often is simply how each candidate is doing, in terms of garnering votes and financial support.

15

THE REPORTER
AS INVESTIGATOR

From reading the early newspaper accounts, it looked like an open and shut case. The New York police had arrested a barely literate black youth named George Whitmore in connection with the attempted rape of one woman and the stabbing death of two others who shared a Manhattan apartment. Not only had the woman in the rape attempt identified Whitmore as her attacker, but Whitmore had confessed to the two killings.

At that point, only one person stood between Whitmore and life imprisonment: a slender, bookish-looking investigative reporter for the old *New York World-Telegram & The Sun* named Selwyn Raab. Raab had been working on a story about police brutality. Going through the clips, he noticed that Whitmore's lawyer claimed his client's confession had been beaten out of him by two detectives. He also found that the district attorney had kept Whitmore at Bellevue Hospital an unusually long time, supposedly for psychiatric testing. To Raab, this was a tip-off that something was fishy. He began an investigation.

It took nine years and produced more than 100 stories. In the end, the DA had to drop the murder case when Raab reported that the police had suppressed evidence placing Whitmore 120 miles from New York on the day of the killings.

But on the charge of attempted rape, Whitmore was convicted—in his third trial, after guilty verdicts in his two earlier trials were reversed by a higher court. Convinced that Whitmore was innocent of rape as well, Raab kept digging. He hunted for clues and witnesses in slum neighborhoods in Brooklyn and in the barrios of Puerto Rico. He finally located a woman who had witnessed the crime and who said Whitmore looked nothing like the man she had seen running from the scene.

In April, 1973, Whitmore walked out of Dannemora prison in upstate New York. He was 28 and had lost ten years of his life, but he was free.

Raab's stories received the Sigma Delta Chi Award that year and provided the pilot for a new CBS-TV police series. In the TV version, the credit for saving Whitmore went not to a reporter but to a fictitious police lieutenant named "Kojak."

A BRIEF HISTORY

Investigative reporters search out news that would ordinarily stay hidden from view. They reveal corruption in business and government: Often it is journalists who expose Medicaid doctors who bill the state for patients they never see, or planning commissioners who recommend that the city build its new parking garage on land secretly owned by their brothers-in-law. Like Selwyn Raab, investigative reporters can also aid the victims of injustice.

In recent years, the names of investigative reporters have become household words. They include Seymour Hersh, the reporter who unearthed the My Lai massacre in Vietnam; Carl Bernstein and Robert Woodward of *The Washington Post*, whose Watergate stories helped depose President Nixon; and Jack Anderson, the Washington columnist whose staff of investigators has dug up stories ranging from CIA plots against foreign leaders to the sexual misadventures of a cartoonist on the college lecture circuit.

So much public attention has been paid investigative reporters of late that we tend to forget that their calling goes back a long time. In 1887, a reporter with the pen name Nellie Bly—her real name was Elizabeth Cochrane—became one of the first journalists to go undercover to get a story. Feigning madness and amnesia, Bly spent ten days in what was then known as the New York State Lunatic Asylum, a forbidding stone fortress on Blackwell's Island in Manhattan's East River. Her expose of the sordid conditions there ran for a week in Pulitzer's *New York World*, generating a major scandal that led to a grand jury investigation and reforms in the treatment of the mentally ill.

At the turn of the century, a Pennsylvania writer, Ida Tarbell, created a national stir with her investigative stories about the ruthless business practices of the monopolies, most notably John D. Rockefeller's Standard Oil Company. Tarbell and other investigative writers—among them her colleague at the crusading *McClure's Magazine*, Lincoln Steffens, the *New York Tribune* reporter Jacob Riis and novelists Frank Norris and Upton Sinclair—exposed the dark side of the American economic system. Their attacks on everything from urban corruption and the suffering of the poor to the rapacity of the railroad builders and the filthy state of Chicago's meat packing plants earned them the label "Muckrakers." The term, first mentioned in a 1906 speech by Teddy Roosevelt, was intended to be derogatory: Roosevelt took it from the "Man with the Muckrake," a character in John Bunyon's *Pilgrim's Progress* who is so busy raking muck that he fails to look up and see the celestial crown over his head. But the investigative reporters took up the epithet and made it a badge of honor.

Some of the most effective muckrakers of modern times never worked for a daily newspaper. Rachel Carson, a marine biologist, created the environmental movement virtually overnight with her 1961 book, *Silent Spring*, which alerted the public to the ecological damage being wrought by pesticides. A year later a freelance writer and socialist named Michael Harrington wrote *The Other America*, a vivid delineation of poverty in the United States that led to the fifteen-year-long federal War on Poverty program. The birth of the consumer movement could be dated from 1963, when a Harvard lawyer named Ralph Nader wrote *Unsafe at Any Speed*, a book that criticized shoddy engineering in American cars.

Today, investigative reporting has become part of the fabric of American journalism. Large papers like the *St. Louis Post-Dispatch* and the *Los Angeles Times* employ reporters who do nothing but conduct investigations. Many smaller papers that cannot afford to hire full-time investigative reporters expect their regular reporters to turn into investigators when promising stories fall their way.

WHAT IT TAKES

General assignment reporters find themselves functioning as investigative reporters whenever they delve beneath the surface of events, into the realm where information is concealed or hard to get. But whereas general assignment reporters do investigative work occasionally, investigative reporters spend nearly all their time digging. Their skills are honed to a fine edge through long use.

One of the characteristics that distinguish investigative reporters is a heightened sense of curiosity. Mike Clancy, a court reporter for the *Albuquerque Tribune* in New Mexico, was jotting down the day's docket of felony cases when he noticed a couple of names that had come up frequently before. Some reporters might have shrugged it off as mere coincidence, but Clancy looked into the matter. Going through the records, he found a pattern of parole decisions that looked decidedly odd. One man with eight felony convictions had been paroled on his last case after serving only seven months in jail. Another, sentenced to serve eighteen to ninety years in jail after eleven convictions, got out of prison after serving only four years.

More digging revealed that the state parole board responsible for these cases was comprised of political hacks who knew little about the purpose of parole. Clancy's story caused such a stir that the state legislature soon voted to set up a parole system employing full-time professionals who would take their jobs more seriously.

Investigative reporters tend also to be unusually persistent. Like diamonds, the best stories are buried deep. Investigative reporters can't afford to get discouraged when promising tips lead only to dead ends, when their questions are resisted or evaded or when they must piece together a story from stray facts so scattered as almost to defy comprehension. Woodward and Bernstein visited a single source *twenty-two times* before she even let them into her house—and then it took hours more to break down her resistance to talking. Stanley Penn, investigative reporter for *The Wall Street Journal*, is a veritable monument to persistence. Reporting his Pulitzer Prize expose of price manipulations by the Occidental Petroleum Company, Penn went regularly to the Federal District Courthouse in New York City. He had heard that a rival oil company was going to file a lawsuit against Occidental, and he thought it might contain documents that could help in his investigation. The lawsuit wasn't filed until *five years later*. When it was, Penn was there waiting for it.

Exposes can lose people their jobs, ruin their reputations and send them to jail. If sloppily reported, such stories can backfire, eroding a newspaper's reputation or costing it libel damages. For this reason, investigative reporters check every fact until they are confident it is dead accurate—and that they can prove it so in court, if necessary. Failing to abide by the thoroughness rule can be expensive. When a Florida newspaper ran a story accusing the county dog warden of smoking marijuana, the warden, furious, sued the paper for libel. The resulting trial revealed that the reporter who wrote the story had not actually seen the alleged pot smoking herself but had relied on secondhand and thirdhand accounts. The jury ruled that the paper had to pay the dog warden $70,000 for damaging his reputation.

Even experienced investigators sometimes fail to use proper caution. In 1972 Jack Anderson wrote that the Democratic candidate for Vice President, Senator Thomas Eagleton of Missouri, had been arrested for drunken driving. As proof, the columnist said he had "located photostats of half a dozen arrests for drunken and reckless driving." When called on to produce the evidence, Anderson said he didn't actually have the photostats in hand, but had been told of their existence by a Missouri state trooper. In the end, the documents were never found. In apologizing for his slip, Anderson said that he had not taken the time to check his facts for fear of getting scooped by a rival reporter.

A thick skin helps; investigators are unpopular among those who have something to hide, and many have encountered threats and insults, even violence. Dan Hicks Jr., publisher of the *Monroe County Observer* in Milledgeville, Georgia, angered so many people that he could hardly keep track of all his enemies. Among the targets of his exposes were Ku Klux Klan members, bootleggers, and corrupt officials in the county roads department. His newspaper office was blasted by a shotgun and twice burned down, and Hicks himself was beaten up by two men who said they were paid for the job with $30 and a gallon of "white lightning."

One of the country's more fearless investigative reporters, Jack Nelson, started at age 24 working for the *Atlanta Constitution* in Georgia. His investigative stories about corruption in nearby Liberty County resulted in two indictments. When Nelson went to cover the resulting trials a deputy sheriff flattened him on the hood of a car and tried to wring his neck while a crowd of onlookers yelled, "Give the little bastard what he deserves." Five years later Nelson wrote a devastating series about a hospital in Georgia where surgery was performed by registered nurses while surgeons attended to their private patients. He won the Pulitzer Prize. He also got slugged by one of the doctors.

Don Bolles, a reporter for the *Arizona Republic* in Phoenix, had written about everything from bribery in the state tax commission to land fraud. Then he began doing stories about Mafia infiltration of the local dog-racing tracks. One day in June, 1976, Bolles turned on the ignition of his car and was blown up by a bomb. In response, dozens of investigative reporters from around the country journeyed to Phoenix to continue covering the stories that Bolles had set out to write.

WHERE TO LOOK

"I never saw anyone confess at a press conference," says investigative reporter Jack Newfield of the *Village Voice*. Reporters have to go out and get the hidden stories. What do they look for?

Consumer Fraud

Every reader is a consumer. Each buys groceries, clothes, transportation, shelter. Journalists render a service by reporting when careless or unscrupulous businesses are selling unnutritious food, baby clothes that catch fire, unreliable tours or driveway "paving" that washes away in the first rain.

One way that investigative reporters cover consumer fraud is by posing as unwitting consumers themselves. A common ploy is to have your car put in perfect working order by a scrupulous mechanic, then take it to a dozen garages, complaining of a minor malfunction, and see how each diagnoses the problem and estimates the charge for fixing it. Reporters for a New York daily telephoned several airlines and were quoted widely different fares for flying the same route; the resulting story, concerning not fraud but confusion, alerted readers not to take the airlines' quoted fares at face value.

Investigative reporters covering consumer affairs watch for advertising claims that seem all but impossible to fulfill. The Famous Writers' School in Westport, Connecticut, a mail-order operation, promised in its advertisements that students who paid its tuition would have their manuscripts looked over by the famous writers pictured in its advertisements; students who did well, the ads implied, would soon be on the road to riches as freelance authors. These claims aroused the suspicion of Jessica Mitford, who enrolled in the course as a student, submitted hopelessly badly written copy and got back encouraging letters, not from the famous writers but from relatively anonymous readers employed by the school. Ultimately, Mitford found that the famous writers never saw the student papers—indeed, their only connection with the school was to allow it to use their names—and that the chances of students making a profit in the writing business were virtually zero. Toward the end of the investigation Mitford interviewed Bennett Cerf, then head of Random House, who was associated with the school, and asked if he had ever published the work of a school graduate. "Oh, come now, you must be pulling my leg," he answered. "No person of any sophistication whose books Random House would publish would have to take a mail-order course to learn how to write." Mitford's exposé, published in 1970 by *The Atlantic*, led to the closing of the school.

Bungling and Inefficiency

Some of the best exposés involve waste and incompetency. A common complaint about the justice system is that more judges are needed to handle the backlog of cases that clog the courts. But how much work do judges do as it is? An investigation by the *Village Voice* found that after arriving late for work, ordering long recesses, eating leisurely lunches, then calling it quits early in the afternoon, many judges put in barely half the day's work they were being paid for. In a series of similar investigative pieces, a reporter who shadowed a sanitation crew for days found that many were loafing instead of picking up the trash.

In investigating waste and mismanagement, an effective tool is *comparison*. Compare an agency in your city with another somewhere else that accomplishes the same tasks with fewer people and less money. Then ask, why the difference? Does your school system give its teachers a lot of "release time" to do chores other than teaching, while another system keeps its teachers in the classroom? How does your police department stack up against others its size as to its "clearance rate"—the number of arrests it makes compared to the number of crimes committed?

Graft and Corruption

"Politics," wrote Ambrose Bierce, a turn-of-the-century newspaper columnist, "is the conduct of public affairs for private advantage." Considering the great number of honest public officials, Bierce's definition seems a trifle cynical. Yet it is hard to deny that, from the Tweed Ring in New York to defense industry profiteers in contemporary Washington, corruption has always persisted in American government.

It takes two to perform an act of graft: the public official who accepts a bribe and the private citizen who offers it. One place to look for evidence of it is at the juncture where government interacts with private enterprise.

Departments of Inspection are notorious for their vulnerability for graft. Some of the most publicized instances have involved inspectors for municipal building departments. Their job is to prevent deterioration of buildings by enforcing the local housing code. An apartment house with a leaky roof, faulty plumbing or falling plaster normally gets a violation notice; failure to make repairs within one or two months can cost the owner a fine. Landlords may find it less expensive to pay off the housing inspector to ignore the violations. Just as often, crooked inspectors put the arm on businesspeople. In the construction of large buildings, thousands of dollars can be lost if the person supposed to inspect the plumbing installation doesn't show up on time, obliging workers to hang around being paid for doing nothing. To ensure against this possibility, the plumbing inspector may solicit an "expediting fee" from the construction supervisor.

Graft thrives in *franchising* and *licensing* situations, where government agencies or officials grant businesspeople privileges that are worth a good deal of money. Franchises provide companies with the exclusive right to run restaurants or gas stations on interstate turnpikes or hotdog concessions at the zoo; they can mean fat profits, and businesspeople may be tempted to bribe their way into landing them. Also valuable is the *license* required to open a hairdressing salon, boat marina or lock repair shop, or to sell liquor. Who grants these privileges? Are they benefitting personally from their position? Where licenses are granted locally, city council members may divide up a city into sections, giving each council member a veto over licenses in his or her area. The kind of graft involved is often more subtle than the outright payment of cash. A would-be restaurateur, for example, may be informed that the council member who could help him or her get a license has a "friend" who runs a linen supply service that the restaurant might find convenient to use once it opens, or that the council member's "cousin" works at an insurance agency that just happens to specialize in fire insurance for restaurants. Such a hint rarely has to be drawn too broadly; the restaurateur usually gets the idea.

Government purchases range from paper clips to fighter bombers, and the government relies on private industry to provide the goods and services it requires. Who sells the city its fifty tons of rock salt every year? Who gets to rent his or her vacant storefront to the new day-care center? Who handles the legal problems of the Industrial Development Commission? The process of deciding just who gets the business invites graft.

To get the best goods and services at the lowest prices, governments are supposed to put purchases up to a public bidding and give the business to the company submitting the lowest bid. But there's plenty of room for finagling in the bidding process. Bidding specifications can be drawn in such a restrictive way that only a single local business—the one that has paid off the officials— can meet the requirements. If city law mandates bidding only on purchases of more than a certain amount, say $5000, a public official need only break a large purchase into several smaller ones, each for less than $5000, then award the smaller contracts to favored "friends." Business, too, can conspire to subvert the bidding process. The *St. Louis Post-Dispatch* exposed a scandal whereby ten of the city's major contractors got together in a hotel room before each big repair job on the country roads. In these meetings they decided what the "low bid" would be on the job and which contractor would be the "low bidder." The others would bid high. Next time around, it would be someone else's turn to get the contract. All profited, because even the "low" bid was fat with profits.

Investigative reporters learn to look closely at whether the government is getting what it pays for. A company may bid artificially low, hoping somewhere along the line to substitute cheaper materials or services for the ones promised, perhaps with the help of corrupt building inspectors. In Rhode Island, for example, a contractor building a new high school tried to save himself $4000 by installing flooring in the boys' gym that was only ¾ inch thick instead of the 1¼ inch flooring listed in the specifications. The substandard flooring was discovered by a member of the school building committee on an unannounced visit—and leaked to a reporter for the *Providence Bulletin*, who wrote a story. The builder, however, explained the discrepancy by saying his workers had only "misread" the specifications. The matter was dropped when the contractor agreed to replace the flooring.

Zoning can have a dramatic impact on the value of land—particularly land in a growing area such as a suburb. The agency involved is usually a local zoning board, created to provide for orderly development of a town by seeing to it that land is not used helter-skelter. Noisy factories should go alongside other factories and not on residential streets; fast-food outlets should be built on commercial strips that can handle the traffic, not between the library and the park bandshell.

Beyond their planning function, zoning designations can alter the land's economic value. To a builder, a five-acre parcel zoned for houses on one acre of land each may be far less valuable than would be the case if the land were zoned so the houses could be put on quarter-acre lots. With the first designation the builder can build only five houses; with the latter, twenty houses. Zoning officials, many of whom serve for little or no pay, may be tempted to augment their incomes by zoning a piece of land the way the developer wants it.

Another common form of zoning graft occurs when the officials in charge of making the zoning decisions—or those who have strong influence over those who are—latch onto a piece of the very land that will increase in value as a result of their own decisions. Typical of this kind of graft was a case uncovered by the *Detroit Free Press* in 1974. Eight city officials in Troy, Michigan, had secretly purchased thirty-seven parcels of land either in or near an area they were about to change from a zone permitting only single-family houses to one allowing far more lucrative commercial development. Two reporters, David Anderson and Peter Benjaminson, got interested in the case when an old man told them he had sold the officials four acres he owned in the section back in 1968. At that time he had checked with City Hall to see if the zoning designation was to be changed. Assured that it was not, he let the parcel go at a relatively low price. Shortly after the zoning officials bought the property, however, a sign went up announcing that it was now "zoned commercial."

Tax assessments determine how much money the government collects in property taxes. What a town collects depends on two things: how much it values, or "assesses," its property and the rate of tax it charges on the valuations. If the tax assessor values a house at $60,000, and the tax rate is $30 for each $1000 of valuation, then the homeowner would pay a yearly property tax of $1800. In one obvious form of graft, businesspeople or officials may exchange money or favors in return for low assessments on their property or that of their friends. If a house on Elm Street owned by the local chairperson of the town Republican Committee is officially assessed at only $50,000 and all the others on the street are assessed at $150,000, chances are that something funny is going on.

HOW TO GET THE STORY

No two investigative assignments work alike, but most may be said to pass through three operational phases. First comes a *clue* that a news story lies hidden somewhere. The clue might be a tip, a leak or just a reporter's or editor's hunch. The second phase consists of *exploration*—searching through documents, talking to people. If a story is there, this is when you'll unearth it. The last phase consists of a *confrontation* with the principals involved. This is when they get a chance to explain their sides of the story, deny the charges, turn you away with a "no comment," or confess.

Clues

A *tip* is a scrap of information that sends a reporter in pursuit of a story. Early in 1976 an electrical engineer named Bo Bryan walked into the *Lufkin News* in Texas to get help finding out the truth about the death of his nephew. At first no one paid any attention to him. Joe Murray, the county editor, was so short of staff that day he had to come in on his day off to get out the paper, and had little time to waste talking with some ear-bender. "When he came in," Murray said later, "I pretended I didn't see him."

But Murray did eventually listen, and what the man had to say was startling. His nephew, 20-year-old Lynn McClure, had died while undergoing basic training at a United States Marine Corps boot camp. The Marines said McClure died of a brain injury he had suffered before entering the Corps. But his uncle had seen the boy's body, and his head seemed to have been battered. He felt sure McClure had been beaten to death.

Murray heard the uncle out, then called over Ken Herman, a 21-year-old reporter on his first newspaper job. Herman interviewed Bryan again. The next day, Herman's obit of the young Marine began:

Lynn (Bubba) McClure, 20, joined the Marines to become a man and make his family proud of him. "I can't wait to show you my uniform," he had written his mother.

Today, wearing that dress blue uniform, he was buried in a flag-draped casket. As he was lowered into his grave, two questions puzzled his family and those who knew him:

They were: How had a tenth-grade dropout with learning disabilities passed Marine entrance tests? And why, despite a protective football helmet and face mask, had McClure suffered fatal brain damage during combat training exercises with padded sticks?

"I GO RIGHT FOR THE DOCUMENTS": JACK NEWFIELD ON INVESTIGATION

Few reporters in the country have made it more uncomfortable for corrupt politicians and the crooked businesspeople who pay them off than Jack Newfield, the chief investigative reporter for New York's weekly *Village Voice*. Judges who take bribes from Mafia figures in exchange for light sentences; nursing home operators who cheat elderly patients out of decent health care while pocketing Medicare payments from the government; the wife of a United States Senator who is secretly lobbying for the interests of a foreign government—these and many more betrayers of the public trust have over the last twenty years felt the sting of Newfield's blistering and highly personal prose. The author of five books, including *Robert F. Kennedy: A Memoir* and a much praised expose of urban corruption entitled *The Abuse of Power*, Newfield became an early proponent of "advocacy journalism," which dictates that reporters should abandon their usual neutrality in favor of openly advocating causes they feel work toward the public good. As an investigative journalist, he said, his hero has always been the muckraker Lincoln Steffens whose theories about public corruption have fueled all of Newfield's work. "The thesis of *The Abuse of Power*," he says, "is that the real decision making power is not held by the people we elect to represent us, but by an unaccountable and permanent clique of law firms, corporations, utilities, politicos, judges, publicists. The only way to combat that infrastructure is by continually exposing it to public view." We talked to Newfield in the living room of his townhouse located in Manhattan's Greenwich Village.

How did you get started in journalism?

It wasn't easy. The most important lesson I learned in my life was to always resist authority. This was something I learned because my father died when I was 4 and I was raised by my mother and an assortment of bizarre relatives all of whom were so odious I got used to never doing what they told me. This attitude, however, constantly got me into trouble with editors, which is why I ended up getting fired from the first three newspaper jobs I had. While I was at Hunter College, for instance, I was a copy boy at the old *New York Mirror*, the Hearst tabloid, and one day I was stripping stories off the wire machines to bring them out to the desk when bells started to go off which means a bulletin is about to come over. It turned out to be the first story about the Bay of Pigs invasion. The other copy boy and I said, "Holy shit, America's invading Cuba," and here we'd placed all this faith in President Kennedy as such a force for good. So I right away burned the first eight takes of the story, set fire to them in protest. Editors ran in when they saw smoke coming out of the wire room, and they fired me on the spot. Ever since then I've called myself the first advocacy copy boy.

Then in 1963 I got a job as editor for a community paper on the West Side of Manhattan. This was during the civil rights movement, and I'd been involved in a thing called the Committee to Defend Martin Luther King, which was a support group for the freedom rides and sit-ins in the South. On July 4 I went down to join a big protest demonstration at a segregated amusement park outside Baltimore, and we all got ourselves arrested. I spent twelve hours in jail with the lawyer Mark Lane and the entire cast of The Living Theatre, and when I got back to New York I found I'd been fired from the newspaper. It was owned by a guy who also ran a lot of porno theatres on 42nd Street. He didn't think journalists should get involved in what they were writing about.

Eventually, I started doing freelance writing for the *Village Voice*—stories from Mississippi, the rise of black nationalism, urban problems—and I've been there ever since.

What got you into investigative reporting?

That was when I started working on a story about the Ten Worst Judges in New York City. Before that no one had ever tried to hold judges accountable and write about them in anything but a highly respectful way. What favors did they do politicians to get themselves appointed? What was their relationship to organized crime? How hard did they work? I mean, there were judges in the City who put in no more than four hours a day, and here's a court system screaming that it's hopelessly bogged down because it doesn't have enough judges! The way the story came about was that I was doing a piece about a cop and what he had to deal with in my old neighborhood in the Bedford-Stuyvesant section of Brooklyn. I was riding around with him at night in his squad car and he told me he had been to court that day and locked up this heroin dealer. It was the third time he locked him up, and this judge still let the guy go with no bail. I began to do research into the judge's other cases and found a pattern of leniency toward organized crime.

Once you've got a tip like that, how do you proceed in an investigation?

I go right for the documents. That was what the judge's story taught me. With that first judge I found that there had been a state legislative hearing two years earlier and the committee had a whole file on the cases he'd sat on—not enough to convict him of a crime, but plenty of stuff for my story. Ever since then, at the start of every investigation, the first thing I find out is where the paper is and how to get my hands on it. Documents are much more trustworthy than people. When I was doing the nursing scandal, I learned there was something called the HE-2 form a nursing home operator submits for Medicaid reimbursement. On that form the owner discloses everything—the salaries supposedly paid his staff that he might be pocketing himself, legal fees, services he's performed for patients. Then you go in and see if what he claimed is really true.

Until I did the story about the senator's wife who was a foreign lobbyist I didn't know there was a foreign agent's registration form in a file in the Justice Department. Until I exposed a school official in Brooklyn who was stealing money from the government I didn't realize that the Board of Education had records of every voucher he'd ever signed, every claim for expenses he'd ever made, all the school equipment he said he'd bought. The City never has time to check up on these things, but a journalist can go into his schools and see if he really bought all this stuff or was just using the vouchers to pay money to himself.

Where do your tips usually come from?

I usually don't get good tips until after I've done several stories on a subject. It's after you've done ten or fifteen stories about a subject that the real inside tipster knows that you are not looking to do a hit-and-run job, that you're really committed to getting to the bottom of something. Only then will he or she pick up the phone and call.

When I began writing about the nursing home scandal, I got a call from a woman who was a nurse at Brooklyn Jewish Hospital who asked me to come out and see her. The guy I was investigating, a man named Bergman, had two nursing homes, the Willoughby and the Oxford, both of which were near the hospital. I'd always been puzzled by the fact that if his homes were as bad as they seemed why was it that, compared to other nursing homes, far fewer elderly people died in his homes than anywhere else? This nurse, however, explained to me that the reason there was a low mortality rate in Bergman's nursing homes was that when elderly patients were about to die they were shipped out to Brooklyn Jewish Hospital. She would get them two days away from dying. She said these patients all suffered from what the staff came to call the "Bergman syndrome." It had three symptoms: malnutrition, dehydration and infected sores. He was getting rid of them so the records would show they died at the hospital and not at his nursing homes. That nurse, though, would never have called if I hadn't already written several articles and shown I was serious about going after this story.

Once you're onto a story, how do you get people to talk?

By knowing something. You can't find out something unless you know something. When I first started working on a story about corruption involving people trying to sell bus shelters to the City, I didn't know how the bidding process worked or how auditing was done. It was only by working long hours to saturate myself in the details and the language of the subject that the real experts started to respect my knowledge enough to want to talk to me. It's the same thing with the courts. It's only when you know the difference between a misdemeanor and a felony, when you can discuss law with lawyers, that they will finally open up. A lot of my sources tell me they don't leak stories to daily reporters because they're afraid the nuances of what they say won't be understood. They're afraid that out of sheer ignorance the reporters will harm them or make them look foolish.

What's the cardinal principle to follow as an investigative reporter?

To be fair, I pride myself on respecting the civil liberties of the people I write about. I always keep in mind the fact that I might be wrong, that they might be innocent. There are a lot of stories I've not written because I felt it would be unfair. A few weeks after I did the first Ten Worst Judges articles, a detective in the Brooklyn DA's office called me up and said he had arrested a middle-level Mafia person the night before, and when he searched the guy he found in his pocket the unlisted number to the private chamber of one of the judges on my ten-worst list. I met with the detective, and he gave me the number, and it was the one to the judge's chamber. Now something like this would certainly not look good if it came out in print, and it would have helped my ten-worst story. But what did it really prove? That the judge knew a hoodlum? Maybe the Mafia guy got the number from the judge's law secretary. Maybe it was an innocent relationship. I ended up not doing anything with the story because even though I personally was convinced the judge was crooked, nothing I had in my possession proved it.

Herman and Murray stayed on the story for ten weeks, working days, nights and weekends. They were lied to by the Marines and chased the story from Texas to California to Washington, D.C. In the end, they proved that what the uncle suspected was true—McClure had indeed been beaten to death, with a Marine pugil stick—and, in the process, they uncovered a scandal involving officers who falsified tests and references in order to fill their recruitment quotas with blatantly unqualified men. The story brought on a presidential inquiry and recommendations by Congress for basic training and recruitment reforms. It also brought the *Lufkin News* Pulitzer Prize for public service reporting.

Tips come most often to those investigative reporters who have demonstrated an interest in a particular field of news. When he was covering a nursing home scandal in New York City, Jack Newfield had already run several pieces in the *Village Voice* detailing the wretched conditions in which elderly people were being forced to live. One of the nursing home owners tried to refute Newfield's account by saying that conditions at his home couldn't be as bad as Newfield said they were because, compared to other establishments, his had had a very low death rate among patients. After that story appeared, Newfield got a call from a nurse who worked at a hospital near one of the nursing homes in question. The reason it had a low death rate, she said, was that the owner shipped dying patients to the hospital so their deaths would not appear on his records. The tip, filled out with appropriate evidence, plugged an important hole in Newfield's account. And it helped send the nursing home owner to jail.

A *leak* consists of confidential information given to a reporter by someone on the inside. Leaks can be useful, but they're also dangerous. When presented with juicy information ask yourself: What is the *motive* behind this boon? Some people leak valuable information out of altruistic motives; others have motives less pure. The Congressional aide who tells you how his or her boss took bribes may be planning to defect to the congress member's opponent—using your smear of his or her former employer to impress the new boss. The friendly police detective who fills you in on an investigation may be trying to sustain a failing operation by getting it some favorable, if inaccurate, publicity. A leak or tip is the *beginning*, not the end, of an investigation.

Exploration

Investigative reporters gather information from paper and from people. Paper is less glamorous, but more efficient. Washington journalist I. F. Stone, whose *I. F. Stone's Weekly* was famous for its many revelations of duplicity and misconduct in government, never bothered to cultivate personal sources at all; he simply read government documents—stacks of them—kept extensive files and followed his instincts.

To learn what kind of records are available, get a copy of the United States Freedom of Information Act. Passed by Congress shortly after the Watergate scandals, it served to open certain government reports and operations to public scrutiny.

Many states have "Sunshine Laws," spelling out what governmental information must be available to the public. Carry a copy of the rules in your pocket and show it to officials who try to block your path. When the law clearly allows you access, don't take "No" for an answer. If necessary go to your editor and get the newspaper to institute court action to open a meeting or get you a document.

Although the law opens up the records, it does not show you how to find what you need. For this, cultivate the clerks and secretaries who work in government record rooms. If you treat them courteously, they will be happy to help out.

Among the documents useful to investigative reporters are *property records*, *audits*, *disclosure statements*, *license applications* and *business records*.

Property Records. Usually located in the city or town clerk's office, property records provide legal evidence of who owns what and how much tax they pay. To an investigative reporter, they contain four other important pieces of information: when the property was bought and from whom; how much was paid for it; how large a mortgage was needed to buy it; and how much interest was charged for the loan.

Warranty deeds are records of the transfer of property. In many states they are filed for every sale of buildings or land. They show the date of purchase and, in most instances, how much was paid for the property. Knowing when someone bought a tract is important in investigating zoning scandals like those we mentioned earlier. They also help to determine whether public officials are using inside knowledge to make money from land speculation—in documenting who made a killing and who got wiped out. Hearing a story from an anonymous tip, you can check warranty deeds to see if it's true.

Mortgage deeds record the amount of money someone was lent for the purchase of a piece of property. They can provide the key to stories involving shady relationships between local banks and public officials.

Where does the town keep its major bank accounts? These can run into millions of dollars, an extremely valuable account for any bank. Find out the name of the public official in charge of choosing which banks get the town's deposits. For any bank executive, that official is an important person to have as a friend. Look into how the bank might have induced the official to throw some business its way. Rarely would the payoff be an outright bribe. A more subtle arrangement would be to grant the official a home mortgage at interest rates below the going market value. Over the twenty or twenty-five year period of a mortgage, a single percentage point can run into tens of thousands of dollars. Another way would be to give the official a mortgage in an amount that exceeded the value of the official's house. Handing out such unsecured loans is an unjustifiable risk—unless, of course, the banker expects to get something in return.

Check into the background of the bank's board of directors as well. Which ones have ties to public officials or, indeed, are officials themselves? Influence over how a bank uses its assets is a powerful tool that more than one politician has used to forge a lucrative career.

One of the biggest property scandals in American history was unearthed in the early 1970s by two reporters for the *Philadelphia Inquirer*, James Steele and Donald Barlett. After spending two months poring over hundreds of warranty and mortgage deeds, Steele and Barlett found the schemes worked something like this: A real estate dealer would buy a dilapidated house in a slum neighborhood for $2500, then resell it to a poor family for $10,000. Because the house wasn't worth $10,000, no bank would give the family a mortgage. But the real estate dealer had a crooked friend who worked for the Federal Housing Administration. The FHA's job is to insure mortgages—that is, to guarantee to the bank or other mortgage lender to pay back the amount of the mortgage if the family defaults. The crooked FHA official, accordingly, would pledge on behalf of the federal government to insure the whole $10,000, whereupon the bank would agree to lend the family the money with which to buy the house from the crooked real estate dealer. The house was usually in such bad shape that it would start falling apart almost before the first mortgage payment came due. With no money to make repairs, the family ended up defaulting on the mortgage and abandoning the building. The bank then would go to the federal government to be reimbursed for the $10,000. The federal government got stuck with the house, which was worth only $2500 and which, in most cases, the city would have declared unfit for human habitation. The scheme was repeated in city after city across the country. By the time the press broke the story, the government had lost an estimated $200 million.

Audits. An audit is an accountant's investigation into the finances of a company or government agency to see if anyone is wasting or stealing money. The mayor's office might audit the city's Recreation Department to see whether its $100,000 summer youth employment grant went to hire poor teenagers, or went, instead, to hire the children of department officials.

Accountants can find at least something to criticize in almost any agency they investigate, so local officials are not always happy to release audits to the press. Investigative reporters therefore get to know the people at the government office in charge of doing audits and get someone to slip them a copy when the audit is completed.

Disclosure Statements. Federal, state and local governments operate under various disclosure laws designed to keep public officials honest. Some of these "ethics" laws require office holders to disclose their finances. Others require elected officials to list the names and contributions of donors to their election campaigns. Often the information released in those statements is kept purposely sketchy. An official who has shady connections, after all, is going to try to conceal that fact. But disclosure statements can provide ample clues to good stories. Going through an official's finances, for instance, check into the companies in which he or she has an interest. Do they do any government business? Is the official in a position to use political power to profit the company?

Financial statements can also be useful for what they *fail* to divulge. Did the lawyers who sit on the city's Parks Board fail to include the fact that one of their clients is the architect who designed the city's new playground? Did the chair of the School Board "forget" to disclose that he or she owns stock in a company that provides remedial reading materials to the town's elementary schools? If you can discover economic dealings that an official chose to omit from the statement, these might be worth investigating.

Examine the lists of campaign contributors. Some people give money to a candidate because they believe in his or her ideals. Others hope to get something in return. Large donors may be suppliers and contractors who regularly do business with the government. Some of them give money to both parties so that no matter who wins they're still in a position to ask for favors. Check into what work they've done for the city and how it might be connected with the candidate they're backing. Or wait and see what business gets thrown their way in the future.

To minimize influence peddling, campaign contribution laws often limit the amount of money one person can contribute to a political candidate or campaign. To circumvent the law, some large supporters split up their contributions among several donors, often by putting donations in the name of employees or relatives. Among the defendants in trials related to the Watergate scandal were companies and executives who had tried to mask their contributions in this manner. They also "laundered" their political donations—that is, they set up dummy accounts that would look as though they were part of the company's legitimate operations when in reality they were secretly being used to dispense cash to candidates.

Another form of contribution involves buying tickets for "testimonial" or "benefit" dinners for a candidate. These provide an advantage to large contributors in that dinner tickets or advertisements in printed programs for such dinners do not have to be reported under most campaign contribution laws. A donor can pick up several dozen tickets to a $100-a-plate supper and send friends to have a good meal. The only person who need know about such a donation is the candidate getting the money. Investigative reporters who cover politics attend these dinners not only to make contacts but also to observe whose money is supporting the guest of honor.

License Applications.   License applications and registrations are easy-to-obtain public records often overlooked by politicians seeking to hide evidence of sudden wealth. A $50,000 cabin cruiser is not a possession that an $18,000-a-year Building Department inspector would like to brag about. Such a vessel, however, must be registered with the state, and the name of the owner, or the owner's spouse, will be on the application.

Business Records.   Business dealings can be delicate and complicated, and companies go to considerable trouble to keep their operations confidential—especially if they're doing something illegal. But a good reporter can find out a lot about people's business connections simply by knowing where to look.

All companies file a DBA, or "doing business as," form, which lists the owners, with the government. Corporations must register their officers with the state; in some states, they must also list the names of their stockholders. A directory exists from which you can learn the names of a lawyer's big clients or find who has secretly purchased stock in a company through someone else. Banks, insurance companies and public utilities are regulated by state commissions and must file detailed documents on their operations. Other businesses are watched over by government agencies because their manufacturing processes pose threats to the environment or expose workers to occupational dangers. Staffers and researchers at these agencies will usually point out to reporters what kinds of records are available.

To learn how companies are run, study one or two basic business and accounting texts. Write for a copy of a pamphlet called "How to Read a Financial Report," put out by the stock brokerage firm Merrill, Lynch, Pierce, Fenner & Smith in New York City. Get to know professors of business law at the state university.

In short, paper is important in exploring a story. But so are people. The relationship between an investigative reporter and a source usually involves a degree of personal trust. Investigative reporter Nicholas Gage, who specializes in covering the Mafia, may see a source socially dozens of times before asking for help on a story. "A source," he says, "won't trust you unless you're close to him."

Some of the most talkative sources are people who have been hurt by the developments that make up a story—an employee who was fired, an underling who was treated unfairly, a businessperson who lost a contract because he or she lacked political connections. In 1973, Joel Weisman of the *Chicago Sun-Times* noticed that the city had just switched its $1.5 million airport insurance contract to a new agency. Knowing that under Mayor Richard C. Daley nothing like this would happen without a reason, Weisman checked into the switch. The first person he called was the agent who had just lost the $1.5 million worth of business. From him, Weisman learned that the new firm had acquired a partner with influence at City Hall: The partner turned out to be Mayor Daley's 25-year-old son, who, Weisman found, had been given a license to sell insurance despite having dismally failed the state insurance examination. Confronted with a blatant case of nepotism, Daley nevertheless fended off the story with bravado. "Any father that wouldn't help his children in a legitimate legal way," he said, "isn't much of a father."

Reporters sometimes get information by exploiting antagonisms between groups. Politicians like to gossip about their opposition, union officials may be willing to talk about a factory that is violating safety standards and college professors can be relied upon to provide criticism, some of it informative, of college administrators. Investigating a corrupt union boss on the Brooklyn waterfront, Jack Newfield got help from an official in the same union who was trying to clean up its corruption. The rival had gone through the boss's trash can one day and discovered a letter from the man's daughter chiding her father for stealing money from the union pension fund. Newfield ran the letter as part of his expose.

Other sources include the members of pressure groups, good government associations, consumer coalitions and private agencies formed to promote causes they feel are in the public interest. These organizations spend time and money gathering information, and they have a decided interest in helping reporters on stories that will bolster their causes. They exist in almost every line of endeavor, from groups promoting prison reform and safer working conditions in factories to those that want to fight welfare cuts. In New York City the Citizens Budget Commission watches out for fiscal finagling in city government. In Chicago, the Better Government Association investigates corruption and reports what it finds. Ralph Nader's Public Interest Research Group has branches in many states and is eager to assist reporters gathering material on consumer issues.

Confrontation

The last stage in reporting many investigative stories consists of confronting the people under investigation. The objective of this meeting depends upon the nature of the story and how much a reporter has learned beforehand. Sometimes the journalist lacks essential material and hopes to fill in the missing pieces. Ideally, the reporter already has enough information to write the whole account and is only giving the person a chance to tell his or her side.

Such a confrontation can be dramatic. While working on a book about his experiences during the McCarthy period of the early 1950s when America was gripped by the fear that communist agents were infiltrating the government, Penn Kimball, a professor at the Columbia University Graduate School of Journalism, employed the Freedom of Information Act to secure copies of the file kept on him by the FBI. Much to his amazement, he found that people he had worked with at *Time* magazine and *The New York Times* had accused him

In theory, public officials are to make themselves available to the press, but in practice they often try to evade reporters if they fear an unfavorable story. © 1978 G. B. Trudeau. (Reprinted with permission of Universal Press Syndicate. All rights reserved.)

behind his back of being a "communist" or "pro-communist." The accusation, which he had never been given an opportunity to refute, led to his classification as a "security risk" and prevented him from getting a job he wanted in the State Department.

The names of his accusers were inked out in the FBI report, but a few remained identifiable nonetheless. Kimball called these individuals one by one and proposed reunion lunches to talk over the good old days. Each lunch progressed cheerfully, until over coffee he pulled out a copy of the FBI report and handed it across the table. Without saying a word, he stared at his accusers as they read it.

Their reactions varied. One stammered that the FBI interviewers had gotten his remarks twisted. Another denied outright that he had talked to the FBI, despite the file. In one case, the person started shaking violently and had to leave the table.

Confrontation interviews seldom need come to such dramatic conclusions. Generally, reporters should stay calm, asking questions in a neutral way and avoiding an accusatory tone. If made to feel guilty, the subjects of investigations may tend to act defensive, clam up, get angry. Dealt with coolly, interviewees may not appreciate the import of what they are saying. In 1973 Brenda Pavlik, a reporter for the *Fort Worth Telegram* in Texas, was investigating shoddy treatment of Vietnam veterans at the local Veterans Administration Hospital—in particular, the practice of releasing psychiatric patients after providing them little or no therapy. Through the help of a psychiatrist who was upset about the situation, Pavlik obtained case histories of the abuses that included stories of early releases who had later committed suicide. In confronting the director of the hospital, Pavlik asked her questions in such a casual, almost sympathetic manner that he readily admitted to most of the practices. When her story appeared, the director was promptly fired.

Another reason to stay cool is that it can help you control your tone of voice. If your tone is persecuting, rude or abusive, that fact might later be used as evidence that you had made up your mind before giving the person a chance to explain—that you acted out of malice rather than in a spirit of objective journalism.

WHO'S AT FAULT?

In some investigative stories it's easy to spot the bad guy. If contractors pay off a city inspector so they can charge for putting down twice as much asphalt in the new City Hall parking lot as they actually did, both the contractors and the inspector deserve all the bad press they get. But in other instances, guilt is not so easily assigned. Some years ago, New York City passed a law known as the J-51 provision of the property tax code. It said that landlords who renovated rundown buildings could get a 90 percent tax abatement for ten years on the cost of improving the building. The law was intended to upgrade deteriorating neighborhoods, largely in Manhattan, but it had an unpleasant side effect: Landlords not only began upgrading their buildings, but they zealously started kicking out poor tenants as well, turning their apartments into high-rent dwellings for the middle and upper-middle classes. If the poor people—often the elderly and the infirm—refused to go, the landlords hired "building cleaners" to get them out, by means of threats, intimidation and, in at least one case, murder.

Several crusading reporters wrote stories that pilloried the more repulsive slumlords. But the property owners weren't the only ones responsible: There was the mayor, who put off trying to change the law lest real estate interests stop contributing to his reelection campaign. There were also the new tenants, who snapped up the apartments as quickly as they became available, with scant thought as to what had happened to the previous tenants.

In their zeal to pin the blame on someone whom readers will find it easy to dislike, investigative reporters should reserve space to remind us that sometimes we're all a little at fault. Investigative reporting is about the society we live in, not just individuals.

SUMMARY

Investigative reporters search out news that would ordinarily stay hidden from view. Whereas general assignment reporters do investigative work occasionally, investigative reporters spend all their time digging.

Most investigations involve rooting out consumer fraud, bungling and corruption among corporate and public officials. Covering them usually involves three stages—a *clue* that there *is* a story, *exploration* of it and *confrontation* with those responsible.

Exploration usually involves a search for public records. These include property deals, audits of public agencies, disclosure statements and general government and business records. The second step of exploration is to find people willing to talk. The final stage, confrontation with the people under investigation, ideally should come only after the reporter already has enough information to write a complete story, for the purpose of offering the person a chance to tell his or her side.

Investigative reporters must beware of scapegoating. Real events seldom are a simple matter of heroes and villains.

PART V   Journalism in the Society

Learning has brought disobedience and heresy into the world; and printing has divulged them and libels against the government.

Official in the Government of Virginia, 1671

Were it left to me to decide whether we should have a government without newspapers, or newspapers without a government, I should not hesitate a moment to prefer the latter. . . .

Thomas Jefferson

16

FREEDOM OF THE PRESS

The First Amendment of the United States Constitution says that "Congress shall make no law . . . abridging the freedom of speech, or of the press. . . ." To the extent that they are put into practice, these words free journalists to report the news as they see fit, without constraint by the government. The tradition of a free press sets the United States apart from totalitarian nations, where the news is subject to censorship and where journalists whose stories offend the government are punished or banished.

And yet, although millions of words have been written by judges, journalists and scholars trying to interpret the words of the First Amendment, there is still no clear consensus as to exactly what is meant by "freedom of the press."

One interpretation holds that the First Amendment means exactly what it says—that there is to be *no* law abridging a free press, that anyone is free to write and publish whatever he or she wishes, without any government interference whatsoever. This was the opinion sometimes enuciated by Supreme Court Justice Hugo Black. Asked to explain the First Amendment, Black simply quoted the words of the Constitution: "Congress shall make *no* law. . . ."

But, in practice, legislatures have imposed, and courts upheld, some limits to press freedom. As legal scholar Ronald Dworkin notes, "It has always been possible for people to sue one another in American courts for libel and slander, for example, and even the most famous defenders of free speech have conceded that no one has a constitutional right to cry 'fire' in a crowded theater or publish troop movements in time of war." Even Thomas Jefferson's first draft of the

First Amendment would have limited its protection to those who publish the truth.

What, then, does freedom of the press mean for the working journalist today? For one thing, it means that journalists are free to report the news, and to decide for themselves what the news *is*. Government officials in Washington, unlike those in Moscow and Beijing, can neither tell the press which stories to cover nor legally penalize journalists whose work offends them.

If freedom of the press means that journalists can print the news as they see fit, then it must mean also that they are free to *gather* the news. As the Justice Department noted in a set of guidelines, "Freedom of the press can be no broader than the freedom of reporters to investigate and report."

The First Amendment applies not just to professional journalists, but to everybody—to the pamphleteer toiling over a mimeograph machine as much as to the editor of *Newsweek*. And the First Amendment figures in nonjournalistic questions as well—questions such as whether comedians ought to be allowed to utter "indecent" words on television, or whether professors sympathetic to communism ought to be allowed to teach in public universities, or whether ex-CIA agents ought to publish books detailing their intelligence careers. But in this chapter we stick to journalism. We examine six of the most problematical areas of press freedom: *News gathering*; *free press and fair trial*; *confidentiality of news sources*; *national security issues*; *illegal and extralegal curbs on press freedom*; and *broadcast news and the First Amendment*.

NEWS GATHERING

Press freedom is meaningful for journalists only if they are free to gather, as well as to report, the news. But just how far does the right to report extend?

Certainly, reporters can go anywhere the general public can go. But how much further? Surely *not* into private homes (see Chapter 17 on the right of privacy) nor into private meetings. Military bases can be declared off limits to the press. So, evidently, can prisons: The Supreme Court held, in *Saxbe v. The Washington Post Co.* (1974), that the press has no constitutional right to interview prisoners.

In government, the picture is mixed. Federal and state "freedom of information" acts guarantee the press access to many sorts of government proceedings and records. The courts have held that these laws permit reporters to see the names of corporation stockholders and of landlords receiving federal rent subsidies, to copy audio and videotapes entered into evidence in a trial, to attend budget discussions at the Nuclear Regulatory Commission and to witness the deliberations of search committees looking for new deans in state universities. But they have also ruled that a reporter could *not* see Justice Department files concerning the death of Karen Silkwood, who was killed in a car crash on her way to give a newspaper reporter documents she said would reveal misconduct by a plutonium processor. And Congress has barred reporters from many committee meetings. As Supreme Court Justice William Brennan writes, "An assertion of the prerogative to gather information must . . . be assayed by considering the information sought and the opposing interests invaded."

Military actions often present First Amendment problems. When United States troops invaded the island of Grenada on October 25, 1983, reporters were barred from the island until the third day of fighting, when the battle was all but over. In the meantime, the public learned what went on only through government channels. In the resulting uproar, a Pentagon committee composed of journalists and military officers decided that a pool of broadcast and print reporters would be allowed on the front lines in future military actions.

Wherever the law permits access by one reporter, it permits access by all. In theory, public officials cannot pick and choose among reporters, admitting those they like and barring those they don't. In practice, they sometimes try to do so, as when Hunter S. Thompson of *Rolling Stone* magazine was barred from obtaining White House press credentials in the Nixon years. If there is "pool" coverage, as when a single reporter is invited to ride with the president in his cabin aboard Air Force One, the pool must be selected from among all concerned journalists. Ted Turner's Cable News Network won this point of law when the White House persisted in selecting pool TV correspondents from among only the three major networks.

FREE PRESS AND FAIR TRIAL

American trials traditionally have been open to the public. Our country's founders felt so strongly about this that they built their courthouses without doors, to ensure that the public could not be locked out. Because the role of journalists is to act as the eyes and ears of the public, it follows that journalists, too, are free to attend trials and report what happens there.

The main reason for open trials is to protect the rights of defendants. "The press does not simply publish information about trials," write Donald Gillmor and Jerome Barron in *Mass Communication Law*; it "guards against the miscarriage of justice by subjecting the police, prosecutors, and judicial processes to extensive public scrutiny and criticism."

But a defendant's Sixth Amendment right to a fair trial can suffer if the press publishes incriminating material that prejudices (the word *means* prejudge) potential jurors. The reality of this danger has been substantiated under controlled conditions: In a University of Chicago study, two groups of jurors were shown identical videotapes of a mock trial. One group read prejudicial news clippings about the case before viewing the tape; of these jurors, 72 percent voted guilty. Among the jurors who had not seen the news clippings, only 44 percent voted guilty.

Strict rules of evidence determine what jurors get to hear in court. Jurors are not, for instance, permitted to consider rumor or hearsay in arriving at a verdict. But the press is free to report rumors and innuendo as well as fact, or even to print editorials suggesting that the accused is guilty. Faced with prejudicial material in the press, a judge who tries a case in court has three choices:

1. The judge can admit to the jury people who have been read the press reports but who say that they will not be swayed by it in reaching a verdict. The trouble with this approach is that a prospective juror's claim to be unprejudiced cannot necessarily be trusted. Some appellate judges have thrown out verdicts reached by a jury that was exposed to potentially prejudicial news reports either before or during the trial, even though the jurors insisted that they had not been influenced by the reports.

2. The judge can exclude from the jury anyone who admits to having read or heard news reports concerning the case. The trouble with this approach is that it tends to limit the jury to those so uninformed and ignorant that they neither read newspapers nor listen to news broadcasts. In *Roughing It*, Mark Twain assailed the exclusion principle this way:

> A minister, intelligent, esteemed, and greatly respected; a merchant of high character and known probity; a mining superintendent of intelligence and unblemished reputation; a quartz-mill owner of excellent standing, were all . . . set aside. Each said the public talk and the newspaper reports had not so biased his mind but that sworn testimony would overthrow his previously formed opinions and enable him to render a verdict without prejudice and in accordance with the facts. But of course such men could not be trusted with the case. Ignoramuses alone could mete out unsullied justice.
>
> When the preemptory challenges were all exhausted, a jury of 12 men were impaneled—a jury who swore they had neither heard, read, talked about, nor expressed an opinion concerning a murder which the very cattle in the corrals, the Indians in the sage-brush, and the stones in the streets were cognizant of! It was a jury composed of two desperados, two low beer-house politicians, three barkeeps, two ranchmen who could not read, and three dull, stupid, human donkeys! . . . The jury system puts a ban upon intelligence and honesty, and a premium upon ignorance, stupidity, and perjury.

3. A third option open to the judge is to grant a motion to try the case somewhere else, away from the glare of publicity. But this remedy is to no avail if the case has received national publicity. Lee Harvey Oswald was so widely described as John Kennedy's assassin that it seems unlikely that he could have received a fair trial anywhere in the United States. (Indeed, it was for the convenience of the press that Oswald was being transferred from the city to the county jail when he was shot and killed by Jack Ruby.) Bruno Hauptmann, on trial for the Lindbergh baby's kidnapping, was described in the national press as "a thing lacking human characteristics" and was slandered in such headlines as:

BRUNO GUILTY, BUT HAD AID, VERDICT OF MAN IN STREET

Due in part to the prejudicial publicity that surrounded the Lindbergh trial, Hauptmann's conviction remains the subject of lively debate even today.

The archetypal case of prejudicial pretrial publicity was the trial of Dr. Samuel Sheppard, who was convicted of murdering his wife. Sheppard's account of the murder—he said an intruder had committed the murder—aroused the skepticism of the journalists, many of whom wrote slanted stories that as much as convicted him in print. Even before the trial, while police were still investigating the murder, the *Cleveland Press* called for Sheppard's arrest in a page one editorial with the banner headline:

WHY ISN'T SAM SHEPPARD IN JAIL?

A coroner's hearing in the case was jammed with reporters and was broadcast live on radio. The newspapers published the names and addresses of all seventy-five prospective jurors, who then received anonymous letters and phone calls from people urging them to declare "Dr. Sam" guilty. "If ever there was a trial by newspaper," said the federal judge who overturned the jury's guilty verdict, "this was a perfect example." Sheppard was convicted and spent ten years in prison before finally being granted a new trial; he was acquitted.

Frustrated in their efforts to hold fair trials under the glare of publicity, judges have increasingly turned to a fourth approach: limiting prejudicial publicity by limiting press coverage of pretrial legal proceedings altogether. In some cases, judges issue "gag orders" requiring that journalists covering pretrial proceedings not report on what they have seen. In others, reporters have been barred from pretrial proceedings altogether. In *Gannett* v. *De Pasquale* (1979), the Supreme Court ruled that court orders of this kind are justified, at least under some circumstances.

The problem is that in today's crowded courts upwards of 80 percent of criminal cases are settled by means of plea bargaining or other determinations before they ever get to trial. To exclude reporters from pretrial hearings in these cases is to exclude them from the entire judicial process. That's why the American Civil Liberties Union reacted to the *Gannett* decision by accusing the court of erecting "an iron curtain between the criminal process and the inquiring press."

Moreover, not every attempt to limit press coverage of hearings has clearly been justified by the risk of prejudicing jurors. Gag orders have been handed down in everything from a murder trial, in which nine prison inmate witnesses feared for their lives if their names were made public, to the proceedings in a paternity suit against comic Flip Wilson. Some gag orders have been sustained on appeal, others not. Confronted with widespread dissent over *Gannett*, the Supreme Court in *Richmond Newspapers* v. *Virginia* (1980) emphasized that "a presumption of openness inheres in the very nature of a criminal trial," and hinted at a more tolerant attitude toward the right of the press to report pretrial proceedings.

The right to cover a trial in open court remains well established, but the situation with regard to pretrial proceedings remains confused. Reporters who are barred from a hearing or who are told by a judge not to report something they have witnessed should call their editors promptly and explain the situation, so that attorneys can be consulted about how to proceed.

CONFIDENTIALITY OF NEWS SOURCES

Some of the most newsworthy stories originate with people who for one reason or another want their names kept out of the newspapers—like "deep throat," the unnamed source who aided Woodward and Bernstein in their Watergate investigations. Confidential sources show up in print via such "blind" attributions as, "A Quaalude addict, who asked that his name not be used, said . . ." or such generalized identifications as, "Sources close to the President said . . ." or such disguised identities as, "Billy Smith (not his real name) has been in and out of reform schools since age 12."

If concerned government officials demand to know where a reporter got certain information, the result can be a confrontation between press and government over the reporter's right to keep his or her sources confidential. Such confrontations are not new—a reporter for *The New York Times* was jailed for refusing to name his sources in 1857—but they have become more frequent since 1972. That was the year the Supreme Court ruled that journalists have no special right to refuse to answer questions before a grand jury, even if the jury demands that they name news sources to whom they have promised anonymity. The Court held that communications between journalists and their sources enjoy no legal privilege like the privilege that protects communications between lawyers and their clients or doctors and their patients. Reporters summoned to court and asked to disclose the names of confidential sources must answer or risk being jailed for contempt of court.

In the years following that decision, dozens of journalists were jailed for refusing to tell judges or grand juries how they had obtained information concerning matters of interest to the law. Other journalists—no one can be sure how many—passed up newsworthy stories rather than face the choice of betrayal or jail. In one instance, a Pulitzer Prize-winning reporter turned down an opportunity to write a book about the bombing of the United States Senate by a group of radicals who, though hiding from the authorities, had agreed to talk to him. Attorneys advised the reporter that he could write the book only if he were prepared either to reveal the names and whereabouts of his confidential sources or to face imprisonment. The book was never written. In legal language, the Supreme Court decision has had a "chilling effect" on the ability of journalists to gather information from people who fear having their names made public.

Many reporters are willing to reveal confidential sources if justice can be served in no other way—if, for instance, a man were on trial for murder and a reporter alone knew of evidence that would prove him innocent. But in a dismaying number of the confidential sources cases, public officials have seemed less interested in serving justice than in striking back at reporters who offended them. A Louisville reporter was called before a grand jury and told to reveal his sources for a news story he had written on the ready availability of hallucinogenic drugs in the community. When the reporter refused to divulge his sources, he was cited for contempt of court. Were the authorities really interested in cleaning up the drug traffic, he wondered, or were they trying to punish the reporter for publishing a story that had embarrassed them by revealing their inability to deal with the drug situation? To limit such abuses by federal authorities, the United States Department of Justice adopted a policy of issuing subpoenas to reporters only at the specific authorization of the attorney general.

Journalists have a common law privilege not to disclose the identity of confidential sources except when the material sought is essential to a fair trial or to fair administration of justice, but in practice, this can be a very limited privilege indeed. Grand juries may demand that journalists, like other citizens, appear before them and testify, as long as their questions are relevant to their legitimate business and they are acting in good faith. If a defendant in a criminal trial can show that he or she needs the information the journalist is concealing, the court can demand that the reporter provide it or go to jail for contempt. Parties to civil actions also can request confidential information from a journalist, and the courts will uphold their requests as long as the information sought could not be obtained from another source and is relevant to the case.

Legislatures in many states have passed "shield laws" to protect journalists against having to testify about confidential information in all but the most crucial cases. Some shield laws protect the identity of the confidential source but not of the information he or she provided; in practice, this means that a judge can demand to see all of a reporter's notes, tape recordings and so forth, from which the identity of a source might well be obtained by inference. Other shield laws do just the reverse: They tend to protect the confidentiality of the information, but not the identity of the source. Shield laws yield before the rights of defendants in criminal actions. A dramatic instance came in 1978, when *The New York Times* was fined $185,000, and its reporter Myron Farber was jailed, for refusing to turn over the notes and documents Farber had used in writing a series of stories that had led to the indictment of a New Jersey surgeon, on charges of murdering five of his patients by injecting them with curare. The surgeon, on trial for his life, maintained that he needed Farber's material to prepare an adequate defense. The surgeon was acquitted; Farber served forty days in jail before being pardoned.

Journalists sued for libel lose their shield law protection whenever they invoke the defenses of truth, fair comment, good faith or lack of malice, or when they assert that they obtained the information from a "usually reliable source." (You can't very well claim that a source was "usually reliable" unless you're prepared to identify the source.) Reporters who rely on the most popular libel defense, *The New York Times* rule (see Chapter 17), may be ordered to hand over notes, memoranda or other material that would constitute evidence of whether they were in malicious states of mind when they wrote the stories that produced the libels. A CBS producer involved in the "60 Minutes" television program actually spent *twenty-six days* answering questions from the attorneys of a man who was bringing a libel action against CBS, and the Supreme Court held that even this depth of inquiry was justified.

The *subpoena*—a document requiring someone to appear in court—is the means traditionally employed to call upon journalists to testify. But in recent years, *search warrants* have been increasingly used as well, a trend that poses a grave threat to freedom of the press. A subpoena can be contested in court before a journalist need surrender film or documents. But police armed with a search warrant can burst in and seize documents, photographs or other material before any appeal is possible.

And they have. A printer in Palo Alto, California, was raided in 1971 by police seeking photographs taken by a college newspaper, the *Stanford Daily*, of a violent demonstration in which nine police officers had been injured. Sixteen similar searches took place in the following ten years. Film clips were seized by police in television studios in San Francisco, Providence, Boise and Dubuque. Police brandishing a search warrant invaded an Associated Press bureau in Helena, Montana, and threatened to break into a reporter's locked desk to obtain a tape recording and notes of a telephone conversation between the reporter and a suspected murderer. In 1978 the Supreme Court upheld such searches, even in cases in which no journalist on the premises had refused to heed a subpoena, and none was suspected of committing any crime.

What troubles journalists most about these developments—even more than the prospect that police officers may come crashing into the newsroom at any time—is that, by making everything reporters learn available to law enforcement agents, they make reporters look like cops themselves. "The decision makes newspapers an arm of the prosecution," said Anthony Day of the American Society of Newspaper Editors. Moreover, subpoenas and search warrants can be used by public officials to thwart investigative journalists who dig too deep. Wilbur Landrey of the St. Petersburg, Florida, *Times* remarked that had it been in effect a few years earlier, President Nixon "easily could have gotten a court order to raid *The New York Times* when it was working with all the Pentagon Papers."

Mindful of these potential abuses, legislatures in many states have enacted laws to limit newspaper searches. And, in 1980, a federal statute signed by President Jimmy Carter sharply limited the circumstances under which police could search newsrooms without first seeking a subpoena.

One effect of the decrease in protection for reporters' confidentiality has been that lawyers are more often consulted by newspaper editors and broadcast news producers. Previously, the rule of thumb, as one broadcast newsman recalled, was "not to call in the company lawyers, because they always say 'no.'" Another effect is to wipe out valuable records: Reporters often destroy notes rather than risk their being seized or subpoenaed. And organizations of journalists, while seeking to institute appropriate state and federal laws limiting subpoenas and searches, worry that such laws may in the long run tend to further erode freedom of the press—because what legislatures give, legislatures can take away.

NATIONAL SECURITY ISSUES

The term "national security" is sufficiently vague that parties on opposite sides of a First Amendment dispute can maintain their devotion to it with equal conviction. The publishers of *The Washington Post*, *The New York Times* and *The*

Boston Globe felt that they were acting in the interest of national security when they published the Pentagon Papers, a secret government study that revealed that the administration had concealed from the American public how badly the war in Vietnam was going: Didn't the public have the right to know the truth about this tragic war? But national security was also on the minds of at least some of the administration officials who tried to prevent the Pentagon Papers from being published: Didn't the public have a right to expect that classified documents would be kept secret? And, of course, motives on both sides may be less laudatory. An editor may publish sensitive information just to get a scoop, without much thought about what is good for the country, and government officials may seek to suppress information not because its publication would endanger national security but merely because it threatens to embarrass them.

When newspapers acquire information that the government feels they ought not to print, the government can react in a variety of ways. One course of action is simply to ask the journalists to voluntarily withhold the information. Many publishers have agreed to such requests. In some cases, their restraint clearly served the public interest. In 1986 CBS and ABC news knew in advance of an American bombing raid on Libya, carried out in reprisal for Libyan-backed terrorist attacks abroad. Both networks kept quiet about it, lest they endanger American pilots. Similarly, advance word of a raid by United States troops on a Bolivian cocaine operation reached the *Los Angeles Times*, *The New York Times*, *The Washington Post* and NBC News, and none ran the story until the raid was over. And, on the afternoon of October 18, 1977, all the news media complied when Reuters and the French Press Agency asked their clients to embargo news that West German commandos had just landed at Mogadishu Airport in Somalia to rescue eighty-six hostages aboard a Lufthansa jet airliner being held by hijackers who had killed the plane's pilot. The CBS radio network said it had withheld the news out of a concern for "human decency." The executive producer of the NBC Nightly News withheld the story, saying, "I really don't care what other people do—I just wouldn't do it." Security intact, the commandos stormed the aircraft, killing the hijackers and rescuing the passengers.

But on other occasions, it has been more questionable whether journalists performed a public service by withholding information at the government's request. For example, *The New York Times* learned from its reporter Tad Szulc in 1961 that anti-Castro troops trained by the Central Intelligence Agency were soon to invade Cuba. Months earlier, *The Miami Herald* and several other publications had learned of the invasion plans, but had withheld the news at the request of administration officials. The *Times* did the same, after its publisher, Orvil Dreyfoos, talked by telephone with President John F. Kennedy. The invasion failed, with great loss of life. Kennedy later mused that the nation might have been better off had the *Times* gone ahead and printed the story. Many journalists agreed. From whom, they asked, had the invasion been kept secret? If one reporter had been able to learn of it in the course of a few days of stalking around Miami, wasn't it likely that Castro too had known about the operation in advance?

Another case of cooperation between journalists and the government involved an attempt by the CIA to raise a sunken Soviet submarine from the floor of the Pacific in order to recover its nuclear warheads, code books and other materials of interest to the American intelligence community. Editors of several of the nation's leading newspapers got wind of the enterprise after the salvage had been attempted, but agreed not to print the story. CIA Director William Colby told them that his men had failed to raise the submarine but might succeed on a second try. This follow-up mission, he argued, would have to be scrapped in the face of Soviet outrage if the story were made public. Consider the subtleties of the situation: The Soviet government must have known something was going on; its surveillance satellites would have observed a strange ship hovering for days in midocean at a site distinguished solely by the fact that a Soviet submarine had sunk here. Nonetheless, journalists were being asked to keep secret a major CIA operation (it cost $350 million) because to print the story might offend not the American people, not the United States government, but the Soviets.

Ultimately, the story was broken by syndicated columnist Jack Anderson, who noted nevertheless that he had sometimes "withheld other stories at the behest of the CIA." That wasn't the end of the affair, however. Months later, reports circulated that the original CIA mission had not failed, as the newspaper publishers had been told, but instead had succeeded brilliantly, netting valuable secret Soviet defense information. If these reports were true, the CIA was engaged in an elaborate effort to leak a false cover story—that the mission had failed to raise the sub—which the CIA director sought to make seem more plausible by exerting himself to keep the false story out of the newspapers. His motive would have been that defense secrets are most valuable when your adversaries don't know you have them, for in their ignorance they may then fail to take countermeasures like altering the codes.

Sometimes government agencies intentionally leak inaccurate information. In 1986, White House officials hoping to weaken the political power of Libyan leader Muammar el-Qaddafi planted false news stories indicating that they were considering a military invasion of Libya. When the deception came to light Bernard Kalb, chief spokesperson for the State Department, resigned in protest against the use of such "disinformation" tactics by the Reagan administration. The American Society of Newspaper Editors declared, in a telegram to the White House, that "this calculated technique of falsehood, commonly employed by totalitarian governments as an instrument of policy, is repugnant to American democratic principles and destructive of the role of the press in a free society."

Among the most dangerous forms of government interference with freedom of the press are intelligence agencies' recruitment of reporters as agents and their placing of agents in journalists' jobs. The CIA is estimated to have paid the salaries of thirty to fifty American journalists and as many as 800 foreign journalists from the end of World War II through the 1970s and to have subsidized more than fifty newspapers, news services, radio stations and magazines at home and abroad. Through these and other conduits, the CIA disseminated scores of distorted or fabricated news items. On one occasion, CIA officers concocted thirty-four paragraphs of text that attributed to Soviet Premier Nikita Khrushchev, and then grafted the paragraphs onto the end of the transcript of a genuine Khrushchev speech. The CIA distributed the falsified speech to the European press, who unwittingly reported the speech as genuine.

The Federal Bureau of Investigation has also recruited reporters—to inform upon the activities of groups and individuals it considered subversive. Cooperative reporters handed over copies of their notes to the FBI; one reporter, covering a conference of the Students for a Democratic Society, an antiwar group that was under FBI investigation, filed no story for her newspaper, but wrote a fifty-page report for the FBI.

The damage done to objective journalism by actions like these is not difficult to discern: If it is known that a few reporters secretly work for intelligence agencies, then every reporter becomes suspect. If a few inaccurate stories are planted in the press by government officials, then every story becomes suspect. The result is a press that may still be free in theory, but that has been hampered in its ability to gather the news and that is thus at least partially discredited in the eyes of its readers.

In addition, government officials on the highest levels sometimes try to counter unfavorable news coverage by taking direct action against journalists. In 1986 former CIA Director William Casey threatened to prosecute *Time*, *Newsweek* and two newspapers under a thirty-five-year-old law for publishing sensitive information about an espionage case, and President Ronald Reagan telephoned Katharine Graham, owner of *The Washington Post*, to say he would support prosecution unless the newspaper complied. President Kennedy, angered over network news reports critical of his handling of a conflict with big steel companies who sought to raise prices, tried to have the Federal Communications Commission threaten network executives with revocation of the licenses of their television stations. The FCC director took no immediate action, and Kennedy cooled off and changed his mind by the next morning. President Johnson castigated reporters who filed stories critical of the Vietnam War, even accusing a few of treason. When a *Time* magazine reporter cabled to New York an accurate report that the White House was planning to raise the number of troops in Vietnam to over 500,000 in 1965, Johnson managed to keep the news out of print by ridiculing the idea to *Time* executives, calling it "sheer insanity." President Nixon, too, became enraged by what he called the "outrageous, vicious, distorted reporting" of the television networks. Working behind the scenes, he sought Internal Revenue audits of the tax returns of journalists critical of his administration and instituted antitrust action by the Justice Department against the major TV networks.

The government can further try to curb freedom of the press by suppressing news before it can be published. The legal term for this is "prior restraint." There have been two important cases of prior restraint in recent American history. The first was the case of the Pentagon Papers, 2.5 million words of information classified "top secret." None of the material in the Pentagon Papers threatened national security—as journalist David Halberstam wrote years later, there were no "secrets which if they got out might cause a ship to be sunk, a battalion to be wiped out, a weapons system to be invalidated"—but much of the contents of the Pentagon Papers was highly embarrassing to administration officials, especially to those who had themselves lied to the American people about the prosecution of the Vietnam War. When *The New York Times*, *The Washington Post*, *The Boston Globe* and other newspapers began printing excerpts from the Pentagon Papers, the Department of Justice obtained injunctions preventing them from publishing any more of the classified material. In an episode unprecedented in American history, the injunctions remained in effect for fifteen days, preventing journalists from printing news they wanted to print. The newspapers won, in a six to three Supreme Court decision, but the fact remained that the prior restraint had been exercised by the government with the sanction, if only a temporary sanction, of the highest court in the land. As columnist James Kilpatrick wrote, "Our side won, but it didn't win much."

A second case of prior restraint came in 1980, when *The Progressive*, a small (circulation 40,000) magazine in Madison, Wisconsin, notified the government that it was planning to publish an article titled "The H-Bomb Secret," containing a general description of how a hydrogen bomb is constructed. The article harbored no classified material. Its author had researched it entirely from sources available to the general public. His point was that if the secret of the H-bomb actually is no longer a secret, the government's purpose in classifying it is not to protect national security but instead to muzzle public debate on nuclear arms.

The Department of Justice, citing the 1954 Atomic Energy Act, promptly obtained an injunction prohibiting *The Progressive* from publishing the article. The injunction remained in effect for six months while the case wound its way through the courts. Eventually the Justice Department dropped the case and *The Progressive* published the piece. The magazine was left with legal bills of over $200,000. The government said it retained the right to ban publication of any nuclear information classified secret. So *The Progressive* case left unresolved the question of whether government officials can circumvent freedom of the press by declaring material "secret" without regard for whether such secrecy genuinely helps guard the security of the nation.

ILLEGAL AND EXTRALEGAL CURBS ON PRESS FREEDOM

Not all the forces that work to limit freedom of the press are as lawful as a subpoena or as overt as stamping a document "secret." Informal pressure can be brought to bear as well.

Often the pressure is financial. Philadelphia Mayor Frank Rizzo cancelled $500,000 in city advertising when the *Philadelphia Bulletin* refused to retract a report of alleged misconduct of his administration. A New York mayor reacted to a critical story in the *New York Post* by threatening to ban *Post* delivery trucks from the West Side Highway, which would delay shipment of the paper to newsstands. The mayor of Utica, New York, once became so enraged at newspaper coverage of his administration that he declared that the city's official records (which are paid for as advertising) would thereafter be published in the Syracuse newspaper, fifty miles away.

Most publishers try to resist such pressures, but few are so fortunate as to be entirely free from them. Publishers of a small-town newspaper that receives 10 percent of its advertising revenues from a single department store may think twice about authorizing an investigative story revealing that the store is a firetrap. Can't we just advise the management of the danger, they may ask, and let them fix it quietly? Pressure from advertisers aside, newspapers face practical limits, imposed by their budgets, upon how extensive their news coverage can be. Few can afford to hire all the reporters they need to cover all the news, and most tend to stay away from digging up news that might take too much time and money. Faced with these constraints, many editors—too many—fall into the habit of sticking with the easy news—covering fires and arrests and the proclamations of government officials—and seldom try to dig any deeper. In theory, these editors still enjoy freedom of the press, but in practice their freedom is of little more use to them than are open skies to birds who have forgotten how to fly.

Influential public officials frequently threaten or cajole the press. President Herbert Hoover, who felt that "only such news as is given out through the stated channels of the executive offices should be printed by the newspapers of the country," required that press conference questions be submitted twenty-four hours in advance; then he ignored the tough ones. One day, the White House reporters got together and all submitted one identical question; Hoover simply tore up the questions and talked about something else. Franklin Roosevelt, irritated by a United Press story, said to UP bureau chief Lyle Wilson, "For the President of the United States to have a feud with the United Press . . . wouldn't hurt me but it would hurt UP and it would hurt you." "That's right, Mr. President," Wilson replied, "It would hurt UP and it would hurt me. But what would hurt us even more is if word got around that you said to kill a story and we did it." Dwight Eisenhower ordered security investigations of reporters whose dispatches irritated him. Lyndon Johnson lied to the press so often that a couple of journalists finally got even by printing a joke that was making the rounds: "Do you know how to tell when Lyndon Johnson is not telling the truth? Well, when he goes like this"—finger beside nose—"he's telling the truth. When he goes like this"—pulling ear—"he's telling the truth. When he goes like this"—stroking chin—"he's telling the truth. But when he starts moving his lips, he's *not* telling the truth."

Social pressure, too, has been brought to bear against the press. A newspaper's job, said Hodding Carter Sr., publisher of the Greenville, Mississippi, *Delta-Democrat-Herald*, is to print the news and raise hell. Neither function is consistently popular. Journalists who reported the tragedy and futility of the Vietnam War risked being called disloyal. Southern reporters who called attention to racial injustice in the South in the early days of the Civil Rights movement faced censure in their homeland. Editorial writers who objected to the quota system in university hiring practices in the 1970s were accused of condoning racism and anti-Semitism.

Violence is the ultimate recourse of those who oppose a free press or feel threatened by its actions. On the average, journalists are the targets of violence somewhere in the world every few months. A number of reporters covering antiwar demonstrations in the 1960s were beaten by police who resented newspaper coverage that they perceived as sympathetic to the demonstrators.

BROADCAST NEWS AND THE FIRST AMENDMENT

When our country's founders convened to draft the Constitution, there were no radio or television networks. Consequently, the First Amendment deals with freedom of the *press*, but says nothing about freedom to broadcast.

Broadcast news does not, as yet, enjoy the full First Amendment protection afforded to print. Radio and television stations must be licensed by the government before they can legally transmit. Licensing originally was necessary in order to police the technical aspects of broadcasting, so that radio station frequencies didn't overlap one another or one station's signal overpower the others. But the government regulated more than the technical aspects of broadcasting. Two of its regulations pertinent to broadcast news—one recently repealed, the other still in effect—were the *equal time provision* and the *fairness doctrine*.

The *equal time provision* requires that political candidates be given "equal opportunities" to be seen and heard over each broadcasting station. If a TV station sells ten thirty-second spots to a congressional candidate, it cannot refuse to sell equal time to the opposing candidate. If the station stages an in-studio debate among the candidates, it must permit all legally qualified candidates to participate. But the equal time rule does *not* apply to newscasts, news interviews or news documentaries: Airing a thirty-second report on a Democrat's speech doesn't obligate the news director to send a crew scurrying over to do thirty seconds on the Republican candidate. Nor does it restrict coverage of debates staged outside the studio—which is why the networks can carry the League of Women Voters debates among the leading presidential candidates without having to include all the minority party candidates as well. But the equal time rule has produced some odd consequences. When Ronald Reagan was running in the 1980 presidential primaries, for instance, the FCC advised a television station in California that if it ran old Reagan movies it would have to make available equal time to his opponents.

The *fairness doctrine* held, in the words of Justice White, "that discussion of public issues be presented on broadcast stations, and that each side of those issues must be given fair coverage." The intent of the doctrine was to ensure that minority viewpoints are aired, rather than being suppressed by a few wealthy owners of radio and television stations. Broadcasters who failed to obey the fairness doctrine could be advised or ordered by the Federal Communications Commission to change their ways or lose their licenses when they come up for renewal. And, the doctrine was sometimes abused. When ABC News carried an interview with a man who said the CIA had ordered him to commit murder, the CIA filed a complaint with the FCC, alleging that ABC had violated the fairness doctrine, and ABC promptly withdrew the story. The FCC repealed the fairness doctrine in 1987.

Regulations like these leave broadcast journalists less free than their colleagues working in print. Anybody with access to a printing press can start a newspaper; no license is required. Newspapers don't have to provide fair coverage to all sides of a controversy, nor equal opportunities to be heard to all candidates. If a newspaper abuses its right, say by systematically slanting the news, the public may react against it, but the government has no power to regulate it.

The power of government over broadcasting becomes increasingly ominous as newspapers die out and television increasingly becomes the main source of news for most Americans. As NBC News correspondent Bill Monroe puts it, "This country is already on the road, without realizing it, to a dual system of mass media: a printed press that is free but shrinking and an electronic press that is growing but unfree."

The fairness doctrine, prior to its repeal in 1987, required that news documentaries present "all sides" of each issue—but the whole point of some of the best news documentaries is to make *one* point, a point worth making that hasn't received sufficient attention. CBS's "The Selling of the Pentagon" was by any standard one of the more thought-provoking documentaries ever aired, but it was roundly attacked by government officials who maintained that it violated the fairness doctrine. NBC's "Pensions: The Broken Promise" was applauded by the critics, but the FCC ruled that it failed "to give both sides," and NBC was ordered to "balance" it with a broadcast reporting that pension systems are "overwhelmingly successful."

Government regulation also makes broadcasters more vulnerable to informal administrative arm twisting, too—as when President Nixon, angered by network coverage of the Vietnam War, threatened television station owners with trouble at license-renewal time unless they pressured the networks to take a more favorable attitude toward his administration.

The growing prosperity of television stations, rather than strengthening their First Amendment rights, has had, if anything, the opposite affect. Many local TV stations are reluctant to air network news documentaries, which tend to garner lower ratings. And the more profitable network television becomes, the less inclined are its executives to emphasize controversial news. ABC-TV's broadcasts of the 1954 Army-McCarthy hearings alerted millions to McCarthy's demagoguery and marked an important step in the maturation of television journalism. But to televise the hearings today would cost each network tens of millions of dollars in advertising revenues, and that, as David Halberstam remarks, "is a higher price for democracy than most network executives would be willing to pay."

The chief rationale for government regulation of television and radio is that there are only a limited number of broadcast frequencies and that, therefore, the government must have some way of deciding who gets to use them. This rationale is weakening with the advent of cable and direct satellite TV, which have the potential to carry hundreds of channels, to "narrowcast" highly specialized programming and to establish computerized "two-way" television, by which viewers can instantly respond to and influence programming. It remains to be seen whether electronic technology, which gave birth to broadcasting, can eventually set it free.

SUMMARY

The First Amendment to the Constitution specifies that "Congress shall make no law . . . abridging freedom of speech, or of the press," but thousands of words have been written during the centuries since in an effort to determine what these simple words really mean. Most people agree that there must be some limitations on press freedom. Controversy centers on just what and how severe these limitations ought to be.

The right to report implies a right to *gather* the news. Generally, journalists cannot be excluded from proceedings open to the public, but they cannot enter private homes, military bases or prisons without permission. The federal Freedom of Information Act opens many public meetings and files to reporters (and to the public), and state "sunshine laws" make government more open to press scrutiny.

The Sixth Amendment right to a fair trial can collide with the First Amendment when excessive publicity threatens the rights of the accused by prejudicing jurors. Judges have been upheld in barring reporters from several sorts of pretrial hearings, a substantial limitation on freedom of the press because most criminal cases today are decided at the pretrial level.

Journalists have no constitutional privilege to keep their sources confidential, if the information is essential to a fair trial or to fair administration of justice. Many, in fact, have been jailed for contempt of court after refusing to testify about what they learned, or from whom, under a promise of confidentiality. Most states now have "shield laws" to protect journalists against having to reveal their sources, but the protection of these laws is far from absolute. When sued for libel, journalists waive their privilege of confidentiality and may have to testify and produce documents relating to their states of mind when the libels occurred. A still more menacing development has been the use of search warrants to obtain notes, photographs, tape recordings and other materials from newspaper and broadcasting newsrooms. The law continues to evolve, and journalists need to familiarize themselves with local legislation. They must also consult with lawyers to be clear about their rights.

"National security" concerns have sometimes impelled journalists to withhold sensitive information: On rare occasions the government has managed to impose "prior restraint," temporarily preventing journalists from publishing news the government wanted to keep secret. Some actions by the CIA and FBI, such as planting agents in reporters' jobs or recruiting reporters to pass along information, have tended to erode public confidence in the impartiality and reliability of the news media.

In addition to legal constraints, illegal and extralegal techniques also can hamper reporters in their work. Government officials sometimes try to penalize newspapers that have offended them by withdrawing government advertising or by using the police to harass them. People who disagree with what the press is doing may ostracize reporters, as did residents of some southern communities during the civil rights movement, or even resort to violence. And most publishers are limited in their exercise of press freedom every day by the limits of budgets, which seldom permit them to cover all the news.

As the number of newspapers decreases, the influence of radio and television news increases, but broadcasters enjoy less freedom than do print journalists. They are regulated by the government, and they must heed, among other regulations, the *equal time provision*, which requires that political candidates be given equal access to air time.

17

LIBEL AND PRIVACY

The law of libel is intended to redress those whose reputations have suffered unwarranted damage in print or broadcast. Privacy law affords a somewhat similar protection against unwarranted invasions of personal life. The law permits those who have been libeled or whose privacy has been violated to sue and, if the harm done them proves to be unjustified, to collect damages—money—from the person or organization that injured them. Libel poses by far a greater limitation on freedom of the press than does privacy, so we discuss libel first and then proceed to privacy.

LIBEL

Like most controversial areas of law, libel represents conflicting rights: the right of society to learn about the issues that concern it and the right of individuals to avoid being victimized by the press. Formulating universally applicable rules is made more difficult by the wide range of circumstances involved. The plaintiff in a libel action may be a saint or a Mafia boss; the defendant may be a newspaper as upstanding as *The Boston Globe* or as sleazy as the Hollywood scandal sheets that wildly brand movie stars as "lesbians" and "cocaine users."

A journalist's risk of being sued for libel is very real: Every year, American reporters, editors, publishers and broadcast producers are called upon to defend themselves against libel actions brought by plaintiffs asking for millions of dollars in damages. Working journalists therefore need to understand the libel laws.

311

If they don't, they may risk either losing costly libel suits out of ignorance of the law or, at the other extreme, being overly cautious and thereby reporting less than all the important news.

But what, exactly, is libel? Briefly, libel is anything published or broadcast that tends to seriously damage someone's reputation. If a newspaper reports that Jane Jones has been accused of theft, it has libeled Jones. If it quotes Bob Brown's secretary as saying he's "a bungling incompetent," it has libeled Brown. It is libelous to report that someone lied, was charged with a crime, suffers from AIDS, is addicted to heroin, has committed treason, has gone crazy or bankrupt. Such stories constitute libel even if the journalists who write them are only passing along information that they gained from another source. They may be libelous today even if they weren't yesterday: Once it was considered acceptable, even meritorious, to be an agent for the Central Intelligence Agency, but, following exposure of improper CIA activities, courts held that it could be libelous to call someone a CIA agent.

From this, you may have gotten the impression that newspapers and broadcasters libel people every day. That impression is correct; the news is full of libel. The question is whether a particular libel is *defensible*—that is, whether a newspaper or broadcaster being sued for libel has a proper defense. *Truth,* for instance, is a defense against having to pay libel damages: You can unconcernedly print libelous information as long as you are prepared to prove that it is true. Another absolute defense is *the privilege of reporting official proceedings*. This permits the publication of libelous information that emerges in the course of official business—such as trials, police investigations and legislative sessions. A third important defense is the *New York Times* rule. This limits the recourse to the libel laws afforded to "public figures" that is, people of public prominence.

When you have a piece of newsworthy information that makes somebody look bad, and are wondering whether it can safely be published, ask yourself these two questions: First: *Is it libelous*? If the answer is yes, then proceed to the second question: *Is it defensible*? If the answer to the second question is yes, you can feel free to publish. Let's look at these two questions more closely.

IS IT LIBEL?

Libel is a form of defamation. Defamation (to de-fame) means badly damaging someone's good name. The New York State Supreme Court described libel as involving "words which tend to expose one to public hatred, shame, obloquy, contumely, odium, contempt, ridicule, aversion, ostracism, degradation or disgrace, or to induce an evil opinion of one in the minds of right-thinking persons, and to deprive one of their confidence and friendly intercourse in society. . . ." The Alabama Supreme Court held that libel occurs "where the words published tend to injure a person libeled by them in his reputation, profession, trade or business, or charge him with indictable offense, or tend to put the individual into public contempt."

That's strong language: To constitute libel, a publication or broadcast must strike hard against a person's reputation. To write that a sheriff bribed voters to win an election is libel; to write that he has done a poor job as sheriff is probably not. To write, as did one student newspaper, that "sex, drugs and booze" are "staples of life" at a college does not libel the college; to write that the college administration condones and sanctions such activities does.

A crusading newspaper, *The American Press*, was sued for libel after it editorialized against a Lake Charles, Louisiana, attorney. Had the newspaper accused the lawyer of making mistakes in handing out financial advice, that would have been mere criticism, not libel. But the editorial went so far as to say that "No bond buyer would buy a nickel's worth of securities on [his] opinion." *That* went to the core of the lawyer's reputation, and he was awarded $150,000 in damages.

For libel to occur, the damaging material must have been made public. If you write a defamatory sentence on a piece of paper, fold it up and tuck it into your shoe, no libel has occurred. But once the words have been published or broadcast the libel laws apply, even if the means of publication is relatively inconspicuous. A tiny advertisement printed in the bottom corner of the last page of a newspaper distributed for free in a supermarket is just as published, in the eyes of the law, as is an editorial in *The Washington Post*. So is anything broadcast, even if murmured into a microphone at 3 o'clock in the morning on a radio station to which hardly anyone is listening. Newspapers have been held to have "published" information that they made public even if the item was never printed. The Alton, Illinois, *Telegraph*, for instance, was ordered to pay $9.2 million in damages to a building contractor who had been driven out of business as the result of a libelous memorandum that two *Telegraph* reporters had merely sent to a government investigator. (The award was reduced to $1.2 million after the *Telegraph* filed for bankruptcy.) Even an epitaph has been deemed a publication: So ruled the Maryland court that awarded $2000 in damages to Gloria Kovatch after her brother inscribed her father's tombstone with the words, "Stanley J. Gladsky, 1895–1977, abused, robbed and starved by his beloved daughter."

Individuals and corporations (which are considered individuals by law) can sue for libel. The dead, generally, cannot. "The dead have no rights and can suffer no wrongs," says an old legal dictum. But several states, among them New York and Pennsylvania, allow libel claims by the deceased to proceed if they were filed when the plaintiff was still alive.

Governments cannot sue for libel. A city, for example, can't sue a television network for broadcasting that it is a "deadly dumping ground" of chemical waste, nor can the federal government sue a pamphleteer who writes that the system is corrupt and should be replaced.

To suffer libel an individual must have been identified in the offending publication or broadcast—but this doesn't necessarily mean identified by name. All the plaintiff in a libel action need prove by way of identification is that some readers, even as few as one or two, were able to recognize him or her. When novelist Gwen Mitchell drew an unflattering portrait of a "nude marathon" psychologist in her book *Touching*, she and her publisher lost a $75,000 libel award to psychologist Paul Bindrim, who convinced a jury that at least a few readers could recognize him as the model for the book's protagonist, even though his name appeared nowhere in the book. *Penthouse* magazine lost a libel suit brought by a former Miss Wyoming over a short story it published detailing the sexual exploits of a fictitious Miss Wyoming who bore many resemblances to the real one—among them that both were baton twirlers who wore blue warm-up suits and blue chiffon dresses and had lived in Laramie. (The decision was reversed on appeal, but on other grounds.)

Mistaken identity is no defense. *The Washington Post* was held liable when it mistakenly identified an innocent District of Columbia attorney as an accused forger, who also was a lawyer. The two men shared the same first and last names but had different middle initials; the judge ruled that the *Post* took insufficient care to verify the forger's identity.

To sum up, libel is anything published or broadcast—either words or pictures—that tends to do serious harm to someone's reputation. It is libelous to write that someone is inept or incompetent; has been charged with or convicted of a crime; is a coward, a traitor or a liar; is unethical, dishonest, stupid or crazy. The libel laws apply to any published item, even if it is published only for a small audience. And they apply as long as any readers can tell who is being libeled, even if the person is not named or if he or she has been inadvertently named through a negligent mistake.

Much of the news tends to damage reputations, and so journalists asking themselves of a given story, "Is it libel?" often answer that question, "Yes." That in itself doesn't mean the item should not be published. It means that they must proceed to ask the second question: Is the libel legally defensible?

IS IT DEFENSIBLE?

The law permits libel when the public's need to know is viewed as more important than the sanctity of individual reputations. These sanctioned areas take the form of *absolute defenses* against libel suits. A defendant who can satisfy any *one* of these defenses need not pay libel damages. The most important libel defenses are *truth*, *privilege*, and the *New York Times rule*.

Truth

"Truth is defense against libel," as the old saying goes: You can feel free to print a libel if you can prove that it is true. Though supremely self-satisfying for journalists, the truth defense has its limitations, and any journalist who relies on it should be mindful of two cautionary points:

First, to qualify for the truth defense an item must not only be true to the reporter's satisfaction, it must be capable of being *proved* true in court. Suppose you are writing a story about a murder for which a suspect, Bob Smith, has been arrested and charged, and the police have three witnesses who say they saw Smith shoot down his victim in the town square at high noon. Can you write that Smith committed the murder? No. Instead, write that Smith was arrested and that he was charged with murder. That alone is what you know to be true—unless you were among those three eyewitnesses. Smith may be acquitted (stranger things have happened) or permitted to plead guilty to a reduced charge. If you were careless enough to have pronounced him guilty, he could turn around and sue you for libel, and the burden of proving the murder charge would then rest on your shoulders.

Demonstrating the truth of a libelous allegation to a judge or a jury can be an expensive and exhausting process. It took columnist Jack Anderson and his associate Britt Hume five years to prove the truth of their report that Edward Carey, an attorney for the United Mineworkers Union, had removed, from UMW headquarters in Washington, a box full of sensitive documents that he subsequently claimed had been stolen by burglars. (Carey had branded the report "a contemptible, despicable lie," and filed a libel action.) Anderson and Hume won, but how many such protracted legal battles does a journalist care to fight?

The other point to remember about the truth defense is that the defendant— that is, the journalist—assumes the burden of proving that the substance of the charge was true. *It is not sufficient merely to prove that you accurately quoted a libelous charge made by someone else.* You must be prepared to prove that the charge *itself* was true.

It's not difficult to understand why journalists must be held responsible for proving the accuracy of any libel they publish, regardless of its source. Otherwise, unscrupulous journalists could libel anyone they cared to, simply by quoting someone foolish or careless enough to utter the libel for them. An insane man may wander down Main Street shouting that his psychiatrist, Dr. Peterson, is a robot whose brain is controlled by communist secret agents, but this doesn't free the newspapers to libel the psychiatrist by printing a story headlined:

DR. PETERSON BRANDED "COMMUNIST" PSYCHIATRIST'S BRAIN UNDER MOSCOW'S CONTROL, LOCAL MAN ALLEGES

For this reason, the truth defense is of little help in covering a controversy when libelous charges are flying back and forth. A group of parents whose children attended a public school on the West Side of Manhattan alleged that the school principal had sexually molested several students. The principal was white and the parents black, a fact evident from the photographs published in the papers, and this gave some readers the impression that the protest was racially motivated. The parents, indignant at this development, demanded that the papers report the real nature of their charges. But the newspapers' lawyers advised that they could not do so. To charge someone with molesting children is about as libelous as anything one can print. If the papers were to publish such charges and the principal then sued for libel, it would not help the papers to point out that they were merely repeating the charge that originated with the parents. (*Accurately reporting a libelous charge made by someone else does not satisfy the truth defense.*) In order to print the charge, the newspapers would have had to be prepared to prove in court that the principal was actually guilty of the sexual crimes—and this they could not do.

Minor errors, however, do not defeat a truth defense. You can prevail if you wrote that Smith was convicted of arson in Kansas City, Missouri, when in fact it was Kansas City, Kansas, or that a juvenile was arrested when he or she was only detained for delinquency. But you must be able to show that the libel was "substantially true." The truth defense is like a blanket: It must be wide enough to cover the scope of the libel itself.

The Privilege of Reporting Official Proceedings

Everything that transpires during an official governmental proceeding can be reported without fear, even if the material involved is libelous, as long as the report is fair and substantially accurate. You can report, for example, that one legislator called another a "liar" during a session of the State Senate, or that witnesses in an arson trial said they saw the defendant set the fire. But what, exactly, is an official proceeding?

Arrests are official acts of a government body—the police department. It's libelous to report that someone has been arrested, because it damages his or her reputation to report that the police think he or she committed a crime, but arrests can be reported without worrying about the legal repercussions, thanks to the official proceedings defense.

Keep these points in mind when reporting arrests:

1. Be sure that the suspect actually has been arrested, not merely detained or brought in for questioning. A suspect who is being questioned has not necessarily been arrested. Nor has someone been arrested who is simply given a summons, such as a speeding ticket, and is then permitted to go about his or her business. An Associated Press reporter covering a murder investigation in New Jersey spotted two plainclothes detectives hustling a local mobster, in handcuffs, into the back door of the police precinct house. The reporter filed a story naming the man and saying he had been arrested. A few hours later, the man was released—having been questioned, but not arrested. The AP reporter was lucky to keep his job.

2. Remember that an arrest is not a conviction. A suspect is presumed innocent until proven guilty. You would write that the suspect was "arrested and charged with rape," not that the suspect was "arrested for committing rape." Nor would you say that the suspect is "an accused rapist." Both these choices of words have the effect of implying guilt, which is a matter for a judge or jury to decide.

3. Take care to be absolutely accurate in identifying those who have been arrested. If you make a mistake and name the wrong person, you may end up

having to pay libel damages. Check the spelling of names in the police blotter against the city directory or telephone book; police blotters are notoriously inaccurate. Include ages and addresses, or equivalent identification, for each person mentioned in the story. If you write that Bob Brown was arrested and charged with auto theft, you have in effect libeled everybody named Bob Brown. If you write that the suspect is Bob Brown, age 28, a mechanic who lives at 12 Greene Street, then you will be libeling only the particular Bob Brown whom police arrested, and you are protected by the official proceedings defense.

When doubt remains about the identity of someone libeled in a story, say so. Write, *"The suspect gave his name as* Robert Smith," or, *"Police identified* the suspect as Robert Smith," or, *"A room clerk at the motel said the man registered as* Robert Smith."

4. Attribute libelous information to its official source. Don't write, "Police found the marijuana in the trunk of Dubrinski's car after they pulled him over because of an expired license plate." Written that way, the report draws two conclusions—that police stopped the car out of innocent motives and that they actually found the drugs—neither of which you know for certain to be true. Instead, write, "Police *said* they found the marijuana in the trunk of Dubrinski's car after pulling him over because of an expired license plate." The habit of employing such attribution is fairer both to readers and to the individual who is being libeled; it sets forth how you came upon the damaging information.

5. An arrest involves an allegation by police that a suspect has committed a crime, and so the word "allegedly" is sometimes used in news stories to refer to the allegation of guilt. Writing "allegedly" reminds readers that the guilt has merely been alleged, not proven. But it does *not* exempt anyone from the libel laws. To write that Babcock "allegedly" murdered Scott is to libel Babcock. If carelessly phrased, "allegedly" may even fail to lighten the burden of assumed guilt. Do *not* write, "Smith, the alleged assailant." To write "alleged assailant" is to say that you think Smith is guilty of the crime: An alleged assailant is, presumably, an assailant, just as a white dog is a dog or a bald editor an editor. Instead, make it, "Smith allegedly assaulted Jones." In any case, there's nothing magical about the word "alleged." You remain answerable at law for the truth and fairness of your report.

Proceedings in open court are official proceedings—trials, for instance. You can report on trials without fear of reprisal under the libel laws—as long as you do so fairly and accurately. The official proceedings defense makes it possible for newspapers covering a murder trial to report one day that Smith testified that she saw Jones kill a man with an axe, then report the next day that Jones took the stand and called Smith a liar. Both charges are libelous, but both can be reported because they were uttered in a court session.

The privilege of reporting official proceedings applies to what goes on in open court. Not all judicial proceedings are covered by it. The secret proceedings of *grand juries* may not be privileged; if you publish a story revealing that a grand jury heard testimony that Brown trafficked in narcotics, you may lose a libel suit even if the grand jury did indeed hear such allegations. (Keeping unsubstantiated and defamatory charges from public view is the main reason why grand jury proceedings are secret.) *Pretrial pleadings* are not privileged in many states, either, to prevent allegations that may never reach trial from being publicized and harming the reputations of the presumably innocent. Neither are many documents associated with a trial—such as depositions—privileged, until they have been read in open court. Also unprotected by the official proceedings privilege are documents that the court has declared secret, such as sealed papers in divorce actions. The general rule is that the press, as a representative of the public, can report whatever the public is permitted to see. Far less often is the privilege extended to permit unfettered reporting of defamatory material that the public was meant *not* to see.

Executive actions are protected. This includes statements by presidents, governors, mayors and other governmental executives, as long as they made the statements in the course of performing their official duties. It was owing to this aspect of the official proceedings defense that newspapers could safely report President Nixon's inadvertent remark, made prior to Charles Manson's having been convicted, that Manson was "guilty directly or indirectly" of murder. The same applied to Chicago Police Chief O. W. Wilson's declaration that Richard Speck, arrested moments earlier, was the "killer" of eight nurses. But privilege may not attach to *secret* legislative proceedings or to proceedings of very low-level executive groups: A reporter who quotes a defamatory statement uttered by an unsalaried member of the local water control commission during its meeting in the back of Frank's Tavern probably cannot rely on the official proceedings defense.

Proceedings of legislatures, legislative committees and government agencies are official proceedings, too. When the city council of a Missouri town discussed whether the police chief had committed statutory rape, newspapers reported it despite the libel to the chief: A city council meeting is an official proceeding, and reporting it is therefore privileged. The same is true if the House Ways and Means Committee hears testimony implying that a prominent banker is guilty of fraud, if a report by the State Board of Agriculture suggests that local grain elevator operators have conspired to inflate prices or if a member of the United States Congress charges that a labor leader hired thugs to bully his way into union office. Each of these libelous accusations can be freely reported, as long as the report is fair and accurate, and the libel was aired in the course of official business.

What is *not* an official proceeding? News conferences usually are not. Private conversations are not: If a police detective confides to you over drinks that he or she is certain a suspect is guilty, you cannot rely upon the official proceedings defense if you report the libelous remark. You may safely report what a witness says on the stand while court is in session, but not what he or she whispers to you in the hallway during recess.

In short, the official proceedings defense bars recovery of libel damages in cases arising from fair and accurate reports of the official actions of governmental agencies—including arrests, proceedings in open court, the actions of governmental executives and the public doings of government agencies, legislatures and committees. But the defense is not a license to air libelous charges that may have been bandied about during closed judicial proceedings or to pass along the libelous utterances of public officials when they step outside their official roles.

The *New York Times* Rule

The freedom to report *issues* of public concern implies the freedom to report on *people* of public concern. So the Supreme Court decided, in a landmark decision in 1964 that created what is called the *New York Times rule*. This rule holds that public figures—people who have "thrust themselves" into public prominence, and even a few who have unwillingly been caught up in the vortex of newsworthy events—cannot recover libel damages in connection with reports of their public conduct unless they can show that whoever libeled them either knowingly lied or acted in reckless disregard of the truth, conduct that the Supreme Court called "actual malice."

The idea behind the *New York Times* rule is to prevent public officials from using the libel laws to discourage criticism of their conduct in office. A rapidly evolving area of libel law, the *New York Times* rule has changed in response to changing judicial sympathy for the relative rights of the public to know and of libeled individuals to protect their reputations. It is a popular defense, because, unlike truth and privilege, it places the burden of proof not on the defendant publisher but on the plaintiff: the person who claims to have been libeled. But it can be treacherous, owing to its confused and rapidly changing status at law.

The rule arose from the civil rights movement of the 1960s. L. B. Sullivan, the head of the Montgomery, Alabama, police department, sued *The New York Times* for libels contained in an advertisement that had been paid for by a civil rights group. (Newspapers are responsible for the content of their advertisements, just as they are for their news stories and editorials.) The advertisement alleged, among other things, that civil rights leader Martin Luther King Jr. had encountered "intimidation and violence" from Montgomery city officials, that his home had been bombed and that he had been arrested by police seven times. In his lawsuit, Sullivan established that King had been arrested not seven times but four, and that there was no evidence linking Sullivan or the Montgomery police to the bombings of King's home. Indeed, Sullivan argued, the police had tried to apprehend the bombers.

Sullivan fared well in the lower courts, but lost when the case reached the United States Supreme Court, which held that those who occupy high public office enjoy less protection against libel than do ordinary citizens. Their reasoning was that the American tradition of free speech, in permitting citizens to criticize their government, implies that people are also free to attack the officials who hold public office without having to worry unduly that they will have to answer for it in court. "Debate on public issues should be uninhibited, robust, and wide-open," the Court said, adding "that it may well include vehement, caustic, and sometimes unpleasantly sharp attacks on government and public officials." Their decision echoed Harry S Truman's remark about criticism directed at him as president: "If you can't stand the heat, stay out of the kitchen."

In its early years, the *New York Times* rule liberated the press to blast away at public officials, secure in the knowledge that, as legal scholar Ronald Dworkin summarized it, "A public figure could not sue a paper for libel even if what that paper had published was both false and damaging, unless the public figure succeeded in showing that the paper had been not merely wrong but either malicious or reckless in what it published." And, at first, the definition of "public official" rapidly expanded, taking in ever more individuals whose recourse to libel actions was, consequently, constrained. People who held no political office but who had achieved positions of public prominence—people like President Nixon's friend Charles G. (Bebe) Rebozo—were held to be public figures; Rebozo was barred from collecting damages when he sued *The Washington Post* for reporting that he had sold shares of IBM stock he knew were stolen. Freelance writers, school board members, sheriffs and a track coach were deemed public figures by the courts as well. The effect of these rulings was to make it easier for reporters to cover the news without worrying about libel, but more difficult for people involved in public affairs to recover damages when libeled.

But then the pendulum began to swing the other way. In a series of landmark decisions, the Supreme Court sharply limited its conception of who constitutes a "public figure" under the *New York Times* rule. First came *Gertz v. Robert Welch, Inc.* The plaintiff, attorney Elmer Gertz, had been libeled in the pages of *American Opinion*, a publication of the John Birch Society, after he became involved in a civil rights case, representing the family of a youth killed by a police officer in a suit against the officer. Gertz was a well-known attorney, author, lecturer and founder of organizations ranging from the Civil War Roundtable to the Henry Miller Literary Society, yet the court held that he was *not* a public figure *in terms of the issue at hand*. (In any case, added the judge, "none of the prospective jurors called at the trial had ever heard of [him].") Gertz won his case. "Absent clear evidence of general fame or notoriety in the community, and pervasive involvement in the affairs of society," said the Supreme Court, "an individual should not be deemed a public personality for all aspects of his life."

The *Gertz* decision deprived the press of much of the freedom it had gained under *Sullivan*—if Gertz isn't a public figure, not many people are—but the press did gain something from the decision: The Court held that, to collect libel damages, nonpublic persons must prove that the libelor acted negligently. Before *Gertz*, it had been enough to demonstrate that libel had occurred and that none of the existing defenses applied.

Next came *Time, Inc. v. Firestone*. Mary Alice Firestone, a prominent socialite and the wife of a millionaire, sued *Time* magazine over an item reporting that her divorce trial had "produced enough testimony of extramarital affairs on both sides, said the judge, 'to make Dr. Freud's hair curl.' " The report contained various substantial inaccuracies. The Supreme Court held that Mrs. Firestone, despite her prominence, was not a public figure, and was therefore entitled to the same protection against libel that is afforded to ordinary citizens.

Gertz, Firestone and decisions that followed left considerable confusion as to who is a public figure. A belly dancer in Rochester, New York, was held to be a public figure; the vice president of a major corporation was not. One court ruled that police officers are public figures, another that they are not. A real estate developer who was embroiled in a public controversy was held to be a public figure, but a scientist who had been accused by a United States Senator of wasting government money was not.

Despite some confusion over just who qualifies as a public figure, the *New York Times* rule clearly restricts libel recovery by people of prominence and high public officials, leaving journalists free to report the tough and often fairly personal allegations that have long been part of public affairs—as when Vermont newspapers reported one mayoral candidate calling another "a jerk," "an idiot" and a "horse's ass."

The defense acts to protect journalists' statements of opinion as well. The common law defense of *fair comment* has been strengthened by the *Times* rule. Journalist Jack Newfield won when he was sued by a New York City trial judge whom he had called "incompetent" and "probably corrupt." "All statements of opinion concerning public officials, no matter how unreasonable, extreme or erroneous," ruled the State Court of Appeals, "are protected if the facts supporting such opinions are set out."

But the *New York Times* rule, like other libel defenses, offers far less protection to the journalist who can be shown to have acted out of malice. Actual malice—deliberately lying, or acting with disregard for the truth—strips one of the *New York Times* defense.

MALICE AND ACTUAL MALICE

Malice in libel is defined by *Black's Law Dictionary* as involving "evil intent or motive arising from spite or ill will; personal hatred or ill will; or culpable recklessness or a willful and wanton disregard of the rights and interests of the person defamed." Here is to be found the distinction between disinterested professional journalists out to report the news and those who would use the power of the press to pursue personal vendettas. This is not to say that the libel laws are meant to punish writers who have a legitimate axe to grind; but it does mean that the law is impatient with libel motivated by a desire to distort the truth or smear people. One of the riskiest things a journalist can do is to libel someone out of malice.

All libel defenses are weakened if malice was involved in the libel: The truth defense collapses if the plaintiff in a libel action can show that the journalist was not motivated by a desire to tell the truth but instead was out to demolish the plaintiff's reputation. The privilege of reporting official proceedings defense holds up only as long as the reporter invoking it can demonstrate that he or she wrote a fair and accurate account. And, as we have seen, *The New York Times* rule is suspended if a journalist acts with such culpable negligence as to be guilty of actual malice.

The role of actual malice—willful or reckless disregard for the truth—was illustrated in two cases decided by the Supreme Court on the same day: *Curtis Publishing Co. v. Butts* and *Associated Press v. Walker*. The first case involved University of Georgia football coach Wally Butts's suing the *Saturday Evening Post* for publishing a story charging that Butts had conspired to "fix" a football game by revealing Georgia's strategy to the coach of the rival University of Alabama team shortly before the game. Reviewing evidence of how the *Post* had put the story together, the Court learned that the story had been based on the affidavit of a single man who claimed to have overheard a telephone conversation between Butts and the Alabama coach. *Post* editors had failed to ask to see the reporter's notes, or to interview a second person said to have been present when the phone call was overheard, or to screen films of the games to see whether Alabama appeared to have acted on inside information or to check the details of the story with anyone versed in football strategy. The Court ruled that the *Post* editors had acted "with reckless disregard of whether it was false or not"—the definition of actual malice—and Butts was awarded $460,000 in damages.

The other suit was brought by Edwin Walker, a former Army general opposed to desegregation. The AP ran a story alleging that Walker had incited a crowd to violence and had led the crowd in a charge against federal marshals who had been sent to the University of Mississippi to enforce integration. Walker testified that he had done no such thing, and that he had instead counseled nonviolence among the anti-integration marchers. This time, the defense won: The Supreme Court noted that the story had originated with an AP reporter on the scene, that it was consistent with what editors who knew of Walker's background might be led to expect and, perhaps most important, that the AP had acted in accordance with "accepted publishing standards" in covering the story under the time available to them.

Both Butts and Walker were deemed public figures. In the Butts case, journalists were held to have acted sufficiently negligently to constitute actual malice. In the Walker case, they were not.

For journalists, the dark side of the malice issue is that it opens a reporter's every word and deed, even his or her thoughts, to potential scrutiny in court. Public figure plaintiffs have been permitted to subpoena tons of reporters' notes and memos as well as outtakes from filmed and taped interviews to establish whether the journalists who libeled them did so out of malice. The result of this close scrutiny has been to turn major libel trials into tests of reporters' fairness and objectivity. When Israeli Defense Minister Ariel Sharon sued *Time* magazine for suggesting that he encouraged Lebanese Phalangists to kill Palestinian civilians in two refugee camps in Beirut in 1982, he won none of the $50 million in damages he sought; the trial nonetheless produced long hours of testimony about whether *Time* editors and correspondents were biased against

Sharon—the sort of question that had not often before been open to official inquiry.

PARTIAL DEFENSES AND MITIGATING CIRCUMSTANCES

When libel has occurred and the major defenses are not satisfied, partial defenses or mitigating circumstances may tend to limit damages. These circumstances include *consent, retractions and corrections* and reliance upon a *usually reliable source*.

Consent

Someone who has consented to the publication of a libelous item cannot expect to subsequently collect damages in connection with the same item. The significance of this rule to a journalist is that if a libeled individual replies to the libelous charges, and the journalist fairly and accurately reports both the charges and the reply, the person libeled has in effect consented to the publication of the libel. Consent is implied because the person responding could not have expected the reporter to print his or her responses without also printing the charges. Here the law supports a basic tenet of objective journalism: If you want to print damaging information, get all sides of the story, give the injured party a chance to reply and afford the reply proper prominence.

Retractions and Corrections

The courts in most jurisdictions will limit libel damages against a publication that inadvertently committed libel and then promptly ran a correction—as long as the correction was made in good faith and was given a prominence, or "play," comparable to that of the item that contained the libel. The publication's case is strengthened still further if the plaintiff had agreed to the correction as a remedy. But when good faith seems lacking, printing a grudging correction does the publication little good. The *National Enquirer* lost a major libel action to actress Carol Burnett even though it had published a correction of a report implying that Burnett had been drunk; the judge noted that despite the correction, the *Enquirer* had shown "absolutely no remorse for its misdeeds."

The Usually Reliable Source

It seems unfair that a newspaper that publishes, say, an AP report originated thousands of miles away should have to pay damages if the report turns out to be indefensibly libelous. Yet exactly that has happened, and often. Annie Oklay, brought into a Chicago court on a drunk and disorderly charge, was mistakenly identified in a wire service dispatch as the sharpshooter Annie Oakley who had toured the country with Buffalo Bill's Wild West show—despite the different spellings of the last name. The real Annie Oakley sued a variety of newspapers that had carried the wire service stories, and she collected from several. To prevent this sort of thing from getting out of hand, many courts have reduced or eliminated damages resulting from publishing wire service dispatches or other material that the journalists involved had good reason to assume was accurate. Several states have passed legislation barring recovery of libel damages from those who relied upon usually trustworthy sources.

PRIVACY

The idea that a "right of privacy" protects people from unwarranted prying by the press was first asserted in its modern form in 1890. It began as a reaction against yellow journalism (see Chapter 2). Particularly offended by the excesses of a leering, rumor-mongering press was Samuel B. Warren of Boston. Gossip about Warren's patrician family had recently been headlined in the tabloids. Warren and his law partner, Louis Brandeis, who later became a justice of the United States Supreme Court, wrote an article in the *Harvard Law Review* asserting that a "right of privacy" should protect people against idle gossip mongering by the press. Wrote Brandeis and Warren:

> The press is overstepping in every direction the obvious bounds of propriety and decency. Gossip is no longer the resource of the idle and of the vicious, but has become a trade, which is pursued with industry as well as effrontery. To satisfy a prurient taste, the details of sexual relations are spread broadcast in the columns of the daily papers. . . . The intensity and complexity of life, attendant upon advancing civilization, have rendered necessary some retreat from the world, and man, under the refining influence of culture, has become more sensitive to publicity, so that solitude and privacy have become more essential to the individual. But modern enterprise and invention have through invasions upon his privacy, subjected him to mental pain and distress, far greater than could be inflicted by mere bodily injury.

Today the press is more responsible than it was in the 1890s, but threats to personal privacy nevertheless loom even larger than when Brandeis and Warren wrote. The reason is that more news gathering is going on today than ever before. A television camera no larger than a paperback book can be used to send live color images all over the world; data stored in computers can reveal embarrassing personal information—that a Catholic woman has had an abortion, say, or that a member of Congress has been treated for alcoholism; and wiretapping and bugging threaten, as Brandeis and Warren foresaw, "to make good the prediction that 'what is whispered in the closet shall be proclaimed from the housetops.' " The press is not solely to blame for these threats to personal privacy, but it is constrained by the growth of legal means to defend against them. Many states now recognize a common law "right to privacy," and several have enacted statutes to defend it.

In this section we discuss privacy as a matter of *law*. For privacy as a matter of *taste*, see Chapter 18, *Facts, Fairness, Ethics and Taste*.

What Is Privacy?

Everyone has a basic right to solitude, to manage his or her life without undue intrusion by government or—as concerns us here—by the press. Society, on the other hand, has a legitimate interest in various sorts of information—news—regardless of whether obtaining that information violates someone's privacy. Privacy lawsuits flourish where these rights conflict.

The individual's right to privacy has been described as "a general 'right to be left alone,' and to define one's circle of intimacy; to shield intimate and personal characteristics and activities from public gaze; to have moments of freedom from the unremitted assault of the world. . . ." The news media, for their part, have a right to report matters "of legitimate public concern," as the courts phrase it. Put these two together and you come up with a working definition like this one, from Paul Ashley's book *Say It Safely*:

> The right of privacy does not suppress the news or fair comment. However it is an aggressive defense against the publicizing of private affairs with which the public has no legitimate concern or the wrongful intrusion (the bad taste, if you please, of an intrusion) into private activities in such a manner as to cause mental suffering, shame, or humiliation to a person of ordinary sensibilities.

Ashley's is an apt thumbnail rule, but to understand this changing field of law, we need look at privacy in greater detail.

PRIVACY AS A MATTER OF LAW

The law designates four kinds of invasion of privacy: *intrusion*, *misappropriation*, *disclosure* and *false light*.

Intrusion

Intrusion means illegal entry, illegal search, wiretapping and the like. A reporter risks losing a costly judgment for invasion of privacy if he or she is so unwise as to secretly photograph people in their apartment through a telephoto lens, bug someone's office with a recording device, eavesdrop on a conversation in a boardroom while disguised as a typewriter repairer or gain entrance to a bereaved home by pretending to be a member of the clergy.

Strictures against intrusion hold regardless of whether the material so obtained is ever published: A reporter trespassing in pursuit of a story is just as liable as a private busybody. "The First Amendment has never been construed to accord newsmen immunity from torts or crimes committed during the course of news gathering," ruled a federal appeals court. "The First Amendment is not a license to trespass, to steal, or to intrude by electronic means into the precincts of another's home or office."

A widely publicized case of unreasonable intrusion by a journalist involved freelance photographer Ron Galella, who specialized in taking candid photographs of Jacqueline Kennedy Onassis and selling them around the world. Galella followed Mrs. Onassis on foot and by car through the streets of Manhattan, buzzed her in a power boat when she was swimming in the Mediterranean, leapt from behind trees late at night to take flash pictures of her and her children, romanced her maid and bribed her servants to learn of her whereabouts. *That*, said the judge, was "unreasonably intrusive" behavior, and Galella was enjoined from approaching Mrs. Onassis. "The First Amendment does not immunize all conduct designed to gather information about or photographs of a public figure," wrote the judge. "There is no general constitutional right to assault, harass, or unceasingly shadow or distress public figures."

Far less offensive behavior has been ruled an unreasonable intrusion. *Life* magazine sent two reporters to the office of a quack doctor, where, concealing their identity as journalists, they photographed him and transmitted his remarks over a hidden radio transmitter. The "doctor" (he pled no contest to a charge of practicing medicine without a license) sued for breach of privacy and won. His office, the court held, was "a sphere from which he could reasonably expect to exclude eavesdropping newsmen. . . . One who invites another to his home or office . . . does not and should not be required to take the risk that what is heard and seen will be transmitted by photograph or recording, or . . . in full living color and hi-fi to the public at large." The court took a similar stance in the case of a television reporter who barged into a restaurant that had been charged with a health violation, accompanied by his crew and with his camera rolling.

Misappropriation

Misappropriation refers to the unauthorized use of someone's name or likeness for commercial gain, as in an advertisement. Misappropriation was at issue when golfer Ben Hogan collected $5000 from the publishers of a golfing book that included photographs of Hogan that were used without his permission. Misappropriation prompted actor Kirk Douglas to sue Walt Disney for broadcasting, on a "Disneyland" TV show, home movies showing Douglas and his two sons riding a toy train at Disney's home. In cases like these, what is involved is not so much a breach of privacy as a misappropriation of someone's commercially valuable endorsement. For this reason, jurists sometimes refer to it as the "right to publicity."

The First Amendment defends the use of people's names and likenesses in news stories, so journalists need worry about misappropriation only when advertising is concerned. Here the courts hold that the advertisement is justified if it reflects the news. That's why quarterback Joe Namath lost when he sued *Sports Illustrated* for running an ad featuring his photograph. The photo had appeared in the magazine as part of a news story; in reprinting it the magazine was exercising its right to advertise as a news publication.

Disclosure

Disclosure means publishing or broadcasting intimate, embarrassing facts. A woman who visited the fun house at a carnival was photographed just as an air jet blew her skirt up. She sued the newspaper that ran the photo. She won. Yet, had she been an actress, model or rock star, publication might well have been protected. Why? Because the courts, in deciding disclosure suits, weigh the embarrassment caused against the *newsworthiness* of the story being covered. If the facts involved are of "legitimate public interest," then the injured party has no recourse at law, however much he or she may have been offended or embarrassed by the publication. A man who was arrested in front of his home—stark naked—sued the television station that broadcast footage of the episode on a nightly news broadcast. He lost. The court ruled that the arrest itself was newsworthy enough to outweigh the man's humiliation at having it broadcast.

A classic case in this regard involved William James Sidis. Raised by a father devoted to developing the boy's mental powers, Sidis was lecturing on mathematics at Harvard when only 11 years old. But soon he dropped out of sight. Twenty-seven years later, *The New Yorker* reported that Sidis was living in a small room in Boston next to an elevated railroad track, collecting streetcar tickets and studying the folklore of a nonexistent Indian tribe. The article was widely read and discussed, and Sidis sued for invasion of privacy. He lost. "Regrettably or not," held the New York court of appeals, "the misfortunes and frailties of neighbors and 'public figures' are subjects of considerable interest and discussion to the rest of the population. And when such are the mores of the community, it would be unwise for a court to bar their expression in the newspapers, books and magazines of the day."

To avoid infringing on the First Amendment by ruling too strictly on what constitutes "legitimate" news, judges have tended to be liberal in interpreting what makes for public interest. *Cosmopolitan* magazine won when sued by a woman who had been quoted, to her embarrassment and without her permission, in an article titled "Would You Wear a Monokini?" Whether to go topless at a public beach might not be the most world-shattering news of the day, but the court held that it was a matter of legitimate public interest. Surfer Mike Virgil failed to persuade the courts that *Sports Illustrated* should pay him damages for invading his privacy in a profile that quoted him as admitting that, while doing construction work, he had intentionally injured himself to collect unemployment benefits so he would have time to go body surfing. A southern California district court held, first, that the "facts are generally unflattering and perhaps embarrassing, but they are simply not offensive to the degree of morbidity and sensationalism," and, second, that the subject, body surfing, was of "legitimate public interest."

Publication of even the most mortifying information is permissible under law—if not by standards of good taste—if the information is newsworthy. The father of a rape victim lost when he sued a television station for naming his daughter in its report of the crime. The Supreme Court held that "The commission of crime, prosecutions resulting from it, and judicial proceedings arising from the prosecutions . . . are without question events of legitimate concern to the public and consequently fall within the responsibility of the press to report the operations of government."

False Light

False light means creating an inaccurate impression of someone. The person so identified may collect damages for invasion of privacy if (1) the material is highly offensive *and* (2) its publisher either knew it was false or acted with reckless disregard for its truth. The former of these two conditions is the same as the definition of invasion of privacy through disclosure, except that here the material is not only embarrassing but also false. The latter part is the definition of actual malice, which we discussed earlier in this chapter under the *New York Times* rule. Indeed, false light invasion of privacy is so similar to libel that some legal scholars would prefer that it be treated as a branch of libel law.

An archetypal false light privacy award came when Margaret Cantrell sued the *Cleveland Plain Dealer* for a Sunday supplement article describing how she and her four children were living in poverty and squalor following the death of her husband in a bridge collapse. "She wears the same mask of non-expression she wore at the funeral," wrote the reporter, adding that she refused to talk about the accident. The trouble was, he hadn't seen her. She was away when he visited the house and talked with one of her children. She was awarded $60,000 in damages.

False light may be cast by misleading statements even if they are technically true. Suppose you write, "Rock guitarist Tony Prang hasn't taken heroin in over a year." If Prang has *never* taken heroin, you've cast him in a false light.

Many false light suits are brought by people whose names or photographs were used to illustrate news stories that did not really involve them and that depicted them inaccurately. An honest cab driver was awarded damages when he brought an invasion of privacy suit against a magazine that printed his photograph to illustrate an article about crooked cab drivers.

Fictionalized accounts, too, can breed false light privacy lawsuits. CBS broadcast a dramatic account of the murder of Rasputin, the Russian mystic who was poisoned, shot twice, then strangled before finally being thrown into the Neva River and drowned. The network was sued by Felix Youssoupoff, one of Rasputin's murderers, who alleged that the show portrayed him in a false light. He won, though he was denied damages under the legal doctrine that a criminal cannot profit from his illegal deeds. In *Time v. Hill*, individuals who had been held hostage by three escaped convicts filed suit against *Life* magazine for publishing a story about a play based on the incident. The play, based on Truman Capote's novel *In Cold Blood*, allegedly portrayed them in a false light. The court found that there was insufficient evidence to prove that *Life* had published the piece knowing that it was inaccurate.

PRIVACY IN PRACTICE

Here are a few points to keep in mind regarding the right to privacy:

In dealing with sensitive material, first ask if it really invades anyone's privacy. Writing about a halfback's cocaine addiction would invade his privacy if he had refused to discuss the matter, but if he's already talked to the press about it, then the subject is no longer private, it's public, and no invasion of privacy will result from your story. A boxer who made a career fighting under the name Canvasback Cohen lost a lawsuit against Groucho Marx, who had said on his radio show: "I once managed a prize fighter, Canvasback Cohen. I brought him out here, he got knocked out, and I made him walk back to Cleveland." The remark was untrue (it was a joke, after all), and it cast Cohen in a false light, but the court ruled that Cohen had already waived his right of privacy by capitalizing on the name during an extremely public career.

If material does seem to invade a genuine realm of privacy, ask whether it's newsworthy. If so, you usually can publish it without fear. A man dropped into a tobacco shop to buy a newspaper; while he was there, police raided a gambling operation in the back room, and his photograph appeared along with stories about the gambling arrests. His privacy was invaded, and he was cast in a false light, but he failed to collect damages. The courts held that the press has a right to report on crime—there is a legitimate public interest in crime—even though the innocent sometimes suffer as a result of such reports.

In privacy as in libel, malice greatly weakens the journalist's standing in court. If you write that Senator Pringle had a homosexual affair thirty years ago while in boarding school, you may escape—*narrowly* escape—paying damages, if the allegation appears in the context of a generally fair and impartial report on the Senator. But if the allegation was part of a vituperative smear, the judge will scowl and you, most likely, will pay. As the head of the Washington State Bar Association told a group of journalists (italics added), "The essence of the wrong will be found in *crudity*, in *ruthless exploitation* of the woes or other personal affairs of private individuals who have done nothing noteworthy and have not by design or misadventure been involved in an event which tosses them into an arena subject to public gaze." The extent to which the right of privacy erodes the protection of the First Amendment in years to come may well depend on whether news reporters indulge in the vulgarity and bad taste of the yellow journalists who midwifed its birth.

DAMAGES

Three sorts of damages may be awarded in libel and privacy actions: *special*, *actual* and *punitive*. *Special* damages (think of the word as meaning "specific") are to repay the injured party for an actual financial loss. Malice is not an issue here. Circulation is; the greater the number of people who read the damag-

QUESTIONS AND ANSWERS ABOUT LIBEL AND PRIVACY

Howard Gilson, the TV star, is in town but he won't give us an interview. The room clerk at his hotel will slip me a key to his room in return for a few bucks. Can I wait for him there?

You're risking an invasion of privacy action if you do; reporters have no special rights to trespass just because they're gathering news. Wait for Gilson in the lobby.

May I libel the dead?

Most courts have held that the dead cannot recover libel damages, but the rule is not uniformly established. In any event, responsible journalists treat the dead as fairly and impartially as they would the living. To do otherwise is to take advantage of the fact that the dead can no longer reply, a tactic that reflects more damagingly upon the libeler than the libelee.

We published a book review in the paper today that inadvertently libeled a novelist. We meant to call her a "sob sister," but owing to a typographical error it came out "sot sister." What do we do now?

Print a correction, and give it the same prominence as the libelous item. A correction evidences good faith, especially in a case like this, in which the error could easily have cropped up despite professionalism and proper care in handling the item.

We published a wire service dispatch from Singapore that said that Jim Jakes, the former middle-weight boxer, had turned into a destitute opium addict. Now it turns out that the wire service reporter had the wrong man. Jakes the boxer runs a sporting goods store in San Diego. He's suing everyone who ran the libelous wire service item. Can he collect from us?

Possibly, though several states have laws protecting newspapers from paying libel damages in connection with wire service dispatches or other items they had good reason to assume were accurate. If sued, you can mitigate damages by pointing out that you harbored no malice, acted without negligence and had no reason to suspect the story, coming as it did from a usually reliable source.

Speaking of malice, our music critic—who just went through a bitter divorce from Lena Lane, the singer—has written a review of her new record that calls her a "catatonic imbecile with a voice like a rockslide." Can we print it?

Is it libelous? You bet. Is it defensible? All defenses are eroded if malice was present. You had better not print this one, unless you think you can prove in court that despite the bitter divorce, your critic was innocent of malice.

---

ing story, the greater the loss to the injured party and the greater, therefore, the damages are likely to be.

Actual (also called "compensatory") damages are to compensate the plaintiff for emotional stress caused by the libel or invasion of privacy. In the Carol Burnett–*National Enquirer* case, the court found no financial loss to Burnett and so awarded her no special damages—but it awarded her actual damages of $50,000.

Punitive damages are intended to punish the party that committed the libel or invasion of privacy. Malice is relevant. In the Burnett case, the court found the *Enquirer's* fabrication of events and bad-faith correction sufficient evidence of malice that it ordered the *Enquirer* to pay $750,000—subsequently reduced to $150,000—in punitive damages.

LIBEL AND PRESS FREEDOM

The number of libel suits filed and the size of the damages awarded against newspapers and broadcasters have skyrocketed in recent years. From 1980 to

---

I have a videotape of an inmate in the state penitentiary saying that the warden takes bribes from prisoners in return for easier treatment. Can I broadcast the tape?

Not unless you're prepared to prove that the warden really does take bribes. The prisoner's statement is no more than hearsay, whether on videotape or signed in blood.

The head of the local Young Republicans Club today held a press conference and called the head of the Young Democrats "so crooked he could hide behind a corkscrew." Can I use the quote in my story on what was otherwise an uneventful press conference?

Is it libelous? Yes. Do you have a defense? No. The head of the local Young Democrats doesn't sound like a lofty enough public figure to be embraced by the *New York Times* rule, and a press conference is not an official proceeding. Truth is a defense only if you can prove the charge yourself.

A bridge that collapsed three days ago, killing two motorists, was designed by an engineer who lives in town. I want to name him as its designer. Can I do so?

You're not saying that he was responsible for the bridge collapse, or that he is incompetent as an engineer, so there's no libel in the first place. Call him and interview him. And stick impartially to the facts; to load up the story with unwarranted assumptions, writing lines like, "His voice revealed no hint of remorse over the terrible accident," would be risking a lawsuit.

I'm writing a profile of Vince Andretti, the health food proponent. He told me that nobody should eat "Bon Voyage" brand vichyssoise because the soup's terrible and will ruin your health. Can I include this comment? He doesn't name any individual, just the corporation.

Corporations are considered individuals at law, and can be libeled. Their products can be criticized, but any attack on the very reputation of the company could constitute libel. It would be best to consult an attorney on this one.

David Carruthers, the famous Shakespearean actor, fell outside the Plaza Hotel last night, while I was standing there, and broke his ankle. He shouted, "The carpet was loose! It's the hotel's fault! Now I won't be able to open on Broadway! I'm going to sue the hotel for everything it has." Can I print his complaint?

Remember to ask yourself first, "Is it libel? Does a loose carpet ruin the reputation of the hotel, besmirch its image, make you feel you'd never book a room there? Probably not; it's an accident that might happen even in the best hotels. So there appears to be no libel, and you probably can print the item. But do call the hotel management and give it a chance to air its side.

1985, damages of $1 million or more were awarded in at least twenty major libel actions, and journalists were kept busy defending themselves in hundreds of lesser suits. The trend reached a climax when General William Westmoreland, in an effort financed by wealthy conservatives opposed to what they saw as a liberal bias in the news media, filed a $120 million libel suit against CBS News over a documentary that alleged that Westmoreland had deliberately underestimated enemy troop strength in Vietnam in order to prevent the Johnson administration from becoming discouraged about prospects for winning the war. Westmoreland withdrew his suit just before the case went to the jury, but concerns about the effect of all these libel actions on the freedom of the press remained.

One concern is that the loss of a major libel suit can drive a small newspaper out of business: A number of papers and at least one syndicated column have folded in the past decade, their pockets emptied to pay libel damages. The tiny Pt. Reyes, California, *Light* won a Pulitzer Prize for its coverage of the Synanon foundation, but in the process it had to fight off four libel suits totalling more than $1 billion in damages, the loss of any one of which would have bankrupted it.

Another concern is with legal fees and court costs; winning a libel suit can be almost as costly as losing one. *The Washington Post* spent over $1 million defending itself in a libel action filed by Mobil Oil president William Tavoulareas, even though the *Post* eventually won. CBS News spent a comparable amount prevailing against the Westmoreland suit. "I have never paid a penny in settlement," says columnist Jack Anderson, ". . . yet I have put out a fortune fending off libel suits that obviously lacked substance." The American Newspaper Publishers Association estimates that its members spend ten times as much for legal fees defending themselves against libel suits as they pay in damages. Libel insurance is available, but as awards grow, so do insurance premiums.

Journalists and First Amendment advocates worry that all these suits tend to have a "chilling effect" on the willingness of broadcasters and newspaper publishers to pursue the sort of hard-hitting stories that produce libel suits. Smaller newspapers and magazines who cannot afford to lose major libel suits are tempted to play it safe by covering only "low risk" news. Said Paul Hogan, managing editor of *The Tampa Tribune*, after his paper paid out damages in two consecutive libel suits filed by a local solar energy company, "We've been a little less aggressive. There are situations we haven't covered that we otherwise might have."

Chilled or not, reporters can spend so much time defending themselves in court that they lack time to do their jobs. A three-reporter investigative team established by the McClatchy chain of *Bee* newspapers to ferret out corruption in Fresno County, California, had to fight so many libel cases that it was forced to disband. "The team no longer exists," said Frank McCulloch, editor of the Sacramento *Bee*, "not because we're afraid to have it, but because its members have become full-time litigants."

"The only way a publisher or news organization can be sure it will not be sued," writes civil rights attorney Martin Garbus, "is to systematically omit controversial material. Under pressure from recent libel decisions, this form of self-censorship is likely to grow more common."

SUMMARY

Libel is anything published or broadcast that defames someone—that is, that tends to make normal people form a highly unfavorable opinion of the person libeled. It is libelous, for instance, to publish an item indicating that someone is inept or incompetent; has been charged with or convicted of a crime; is a coward, a traitor or a liar; is unethical, dishonest, stupid or crazy; or is a Nazi.

If you pick up almost any newspaper, you will find libelous items scattered through it. This is possible because the law provides a variety of defenses available to journalists and others who are sued for libel. If you qualify for one of these defenses, you need not pay libel damages.

The most important defenses are *truth, the privilege of reporting official proceedings*, and the *New York Times* rule. To satisfy the truth defense, you must be prepared to prove in court that the essence of the libel was true: It is *not* sufficient merely to show that you accurately quoted a libel that originated with someone else. The official proceedings defense permits fair and accurate reporting of all government proceedings—such as *arrests, executive actions, legislative matters* and *trials* in open court—even though these may contain libelous material. The *New York Times* rule holds that public officials, and some people who have sought out positions of prominence involving the issue at hand, can collect damages for libels relating to their public conduct only if they can show that they were libeled out of "actual malice"—which means knowing or reckless falsehood.

These defenses, and the lesser defenses in libel actions as well, are severely weakened if the journalist can be shown to have been guilty of *malice*. Don't commit libel carelessly or in the heat of anger.

Privacy law protects people from unwarranted intrusion or exposure by the news media. It awards damages if reporters *intrude* where they have no right to be, even if in pursuit of a story. *Disclosure* of embarrassing facts, even if true, is actionable except when the facts relate to matters of legitimate public interest. If the disclosures cast a *false light* and are highly offensive, the question becomes much like one of libel, and the *New York Times* rule applies. When concerned with privacy, be sure the material involved is newsworthy, and that in publishing or broadcasting it you are acting without negligence and free from malice.

Three sorts of *damages* may be awarded in libel and privacy suits: *Special* damages are to repay actual loss; *actual* damages compensate for emotional injury; and *punitive* damages punish the libeler.

18

FACTS, FAIRNESS, ETHICS AND TASTE

Most journalists agree that they should try to report the facts objectively and to conduct themselves ethically. The problem lies in determining just how to put these sentiments into practice. In this chapter we examine the foundations of the journalistic ideals of factual accuracy, sound reasoning, fairness and objectivity, and ethical conduct.

FACTS

A fact is a true statement about the real world. By the "real world" we mean the world of shared experience, the realm of "objective" reality. Facts in the abstract may be unambiguous (pi equals 3.14159) but in the jumbled realm of human affairs, the truth, as Oscar Wilde said, "is rarely pure, and never simple." People still disagree on the facts of major news stories like the Alger Hiss case (was he guilty of espionage?) and the Lindbergh baby (was the man convicted of the kidnapping really guilty?), and those stories were thoroughly reported at the time and have been scrutinized by journalists and historians ever since.

Among the leading obstacles to finding the facts are *lies, half-truths, misconceptions and preconceptions, quantitative errors and logical fallacies*.

Lies

Lies—falsehoods conveyed with the knowledge that they are false—are commonplace. The prudent journalist remembers this sad fact.

The more the truth hurts, the more tempting it is to lie to reporters who are after the truth. On March 17, 1968, *The New York Times* published a Vietnam dispatch that began: "American troops caught a North Vietnamese force in a pincer movement on the central coastal plain yesterday, killing 128 enemy soldiers in daylong fighting." Fully twenty months passed before a freelance journalist unearthed the true story—that at least 109 of the "enemy soldiers" killed were in fact unarmed civilians, many of them women and children, who had been herded into a ditch in the village of Mylai and massacred by American soldiers. The fallacious account had been relayed to the press by military authorities in the course of a daily Saigon press briefing so notorious for its inaccuracies that reporters called it "The Five O'Clock Follies."

The extremely high stakes of top-level national and international politics generate the most grandiose of falsehoods, the "big lie." This consists of repeating a lie so often and disseminating it so widely that people eventually assume that it must be true. Hitler employed the big lie when he blamed Germany's economic troubles on an imaginary conspiracy of communists and Jews. The Soviet Union employed it when it said it invaded Afghanistan at the request of the Afghani people—this at a time when the Afganis themselves were busy shooting at Soviet soldiers every chance they got.

A free and independent press can mitigate the effect of propaganda, but is hardly immune to its effects. In foreign affairs especially, journalists may unwittingly adopt the government's way of seeing and talking about things. During the Eisenhower administration, for example, an American U-2 spy plane was shot down over Russia. The White House issued a statement saying that the U-2 was on a scientific mission, studying the weather, and had strayed into Soviet airspace by mistake. *The New York Times*, reporting the White House position, at first described the aircraft as a "weather" plane, using quotation marks and attributing the designation to the administration. But as days passed and the White House stuck to its story, the *Times* dropped the quotation marks, giving readers the impression that the U-2 was a scientific craft in fact, and not just in the words of the White House. This soon proved embarrassing: the Soviets produced the U-2's pilot, its cameras and other evidence proving that it was a spy plane.

Half-Truths

Journalists often are tripped up by half-truths, statements that are calculated to mislead though they may be technically accurate. Lyndon Johnson was asked at a White House press conference whether he was looking for someone to replace Henry Cabot Lodge as ambassador to Saigon. Seizing upon the opportunity presented by the wording of the reporter's question, Johnson replied, "No, there is no truth that I am looking for a successor." A few days later he replaced Lodge with Ellsworth Bunker. Johnson's press secretary, George Christian, defended the President's reply as "absolutely accurate." Christian pointed out that when asked the question, Johnson had already decided to give Lodge's job to

Bunker, and so, having found a successor to Lodge, was not "looking" for one. As the *Chicago Daily News* noted in an editorial, Johnson's remark was "accurate, perhaps, but not truthful."

A favorite form of half-truth among government officials is the "trial balloon." Johnson was a master of trial ballooning. If he were thinking of raising taxes, he might leak an anonymous report that a tax increase was imminent, then see how the report was received. If Congress and the people seemed to accept it, fine; if they loudly opposed it, Johnson could always claim that the press had erred and that he had never intended to raise taxes in the first place. A variation is to inflate the trial balloon: A president who is planning to ask Congress for a 3 percent hike in taxes can leak a story that he's going to ask for a 7 percent tax increase. If the public is outraged, fine: A 3 percent increase may then seem like a comparatively good deal.

Misconceptions and False Preconceptions

Misconceptions and false preconceptions afflict us all, from the simplest level on up. How many of these homey examples were you taught in school?:

Columbus proved that the world is round.

Sweden has the world's highest suicide rate.

The U.S. has the world's highest standard of living.

Mussolini made the Italian trains run on time.

George Washington as a lad chopped down a cherry tree, then admitted to his deed with the words, "I cannot tell a lie."

All these stories have been around for years, have appeared repeatedly in print, are accepted by millions—and they're all false.* They illustrate our tendency to believe what we *want* to believe—that heros like Columbus and George Washington don't make mistakes, that socialism is gloomy and fascism efficient though oppressive and that our country is the best of all.

We tend to fall victim to the misconceptions that best suit our preconceptions; we're liable to assume that something *must* be true merely because we feel that it *ought* to be true. When reggae singer Bob Marley died, the cause of his death was widely reported to be lung cancer. Marley was known to have smoked large quantities of marijuana daily throughout his adult life, and many journalists jumped to the conclusion that the cancer that killed Marley *must* have been

---

*Columbus was out to prove not that the world was round (something educated people had known for 2000 years) but that it was only 8000 miles in circumference—about one-third the correct figure; that's why he thought he could reach Asia by sailing west in three tiny ships. The American standard of living is high, but not the world's highest. Sweden, despite its dank climate, is not the leader in suicide. Italian trains ran late even under Mussolini's iron hand. The George Washington story was the invention of an adoring biographer.

PEANUTS

(Reprinted with permission of United Feature Syndicate, Inc.)

lung cancer. But it wasn't: Marley died of melanoma, a rapidly metastasizing form of cancer that began as a tumor in his foot.

Once a misconception appears in print it tends to propagate. Have you ever heard of Nikolai Lenin, leader of the Russian Revolution? Many readers of American newspapers have; Nikolai still turns up regularly in print. But that wasn't Lenin's first name. The communist leader signed his manifestoes N. Lenin, and a New York newspaper editor facing a deadline years ago guessed that the initial stood for the common Russian name Nikolai. Actually, like the "S" in Harry S Truman, the "N" stood for nothing at all. Lenin's real first name was Vladimir, and his last name was Ulyanov. "Lenin" was a pseudonym he adopted to disguise his identity during the days he was helping to organize the communist party while in exile in Siberia.

The solution? Check the facts out. And be most skeptical of your assumptions precisely when you most want to believe them.

Quantitative Errors

The ways of the world, and therefore of journalism, are increasingly dominated by the need to think accurately in terms of *quantities*. In ancient societies it may not have mattered whether one understood the difference between a million and a billion or could calculate statistics of probability. But today, when the federal budget runs to hundreds of billions of dollars and public opinion polls influence everything from presidential elections to soft drink recipes, journalists need to better understand quantitative relationships.

Can you spot the errors in these examples, drawn from *The New York Times* house organ *Winners & Sinners*? (Answers appear on page 359)

1. A story about a Nebraska woman going on 80 began, "Hanna Sanger should have died 7.05 years ago, according to the statistics. . . ."
2. "In general," said the story, "according to the committee, generic drugs are 300 to 700 percent cheaper than their brand-name counterparts."
3. "White Plains, for example, had no homicides last year, but has had one so far in 1976. That is an increase of 100 percent. . . ."

4. "Mount Lebanon . . . did not have a single robbery in 1974, but there were three last year, producing an increase of 300 percent."
5. "Medicaid payments to all nonconforming nursing homes would double, rising from $8.4 million a year to $25.2 million."
6. "The vessel, measuring 500 by 100 feet, almost the size of two football fields. . . ."
7. ". . . the results of a national poll reported yesterday by the Gallup organization suggested that the majority of Americans favor Federal loan guarantees for the city. . . . The survey . . . found that guarantees were favored by a margin of 41 percent."

Logical Fallacies

An illogical argument is invalid even though it may be based on fact. Consider this imaginary speech by a Democratic presidential candidate:

My fellow Americans, do you remember how Richard Nixon conducted himself when he was president? How he lied to you, and had to resign from office under threat of impeachment?

You know, he was leader of the Republican party. And my opponent is a Republican, too. He belongs to the party of Richard Nixon. And if you vote him into office, he'll act just like Nixon did.

The Democrat may have stated the facts correctly—Nixon was a Republican, and he did resign rather than face impeachment—but the argument is logically unsound. Stripped to the essentials, it goes like this:

Nixon, a Republican, resigned the presidency in disgrace.
My opponent is a Republican.
Therefore my opponent, if elected, will resign the presidency in disgrace.

The logical fallacy here is the *non sequitur*—Latin for, "It doesn't follow," meaning that the conclusion doesn't follow from the premises. To see the error more clearly, let's change its subject while retaining its logical structure:

Birds breathe air and eat worms.
My opponent breathes air.
Therefore my opponent eats worms.

Other logical fallacies journalists frequently encounter include *ad hominem* attacks, the fallacy of *false cause*, the *strawman* and the *appeal to authority*.

Ad hominem means "to the man." It refers to the fallacy of attacking someone personally over an issue that does not concern personality. If a mathematician says that the sum of the angles of a triangle is not necessarily 180 degrees, it is irrelevant to dispute him by saying he is a communist or a drug addict: the issue is the triangle, not the mathematician. Mayor Richard Daley of Chicago was indulging in an *ad hominem* argument when he referred to antiwar demonstrators as "bums;" so were the protestors who called the Chicago police "pigs."

Neither slur had much to do with the issue at hand, which was whether the United States ought to have continued to prosecute the war in Vietnam.

When one side in a dispute stoops to the *ad hominem* argument the other side may respond in kind, with what is known as the *tu quoque*, meaning "You're another." Many a political campaign has stumbled down this dismal trail.

Journalists can help rescue public affairs from the morass of the *ad hominem* and the *tu quoque* by resisting true temptation to make spicy headlines out of irresponsible quarreling. In 1983, Chicago's first black mayor was locked into a bitter conflict with his predominantly white city council. With the mayor and council unable to agree on a tax measure, the city ran out of funds, and hundreds of city employees had to be laid off. Some journalists reported this as merely another round in the fight between the mayor and the council, almost as if it were a sporting event. But other journalists, taking a more considered view, emphasized the fact that the conflict was bringing city government to a standstill; their restraint helped keep the newspapers from being reduced to an arena for endless mud slinging.

The fallacy of *false cause* rears its head when events that may have been sheer coincidence are linked together as if one had caused the other. That's what the preacher in Shakespeare's time did when he blamed the theater for an epidemic of the plague: "The cause of plagues is sin, if you look to it well; and the cause of sin are plays; therefore the cause of plagues are plays." In his autobiography, Mark Twain satirized this sort of thinking when he noted that his birth had boosted the population of his tiny hometown of Florida, Missouri, by 1 percent, adding: "I did it for Florida and it shows that I could have done it for any place—even London, I suppose."

Journalists fall victim to the fallacy of false cause when they allege a connection between events without really knowing that the connection is there. A political reporter who visited China wrote a column saying that the Chinese punish criminals swiftly and brutally, and that, *therefore*, there is less crime in Peking than in New York. But Peking is very different from New York; it never had New York's high crime rate, not even before more stringent anticrime laws were imposed.

It's best to avoid jumping to conclusions. When an elderly woman with a weak heart was found dead in her locked New York apartment, veteran reporters stopped short of writing that a heart attack *caused* her death. And a good thing, too: An autopsy revealed that she had been strangled.

In the *strawman* fallacy, an artificial argument is attributed to the opposition solely for the purpose of knocking it down. The idea is to make the opponent's case look so unappealing that the audience will flee into the arms of one's own case instead. To avoid being taken in by the strawman fallacy, make it a practice to seek people's opinions from the people themselves and not from their opponents. If you want to know what the Secretary of the Navy thinks about arms control, look up his papers and speeches on the subject, rather than relying upon an account of his views provided by a special interest group. If you want to know how the principal of the junior high school feels about dress regulations, call and find out; don't parrot what the students have told you is the principal's position. The argument Brown attributes to Jones may not be Jones's argument, any more than someone's leaving a basket of kittens on your doorstep means that you asked for the kittens.

The *appeal to authority* involves asking that we accept an argument not on its merits, but because it has been endorsed by someone knowledgeable, powerful or famous. On a trivial level, the appeal to authority asks us to believe that winning the Super Bowl turns a quarterback into an expert on aftershave lotion, or that selling a million records makes a pop star a philosopher. Such an appeal turned more serious when President Johnson asked the American public to support the war in Vietnam because, he said, he was privy to classified information that proved the war could be won.

Journalists learn to be skeptical about "authorities" in general and "experts" in particular. Anyone can be labeled an expert. UFOs ARE PILOTED BY AN-GELS FROM GOD, EXPERTS REVEAL read the front-page headline on an issue of the *Weekly World News*, a tabloid of the *National Enquirer* genre. Among the "experts" cited in the story were a "Hampton, New Hampshire, chemist," an "inventor-evangelist," and a "pastor of the Northminster Presbyterian Church of Endwell, N.Y." Not all empty appeals to authority are this silly, of course, but all serve to remind us that nothing is so just because somebody *says* it's so.

OBJECTIVITY

The press has tremendous power to help people; ask Billy Graham, who was boosted toward evangelical superstardom when William Randolph Hearst sent the editors of his many newspapers a two-word telegram reading, "Puff Graham." And it has tremendous power to hurt people; ask Gary Hart, whose 1987 presidential bid collapsed when newspaper reporters indicated that he was involved in at least two extramarital affairs. The press can push the nation toward war, as Hearst's newspapers did prior to the Spanish-American War, or help guide it toward peace, as some newspapers and broadcasters did in the Vietnam years.

Aware of their power, many journalists concede that they should try to be "objective." "Objectivity in reporting the news," reads the code of ethics of Sigma Delta Chi, the society of professional journalists, ". . . serves as the mark of an experienced professional. It is the standard of performance toward which we strive."

But what does "objectivity" mean? Webster's unabridged dictionary, second edition, defines "objective" as "emphasizing or expressing the nature of reality as it is apart from self-consciousness; treating events or phenomena as external rather than as affected by one's reflections or feelings; expressing facts without distortion from one's personal feelings or prejudice." But how close can working journalists come to this ideal?

Publishers sometimes talk of objectivity in almost metaphysical terms, as though their newspapers reported only ultimate truth. Such a state of absolute impartiality, which might be termed "Objectivity with an upper-case 'O,'" is seldom to be found in journalism. A few individuals with the perspective of Socrates, Lao Tzu or Jesus may view the world with genuine impartiality, from a peak high above the social jumble, but the publisher who demands *that* objective an outlook from every reporter is going to have a hard time putting together a staff. Most of us are products of our time and place, imbued with assumptions, opinions, judgments and biases, however much we may try, when writing, to set our personal prejudices aside.

For the working journalist, this more feasible goal could be called "'objectivity' with a lower-case 'o.'" It's the objectivity of journalists who want to tell the truth as best they can ascertain it, without bias or prejudice, while understanding that they can but approximate the ideal of absolute impartiality. As the Sigma Delta Chi code says, objectivity is an ideal "toward which we strive," not a standard that every reporter must meet before he or she can write a lead.

Henry Luce, founder of *Time* magazine, preferred the word "fairness" to objectivity, yet *Time* under Luce was often unfair. It called the celebrated American author Henry Miller "that old pornographer," and dismissed Jean Paul Sartre, the eminent French philosopher, as "long a communist crony." When Theodore H. White, later to become author of the *Making of the President* books, quit his post as a *Time* staff reporter, Luce responded to the defection of one of his favorite correspondents by labelling White a "pinko."

The effort to be fair and objective is an ongoing process, more like weeding a garden than carving a monument. Among the more virulent "weeds" that afflict the process are *regional* and *political bias*; *prejudice* in matters of *race, ethnic origin, religion, sex* or *age*; and *news bias*, produced simply by the desire to get a good story.

Regional Bias

Regional bias is prevalent on the national level; most nations indoctrinate their young with patriotic beliefs, and journalists, like other citizens, tend to grow up with a nationalistic bias. Nationalistic bias is responsible for the tendency of many American newspapers to call anti-American leaders "strongmen" and "bosses" but to describe the dictators of friendly regimes as "statesmen." As Robert E. Smith of *Newsday* points out, the American press habitually refers to the "*regimes* of unfriendly countries and the *administrations* of friendly countries; *military muscle* in Soviet May Day parades, *colorful marching units* on July Fourth in this country; *puppet governments* among Communist nations (like North Korea), and *allies* among non-Communist nations (like South Korea)."

On the local level, regional bias may take the form of "boosterism," the feeling that journalists ought not to write anything that's bad for business in the community. The Associated Press Managing Editors Code of Ethics states that a "newspaper should report the news without regard for its own interests. It should not give favored news treatment to advertisers of special-interest groups. . . .

Concern for community, business or personal interests should not cause a newspaper to distort or misrepresent the facts." Yet many an editor has instructed reporters to ignore news that might offend a major advertiser. This doesn't make the editor a villain; the very survival of the newspaper may be at stake. But it does make life difficult for the reporter trying to do his or her job. If you're told to forget about covering, say, asbestos cancer in a town whose major employer is an asbestos plant, you can object and argue and grumble about the decision, but ultimately there isn't much else to do except to start looking for a job on a paper whose sacred cows are fewer, or smaller.

Political Bias

Reporters who let their own political bias or that of their publishers affect how they write a straight news story can wind up looking pretty foolish. When Upton Sinclair, a socialist, ran for governor of California in 1934, the *Los Angeles Times*, then rabidly Republican, simply ignored him. Times readers learned of his existence only in occasional items suggesting that he was a threat to motherhood, the home and the church. Meanwhile, the *Times*'s chief political correspondent produced a series of phony newsreels, distributed to movie houses throughout the state, that contained faked footage damaging to Sinclair. In one episode, a bearded "radical" announced that he planned to vote for Sinclair because, "Vell, his system vorked vell in Roosia, vy can't it vork here?" Sinclair lost the election, but the *Times* lost, too; its tactics tarnished the paper's reputation for years thereafter.

Avoid loaded language. Are the candidates "left-wingers," which sounds derogatory, or are they "liberals," which has a more neutral tone? Did the Nazi marchers constitute a "mob," implying that they were disorderly, or just a "gathering"? Was that a "smirk" on the candidate's face, or a "smile"?

Racial, Ethnic and Religious Prejudice

Racial, ethnic and religious prejudice have eased in the press, as in American society generally; the days are gone when the New York *Daily News* considered blacks newsworthy only if they broke either an athletic record or the law, and when *The New York Times* refused to print the bylines of Jewish reporters for fear the paper might appear to be "too Jewish." But problems persist. Some newspapers, for instance, still habitually report the race of criminal suspects when they are black but not when they are white. As journalist Ernest Dunbar writes, "If the purpose of identifying a suspect by race is to help in his or her apprehension, to say that a suspect is 'Black' is patently meaningless. Blacks come in all colors, sizes, and shades and to simply give the description 'Black' only narrows the special list to 25 million people."

Generally, journalists should report the race of the people they write about only when race is relevant to the news at hand. As the Code of Broadcast

News Ethics puts it: "Factors such as race, creed, nationality or prior status will be reported only when they are relevant."

Language offensive to religious and ethnic groups frequently arises inadvertently, from ignorance. Moslems no more like to be called Mohammedans than Christians like being called Jesus freaks. The appropriate terms are Chinese, not Chinaman, and Scot not Scotchman. Avoid such ethnic stereotypes and cliches as "repressed WASP," "drunk as an Indian," "Papist" for Catholic, or any other description that tends to portray the members of a given racial, religious or ethnic group as if all were the same and somehow inferior. Offensive language—*Pollack, Wop, Kike, Mick, Wetback*—belongs in print only when its context makes it obviously newsworthy—as when Secretary of Agriculture Earl Butz told friends a crude joke about "niggers," reports of which led to his resignation.

When in the slightest doubt about the propriety of a word or phrase that might prove offensive, try it out on yourself and see how you like it. Then try it out on the reporter sitting at the next desk—or on the copy editors.

Sexual Prejudice

Sexual prejudice used to be widespread in newspapers. Tabloids ran "bathing beauty" photos daily, and the "women's pages" were dumping grounds for trivia. Today, most papers try to be more even-handed in their treatment of the sexes. A few guidelines can help you avoid sexual prejudice:

Apply the same standards to describing the appearance of women and men. A good test is to reverse the sex of your subject and see how the description then sounds. If you describe the female defense attorney in a trial as "stunning," "well coiffeured" or "statuesque," you'd better be prepared to use language of equivalent emotional content to describe the male prosecutor. If Goldie Hawn is "sexy," then so, presumably, is Burt Reynolds. To write otherwise is to turn a blind eye on the sexual perspective of half your readers.

Avoid language that inaccurately assigns jobs or social roles by sex. A secretary or telephone operator is not necessarily "she," any more than an auto mechanic is necessarily "he." A third of the guards at the maximum-security San Quentin prison, including those serving on the "goon squad," for example, are women. "Girl" is appropriate only when "boy" is too; avoid gaffs like that of the Burlington, Vermont, *Free Press*, which headlined a story about an 18-year-old, BRATTLEBORO MAN FOUND DEAD, while reporting the death of a 26-year-old woman, MONTPELIER GIRL FOUND DEAD.

No purpose is served by writing "policemen" for a patrol force that's 20 percent women, or "chairman" if the chair is held by a female. "Humankind" is less discriminatory than "mankind." Some degree of sexual discrimination, however, is built into English, as in the use of indefinite personal pronouns ("Who among us knows the day of *his* death?"). The details of how to resolve these questions seem relatively unimportant, as long as journalists resolve to abjure stereotypes in general.

Sexual preference—for example, homosexuality—is nobody's business except insofar as newsworthy issues are involved. When a congressman who had publicly attacked homosexuality admitted to having a homosexual affair with a congressional page, the issue that made the story legitimate news was hypocrisy, not sexual preference.

Age Prejudice

Prejudice about age, like other forms of prejudice, can arise despite a newswriter's good intentions. Columnist Nicolas von Hoffman meant no harm when he disparaged television commentators by remarking that, "You probably could have heard stronger opinions in the nation's nursing homes," but, as a number of his older readers wrote in to remind him, the residents of nursing homes can have strong opinions just like anyone else. The reporter who referred to a retiree as "still spry at 70" failed to understand that plenty of people are spry at 70, and don't appreciate the suggestion that they aren't supposed to be. Slurs like "dottering" or "senile" and patronizing euphemisms like "golden agers" have no place in professional newswriting.

"News" Bias

"News" bias is unbalanced coverage arising from the burning desire to get a good story. It takes several forms. One form is the temptation to "hype" or embellish the facts in order to beef up a story—for example, by "improving" a quotation. This quote is from a report of a visit by Richard Nixon to the Philippines: "Said one Filipino, 'There goes the symbol of American friendship and resistance to Communist aggression.'" The quote may have made its heavy-handed point, but does it sound like any Filipino—or anybody else—you know? Another symptom of news bias is blatant exaggeration. When an electrical power failure blacked out New York City for fifteen hours in 1977, the *New York Post* headlined its story about the resulting looting spree REIGN OF TERROR— this about a night when no one was killed, few were injured, and there was no panic. When a transit worker's strike inconvenienced New Yorkers, the *Post* headline read, CHAOS. The truth was that most people had managed to get to work and back in fairly good humor and without serious mishap.

Even when there is no deliberate exaggeration, distortion can result from selective emphasis upon the most "newsworthy" elements of a story. S. I. Hayakawa, a political conservative, was president of San Francisco State College during a period marked by student protests against the Vietnam War. Photographers and film editors zeroed in on an incident in which Hayakawa climbed atop a sound truck and ripped out its wires amid a crowd of hostile students. Reviewing coverage of the story, the National Commission on the Causes and Prevention of Violence reported:

> The television newscast gave the impression that the entire university was in turmoil. If the viewer read the *Los Angeles Times* account the next day, he learned that the

event on television reported only one episode that lasted eight or ten minutes. The rest of the day, Dr. Hayakawa was in his office receiving groups of students seeking to restore order on campus. The same day, 16,000 students attended class and did not participate in the disturbances.

A *Washington Post* account of racial disorders in York, Pennsylvania, was accompanied by a photograph of a black youth riding a motorcycle with a rifle strapped across his back. "The implication was that the 'armed rider' was up to no good, at best, or a possible sniper, at worst," notes Hillier Krieghbaum in *Pressures on the Press*. "Actually it showed a sixteen-year-old boy who was fond of hunting groundhogs. He strapped a rifle across his back with a hunting license dangling so that all would see he was hunting animals, not people. Unfortunately, that was not the impression readers got." The story had been "hyped" at the expense of the truth.

The "scoop mentality"—which emphasizes getting the story first over getting it accurately—is another source of news bias. President Reagan's decision on the highly controversial question of how to base MX missiles was widely, and inaccurately, reported a day in advance of its being announced. George Skelton of the *Los Angeles Times* recounts how the scoop mentality led journalists astray:

> Everybody smelled a great story and the goal was to get it first.
> The television networks moved first, reporting the [erroneous] plan on the nightly news shows. Then, the major wire services jumped on it and moved stories to the newspapers. Newspaper editors, wanting to use stories by their own reporters, urged their Washington bureaus to "match" the wire stories. And many reporters did—matching similar inaccuracies.
> The sources identified as "Administration officials" basically were Pentagon or other national security establishment personnel who obviously thought they knew what was going on but didn't. The many "congressional sources" also clearly were guessing.
> Was the White House upset about the inaccurate information being distributed to the American public? Not really. There was a collective chuckle from some strategists, who saw this as a good opportunity to "teach" the news media a lesson: that they should not try to report news until the White House is ready to make it.

Reporters have staged events to "improve" the quality of their video or audio tapes. A photographer covering an urban riot, for instance, encouraged a young black boy to throw a rock for the cameras. A radio reporter suggested to a group of picketers that they chant a slogan of his own devising, telling them it would make "good audio." To prevent such abuses, the television networks and other major news organizations insist that their reporters not stage or try to influence the events they cover. A reporter about to tape an interview may outline intended questions or suggest which general subjects the interview is to cover, but most broadcast news departments forbid actually rehearsing interviews.

Objectivity and Advocacy

Covering the news fairly and objectively doesn't mean abandoning your emotions and opinions. Nobody expects you to remain untouched when you see an innocent person sent to death row, a child terrified by a prowler, or the pensions

---

**PLEBES SCORE ROME PRESS; DEMAND OBJECTIVE
COVERAGE OF CAESAR FUNERAL ORATION**

Suppose that reporters from three newspapers have been assigned to cover the funeral of
Julius Caesar. The story (as recreated by Shakespeare from an account in Plutarch) is this:

Caesar has been assassinated by a band of high-ranking conspirators, among them a
magistrate, Marcus Brutus. A crowd of plebeians has assembled in the Forum to hear the
funeral orations. Brutus speaks first. He convinces the crowd that Caesar was an ambitious
tyrant who deserved to die. He says he helped plot the assassination "not that I loved Caesar
less, but that I loved Rome more." Confident that he has the crowd on his side, Brutus departs
after introducing Mark Antony, a senator loyal to Caesar.

In a masterful display of rhetoric, Antony stirs the crowd to sympathy for Caesar and outrage
against the assassins. "Friends, Romans, countrymen, lend me your ears," he begins. At first
he is restrained. He says that he regards Brutus as "an honorable man." But the phrase
begins to sound increasingly ironical, as Antony recounts Caesar's many deeds on behalf of
Rome and then recalls the brutality of his murder. When Antony reads Caesar's will, with its
provisions for all citizens, the enraged crowd rushes from the square, vowing revenge against
the assassins.

The first of the three reporters to file his story is Righteous. A reedy, high-strung man
worried about paying the rent on his summer villa, Righteous works for the Rome *Morning
Standard*, a paper editorially sympathetic to Caesar and opposed to the assassins. Hoping to
curry favor with his publisher by slanting his story to suit the newspapers' political stance, he
files a dispatch that begins:

Upstanding Romans by the thousands today
vowed revenge upon the vile assassins who murdered Julius Caesar in the Senate chamber March
15.

Shouting, "Let not a traitor live!" the indignant
Romans fanned out across the city following a display of Caesar's body at the Forum. Their pursuit
sent the craven traitors into hiding.

Their anger had been kindled by a magnificent
funeral oration delivered by Mark Antony, who said
of Caesar, "He was my friend, faithful and just to
me." Antony dramatically drew back the shroud covering Caesar's body and displayed to the crowd the
slain hero's body rent with cruel knife wounds.

"Let me not stir you up to such a sudden flood
of mutiny," Antony implored the crowd. But the people in their wisdom were quick to see the truth in
his praise of Caesar and to pledge that they would
avenge his murderers.

In a generous will revealed by Antony, Caesar
awarded seventy-five drachmas to each Roman citizen, and left to the public his orchards and gardens
along the Tiber.

Earlier the plebeians had been addressed by
Marcus Brutus, a leader among the assassins, but
his facile words failed to sway them for long. It was
Antony, that "plain blunt man" as he called himself,
who saved the day . . .

And so on. Notice that for all its heavy-handedness, Righteous's biased dispatch contains
nothing that is necessarily false. The Romans in the crowd may in fact have been "upstanding,"

---

of retirees stolen by mobsters. Joseph Pulitzer inscribed on the cornerstone of
the *New York World* building the words, "Forever fighting every form of wrong,"
and idealistic motives like Pulitzer's remain strong among journalists today. But
in the long run, the most effective way to pursue these goals is to be factual
and fair. Anything less is like playing tennis with a lowered net: ineffective
against your adversaries, useless in building your skills.

Howard James of the *Christian Science Monitor* was outraged by the ineptitude
and arrogance he found among the nation's worst judges. But he wrote in
terms of facts, not opinions. One judge, he reported, read comics and filled

the assassins "vile" and Brutus "facile." But rather than let us arrive at these conclusions for ourselves, Righteous tries to force them on us.

Also covering the speech is Leftous. Fat, sweaty, addicted to wine, Leftous works for the Rome *Progressive*, a newspaper owned in part by Brutus and highly sympathetic to the assassins. He writes what he thinks *his* publisher will want to read. His story begins:

Marcus Brutus, a leader of the revolutionary vanguard that has delivered Rome from the tyranny of Julius Caesar, today told cheering throngs at Caesar's funeral that he had acted "not that I loved Caesar less, but that I loved Rome more."

Thousands in the Forum shouted, "Live, Brutus, live!" when the tall, handsome senator offered to kill himself if they disapproved of Caesar's slaying.

"Who here is so vile that will not love his country?" Brutus asked the crowd. "If any, speak; for him have I offended."

The crowd responded, "None, Brutus, none!"

Brutus then generously yielded time to Caesar's friend Mark Antony, who in a funeral oration extolled Brutus and his comrades as "honorable men . . ."

Here, too, the bias is obvious. Like Righteous, Leftous is basically factual, but his choice of *which* facts to include seriously distorts the story. We hear of Brutus's speech, but learn nothing of how Antony transformed the crowd's sympathies shortly thereafter.

The third journalist on the scene is Objectivus, a reporter for the Rome *Times*—known for its fair, objective reporting and its freedom from favoritism, bias or expressions of personal opinion. His story begins:

Thousands of Romans calling for revenge against the assassins of Emperor Julius Caesar stormed out of his funeral at the Forum today, shouting that they would burn the homes of the men who stabbed him to death in the Senate chamber March 15.

Cries of, "Let not a traitor live!" echoed through the streets after the crowd of plebeians heard an impassioned oration by Caesar loyalist Mark Antony.

Antony drew back the funeral shroud to display Caesar's body, rent with multiple stab wounds. He read the crowd a will in which the emperor left each Roman citizen seventy-five drachmas and deeded to the public his gardens and orchards along the near banks of the Tiber.

Immediately before Antony spoke, Marcus Brutus, a leader of the assassins, told the crowd he acted out of patriotic motives when he took part in the plot to kill the emperor, whom he described as "ambitious." Onlookers cried, "Live, Brutus, live!" when the chief magistrate said he would kill himself if they disapproved of the assassination, and cheered when he said he had agreed to the plot "not that I loved Caesar less, but that I loved Rome more."

But after hearing Antony, the crowd called for the assassins' blood, despite Antony's characterization of Brutus and his collaborators as "honorable men," and his caution to the plebeians, "Let me not stir you up to such a sudden flood of mutiny."

Objectivus's account gives us both sides of the story and lets us draw our own conclusions; we aren't told whom to like or hate. And it's at least as compelling as the other two dispatches. Fairness and objectivity need not mean dullness.

out a crossword puzzle while a woman in the witness stand testified in a criminal trial. Another, annoyed at an attorney who failed to appear in court, jailed the attorney's client. Another humiliated a woman who appeared in court with her children to plead that she could not afford to pay an $18 traffic fine. Facts like these, dispassionately reported, made their point more powerfully than any expression of editorial outrage.

Gene Miller of *The Miami Herald* worked doggedly for twelve years to free two men convicted of a murder they did not commit. He was ridiculed by public prosecutors and punched in the nose by a nephew of one of the murder victims, but he didn't waste space in his stories proclaiming the convicts' innocence or complaining that he was being persecuted for trying to help them. Instead, he stuck to the facts. When the facts at last prevailed and the two finally were freed, Miller's last account was as objective in tone as those that had preceded it. It began:

> Freddie Pitts and Wilbert Lee walked away from the shadow of death at 37 minutes past noon Friday. They did not look back.
> The clamorous din of the men behind bars faded behind them. A wave of men behind cameras receded before them. Unsmiling, Pitts and Lee acknowledged neither.
> After 12 years and 48 days of imprisonment for another man's crime, they walked into the world as free men, a Xerox copy of the governor's pardon folded in their billfolds.
> "I've had enough of this hotel," Pitts said mildly. "They have very poor accommodations."

James and Miller let the facts speak for themselves. Both their efforts won them Pulitzer Prizes.

The more passionately reporters believe in their stories, the more closely they need to guard against being unfair. In the CBS documentary, "The Uncounted Enemy: A Vietnam Deception," producer George Crile was so convinced that his thesis was true—that during the Vietnam War General William Westmoreland had conspired to deceive the President and the American people about the enemy's troop strength—that he gave short shrift to the general's side of the story. The documentary was lopsided—the general and his one defender got six minutes on the air, while his nine accusers were on screen for over nineteen minutes—and the general's critics were allowed to rehearse their interviews while the general himself was subjected to a withering grilling. Moreover, omitted from the documentary was testimony from President Lyndon B. Johnson himself that he was aware of the enemy's full troop strength during the period that Westmoreland was said to have been falsifying those figures. Had the documentary been more even-handed, it might have convinced more people of its case. As it was, the network's own investigation of the program reached conclusions not far from the general's complaint that he had been the victim of a hatchet job. (General Westmoreland's libel suit against CBS is discussed in Chapter 17, *Libel and Privacy*.)

ETHICS

In the comedy film *The Producers*, Zero Mostel tries to ensure an unfavorable review for a play by slipping the leading newspaper drama critic $20 on opening night. The critic is, of course, appalled by the attempted bribe. Yet theater and film critics routinely accept free tickets to plays and attend parties, screenings and other promotional events at which the food and drinks are paid for by the producers. Where, between the extremes of out-and-out bribery and routine professional courtesy, can we draw a line dividing ethical and unethical behavior?

Some cases are fairly clearcut. No journalist rose to defend *Washington Post* reporter Janet Cooke when she was found to have fabricated her 1981 Pulitzer Prize-winning story about an 8-year-old heroin addict. Nor did any journalist applaud the freelancer, whose supposedly on-the-scene story about suffering in Cambodia, published in *The New York Times Magazine*, turned out to have been written from his home in Spain and to have incorporated long, unattributed passages from a 1930 novel by the French author André Malraux.

Disagreements about ethics arise not in such obvious cases, but in the grey areas between what is clearly right or wrong. Here, even seasoned professionals can and do differ. In a survey conducted in 1984 for Sigma Delta Chi, the journalistic honor society, 819 newspaper editors and broadcast news executives were asked to make ethical judgments on thirty examples of journalistic behavior. In one of the instances cited in the survey, a reporter got her newspaper to provide special coverage of her personal protest against a local school board. In another, a reporter impersonated the relative of an accident victim to get information on her injuries from the hospital. In a third, an editor had to decide whether to print the fact that the son of a conservative candidate for governor was a homosexual. When the answers were tallied, it turned out that in *none* of the cases did the editors unanimously agree whether the conduct was ethical. In nearly a quarter of the cases, about half the editors thought the conduct in question was ethical and the other half thought it was not.

Three persistent grey areas in journalistic ethics are *conflict of interest*, *public relations and news manipulation* and *ethics of reporting*.

Conflict of Interest

A prevalent source of conflict of interest is the *freebie*—anything of financial value given to journalists by those who stand to benefit from favorable press treatment. Freebies can range from a bottle of Scotch sent to a columnist by the governor as a "Seasons greetings" gift, all the way up to computers, cars and even homes "loaned" to reporters by the people whose businesses they are covering. Most journalists would agree that there's nothing wrong with getting a $2.98 plastic datebook free in the mail, but that there *is* something wrong with accepting the loan of a car or a house. But where do we draw the line?

Some journalists deal with this issue by flatly refusing to accept any freebie, however insignificant. "There's no such thing as something for nothing," reads the ethics code of the San Bernardino, California, *Sun*. "As professional journalists, we have no reason to expect, to seek, to want or to accept extra money, extra privileges, gifts, comps, favors, or freebies from anyone." The *Philadelphia Inquirer* ethics code says, "We pay our own way. If it is newsworthy, we can afford it. If it is not, we can get along without it." This position is unambiguous, but can be awkward to enforce. If a bank sends every reporter on the paper a little plastic card bearing emergency phone numbers and the bank's slogan, must the staff take the trouble of mailing all the cards back? The *Des Moines*

Register and Tribune "recognizes that questions will arise about the acceptance of such things as a cup of coffee, a hot dog or a meal in an individual's home. The key to such situations is judgment. . . . We think it is logical that when one is invited by an individual or firm to lunch or dinner, it would be neither discourteous nor unprofessional to say something to the effect, 'Yes, I'd be happy to meet you, but I want to say beforehand that our policy here on such things is that I pay for my own meal.'"

Other news organizations set a maximum dollar value on the freebies their staff members are permitted to accept. At *Newsweek*, the limit is $50. The *Minneapolis Star* requires that free review copies of books and records be donated to charity.

Junkets—free trips for journalists—are an especially problematical form of freebie. Distillers offer reporters complementary tours of gourmet restaurants, garment makers fly them to Paris fashion shows, wealthy politicians wine and dine them at their country estates. Accepting such junkets can create at least the appearance of corruption: "I own every fashion editor in America," boasted one fashion industry public relations expert who had conducted many junkets.

Some newspapers prohibit junkets, period. But others accept them, arguing that if it weren't for junkets, they couldn't afford to send reporters to cover as many out-of-town stories.

Newspapers and broadcasters that accept junkets usually insist that each be cleared with ranking editors. No staff reporter should accept a junket, or any freebie of value, without consulting the boss.

More serious is the obvious conflict that arises when a business reporter plays the stock market, or a real estate editor invests in a development scheme. A number of newspapers and magazines, among them *Forbes*, *Business Week*, the *Chicago Tribune*, *The Washington Post* and *The New York Times*, require their business staff reporters and editors to file disclosures of their finances with management. Others, including the *Los Angeles Times*, *The Miami Herald*, the Associated Press and CBS, ABC and NBC News, do not require disclosure but advise their reporters to report any holdings that might involve a conflict of interest. As the ethics code of *The Milwaukee Journal* puts it, "Financial investments or other outside business activities by *Journal* staff members that would conflict with *The Journal's* ability to report the news, or that would create the impression of such a conflict, must be avoided."

Freelancing—writing for a publication that doesn't employ you full-time—would not pose conflict of interest questions were it not for the suspicion that some freelance assignments are so cushy and high-paying as to constitute a freebie in disguise. There's nothing wrong with freelancing in itself: Nobody objects if, say, an *Atlanta Constitution* reporter writes a book review for the *New Republic*. But what happens when a political reporter is paid by a candidate to write an adoring campaign biography, or when a travel writer makes thousands of dollars writing articles for a magazine published by a hotel chain? Even if the reporters involved don't feel that their independence has been compromised, the public may think otherwise.

Sports columnist Jerry Izenberg of the Newark *Star Ledger* wrote articles for *Pro* magazine, published by the National Football League, until NFL commissioner Pete Rozelle called one day, complained about a *Star Ledger* story, then mentioned Izenberg's contributions to the high-paying *Pro*. Concerned that NFL officials might think that their freelancing fees entitled them to special consideration, Izenberg stopped writing for *Pro*.

Some newspapers forbid their employees to freelance, but this approach tends to drive away some of the most talented and productive writers. One solution is to avoid writing for publications that might imply a conflict of interest: If you expect to be thought impartial when you write about gun control, don't pad your income by freelancing for *Guns & Ammo*.

Financial pressure from advertisers is a chronic threat at smaller newspapers, where the loss of a single major advertiser can cripple the paper. As the editor of one small weekly put it, "News stories inform the ordinary citizen, but he is only paying 35 cents, so the advertiser may have greater leverage. It takes a strong-minded editor to damn the torpedoes without considering the impact on advertising." Professor Timothy Hubbard of the University of Missouri polled 162 business and financial editors and found that fully 20 percent admitted to routinely altering stories at the request of advertisers. At the *Florida Times-Union* in Jacksonville, owned by the Atlantic Coast Line railroad, photoengravers were ordered to airbrush the railroad's logo from the sides of boxcars in photographs of a wreck. A local joke had it that Jacksonville was "a city where trains don't hit cars, cars hit trains."

A useful rule to follow in confronting potential financial conflicts of interest is the one often applied to judges—to avoid not just the impropriety, but the *appearance* of impropriety. In 1983 the *Village Voice* learned, to its embarrassment, that Alexander Cockburn, a *Voice* columnist seldom sympathetic to the state of Israel, had accepted $10,000 from an Arab foundation as an advance on a book he was to write. Cockburn never wrote the book but was permitted to keep the money, an unusual practice in the publishing world. Fellow journalists who knew Cockburn's high ethical standards never seriously believed that his opinions were being bought, but the *Voice*, concerned with what readers would think, ordered Cockburn suspended indefinitely, and he soon went to work elsewhere. As the *Chicago Tribune* cautions in its ethics code, staffers "are expected to avoid any compromises of their journalistic integrity. This must include *even the appearance* of compromise" (emphasis added).

Reporters who specialize in covering business and financial news bear a particularly heavy burden in this regard. Knowing that a favorable (or unfavorable) story you are writing about a corporation will, when published, surely drive its stock prices up (or down) poses a genuine temptation: You or your friends could profit handsomely by playing the market, or by selling the information to other investors. In the 1960s and 1970s the Securities and Exchange Commission found that this sort of temptation had proved too much for business writers at *Time* magazine and the *Los Angeles Herald-Examiner*, and both men lost their jobs. In 1984, a *Wall Street Journal* columnist who had tipped off stock traders to inside information prior to its appearance in the column was convicted of stock manipulation and sentenced to a prison term.

Just as hard to deal with as financial conflicts of interest are appeals that involve not money but friendly persuasion—what might be called "interpersonal" conflict of interest. Political reporter Haynes Johnson found himself becoming so friendly with Senator Robert Kennedy that Kennedy called him at 2 A.M. one night to ask his advice about whether he should run for the presidency. Acting as a journalist and not as a confidant, Johnson promptly filed a story reporting that Kennedy was thinking about running. Kennedy offered Johnson a job; Johnson turned him down. Eventually Johnson handled the matter by taking himself off the Kennedy campaign story for a while.

Here again, the appearance of impropriety can be as damaging as the substance. When columnist George Will revealed that he had helped brief Ronald Reagan for his 1980 campaign debate with President Carter, few, if any, editors questioned Will's personal integrity, but a number of newspapers cancelled his column anyway, saying that his relationship with Reagan just looked a little too cozy.

Public Relations and News Manipulation

Reporters risk being seduced by the sheer glamour and persuasive power of the rich and famous people they sometimes cover. "Power is an insidious commodity," writes journalist Molly Ivins:

> It's fascinating. Once you get into who's doing what for whom, it's as addictive as smack. And it works the same way: you need more and more of it and you produce less and less. You start to identify with your sources, and then you're gone. . . . You get fascinated by it and pretty soon you can't see anything else, just the top, just the power. And the others, the people, the readers, matter so little that you don't even bother to let them know what's going on.

Journalists must put the interests of their readers above those of the people they cover. As the Sigma Delta Chi code says, journalists' "responsibilities to the public are paramount. That is the nature of their profession."

Journalists are sometimes asked to alter or suppress news for the good of the community. When a burglary ring in Staten Island, New York, began preying on people who had suffered a death in the family, knowing that they would be away from home on the day of the funeral, the police asked the local paper, the *Staten Island Advance*, to omit exact addresses when listing survivors in obituaries. The paper agreed. Similarly, journalists may refrain from printing the names of witnesses to serious crimes, for fear that the criminals might try to intimidate or kill the witnesses.

But journalists more often resist the entreaties of public officials who cite civic responsibility as a justification for concealing the facts. The mayor of a small city in Rhode Island asked the *Providence Journal* to hold off running a story about mismanagement in the local Sewer Authority until the city could obtain a badly needed federal grant to construct a new sewer system. The paper refused. As it turned out, the city got the grant anyway, but with it came stern warnings for the Sewer Authority to clean up its act.

Ethics of Reporting

In the movie *Absence of Malice* Sally Field plays a reporter who will go to almost any length to get a story: She wears a concealed tape recorder, has an affair with a man she's covering, betrays the confidence of a source. . . .

How much of this is ethical? How far *should* a reporter be willing to go to get a story? Opinions differ. Most reporters, for instance, believe that they shouldn't break the law. But what about the team of reporters from the Wilmington, North Carolina, *Morning Star* who in 1984 dressed up as bearded terrorists and infiltrated the U.S. Marine base at Camp Lejeune? One "terrorist" reporter even sauntered into a general's home and persuaded his wife to let him use the bathroom. The law the reporters broke was a stern one prohibiting trespassing on military installations. But the point they made in their subsequent story was important—that the Marines were not protecting themselves adequately against domestic terrorism.

Not many reporters lie to get a story, and yet impersonating people—"going undercover"—is a time-honored journalistic technique. Gloria Steinem took a job as a Playboy Club bunny in order to write a story for *Harper's* magazine. Lindsay Van Gelder of the *New York Post* wrote a feature on the chorus girls who make up the Rockettes at Radio City Music Hall by becoming a Rockette herself, and Cameron Crowe, posing as a student, attended classes at his old high school for a *Rolling Stone* article. Nobody was hurt by these mild deceptions, and all produced lively first-person stories. (Crowe's piece was made into the movie *Fast Times at Ridgemont High*.)

A reporter may, of course, attend a public meeting without revealing that he or she is a reporter, provided that no vote has been taken to exclude the press. But if the meeting is obviously of a sensitive nature—Alcoholics Anonymous, for instance, or a group of rape victims—then the ethical thing is for the reporter to identify him- or herself and ask permission to stay.

But suppose you're investigating what you suspect to be a fraudulent scheme for recruiting door-to-door salespeople, run by a bogus outfit that holds lavish recruitment meetings at which it promises people a chance to get rich quick, sells them expensive sales kits and then leaves town. You respond to an ad in the paper, and attend a recruitment meeting without identifying yourself as a reporter. Later, interviewing a promoter of the scheme who wasn't present at the meeting, you ask questions about recruitment methods without first revealing that you attended the meeting, to see whether his or her account squares with what you saw.

This level of concealment may seem defensible. But what if you conceal yourself in a closet and watch the meeting from there? Or what if you carry a concealed tape recorder into the meeting hall?

By this point, many reporters would have drawn the line. "I might get the story," says one veteran, "but I'd feel a little ashamed to admit *how* I got the story." The law agrees; in several jurisdictions, deliberate eavesdropping and using a concealed tape recorder are illegal.

Suppose that you're confronted at the sales meeting by a person who demands to know if you're a reporter. If you deny it, you're guilty of telling an outright lie. Most reporters agree that so bald a deception is unethical, at least most of the time, but many are prepared to employ at least a trace of deception when circumstances seem to warrant it. A police reporter phoning a patrol officer at the scene of a murder might identify him- or herself by saying only, "This is Connors, down at headquarters," in hopes that the patrol officer will assume he or she is talking to another police officer. If the reporter goes further and says, "This is *Captain* Connors," he or she is risking arrest for impersonating a police officer. In 1985 a reporter for the Morristown, New Jersey, *Daily Record* was found guilty by a municipal court judge of telling the mother of a girl who had been stabbed to death that she was an official from the county morgue in order to gain intimate details of the girl's life. The reporter was fined $500 and sentenced to perform thirty days of community service.

"Perhaps the best and easiest test for deciding whether to use deception in a journalistic investigation," says Deni Elliott, a philosopher at Wayne State University who specializes in journalistic ethics, "is to proceed only if the deception will be aggressively defended by the readers in the light of the seriousness of the information to be uncovered." But what if a promising story later fails to pan out? In 1978 Beth Nissen, then a 20-year-old cub reporter for *The Wall Street Journal*, took a job as a factory worker for Texas Instruments in Austin, Texas, to learn whether the company was engaged in illegal union busting. Nissen worked for two weeks soldering component boards, then was fired after walking in one day wearing a T-shirt emblazoned with the logo of the United Auto Workers union. But Nissen nonetheless came up with little evidence that the company was doing anything that would have been considered illegal by the National Labor Relations Board, and she later had second thoughts about her undercover activities. "If I had to do it again, I don't think I would," said Nissen, later an instructor at the Columbia Graduate School of Journalism. "Here I was engaging in the same kind of underhanded conduct we suspected the company of. Somehow it just didn't seem right."

Besides deception, another reporting technique that raises ethical issues is reporters' involvement in a *quid pro quo*, which means "tit for tat"—the exchange of one thing for another. Swapping information is standard practice for many beat reporters and investigative reporters, but it can be ethically treacherous. A public prosecutor may be willing to trade inside information on an investigation in return for a reporter's telling him or her what one of the suspects said during an interview, but such deals tend to make reporters look like prosecutors themselves, a stigma that can destroy public trust in journalism as an independent estate. People in power often seek to use the news media to their advantage— like the influential attorney in the film *The Verdict*, who exploits his journalistic contacts to plant a flattering newspaper profile of a doctor he's defending in a malpractice suit. Reporters who fall for such arrangements aren't reporting—they're being used.

The situation becomes even more questionable when the medium of exchange is money. "Checkbook journalism"—paying for information—poses at least three dangers: First, if sources are being paid for information, they may be tempted to exaggerate or fabricate in order to justify (or boost) their fees. Second, by putting a price tag on hot news, checkbook journalism tends to restrict access to major stories to the big news organizations that can afford to outbid the competition. And checkbook journalism doesn't always pan out. David Frost paid Richard Nixon more than a million dollars to submit to over twenty-eight hours of videotaped interviews; Nixon then evaded most of Frost's questions. Don Hewitt, founder of "60 Minutes," paid $10,000 to a source who promised to disclose how labor boss Jimmy Hoffa had been murdered and where his body was buried, but the "source" absconded with the money.

TASTE

Standards of taste are notoriously difficult for people to agree upon, and journalists vary widely in their opinion of just what constitutes bad taste in newswriting.

Profanity presents recurring problems. When Florida State Senator Dempsey Barron told Senate President W. D. Childers, "You little shit, I'm going to whip your ass and throw you out of the Senate right now," *The Miami Herald* and *The Tallahassee Democrat* printed his exact words. Many other papers in the state, among them the Ft. Lauderdale *Sun-Sentinel* and *The St. Petersburg Times*, did not. Some replaced the profane words with dashes. Others paraphrased them. The Associated Press reported the quotation this way: "Barron called Childers a vulgar name, told him graphically what he was going to whip and threatened to "throw you out of the Senate right now."

Recognizing that their individual tastes differ, editors try to decide questions of taste by considering, first, whether the material in question will offend many readers, and, if so, whether it's newsworthy enough to run it anyway. As guidelines at *The Washington Post* put it, "We shall avoid profanities and obscenities unless their use is so essential to a story of significance that its meaning is lost without them." Managing editor Heath Meriwether noted that *The Miami Herald* publishes objectionable language only in rare instances, but, he added, "We quickly decided that this was one of those exceptional cases. Only Barron's exact words could convey the true anger and emotions that almost resulted in a fight on the Senate floor between two of the most powerful men in Florida." The editor of the *Palm Beach Post* agreed that the quotation was newsworthy, but chose not to run it, considering his rather different audience. "Our average reader is probably a 62-year-old woman," he said. "We've got to have compassion for [those] readers."

Violence, too, poses questions of taste. Here again the agreed-upon standard appears to be a matter of weighing offensiveness against news value. A report of a brutal axe murder may rank as news, but it would be in poor taste, and would serve no useful purpose, to include all the grisly details. In contrast, AP photographer Eddie Adams's photo of a South Vietnamese national police chief's casually executing a Viet Cong officer with a pistol shot to the head may have shocked and offended many, but it ran in thousands of newspapers and magazines and became a lasting symbol of the brutality of war.

The American Society of Newspaper Editors' canons deplore "deliberate pandering to vicious instincts." The operative word here is *pandering*, which means catering to base instincts. Pandering is the word for headlines like these, from the *New York Post*, that aim to use violence to sell newspapers:

HEADLESS BODY IN TOPLESS BAR

UNCLE TORTURES TOTS WITH HOT FORK

When does a reporter's probing into people's lives becomes an unjustified violation of privacy—as a matter not of law (see Chapter 18 on the right of privacy), but simply of good taste? "Don't the news media have any moral responsibility?" wrote Lynn Mills of Redondo Beach, California. "Don't people have the right to privacy and dignity?" She had just seen, on KNXT TV news, videotape "that showed on camera a man's reaction to the news that his wife had shot and killed their two young children while he was out." The answer, of course, is yes. People do have a right to privacy and dignity, and reporters do have a right to report the news. The question is how to weigh these two considerations.

The videotape to which Lynn Mills objected, showing a man at the moment that he learned that his wife had killed their children, was aired that night by every television station that had the tape. Steve Cohen, the news director of KNXT, defended his decision this way:

> I felt that this was exactly what TV is all about—the opportunity, within limits, to show the full range of human emotions. It's so occasional that any of us show ourselves for what we really are, emotionally. Our lives are guarded lives. TV news nearly always presents the pseudo world, the world of information from official sources. Here we had the opportunity to mirror one slice of what we really are like, as human beings.

Tasteless reporting practices generate as much public outrage as does the content of controversial news reports. The families of the 239 Marines who died in a terrorist attack in Lebanon were virtually held prisoner in their homes in America by reporters and camera crews clambering to get the "reactions" to the tragic news. At Camp Lejeune, North Carolina, a TV crew paid children to go into a housing area from which the press was barred and search out the families of the dead Marines. "You people will stop at nothing," an angry Marine told reporters. "Everywhere you go, you leave a smell."

Sensitive to complaints about violations of privacy, the Radio-Television News Directors Association code of ethics states that "broadcast newspeople shall at all times display humane respect for the dignity, privacy and the well-being of persons with whom the news deals." CBS TV guidelines hold that "We do not interview or attempt to interview a person who appears to be in a state of shock. Whenever possible, do not attempt to conduct an interview until permission has been obtained from the interviewee."

Ethical questions can arise from *not* reporting news, as well as from reporting it. Most newspapers withhold the names of rape victims, to spare them further humiliation. Yet even this humane policy has generated controversy. "As long as we do not report the names of [rape] victims, we are perpetuating the mythology that the rape victim is somehow to blame for what happened to her," says Eileen Shanahan of the *Pittsburgh Post Gazette*. Sociologist Gilbert Geis of the University of California at Irvine agrees: "The anonymity provision suggests that the public will . . . conclude that the victim in a way contributed to her own fate," he says.

In 1980, Berkeley police officer Raymond Randle was sentenced to three years in prison for allegedly having forced Susan Bird to perform an oral sex act in the men's room of a San Francisco discotheque. The jury was unconvinced by his testimony that she had agreed to perform the act for $6. Newspapers following the customary policy in stories of this sort would have withheld Ms. Bird's name, viewing her as an innocent victim who need not be humiliated by such publicity. But *The San Francisco Chronicle* broke with its usual policy and printed Bird's name in its report of the verdict. In response to the story, a total of seventeen men eventually came forth, all saying they knew Bird as a woman who solicited sex for money. Had the *Chronicle* not printed Bird's name, Randle might well have gone to jail.

A prominent Illinois state official died of a heart attack in the residential hotel he occupied in Springfield. He died in bed—not in his room but in that of his secretary. She called a few friends, who carried his body back to his room before informing the authorities. While in the room, one of the friends opened a closet and discovered that it was filled with shoe boxes stuffed with cash. One newspaper omitted the exact location of his death, to spare his wife embarrassment. Would you have done the same?

ETHICS IN ACTION

As we have seen, the leading journalistic societies, as well as most major news organizations, have codes of conduct that warn against at least the most obvious sorts of unethical or tasteless conduct. Violations may bring warnings, reassignments to less sensitive beats or more substantial action: A New York TV weatherman who took a ski weekend paid for by a resort that he then mentioned glowingly on the air was suspended for two weeks. A wine critic who freelanced a promotional book for a wine distributor was asked to resign his newspaper post.

Newspapers have become more responsive to public criticism. As late as 1973, only a quarter of America's newspapers routinely published corrections of their errors; a decade later, more than three-quarters did. Most of the corrections involved mechanical or factual mistakes, but many newspapers have also begun publishing admissions that they failed to be fair or complete in covering a story. *The New York Times*, for example, published an "Editor's Note" saying that the paper had violated its "standards of news judgment and fairness" in a story about a CBS documentary that had been "too long and too prominently displayed," giving readers an inflated impression of its significance. Another *Times* Editor's Note said that a headline had "failed to reflect the . . . overall theme" of the story. When the June 10, 1983, edition of the *Chicago Tribune* carried a column, an editorial and an editorial cartoon criticizing schoolteachers, some teachers felt that the paper was campaigning against them. Editor James Squires responded with an explanation, headlined "Corrections and Clarifications," reassuring the teachers that the three items had been prepared individually, and that their combined effect was unintentional. A growing number of newspapers regularly publish editors' accounts that defend controversial stories, apologize for lapses in balance or taste or explain why decisions—like *The Miami Herald*'s decision to publish rough language in a quotation—were made.

SUMMARY

Journalists agree that they have an obligation to report the facts fairly and objectively and to act according to the dictates of ethics and taste, but questions naturally arise about how to apply these ideals in practice. Among the leading obstacles to finding the facts are *lies, half-truths, misconceptions* and *false preconceptions, quantitative errors* and *logical fallacies*. Commonplace logical fallacies include the *non sequitur*, which means that the conclusion doesn't follow from the premise; the *ad hominem*, which argues personalities instead of issues; *false cause*, which links unrelated incidents together as if one were responsible for the other; the *strawman*, which is an artificial argument set up solely in order to knock it down, and the *appeal to authority*, which advances an opinion not on its merits but on the basis that it is held by someone famous or powerful.

Quantitative errors, always a hazard to journalists, are becoming more so with the growth of technology and science. Statistical errors are their most common form.

The power of the press to either inform or mislead prompts journalists to seek to use that power without bias or favoritism—that is, to be "objective." This somewhat ambiguous word may be taken to mean that journalists recognize their human biases and blind spots and try to excise them from their straight news writing. They seek to avoid *regional bias*, such as writing about America and its allies in favorable language while writing of our purported adversaries in derogatory language; *political bias*, ventilating their own or others' political views via the news; *racial, ethnic* and *religious prejudice*, including stereotyping people according to their race or creed; *sexual prejudice*, such as demeaning women by referring to them in overly familiar or condescending terms; and *age prejudice*, applying cliches about the old. The desire for a good story can itself lead to distortion, if the most "newsworthy" elements are excessively emphasized at the expense of the whole truth; this might be called *news* bias.

Ethical questions arise not so much over obvious offenses like a journalist's taking a bribe or inventing a news story—though these abuses do occur—as in ethical "grey areas" where reasonable people may differ in their estimation of just what is ethical. These include financial and interpersonal *conflicts of interest*, the effects of *public relations and news manipulation* and the *ethics of reporting*. In matters of *taste*, journalists weigh the offensive nature of a photograph or piece of information against its news value. The answers to questions of ethics and taste in journalism are best found by looking beyond journalism itself, and acting according to what satisfies personal codes and benefits society as a whole.

Here are the answers to the statistical problems on pages 337–38. The comments are based upon those of *The New York Times* copy editors.

1 It makes a cute lead, but it's a safe bet that the Federal statistics indicate life expectancy for persons born in 1974 or thereabouts, not those born 80 years ago. The life expectancy for persons born when Hanna Sanger was born was probably closer to 48 years. And in any case the statistics apply to the Nebraska population in general, not to an individual.

2 If generic drugs are 100 percent cheaper than brand-name drugs, they are free; if they are 700 percent cheaper, the druggist pays you to take them away.

3 100 percent of zero is zero. 300 percent of zero is also zero.

4 Wouldn't "triple" be nearer right?

5 The area of the vessel is 50,000 square feet; the area of one football field alone is something like 48,000 square feet, not counting the end zones.

6 A "majority" would not be 45%; it would have to be more than 50 percent. In an election, if A gets 45 votes, B gets 41 and C gets 14, A does not have a majority; he has a plurality.

APPENDIX: STYLE MANUAL

How do you abbreviate "Colorado"? Is it "Col.," "Co.," or "Colo."? When do you write the numeral "10," and when do you spell it out? Do you always capitalize the *President* of the United States? How about the *president* of Venezuela? It makes little difference which way you do it when you are writing college essays or a letter to a friend; they're all correct English. But on a newspaper everything must be written the same way—all the time. Style manuals contain the rules to ensure such uniformity. Some newspapers, such as *The Washington Post* and *The Chicago Tribune*, have style manuals of their own. Others, mostly smaller ones, use the style rules adopted by the wire services.

Following is a sample style manual that combines the basic rules governing stories written for the Associated Press and United Press International.

I: CAPITALIZATION

1.1 CAPITALIZE titles preceding a name: Secretary of State George P. Shultz. LOWER CASE title standing alone or following a name: George P. Shultz, secretary of state. EXCEPTION: Incumbent president of the United States is always capitalized. Do not capitalize candidate for president, no president may seize, etc.

1.2 CAPITALIZE government officials when used with name as title: Queen Elizabeth II, Premier Chirac, etc. LOWER CASE when standing alone or following a name: Chirac, premier of France.

1.3 CAPITALIZE Pope in all usage; pontiff is lower case.

1.4 CAPITALIZE foreign religious leader titles Imam, Patriarch, etc., but LOWER CASE standing alone or following a name. EXCEP-

TION: Pope and Dalai Lama capitalized in all usage. (See Section VIII)

1.5 CAPITALIZE titles of authority before name but LOWER CASE standing alone or following a name: Ambassador John Jones; Jones, ambassador; the ambassador. (See 1.12, 3.31)

1.6 Long titles should follow a name: John Jones, executive director of the commercial department of Blank & Co. Richard Roe, secretary-treasurer, Blank & Co. (See. 6.5)

1.7 LOWER CASE occupational or "false" titles such as day laborer John Jones, rookie left-handed pitcher Bill Wills, defense attorney John Jones. (See 2.14)

1.8 CAPITALIZE Union, Republic, Colonies referring to the United States; Republic of Korea, French Fifth Republic. (See 2.12)

1.9 CAPITALIZE U.S. Congress, Senate, House, Cabinet; Legislature when preceded by name of state; City Council; Security Council. LOWER CASE when standing alone: The legislature passed 300 bills.

The building is the Capitol, the city is capital.

Do not capitalize "congress" when it is used as a synonym for convention. (see 1.20)

1.10 CAPITALIZE committee in full names: Senate Judiciary Committee, House Ways and Means Committee, etc. LOWER CASE "subcommittee" in titles and standing alone, also "committee" standing alone.

In some shortened versions of long committee names, do not capitalize: Special Senate Select Committee to Investigate Improper Labor-Management Practices often is rackets committee, not capitalized.

1.11 CAPITALIZE full titles: Interstate Commerce Commission, New York State Thruway Authority, International Atomic Energy Authority, etc., LOWER CASE authority, commission, etc., standing alone. (See 2.1)

1.12 CAPITALIZE Supreme Court, Juvenile Court, 6th U.S. Circuit Court of Appeals, etc. (See 4.2) Specify which U.S. Court such as district, patent, tax, etc. It is Juvenile Court Judge John Jones and not Juvenile Judge John Jones.

1.13 CAPITALIZE Social Security (Administration, Act) when referring to U.S. system: He

was receiving Social Security payments. LOWER CASE use in general sense: He was an advocate of social security for old age.

1.14 CAPITALIZE U.S. armed forces: Army (USA), Air Force (USAF), Navy (USN), Marines (USMC), Coast Guard, National Guard but LOWER CASE all foreign except Royal Air Force (RAF) and Royal Canadian Air Force (RCAF); French Foreign Legion, no abbreviation.

CAPITALIZE Marine, Coast Guardman, Swiss Guard, Evzone, Bengal Lancer, etc. LOWER CASE soldier, sailor, etc. NOTE: It is Coast Guardman (no "s") if member of U.S. Coast Guard.

CAPITALIZE Irish Republican Army (political). (See 1.20)

1.15 CAPITALIZE Joint Chiefs of Staff but LOWER CASE chiefs of staff.

1.16 CAPITALIZE holidays, historic events, ecclesiastical feasts, fast days, special events, hurricanes, typhoons, etc. Mother's Day, Labor Day, Battle of the Bulge, Good Friday, Passover, Christmas, Halloween, National Safety Week, Hurricane Hazel, Typhoon Tilda, New Year's (Day, Eve) but LOWER CASE: What will the new year bring? At the start of the new year, etc.

1.17 CAPITALIZE Antarctica, Arctic Circle but not antarctic or arctic.

1.18 CAPITALIZE specific regions: Middle East, Mideast, Middle West, Midwest, Upper Peninsula (Michigan), Southern (Illinois, California), Texas (Oklahoma) Panhandle, Orient, Chicago's near South Side, Loop, etc.

1.19 CAPITALIZE ideological or political areas: East-West, East Germany, West Germany. LOWER CASE mere direction: Snow fell in western North Dakota.

1.20 CAPITALIZE political parties and members but not "party." Democrat, Democratic, Republican, Socialist, Independent, Nationalist, Communist, Congress (India) etc. LOWER CASE democratic form of government, republican system, socialism, communism, etc.

CAPITALIZE Red when used as political, geographic, military, etc., descriptive.

LOWER CASE nationalist in referring to a partisan of a country.

CAPITALIZE Algerian Liberation Front (FLN) and Irish Republican Army (IRA). (See 1.14)

1.21 CAPITALIZE names of fraternal organizations: B'nai B'rith (no abbreviation), Ancient Free & Accepted Masons (AF&AM), Knights of Columbus (K. of C. as departure from 2.1). (See 2.5)

1.22 CAPITALIZE Deity and He, His, Him denoting Deity but not who, whose, whom. CAPITALIZE Talmud, Koran, Bible and all names of the Bible, confessions of faith and their adherents. (See Section VIII)

CAPITALIZE Satan and Hades but not devil and hell.

1.23 CAPITALIZE Civil War, War Between the States, Korean War, Revolution (U.S. and Bolshevik), World War I, World War II, etc.

1.24 CAPITALIZE names of races: Caucasian, Chinese, Negro, Indian, etc. LOWER CASE black, white, red (See 1.20), yellow. Do NOT use "colored" for Negro except in National Association for the Advancement of Colored People. Colored is correct in African usage.

Identification by race should be made when it is pertinent.

1.25 CAPITALIZE common noun as part of formal name: Hoover Dam, Missouri River, Barr County Courthouse. LOWER CASE dam, river, courthouse, etc., standing alone. CAPITALIZE Empire State Building, Blue Room, Carlton House (hotel), Carlton house (home), Wall Street, Hollywood Boulevard. (See 4.1)

Plurals would be: Broad and Main streets.

1.26 CAPITALIZE species of livestock, animals, fowl, etc., but LOWER CASE noun: Airedale, terrier, Percheron, horse; Hereford, whiteface, etc.

1.27 CAPITALIZE names of flowers: Peace rose, etc. If Latin generic names are used CAPITALIZE the genus (camellia, Thea japonica).

1.28 CAPITALIZE trade names and trademark names: Super Sabre Jet, Thunderjet, but Boeing 707 jet (jet descriptive, not part of name), Pan Am Clipper.

"Coke" is a registered trademark of Coca-Cola and is not a synonym for soft drinks.

"Thermos" is a registered trademark. Use vacuum bottle (flask, jug) instead.

Use generic, or broad, term preferably in all trademark names.

1.29 Some proper names have acquired independent common meaning and are not capitalized. They include paris green, dutch door, brussels sprouts, etc. Check dictionary.

1.30 CAPITALIZE titles of books, plays, hymns, poems, songs, etc., and place in quotation marks: "The Courtship of Miles Standish." (See 3.26)

The words a, in, of, etc., are capitalized only at the start or end of a title: "Of Thee I Sing" and "All Returns Are In" as examples.

1.31 CAPITALIZE first word of a quotation making a complete sentence after a comma or colon: Franklin said, "A penny saved is a penny earned." (See 3.16)

1.32 CAPITALIZE names of organizations, expositions, etc., Boy Scouts, Red Cross, World's Fair, Iowa State Fair but LOWER CASE scout, fair standing alone.

1.33 CAPITALIZATION of names should follow the use of preference of the person. In general, foreign particles are lower case when used with a forename, initials or title: Charles de Gaulle, Gen. de Gaulle, but De Gaulle without forename or title. (See 3.5, 6.4)

In anglicized versions the article usually is capitalized: Fiorello La Guardia.

It is E. I. du Pont de Nemours and Du Pont; Irenee du Pont but Samuel F. Du Pont (his usage).

1.34 CAPITALIZE fanciful appellations: Buckeye State, Leatherneck, Project Mercury, Operation Deep Freeze (Deepfreeze, one word, is trademark.)

1.35 CAPITALIZE decorations, awards, etc. Medal of Honor, Nobel Peace Prize.

II: ABBREVIATIONS

2.1 First mention of organizations, firms, agencies, groups, etc., should be spelled out. Exception: AFL-CIO. In names that do not have commonly known abbreviations, the abbreviation should be bracketed after the spelled name. Thereafter in the story the abbreviation may be used. Example:

The desire was expressed in the Inter-American Economic and Social Council (IA-ECOSOC) of the Organization of American States (OAS) in considering the European Economic Cooperation Organization (ECCO).

Distant Early Warning line (DEW line). General Agreement of Tariffs and Trade (GATT).

2.2 ABBREVIATE time zones, airplane designations, ships, distress calls, military terms, etc. EDT, CST, MIGl7, B60, Military Police (MP), absent without official leave (AWOL), SOS (but May Day), USS Iowa, SS Brasil. (See 3.3, 6.15)

2.3 ABBREVIATE business firms: Warner Bros.; Brown Implement Co.; Amalgamated Leather, Ltd.; Smith & Co., Inc. (See 3.40)

2.4 ABBREVIATE St., Ave., Blvd., Ter., in addresses but not Point, Port, Circle, Plaza, Place, Drive, Oval, Road, Lane. Examples:

16 E. 72nd St. (single "E" with period); 16 Gregory Ave. NW (no periods in "NW"); Sunset Boulevard, Main Street, Fifth Avenue (no addresses). (See 1.25, 4.1)

2.5 Lower case abbreviations usually take periods. The rule of thumb is if the letters without periods spell words, periods are needed. Examples: c.o.d., f.o.b., etc. However, m.p.h., a.m., p.m.

Periods are not needed in 35mm (film), 105mm (armament), ips (tape recording).

In news stories first mention of speed should be "miles an hour" or "miles per hour" and thereafter in story use m.p.h.

ABBREVIATE versus as vs. (with period).

2.6 ABBREVIATE states which follow cities (towns, villages, etc.), airbases, Indian agencies, national parks, etc. (See 3.23)

2.7 Standard abbreviations for states (rule of thumb is abbreviate none of six letters or less except Texas):

Ala.	Colo.	Ga.	Ky.
Ariz.	Conn.	Ill.	La.
Ark.	Del.	Ind.	Md.
Calif.	Fla.	Kan.	Mass.

Mich.	N.C.	Ore.	Vt.
Minn.	N.D.	Pa.	Va.
Miss.	N.H.	R.I.	Wash.
Mo.	N.J.	S.C.	Wis.
Mont.	N.M.	S.D.	W.Va.
Neb.	N.Y.	Tenn.	Wyo.
Nev.	Okla.	Tex.	

Do not abbreviate Alaska, Hawaii, Idaho, Iowa, Ohio, Maine or Utah.

All states are spelled standing alone: He went to Minnesota at the turn of the century.

2.8 ABBREVIATIONS:

C.Z.	V.I.	B.C.	N.S.
Que.	Sask.	N.B.	P.E.I.
P.R.	Alta.	Man.	
Ont.	Nfld.	B.W.I.	

but obscure ones should be spelled in story, such as Prince Edward Island, etc.

2.9 B.C. as abbreviation of Canadian province must be preceded by town name; B.C., the era, must be preceded by a date.

2.10 ABBREVIATE U.S.S.R. in datelines.

2.11 ABBREVIATE United Nations and United States in titles: U.S. Junior Chamber of Commerce (Jaycees as exception in abbreviation by letters), U.N. Educational, Scientific and Cultural Organization (UNESCO). (See 2.1, 3.3)

2.12 Spell United States and United Nations when used as a noun. U.S.A. and U.N. as nouns may be used in texts or direct quotations.

2.13 ABBREVIATE and capitalize religious, fraternal, scholastic or honorary degrees, etc., but lower case when spelled: B.A., bachelor of arts.

2.14 ABBREVIATE titles and capitalize: Mr., Mrs., Ms., M., Mlle., Dr., Prof., Sen., Rep., Asst., Lt. Gov., Gov. Gen., Supt., Atty. Gen., Dist. Atty., in titles before names but not after names. Do not abbreviate attorney in: The statement by defense attorney John Jones, etc. (See 1.7)

2.15 Mr. is used only with Mrs., or with clerical titles (except in texts or verbatim quotes).

2.16 Do NOT abbreviate port, association, point, detective, department, deputy, commandant, commodore, field marshal, general manager, secretary-general, secretary, treasurer, fleet admiral or general of the armies (but Adm. Nimitz or Gen. Pershing is correct). (See 2.21) Do NOT abbreviate "guaranteed annual wage" and do NOT abbreviate Christmas.

2.17 ABBREVIATE months when used with dates: Oct. 12, 1492; but spell out otherwise as October, 1492. Abbreviations for months are Jan., Feb., Aug., Sept., Oct., Nov., Dec. Do not abbreviate March, April, May, June or July except in tabular or financial routine where the abbreviations are Mar, Apr, Jun, Jly and spell May.

2.18 Days of the week are abbreviated only in tabular matter or financial routine where they are Mon, Tue, Wed, Thu, Fri, Sat, Sun. The proper word division for Wednesday is: Wednes-day.

2.19 ABBREVIATE St. and Ste. as in Sault Ste. Marie, St. Louis, St. Lawrence, etc. (except Saint John, N.B.). Abbreviate the mountain but spell the city: Mt. Everest, Mount Vernon. Abbreviate army post but spell city: Ft. Sill, Fort Meyer.

2.20 Do not abbreviate Alexander, Benjamin, Charles, Frederick, William, etc., as Alec, Alex, Ben., Benj., Chas., etc., unless person does so himself. Follow person's preference.

2.21 Military abbreviations:

ARMY

General	Gen.
Lieutenant General	Lt. Gen.
Major General	Maj. Gen.
Brigadier General	Brig. Gen.
Colonel	Col.
Lieutenant Colonel	Lt. Col.
Major	Maj.
Captain	Capt.
Lieutenant	Lt.
Chief Warrant Officer	CWO
Warrant Officer	WO
Sergeant Major	Sgt. Maj.
Specialist Nine	Spec. 9
Master Sergeant	M. Sgt.
First Sergeant	1st Sgt.
Specialist Eight	Spec. 8
Platoon Sergeant	Platoon Sgt.
Sergeant First Class	Sgt. 1.C.
Specialist Seven	Spec. 7
Staff Sergeant	S. Sgt.

Specialist Six	Spec. 6
Sergeant	Sgt.
Specialist Five	Spec. 5
Corporal	Cpl.
Specialist Four	Spec. 4
Private First Class	Pfc.
Private	Pvt.
Recruit	Rct.

NAVY, COAST GUARD

Admiral	Adm.
Vice Admiral	Vice Adm.
Rear Admiral	Rear Adm.
Commodore	Commodore
Captain	Capt.
Commander	Cmdr.
Lieutenant Commander	Lt. Cmdr.
Lieutenant	Lt.
Lieutenant Junior Grade	Lt. (j.g.)
Ensign	Ens.
Commissioned Warrant Officer	CWO
Warrant Officer	WO
Master Chief Petty Officer	M.CPO
Senior Chief Petty Officer	S.CPO
Chief Petty Officer	CPO
Petty Officer 1st Class	PO 1.C.
Petty Officer Second Class	PO 2.C.
Petty Officer Third Class	PO 3.C.
Seaman	Seaman
Seaman Apprentice	Seaman Appren.
Seaman Recruit	Seaman Rct.

MARINE CORPS

Commissioned officers are abbreviated the same as Army, warrant officers the same as Navy. Noncommissioned designations are the same as Army except specialist and:

Master Gunnery Sergeant	Mgy. Sgt.
Gunnery Sergeant	Gunnery Sgt.
Lance Corporal	Lance Cpl.

AIR FORCE

Air force commissioned officers are abbreviated the same as Army. Noncommissioned designations include:

Chief Master Sergeant	CM. Sgt.
Senior Master Sergeant	SM. Sgt.
Master Sergeant	M. Sgt.
Technical Sergeant	T. Sgt.
Staff Sergeant	S. Sgt.
Airman 1st Class	Airman 1.C.
Airman 2nd Class	Airman 2.C.
Airman 3rd Class	Airman 3.C.
Airman Basic	Airman

The Air Force also may designate certain other descriptions as radarman, navigator, etc., but such designations are not abbreviated.

The Navy has numerous ratings such as machinist, torpedoman, etc., and they are not abbreviated.

The Army, Coast Guard and Marine Corps also may describe personnel by specific duty in addition to rank.

III: PUNCTUATION

Punctuation in printing serves the same purpose as voice inflection in speaking. Proper phrasing avoids ambiguity, insures clarity and lessens need for punctuation.

The Period

3.1   The period is used after a declarative or imperative sentence: The facing is Vermont marble. Shut the door.

The period is used after a question intended as a suggestion: Tell how it was done.

The period is used in summary form: 1. Vietnam War. 2. Domestic policy. A. Punctuate properly. B. Write simply.

3.2   The period is used for ellipsis and in some columnist material. Ellipsis: The combine . . . was secure.

Column: Esther Williams gets the role. . . . John Hay signed a new contract. Rephrasing to avoid ellipses is preferable.

3.3   The period is used in abbreviations: U.S., U.N., c.o.d., etc. (See Section II for variations)

3.4   The period separates integer and decimal: 3.75 per cent; $8.25; 1.25 meters.

3.5   The period is omitted after a letter casually used as a name, and where a person omits the period in his name:

A said to B that he was not watching.

Herman B Wells (his usage). (See 1.33)

The Comma

3.6   The comma separates words or figures: What the solution is, is a question.

Aug. 1, 1960.   1,234,567

The comma serves in a series:

The woman was short, slender, blonde, well-dressed and old.

x, y and z.   1, 2 and 3.

The Selma, Ala., group saw the governor.

3.7   Do not use comma before "of": Brown of Arkadelphia.

3.8   Newspaper usage has, in most cases, eliminated the comma before "and" and "or" but this practice does not lessen the need for the mark in:

Fish abounded in the lake, and the shore was lined with deer.

3.9   The comma is used to set off attribution: The work, he said, is exacting. It is used in scores: Milwaukee 6, St. Louis 5.

3.10   The comma is used to separate in apposition or contrast:

Smithwick, the favorite, won handily.

But: The car that failed had been ahead.

3.11   The comma is omitted before Roman numerals, Jr., Sr., the ampersand, dash, in street addresses, telephone numbers and serial numbers: Louis XVI, John Jones Jr., Smith & Co., ORegon 3–3617, 12345 Oak St., A1234567. (See 4.4)

The Semicolon

3.12   The semicolon separates phrases containing commas to avoid confusion, and separates statements of contrast and statements too closely related:

The draperies, which were ornate, displeased me; the walls, light blue, were pleasing.

The party consisted of B. M. Jordan; R. J. Kelly, his secretary; Mrs. Jordan; Martha Brown, her nurse; and three servants. (Without the semicolons, that could be read as nine persons.)

The Apostrophe

3.13   The apostrophe indicates the possessive case of nouns, omission of figures, and contractions.

Usually the possessive of a singular noun not ending in "s" is formed by adding the apostrophe and "s"; the plural noun by adding the "s" and then the apostrophe: boys' wear, men's wear.

The apostrophe also is used in the plural possessive "es"; Joneses' house.

The "s" is dropped and only the apostrophe used in "for conscience' sake" or in a sibilant double or triple "s" as "Moses' tablet." In single letters: A's.

3.14 The apostrophe is used in contractions: I've, isn't; in omission of figures: '90, '90s, class of '22. (See 4.3)

3.15 The apostrophe use or lack of should follow the official name of group, institution, locality, etc.: Johns Hopkins University, Actors Equity Association, Court of St. James's (variation of possessive ending).

The Colon

3.16 The colon precedes the final clause summarizing prior matter; introduces listings, statements and texts; marks discontinuity, and takes the place of an implied "for instance":
The question came up: What does he want to do? (See 1.31)
States and funds allotted were: Alabama $6,000; Arizona $4,000, etc.

3.17 The colon is used in clock time: 8:15 P.M. (See 4.9)

3.18 The colon is used in Bible and legal citations:
Matt 2:14. Missouri Statutes 3: 245–260.

The Exclamation Point

3.19 The exclamation point is used to indicate surprise, appeal, incredulity or other strong emotion:
How wonderful! What! He yelled, "Come here!"

The Question Mark

3.20 The question mark follows a direct question, marks a gap or uncertainty and in the latter use is enclosed in parentheses:
What happened to Jones?
It was April 13 (?) that I saw him.
The mark also is used in public proceedings, interviews, etc.:
Q. Were you there? A. I don't recall.
Exception: Where, in interviews, the question or answer is of some length, it is preferable to paragraph both Q. and A.

Parentheses

3.21 Parentheses set off material, or an element of a sentence.
It is not the custom (at least in the areas mentioned) to stand at attention.

3.22 Where location identification is needed but is not part of the official name: The Springfield, Ohio, Historical Society edition, etc. It is not necessary to bracket: The Springfield, Ohio, area population, etc.

3.23 Parentheses are not used around political-geographical designation: Sen. Wendell H. Ford, D-Ky., and Rep. Hal Daub, R-Neb. were invited. (See 2.6)

3.24 Parentheses set off letters or figures in a series: The order of importance will be (a) general acceptance, (b) costs, and (c) opposition.

3.25 Where part of a sentence is parenthetical and the punctuation mark comes at the end of the sentence, it goes outside:
He habitually uses two words incorrectly (practical and practicable).
Ordinarily the mark goes inside: (The foregoing was taken from an essay.)
Several paragraphs of parenthetical matter start with the opening mark on each paragraph and the final paragraph is ended with a closing parenthesis with the punctuation inside.

Quotation Marks

3.26 Quotation marks enclose direct quotations; are used around phrases in ironical uses; around slang expressions; misnomers; titles of books, plays, poems, songs, lectures or speeches when the full title is used; hymns; movies; TV programs, etc. (See 1.30)

3.27 Use quotation marks instead of parentheses around nicknames apart from the name: Smith, who weighed 280, was called "Slim."
Harold "Red" Grange.
The comma and period are placed inside the quotation marks. Other punctuation is placed according to construction:
Why call it a "gentlemen's agreement"?
The sequence in multiple quotations:
"The question is 'Does his position violate the "gentlemen's 'post-haste' agreement" so

eloquently described by my colleague as "tommyrot"?' "

The Dash

3.28 The dash indicates a sudden change. Examples:

He claimed—no one denied it—that he had priority.

It can be used instead of parentheses in many cases: 10 pounds—$15—paid.

If that man should gain control—God forbid!—our troubles will have only begun.

The monarch—shall we call him a knave or a fool?—approved it.

3.29 The dash is used after the logotype and before the first word of a story:

NEW YORK (logotype)—Mayor, etc.

3.30 The dash also is used as the minus sign in temperatures to indicate below-zero temperature: Duluth —12.

The Hyphen

3.31 The hyphen is one of the least correctly used, and most abused, marks. It is used properly to form compound words, to divide words in composition, in figures, in some abbreviations, and to separate double vowels in some cases.

The general rule for hyphens is that "like" characters take the hyphen, "unlike" characters do not.

A-bomb, U-boat, 20-20 vision, 3D, B60, MIG17, 3-2 (odds and scores), secretary-treasurer, south-southwest, north-central.

Exception: 4-H Club.

3.32 Adjectival use must be clear. (See 5.6)

The 6-foot man eating shark was killed (the man was).

The 6-foot man-eating shark was killed (the shark was).

3.33 Suspensive hyphenation:

The A- and H-bombs were exploded.

The 5- and 6-year-olds attend morning classes.

3.34 Ordinarily in prefixes ending in vowels and followed by the same vowel, the hyphen is used: pre-empt, re-elect. (Check dictionary for exceptions such as cooperate, coed, coordinates, etc.)

3.35 NEVER use the hyphen with adverb ending in "ly" such as badly damaged, fully informed, newly chosen, etc.

3.36 The hyphen also serves to distinguish meaning of similarly spelled words: recover, re-cover; resent, re-sent.

3.37 The hyphen also separates a prefix from a proper noun: pre-Raphaelite, un-American, etc.

3.38 The prefix "ex" is hyphened: ex-champion.

3.39 The hyphen has been abandoned in newspaper usage in weekend, worldwide, nationwide, etc.

The Ampersand

3.40 The ampersand is used in abbreviations and firm names: Jones & Co., AT&T, etc. (See 2.3)

IV: NUMERALS

In general, spell below 10, use numerals for 10 and above.

4.1 Numerals are used exclusively in tabular and statistical matter, records, election returns, times, speeds, latitude and longitude, temperatures, highways, distances, dimensions, heights, ages, ratios, proportions, military units, political divisions, orchestra instruments, court districts or divisions, handicaps, betting odds and dates (Fourth of July and July Fourth acceptable).

Use figures in all man or animal ages. Spell under 10 for inanimates: four-mile-trip, four miles from the center, etc.

Exceptions Fifth Avenue, Fifth Republic of France (See 1.25, 2.4), Big Ten, Dartmouth eleven.

The forms: 3-year-old girl, the girl is 3, 5 feet 2, 5-foot-2 trench, Washington won, 6–3; $10 shirt, seven-cent stamp, eight-hour day, five-day week, 60 cents (See 4.6), .38-caliber pistol.

6:30 P.M. or 6:30 o'clock Monday night (never 6:30 P.M. Monday night, or 6:30 P.M. o'clock). (See 6.15)

The vote was 1,345 for and 1,300 against.

The ratio was 6 to 4, but the 6–4 ratio.

It is 20th century but Twentieth Century Limited (train).

In series, keep the simplest related forms: There are 3 ten-room houses, 1 fourteen-room house, 25 five-room houses and 40 four-room houses in the development.

$4 million but four million persons—the $ is equivalent of second numeral.

4.2 Numerals: 6th Fleet, 1st Army, 2nd Division, 10th Ward, 22nd District, 8th U.S. Circuit Court of Appeals.

Arabic numerals for spacecraft, missiles, etc.

4.3 Casual numbers are spelled:

A thousand times no! Gay Nineties. (See 3.14)

Wouldn't touch it with a ten-foot pole (but: The flag hung from a 10-foot pole—an exact measure).

4.4 Roman numerals are used for personal sequence, Pope, war, royalty, act, yacht and horse: John Jones III (some may prefer and use 3rd), Pope John Paul II, World War I, King George V, Act II, Shamrock IX, Hanover II. (See 3.11)

4.5 Highways: U.S. 301, Interstate 90, Illinois 34.

4.6 In amounts of more than a million, round numbers take the dollar sign and million, billion, etc., are spelled. Decimalization is carried to two places: $4.35 million.

Exact amounts would be: $4,351,242.

Less than a million the form: $500, $1,000, $650,000, etc.

The same decimalization form is used for figures other than money such as population, automobile registration, etc. (See 4.1)

Spell "cents" in amounts less than a dollar. (See 4.1)

In ranges: $12 million to $14 million (or billion) not $12 to $14 million (or billion).

4.7 The English pound sign is not used. Spell "pounds" after figures and convert to dollars. (See 3.28)

4.8 Fractions in Teletypesetter are confined to matrices of 8ths: ⅛, ¼, ⅜, ½, ⅝, ¾, ⅞. Other fractions require the hyphen 3-16, 9-10, 1-3, etc.

Fractions used alone are spelled: three-fourths of a mile.

If the diagonal or slash (/) is incorporated

in Teletypesetter operation, that symbol will replace the hyphen in fractions other than 8ths. The "plus" sign now occupies that casting-machine channel in the agate font and the hyphen will continue to be used in the agate font for fractions other than 8ths.

Stories dealing with percentages use figures; an isolated one-time reference under 10 is spelled as: four per cent of the population is illiterate.

4.9 Time sequences are given in figures: 2:30:21.6 (hours, minutes, seconds, tenths). (See 3.17)

4.10 Metric measurements use the comma in three-figure sequences except that kilocycles and meters in electronics are printed solid unless 10ths are included and the 10ths are set off by a period.

4.11 Serial numbers are printed solid: A1234567.

4.12 Write it No. 1 boy. No. 2 candidate, etc.

V: SPELLING

The first preference in spelling is the short version in Webster's New International Dictionary with exceptions as given in this section; the U.S. Postal Guide; The U.S. Board of Geographic Names and National Geographic Society with exceptions as given in this section. The news services have agreed on some spellings where authorities do not agree.

5.1 The following list includes agreed spellings:

Algiers	Cameroon	The Hague
Antioch	Cape Town	Hamelin
Antwerp	Coblenz	Hannover
Archangel	Cologne	Hong Kong
Athens	Copenhagen	Jakarta
Baghdad	Corfu	Katmandu
Bangkok	Corinth	Kingstown
Basel	Dunkerque	Kurile
Bayreuth	Florence	Leghorn
Beirut	Formosa Strait	Lisbon
Belgrade	Frankfurt	Macao
Bern	Genoa	Madagascar
Brunswick	Goteberg	Marseille
Bucharest	Gulf of Riga	Mt. Sinai

Mukden	Romania	Tiflis
Munich	Rome	Turin
Naples	Saint John, N.B.	Valetta
North Cape	St. John's, Nfld.	Mt. Vesuvius
Nuernberg	Salonika	Vietnam
Peking	Sofia	Warsaw
Pescadores I.	Taipei	Wiesbaden
Prague	Tehran	Zuider Zee
Rhodes	Thailand	

5.2 Where old and new names are used, or where quoted material uses a different form, one is bracketed: Formosa (Taiwan); Gdansk (Danzig), etc.

5.3 In Chinese names, the name after the hyphen is lower case: Chiang Kai-shek, Mao Tse-tung.

It is Peking People's Daily, People's Republic, etc.

5.4 Often used and frequently misspelled: (*preferred spelling)

adviser	drought	old-timer
accommodate	drunken	per cent
anyone	employe*	percentage
Asian flu	embarrass	permissible
ax	eyewitness	post office
baby-sit	fallout	propeller
baby sitter	fire fighter	restaurant
baby-sitting	fulfill	rock 'n' roll
baritone	goodby*	schoolteacher
blond, male	good will, noun	sit-down
blonde,	goodwill, adj.	skillful
female, hue	hanged	strait jacket
box office	harass	strong-arm
box-office	hitchhiker	subpoena
sales	homemade	swastika
cannot	home town	teen-age
cave-in	impostor	under way
chauffeur	ionosphere	vacuum
cigarette	isotope	wash 'n' wear
clue	judgment	weird
consensus	jukebox	wheel chair
consul	kidnaping	whisky
copilot	likable	wiretapping
copter	machine gun	X ray, noun
council	missile	X-ray, adj.
counsel	naphtha	
disc		

Disc is a phonograph record, National Council of Disc Jockeys is the trade organization.

It is drunken driving.

Be sure of words ending in ise, ize, and yse.

It is GI and GIs for persons, GI's and GIs' for possessive.

A consonant after a vowel and ending in a final accented syllable is doubled: corral, corralled; transfer, transferred; canal, canalled.

A consonant is not doubled when the accent falls on an earlier syllable: total, totaled; kidnap, kidnaped; channel, channeled; cancel, canceled.

It is bus and buses—buss is not a vehicle.

5.5 In compounding, meaning should be the guide. A great grandfather means he is great; a great-grandfather is lineage. Three-piece suits at $100 a piece would be $300 each; three-piece suits at $100 apiece would be $100 each.

It is right-hander, right-handed, left-wing group, left-winger but the left wing of the party.

5.6 "Air" is solid in airplane, airline, airport, airwave, airship, etc. Some corporate names divide airline: Eastern Air Lines (EAL), United Air Lines (UAL).

5.7 Some of the general rules for prefixes and suffixes:

all (prefix) hyphenated: All-Star.

ante, anti (prefix) solid: antebellum, anti-aircraft—except in proper noun usage which is anti-American, etc.

bi (prefix) solid: biennial, bifocal.

co (prefix) usually solid: copilot, coed, etc.

counter (prefix) solid; counterfoil, etc.

down (prefix and suffix) solid: down-stroke, touchdown.

electro (prefix) solid: electrolysis.

ex (prefix) hyphenated: ex-champion.

extra (prefix) solid: extraterritorial.

fold (suffix) solid: twofold.

goer (suffix) solid: churchgoer.

in (prefix) solid: insufferable; (suffix) hyphenated: stand-in

infra (prefix) solid: infrared.

inter (prefix) solid: interstate.

intra (prefix) solid: intrastate, intramural.

multi (prefix) solid: multimillion, multifaced.

non (prefix) solid: nonpartisan, nonsupport.

out (prefix) hyphenated: out-talk, out-box.

over (prefix and suffix) solid: overcome, pushover.

post (prefix) solid: postwar (but it is postmortem).

pre (prefix) solid: predetermined, predawn.

self (prefix) hyphenated: self-defense.

semi (prefix) solid: semiannual.

sub (prefix) solid: subzero.

super (prefix) solid: superabundance, superman.

trans (prefix) solid: transatlantic, transcontinental (but trans-Canada with proper noun of country).

tri (prefix) solid: trifocal.

ultra (prefix) solid: ultraviolet.

un (prefix) solid: unshaven, unnecessary (but un-American with proper noun).

under (prefix) solid: underground, underdog, undersold.

uni (prefix) solid: unicolor.

wide (suffix) solid: worldwide, nationwide.

VI: MISCELLANEOUS

6.1 Engine is correct, not motor, in aviation; twin-engine, six-engine, etc. Exception: Trimotor, an obsolete plane but it still occurs in news stories. In railroading, power plants are locomotives—electric, steam, diesel. Diesels also may be called units, or engines.

6.2 Jet planes are driven solely by turbine engines. If the jet engine turns a propeller, it is a turboprop.

Flier is an aviator, flyer is a train.

6.3 A wife becomes a widow on the death of her husband. It is redundant to say "widow of the late." "John Jones is survived by his widow" (not wife).

6.4 Include in first reference the first name and initials, or names or initials according to preference of person: Sen. Theodore Francis Green, D. H. Lawrence. (See 1.33, 9.7)

Correct spelling: Randolph McC. Pate. Howard McC. Snyder.

6.5 Long titles: (See 1.6)

International Brotherhood of Teamsters, Chauffeurs, Warehousemen and Helpers is shortened to Teamsters Union, and in subsequent references to Teamsters.

Cemetery Workers and Green Attendants Union of the Building Service Employes International Union is shortened to Cemetery Workers Union.

6.6 An automatic is not a revolver and vice versa, but "pistol" describes either. A bullet is the metal projectile of a cartridge which includes the propellant powder, casing and primer.

Shell describes military and naval or shotgun ammunition.

6.7 Weather: See Webster for Weather Bureau wind scale which has replaced the Beaufort wind scale.

Be certain in the use of tornado, cyclone, typhoon, monsoon, hurricane, etc. The U.S. Weather Bureau defines a blizzard:

"Generally when there are winds of 35 m.p.h. or more which whip falling snow, or snow already on the ground, and temperatures are 20 degrees above zero Fahrenheit, or lower.

"A severe blizzard is where winds are 45 m.p.h. or more, temperatures 10 degrees above zero or lower, and great density of snow either falling or whipped from the ground."

Neither is a hard and fast rule, the bureau says, because winds and temperatures may vary but blizzard-like conditions may prevail.

Rule of thumb: Do not call a snowstorm a blizzard unless the Weather Bureau describes it as such.

In weather stories, with addition of Alaska and Hawaii as states, it is incorrect to refer to highest or lowest temperatures "in the nation" if figures from those two states are not included. The Weather Bureau has a phrase to cover the omission: It refers to minimums and maximums in the "48 contiguous states."

6.8 There are officers, detectives, deputies, investigators, etc., but not "lawmen."

6.9 Avoid making verbs out of nouns: shotgunned to death, suicided, etc.

Avoid trite phrases of dialect, especially "Sure and it was" and "begorra" etc., in March 17 stories.

If a record is set it is new—"new record" is redundant.

6.10 In describing someone or something from Washington, make clear it is the state or District of Columbia.

6.11 Fahrenheit is used most frequently to measure degrees of heat and cold. If centigrade occurs in foreign, or scientific, copy conversion to Fahrenheit is nine-fifths times centigrade plus 32.

The Kelvin scale of temperature will come into use oftener. Temperatures are referred to in this scale as "degrees absolute" or "degrees Kelvin." Absolute zero in the Kelvin scale is 460 degrees below Fahrenheit zero; 273 degrees below centigrade zero.

6.12 A knot is a unit of speed and is equivalent to 6,076.10 feet an hour. The knot is a nautical mile computed as the length of one minute of the meridian. To convert knots into approximate statute miles per hour, multiply knots by 1.15. It is incorrect to say "sailed 14 knots an hour."

6.13 Gross tonnage is a necessary part of any story dealing with commercial shipping as the accepted basic measurement of size. Naval vessels list "displacement tonnage."

6.14 Red-headed means a red head; red-haired means hair of that color. A person may be called a "red-head" jocularly but is not properly described as "red-headed."

6.15 It is not necessary to bracket time zones in ordinary happenings such as accidents, shootings, etc. It is sufficient to say something occurred at 11 P.M. (See 4.1)

Zone should be included in earthquakes, radio and TV broadcast times. Convert to EST.

Informative notes to editors giving times should include the zone.

6.16 G, G-force, is gravitational pull equal to about 32 feet per second, a second, in acceleration. Thus a flier (plane, rocket, etc.) subjected to a force of 5 G's is accelerating at five times the force of gravity at the earth's surface, or roughly at a 160-foot-a-second, per-second, rate.

6.17 Mach numbers refer to the speed of a body (aircraft, missile, etc.) in relation to the speed of sound. Mach 2 would be twice the speed of sound. A rule of thumb for speed of sound is 750 miles an hour at sea level, and 660 miles an hour at 30,000 feet.

6.18 Thrust is the measure of a driving force, or power, expressed in pounds. Jet engine and rocket powers are expressed in pounds. Thrust in pounds times speed in miles per hour divided by 375 converts thrust to horsepower.

GLOSSARY

Actuality. A broadcast news segment read into the microphone by a reporter at the scene. Known in radio as a *voicer*, in television as a *stand-up*.

Actual malice. Legal term for lying or acting with reckless disregard for the truth. When sued for libel, actual malice deprives journalists found guilty of it from the protection of the *New York Times* rule (see Chapter 17).

Add. Additional copy, as when wire services follow the lead of a breaking story with a "first add" containing the next few paragraphs of the story.

Advance. Information distributed prior to the event to which it is related. For instance, before the inauguration of a president the wire services move advances detailing who will be sitting where on the dais, who is in the parade and so forth, so that this background information need not clutter the wires while the inauguration actually takes place.

AMs. Morning newspapers. They "go to bed"—that is, start printing—the night before.

Angle. The theme, thesis or point of a news story.

AP. The Associated Press.

Art. A catchall term used in journalism to designate all illustrations—from photographs to maps or charts—that may accompany copy.

Associated Press. One of the two major wire services in the United States.

Attribution. The identification of the source of information in a news story. Quotations, for instance, are attributed by naming who said the words quoted.

Background. Information offered to journalists on the condition that it not be attributed to its source by name.

Banner. A headline that extends across the top of the page of a newspaper.

Beat. An area of news in which a reporter specializes, such as local politics, the law, business, the police, science or agriculture.

Bite. In broadcasting, a piece of film, videotape or sound tape, usually from an interview, made on the scene. Also known as a *sound cut*.

Blind quote. A quotation lacking attribution to its source. Also known as an *orphan* quote.

Blotter. A police record of complaints, crimes reported and arrests.

Body. The part of a news story that follows the lead.

Boil down. Shorten copy, as in, "Boil this story down to three 'grafs for the late edition."

Box. An enclosed piece of copy, such as a short sidebar boxed to help distinguish it from the main story.

Breaking news. Fresh news, in which timeliness is important. Much of the content of the front page of a newspaper on a typical day is breaking news.

Bridge. In print, the transition from one part of a story to another, as in, "Elsewhere in the city, the rains did less damage." In broadcasting, the transition from one story to another, as in, "The President's remarks drew comment from NATO ministers gathered in Brussels. Here with that story is. . . ."

Bright. A light or humorous story that may have little news value but offers relief from the more sobering developments that make up most of the news.

Budget. A list of the main stories of the day. Also called a *schedule*.

Bulldog. The first edition of a newspaper.

Bulletin. In the wire services, an important story given precedence over other news. In broadcast, a news story important enough to interrupt regular programming.

Bureau. A news-gathering office away from home. The major newspapers and general wire services have bureaus around the world.

Byline. The author's name, printed atop a news story.

Cable-ese. Specialized usage and spelling designed to save words and minimize misunderstandings and messages transmitted between bureaus and the home offices of news-gathering organizations. Examples of Cable-ese include *TK* for "to come," as in, "CANCER CURE UPDATE TK"; *lede* for "lead," as in, "NEW LEDE LEAD POISONING STY FOLOS"; abbreviations like *SCOTUS* for "*Supreme Court of the United States*"; and combined words intended to prevent garbled massages should a word be dropped, as in, "SUGGEST DOWNPLAY FIRE UPPLAY QUAKE AND MOVE NEW LEDE SOONEST."

Caption. Copy written to accompany a photograph or illustration.

Chain. Several newspapers under one ownership.

City desk. The desk responsible for covering local news, overseen by a city editor. Also known as the *local* or *metropolitan* desk.

Clips. Stories clipped from newspapers. Newspaper libraries store clips, and most reporters keep a collection of their own clips.

Cold type. A process employing images on paper as the print medium, as in the offset process, in which each page of the newspaper is photographed for duplication. Compare *hot type*.

Composing room. The area of a newspaper office where type is set and the pages organized.

Copy. The words written by a journalist for publication in a newspaper or airing in a news broadcast.

Copy desk. The desk where news copy is reread and where headlines and subheads are added. Copy editors work this desk.

Correspondent. A reporter filing copy from a location far from the home office.

Cover. To investigate with the aim of producing a news story. Reporters may be assigned to cover specific developments—for example, a news conference—or a general area, as when a beat reporter is assigned to cover the criminal courts.

CQ. Note inserted in cables and wire service dispatches to inform editors that an unfamiliar or seemingly erroneous spelling or set of facts is indeed correct.

Crop. To trim a photograph, eliminating part of its original content.

CRT. The display screen on a computer terminal.

Cub. A reporter just beginning his or her career.

Cutline. Copy accompanying a photograph or illustration; caption.

Dateline. Name of the location of a news story placed at the beginning of the lead, as in, "TOLEDO, OHIO—A typesetter's strike today halted publication of three newspapers. . . ." Most newspapers employ datelines for stories originating from beyond their localities. These often include the date, which is especially important for international stories that otherwise may become confused because of the time and date differences around the globe.

Deadline. The time when news copy is due. A reporter working to finish writing and editing a story in time to make the next edition of the paper or an upcoming newscast is said to be "writing on deadline."

Deadwood. Excess words in news copy. For example, "Patrol officer engaged under the auspices of the Police Department," would be deadwood for "police officer."

Deep background. Information offered to journalists on the condition that it not be attributed to its source in any way. Compare *background*.

Defamation. The act of seriously damaging someone's reputation. Spoken defamation is slander; if printed or broadcast, libel.

Delete. Take out, remove from copy.

Desk. The basic unit of organization in the editorial department of a news-gathering organization. A newspaper typically will have a city desk, state desk, national and international desk, copy desk, etc.

Developing. Ongoing, in the sense that more developments are expected. For instance, a murder trial in which the jury is still out is said to be developing, because more news will arise when the jury returns and announces its verdict.

Dig. To go deeply into a potential news story.

Dingbat. An asterisk, dot or other typographical symbol employed to separate parts of copy. Its use as a term of derision derives from the relative unimportance of dingbats among the bits of type in the typesetter's drawer.

Ear. The upper two corners of the front page of a newspaper. In *The New York Times*, for example, the right ear contains a summary of the day's weather forecast; the left ear, the newspaper's motto: "All the news that's fit to print."

Editor. A journalist with authority to edit other journalists' copy. The hierarchy of editors includes those with many sorts of responsibilities, among them assigning stories and helping to decide which news goes into each day's newspaper or broadcast.

Editorialize. To express an opinion. Editorializing usually is confined to the editorial pages and to columns or analysis pieces clearly labelled to distinguish them from news stories, which should contain no editorializing.

Feature story. A report typically more interesting than timely or important, written in a format other than the inverted pyramid.

File. To send a dispatch to a newspaper from far away; in the wire services, to transmit a story to clients, as in, "She filed her story by the noon deadline."

Filler. Relatively unnewsworthy material printed to fill empty space at the bottoms of columns of a newspaper.

Flash. A wire service bulletin of the greatest importance.

Follow-up. A report of further developments in a news story already reported.

Freedom of Information Act. A law in federal and some state statutes providing for access to many sorts of government documents.

Freelance. In journalism, a writer or photographer who works on his or her own rather than being employed by a news-gathering organization. Some of the best and some of the worst journalists work freelance.

Futures file. A collection of reminders of upcoming events, maintained by editors and beat reporters.

Galley proof. Copy set in type and available for final proofreading before the newspaper is printed.

Glossy. Photograph with glossy finish, preferred for reproduction in a newspaper.

'Graf. Journalist's slang for paragraph.

Gutter. The white space between the opposite pages of a newspaper.

Hellbox. A bin holding discarded type.

Hot type. Method of typesetting using type cast from molten metal. The method today is yielding to the more popular *cold type*.

Human-interest story. A report considered newsworthy more for its interest to readers than for its impact upon them.

Hype. A potential story misrepresented in order to exaggerate its apparent news value.

Invasion of privacy. Violation of an individual's right to reasonable security from prying by the press.

Inverted pyramid. Structure of a news story in which events are recounted in the order of their importance, the most newsworthy elements at the top.

Investigative reporting. Seeking out newsworthy information that has been concealed from the public view.

Jump. The point at which copy is interrupted on one page of a newspaper, to be continued on a later page in the same edition.

Keys. Wording superimposed on a television screen. From chromakey, an electronic process sometimes employed in superimposing images. See *mattes*.

Kill. To withdraw a story previously intended for publication or broadcast, as in, "The publisher killed the story on her daughter's abortion." or, "The AP killed that gory footage of the air crash."

Layout. The arrangement of copy, photographs and illustrations on each page of a newspaper. Layout is the work of the composing room.

Lead. The first paragraph of a news story. Also, the first news item in a broadcast or the top story on page one of a newspaper, as in, "Let's lead with the Mideast conflict." Sometimes spelled *lede*.

Lead-in. Radio or television copy that sets up an *actuality*, reported from the scene.

Lead-out. Radio or television copy that follows an *actuality*, reported from the scene.

Libel. Defamation in print or broadcast. See *defamation*.

Makeover. To redo the layout of a newspaper page, as in, "We had to makeover page one when the bulletin came in."

Managing editor. The highest-ranking newspaper editor who normally reads all or most daily copy prior to its publication.

Masthead. A statement of the names of a newspaper's owners and higher-ranking editors, printed daily, usually on the editorial page.

Mattes. Letters superimposed on the television screen. Also called *supers*, *IDs* and *lower thirds*.

More. Word appearing at the bottom of a page of copy, or at the end of part of a wire service dispatch, indicating that additional copy in the same story is to follow.

Morgue. A newspaper library.

MOS. Film without sound.

Move. To dispatch copy, as when a wire service editor remarks, "We should move the farmworkers' story within the hour."

News conference. An event called to convey information to journalists. Also known as a *press conference*.

News hole. The amount of space normally allotted in each edition of a newspaper to news copy, as opposed to advertisements and other nonnews copy.

News media. General term for all journalistic organizations. Compare *press*.

News peg. The news element that gives relevance to a story, as in, "Peg the abortion report to today's antiabortion statement by the Right-to-Life Conference."

Newsroom. The place where editors and reporters have their desks. Sometimes called the *city room*.

Not for attribution. Information offered journalists on the condition that it not be attributed to its source.

Obituary. An account of a life published as an announcement of death. Also called *obit*.

Off the record. Information supplied to journalists on the condition that it be used only for their personal knowledge and that it not be reported to the public.

One-shot. A news story that exhausts itself within a single day.

Op-ed page. Page opposite the editorial page, usually containing syndicated columns and letters from readers.

Orphan quote. See *blind quote*.

Pad. To add to the length of a story, as by introducing material of questionable newsworthiness. The opposite of *boil down*. Usually derogatory.

Piece. A news article or story.

PIO. Public Information Officer. See *public relations*.

Pipe. To invent, embellish or unduly emphasize elements of a story in order to exaggerate its news value. Similar to *hype*.

Pix. Cable-ese for pictures, photographs.

Play. The prominence given to each news story, as in, "The UPI story on the home-contracting fraud got good play in papers around the country."

PMs. Afternoon and evening newspapers. Typically they print a first edition in mid or late morning, other editions that afternoon.

Pool. A single reporter or small group of reporters delegated to represent their colleagues in a situation in which all interested journalists cannot be present. For instance, most of the press corps covering a presidential primary might ride in a press airplane while a few pool reporters, selected anew each day, ride with the president in his plane.

PR. See *public relations*.

Precede. A passage introducing a story and appearing before the lead. In wire service journalism, a lead intended solely to alert editors to an important upcoming story.

Press. Term often used for journalists generally. Because it stems from the press on which newspapers are printed, electronic journalists sometimes object to the term as tending to exclude them.

Press release. A document provided to journalists by people or organizations that hope it will interest them. Press releases range from notices that the garden show will open next Monday to thick packets of information handed out to reporters covering a Space Shuttle launch.

Press run. The number of copies of a newspaper printed on a given day.

Profile. A news story, usually a feature, that concerns an individual.

Proofreader. One who reads copy to check for spelling, punctuation and style.

Public figure. Someone who has sought and achieved prominence. Under the *New York Times* rule, public figures have more restricted opportunity to recover libel damages than do ordinary citizens.

Publicist. Someone who represents individuals or organizations to the news media. Some operate freelance, selling their services to clients who want to encourage or shape the way they will be viewed through the press. Others are employed full time by a single client. Also sometimes known as *press agents*.

Public relations. The department of an organization concerned with representing that organization to the society at large. A reporter approaching an organization with routine questions often begins by calling the public relations, or *PR*, person. Compare *publicist*.

Publisher. The highest-ranking executive on a newspaper.

Recover. To overcome the consequences of having missed covering an important news development. If, say, a reporter's car breaks down and he or she misses a press conference by the mayor, the reporter can recover by quickly calling the mayor and trying to arrange an interview.

Reporter. A journalist who covers news stories. Years ago, some reporters did little writing, and instead gathered the news and telephoned it in to the city desk where a *rewrite* person hammered out the story. Today, most reporters write their stories as well, except on major breaking news when several reporters may provide material that is rewritten in the newsroom.

Rewrite. The function of turning raw material into a finished news story. The material may consist of notes gleaned from reporters' telephone calls from the scene of the story, wire service dispatches, press releases or all these combined. Compare *reporter*.

Rip and read. In broadcasting, to air copy—usually wire service copy—without fully understanding or adequately editing it beforehand.

Roundup. A news story summarizing a number of scattered developments, such as damage wrought by a dozen small tornados or the contents of the night's police blotter.

Running story. A news story extending over more than one day.

Second-day lead. The beginning of a story updating a news development reported the day before. If a bridge collapsed yesterday, the second-day story might report on the condition of the injured and the progress of inquiries into who was responsible.

Second front. The first page of the second section of a newspaper.

Series. Several stories running over a period of more than one day on a single topic, such as a three-part series on rising fuel costs or a five-part series on drug addiction.

Shield laws. Statutes enacted to permit journalists to maintain the confidentiality of their news sources in the face of inquiries by the judiciary. These were enacted in many states after the United States Supreme Court ruled that journalists have no constitutional right to refuse to name their sources.

Sidebar. A story accompanying a main news story and relating to one of its aspects. For example, a story on a citywide power failure might be accompanied by a sidebar on how hospitals kept functioning during the crisis.

Slug. A one or two word label identifying a story, usually typed in the upper left corner of each page. Typical slugs might be *pols* for the day's political wrap-up, or *cure* for a story concerning an alleged cancer cure.

SOF. Sound on film.

SOT. Sound on tape.

Sound cut. In broadcasting, a piece of tape, usually from an interview, made on the scene. Also known as a *bite*.

Source. The people from whom journalists get newsworthy information. Reporters may have sources they will readily identify, such as the public relations person at the hospital, and others they would prefer to keep confidential, such as the corporate accountant who tipped them off to price fixing in the steel industry.

Spike. To remove a story or document from consideration for publication or broadcast, as in, "The managing editor spiked the garden club press release." The term comes from the metal spike many editors keep on their desks and use to impale papers they doubt that they want, but are not quite ready to throw away.

Squib. A short item published as filler.

Staffer. Staff reporter in a news-gathering organization.

Stand-up. A television segment in which a reporter is seen talking into the camera. See *voicer*.

Story. Journalists employ the term to mean almost any sort of news item.

Straight news. Basic reportage, usually in the inverted-pyramid format, without interpretation or background; same as *hard news*.

Stringer. A part-time reporter paid by the story. Major newspapers often use college newspaper editors as stringers, and the wire services use full-time reporters for local newspapers as stringers for the wires.

Subhead. A minor headline used to break up long passages of copy. Subheads normally are written at the copy desk.

Sunshine laws. State or local laws guaranteeing public access to many government meetings and documents.

Supers. Words superimposed on a television screen. See *mattes*.

Tabloid. A newspaper with half-sized pages, like the New York *Daily News*, as compared to one with full-sized pages, like *The New York Times*.

Take. A single page of copy.

Takeout. A lengthy news story, so called because it may be printed on several pages by itself, encouraging readers to remove it from the paper to read at leisure or to keep for future reference.

Tease. A brief mention of an upcoming story on a newscast, intended to attract listeners' interest and keep them tuned in.

30. Journalists' symbol for the end of a story.

Trim. To cut the length of a news story.

Typo. Typographical error.

UPI. United Press International, one of the two general wire services in the United States.

Upper case. Capital letter. Abbreviated u.c.

Voicer. A radio news segment in which the reporter at the scene talks into the microphone. Known in television as a *stand-up*.

Wire services. News-gathering organizations that transmit news to client newspapers and broadcasters. In the United States there are two general wire services—United Press International (UPI) and the Associated Press (AP)—plus many specialized wire services, such as those operated by major metropolitan dailies, that sell their material to smaller papers around the country.

Yellow journalism. Journalism that panders to the lowest denominator of audience, emphasizing sex, scandal, violence and rumor.

SUGGESTIONS FOR FURTHER READING

AGEE, WARREN, PHILLIP AULT, and EDWIN EMERY, *Maincurrents in Mass Communications* (New York: Harper & Row, 1986).

ALLEN, ROBERT J., ed. *Selections from the Tatler and the Spectator* (New York: Holt, Rinehart & Winston, 1965).

ANDERSON, DOUGLAS, and BRUCE ITULE, *Contemporary News Reporting* (New York: Random House, 1984).

ASHLEY, PAUL P., *Say It Safely* (Seattle: University of Washington Press, 1976).

BAKER, BOB, *Newsthinking: The Secret of Great Newswriting* (Cincinnati: Writer's Digest Books, 1981).

BARTLETT, JOHN, *Bartlett's Familiar Quotations* (Boston: Little, Brown).

BERNER, R. THOMAS, *Language Skills for Journalists* (Boston: Houghton Mifflin, 1984).

BERNSTEIN, CARL, and BOB WOODWARD, *All the President's Men* (New York: Simon & Schuster, 1974).

BIERCE, AMBROSE, *The Devil's Dictionary* (New York: Hill and Wang, 1957).

BLISS, EDWARD, and JOHN M. PATTERSON, *Writing News for Broadcast* (New York: Columbia University Press, 1978).

BRIAN, DENIS, *Murderers and Other Friendly People: The Public and Private Worlds of Interviewers* (New York: McGraw-Hill Book Co., 1973).

BROOKS, BRIAN, GEORGE KENNEDY, DARYL MOEN, and DON RANLY, *News Reporting and Writing* (New York: St. Martin's Press, 1985).

BURKIN, JUDITH, *Introduction to Reporting* (Dubuque, Iowa: William C. Brown, 1976).

CAPOTE, TRUMAN, *In Cold Blood* (New York: Random House, 1965).

CHARNLEY, MITCHELL, and BLAIR CHARNLEY, *Reporting* (New York: Holt, Rinehart & Winston, 1979).

CROUSE, TIMOTHY, *The Boys on the Bus* (New York: Ballantine Books, 1974).

CREWS, FREDERICK, *The Random House Handbook* (New York: Random House, 1977).

DRECHSEL, ROBERT, *News Making in the Trial Courts* (New York: Longman, 1983).

EPHRON, NORA, *Crazy Salad* (New York: Knopf, 1975).

EPHRON, NORA, *Scribble, Scribble* (New York: Knopf, 1978).

FEDLER, FRED, *Reporting for the Print Media* (New York: Harcourt Brace Jovanovich, 1984).

FENTON, CHARLES A., *The Apprenticeship of Ernest Hemingway* (New York: New American Library, 1954).

FOWLER, H. W., *A Dictionary of Modern English Usage* (New York: Oxford University Press, 1965).

GRAVES, ROBERT, and ALAN HODGE, *The Reader over your Shoulder: A Handbook for Writers of English Prose* (New York: Vintage Books, 1979).

HAGE, GEORGE, EVERETTE DENNIS, ARNOLD ISMACH, and STEPHEN HARTGEN, *New Strategies for Public*

Affairs Reporting (Englewood Cliffs, N.J.: Prentice-Hall, 1976).

HALBERSTAM, DAVID, *The Powers that Be* (New York: Dell, 1979).

Harbrace College Handbook (New York: Harcourt Brace Jovanovich, 1972).

HARRIS, JULIAN, B. KELLY LEITER, and STANLEY JOHNSON, *The Complete Reporter* (New York: Macmillan, 1985).

HOHENBERG, JOHN, ed., *The Pulitzer Prize Story* (New York: Columbia University Press, 1980).

HULTENG, JOHN, *Playing It Straight* (Chester, Conn.: The Globe Pequot Press, 1981).

KEIR, GERRY, MAXWELL McCOMBS, and DONALD SHAW, *Advanced Reporting* (New York: Longman, 1986).

KEMPTON, MURRAY, *America Comes of Middle Age* (Boston: Little Brown, 1963).

KENNEDY, GEORGE, DARYL MOEN, and DON RANLY, *The Writing Book* (Englewood Cliffs, N.J.: Prentice-Hall, 1984).

KESSLER, LAUREN, and DUNCAN McDONALD, *When Words Collide: A Journalist's Guide to Grammar and Style* (Belmont, Calif.: Wadsworth, 1984).

KNIGHTLEY, PHILLIP, *The First Casualty* (New York: Harcourt Brace Jovanovich, 1975).

KRIEGHBAUM, HILLIER, *Pressures on the Press* (New York: Thoman Y. Crowell, 1972).

LIEBLING, A. J., *Mollie and Other War Pieces* (New York, Ballantine Books, 1964).

LIEBLING, A. J., *The Press* (New York: Ballantine Books, 1964).

LIPPMANN, WALTER, *The Essential Lippmann* (New York: Random House, 1963).

MAILER, NORMAN, *The Armies of the Night* (New York: New American Library, 1968).

MAILER, NORMAN, *The Presidential Papers of Norman Mailer* (New York: Bantam Books, 1964).

McCOMBS, MAXWELL, DONALD LEWIS SHAW, and DAVID GREY, *Handbook of Reporting Methods* (Boston: Houghton Mifflin, 1976).

McPHEE, JOHN, *The Deltoid Pumpkin Seed* (New York: Farrar, Straus and Giroux, 1973).

McPHEE, JOHN, *Levels of the Game* (New York: Farrar, Straus & Giroux, 1969).

MENCHER, MELVIN, *Basic News Writing* (Dubuque, Iowa: William C. Brown, 1986).

MENCHER, MELVIN, *News Reporting and Writing* (Dubuque, Iowa: William C. Brown, 1984).

MENCKEN, H. L., *Newspaper Days* (New York: Alfred A. Knopf, 1941).

MENCKEN, H. L., *The Vintage Mencken* (New York: Vintage Books, 1955).

METZ, WILLIAM, *Newswriting from Lead to "30"* (Englewood Cliffs, N.J.: Prentice-Hall, 1985).

METZLER, KEN, *Newsgathering* (Englewood Cliffs, N.J.: Prentice-Hall, 1979).

MEYER, PHILIP, *Precision Journalism* (Bloomington: Indiana University Press, 1973).

NEWBY, ERIC, *A Short Walk in the Hindu Kush* (New York: Penguin Books, 1959).

ORWELL, GEORGE, *A Collection of Essays* (Garden City, New York: Doubleday Anchor Books, 1957).

ORWELL, GEORGE, *Down and Out in Paris and London* (New York: Medallion Books, 1961).

OVERBECK, WAYNE, and THOMAS PASQUA, *Excellence in College Journalism* (Belmont, Calif.: Wadsworth, 1983).

PHELPS, ROBERT, and E. DOUGLAS HAMILTON, *Libel: Rights and Responsibilities* (New York: Dover, 1978).

POLKING, KIRK, and LEONARD MERANUS *Law and the Writer* (Cincinnati: Writer's Digest Books, 1981).

POLLACK, RICHARD, ed., *Stop the Presses, I Want to Get Off* (New York: Random House, 1975).

RICHARDS, PHIL, and JOHN J. BANIGAN, *How to Abandon Ship* (New York, Cornell Maritime Press, 1941).

RIVERS, WILLIAM, *News in Print* (New York: Harper & Row, 1984).

ROOT, HENRY, *The Further Letters of Henry Root* (London: Weidenfeld and Nicolson, 1980).

RUEHLMANN, WILLIAM, *Stalking the Feature Story* (New York: Vintage, 1979).

SIMS, NORMAN, *The Literary Journalists* (New York: Ballantine Books, 1984).

SLOAN, WILLIAM DAVID, VALARIE McCRARY, and JOHANNA CLEARY, eds., *The Best of Pulitzer Prize Reporting* (Columbus, Ohio: Publishing Horizons, 1986).

STEFFENS, LINCOLN, *The Autobiography of Lincoln Steffens* (New York, The Literary Guild, 1931).

STEIN, M. L., *Getting and Writing the News* (New York: Longman, 1985).

STEPHENS, MITCHELL, *Broadcast News* (New York: Holt, Rinehart & Winston, 1980).

STRUNK, WILLIAM, and E. B. WHITE, *The Elements of Style* (New York: Macmillan, 1972, 1979).

SWANBERG, W. A., *Citizen Hearst* (New York: Bantam Books, 1963).

TALESE, GAY, *Fame and Obscurity* (New York: Bantam Books, 1963).

TALESE, GAY, *The Kingdom and the Power* (New York: World Publishers, 1969).

TERKEL, STUDS, *American Dreams: Lost and Found* (New York: Ballantine Books, 1980).

TERKEL, STUDS, *Division Street: America* (New York: Avon Books, 1967).

THOMPSON, HUNTER S., *Hell's Angels* (New York: Ballantine Books, 1977).

THOMPSON, WILLIAM IRWIN, *At the Edge of History* (New York, Harper & Row, 1971).

WARD, HILEY H., *Professional Newswriting* (New York: Harcourt Brace Jovanovich, 1985).

WAUGH, EVELYN, *Scoop* (Boston: Little, Brown, 1977).

WEINBERG, ARTHUR, and LILA WEINBERG, eds., *The Muckrakers* (New York: G. P. Putnam's Sons, 1964).

WILLIAMS, PAUL N., *Investigative Reporting and Editing* (Englewood Cliffs, N.J.: Prentice-Hall).

WILSON, EDMUND, *The American Earthquake* (New York: Farrar Straus Giroux, 1958).

WIMER, ARTHUR, and DALE BRIX, *Radio and TV News Editing and Writing* (Dubuque, Iowa: William C. Brown, 1975).

World Almanac and Book of Facts (New York: Newspaper Enterprise Association, Inc., annual).

ZINSSER, WILLIAM, *On Writing Well* (New York: Harper & Row, 1980).

INDEX

ABOUT THE AUTHORS

Timothy Ferris, a graduate of Northwestern University, is professor of journalism at the University of California, Berkeley. He has taught as well at the University of Southern California, the California Institute of Technology, and Brooklyn College, and has worked as a reporter for United Press International and *The New York Post* and as New York bureau chief for *Rolling Stone* magazine. Articles by Ferris have appeared in *Life*, *The New York Times Magazine*, *The New York Times Book Review*, *Esquire*, *Rolling Stone*, *Reader's Digest*, *Harper's*, and many other magazines and newspapers. His books include *Galaxies*, *The Red Limit*, *SpaceShots*, and *Coming of Age in the Milky Way*. He has received the American Institute of Physics Prize and was twice awarded the American Association for the Advancement of Science writing award, once for print and once as author and host of "The Creation of the Universe," a 90-minute PBS television special.

Bruce Porter, a graduate of Hamilton College and the Columbia University Graduate School of Journalism, has worked as a reporter on five newspapers, among them the *Hartford Courant*, *Providence Journal*, and the *New York World Telegram & The Sun*, and as urban affairs editor of *Newsweek*. His articles have appeared in *The New York Times Magazine*, *Playboy*, *Saturday Review*, *Connoisseur*, *New York*, *Ms.*, *Psychology Today*, and other magazines. He is a consultant to the Ford Foundation on civil disorders and has written two books on that subject, *Blackout Looting!* and *The Miami Riot of 1980*. Porter has received awards from the New York Society of Silurians and the Associated Press Managing Editors for urban reporting, and from the Charles Stewart Mott Foundation for magazine writing. He is director of the Journalism Program at Brooklyn College, and an adjunct professor of magazine writing at the Columbia Graduate School of Journalism.